THE DEVELOPMENT OF LEGAL INSTRUMENTS TO COMBAT RACISM IN A DIVERSE EUROPE

IMMIGRATION AND ASYLUM LAW AND POLICY IN EUROPE

Volume 6

Editors

Elspeth Guild
Kingsley Napley Solicitors, London,
Centre for Migration Law, Katholieke Universiteit, Nijmegen

Jan Niessen
Migration Policy Group, Brussels

The series is a venue for books on European immigration and asylum law and policies where academics, policy makers, law practitioners and others look to find detailed analysis of this dynamic field. Works in the series will start from a European perspective. The increased co-operation within the European Union and the Council of Europe on matters related to immigration and asylum requires the publication of theoretical and empirical research. The series will contribute to well-informed policy debates by analysing and interpreting the evolving European legislation and its effects on national law and policies. The series brings together the various stakeholders in these policy debates: the legal profession, researchers, employers, trade unions, human rights and other civil society organisations.

The titles published in this series are listed at the end of this volume.

The Development of Legal Instruments to Combat Racism in a Diverse Europe

Edited by

JAN NIESSEN

and

ISABELLE CHOPIN

MARTINUS NIJHOFF PUBLISHERS
LEIDEN/BOSTON
2004

A C.I.P. Catalogue record for this book is available from the Library of Congress.

Printed on acid-free paper.

ISBN 90-04-13686-X

Typeset by jules guldenmund layout & text, The Hague

Brill Academic Publishers incorporates the imprint Martinus Nijhoff Publishers.
http://www.brill.nl

Printed and bound in The Netherlands

TABLE OF CONTENTS

Jan Niessen and Isabelle Chopin

INTRODUCTION

In post World War II equality and anti-discrimination were enshrined in international and European conventions to which most European countries are party. These conventions inspired national policies to combat all forms of discrimination. Racial and ethnic discrimination, never totally eliminated in Europe, resurfaced at a time when European societies were becoming increasingly diverse as a result of continuous intra and extra European migration. Migration and immigrant integration, of which equality formed a cornerstone, began to rank high on the national and European policy agendas.

The 1990s bore witness to a disturbing rise of acts of direct and indirect discrimination and racially motivated violence against ethnic minorities, immigrants and asylum seekers in many European countries. Aggressive nationalism and right-wing political parties using migrants as scapegoats were rising. As European governments stepped up their attempts to restrict the admission of immigrants and refugees, those already there found themselves subject to often terrifying attacks in a climate that was increasingly xenophobic.

Both the Council of Europe and the European Union quickly became aware of the urgent need to act against racism. The heads of State and government of the member States of the Council of Europe meeting at the Vienna summit in October 1993 expressed their alarm at the resurgence of racism, xenophobia and anti-Semitism, the development of a climate of intolerance, and the increase in acts of violence, notably against migrants and people of immigrant origin. They adopted a declaration and plan of action on combating racism, xenophobia, anti-Semitism and intolerance, including the creation of the European Commission against Racism and Intolerance (ECRI), and resolved to enter into political and legal commitments relating to the protection of national minorities in Europe.

Earlier that year, the European Union's Copenhagen European Council had called for an intensification of efforts to identify and root out the causes of racism and pledged to do the utmost to protect immigrants, refugees and others against expressions and manifestations of racism and intolerance. The EU Con-

Jan Niessen, Isabelle Chopin (eds.), The Development of Legal Instruments..., *vii-xi*

sultative Commission on Racism and Xenophobia was subsequently established at the European Council summit in Corfu in 1994, which vowed to develop a global strategy at Union level aimed at combating acts of racist and xenophobic violence. The European Parliament, which had been active in the fight against racism since 1984 when it commissioned the Evrigenis report to look into the rise of racism and fascism in Europe, adopted several resolutions on racism and xenophobia and warning against the dangers of right-wing violence. Harmonisation of Member States' measures to combat racism was felt to be important in establishing the principle of equal treatment, ensuring the same level of protection across the EU and also in guaranteeing an equal level of ethnic minorities and immigrants across the Union and proposals for concrete legal measures to this end were presented by the 'Starting Line Group'.

Ten years on, Europe has come a long way at least in the institutional response to racism. This book describes the responses of the Council of Europe and the European Union to the worrying trends of the 1990s, and considers the prospects for combating discrimination in Europe using tools that have emerged as a result. Part one looks at the evolution of the Council of Europe apparatus to combat discrimination and the anti-discrimination standards prescribed by its institutions. Part two considers the legislative measures recently adopted by the European Union. The contributions in part three take a comparative perspective of all measures adopted at European level to combat racial and ethnic discrimination.

In Chapter 1 Janneke Gerards sets out the content and meaning of Article 14 of the European Convention on Human Rights (ECHR) and discusses the methods used by the European Court of Human Rights in interpreting Article 14. Gerards submits that while the court has over time developed an elaborate decision model to deal with Article 14 complaints, there are inconsistencies in its application of this model. Gerards proposes amendments to the Court's doctrine that could result in an enhanced role for the non-discrimination principle in Convention law.

In Chapter 2 Jeroen Schokkenbroek, head of the Council of Europe's Human Rights Law and Policy Division of the Directorate General of Human Rights, presents an overview of the genesis of Protocol 12 to the European Convention on Human Rights, which was adopted on 26 June 2000. Although the Convention had prohibited discrimination since its adoption in 1950, the limits of Article 14 ECHR as an accessory provision that can only be invoked if the facts of the case fall within the ambit of one of the Convention's substantive provisions were well known. The European Court of Human Rights is unlikely to examine a discrimination complaint if it has already found a violation of one of the Convention's substantive provisions, and complaints of discrimination in the enjoyment of social and economic rights – which are not guaranteed under the Convention – have been excluded altogether. 50 years on, Protocol 12 seeks to fill this gap in protection, creating an encompassing general prohibition against discrimination on grounds such as sex, race, colour, religion, political or other opinion, national or social origin, association with a national minority, property, birth or other status, at least in vertical relationships. Schokkenbroek highlights aspects of the drafting history of Protocol 12 which explain its intended content and scope, considering in particular whether it gives rise to positive obligations of member States to take active steps to prevent and remedy discrimination, including discrimination between private persons (horizontal effects).

On 13 December 2002 the Parliamentary Assembly of the Council of Europe adopted the European Commission against Racism and Intolerance General Policy Recommendation No.7 on National Legislation to Combat Racism and Racial Discrimination, as a follow up to the European Conference against Racism of 11-13 October 2000 and the World Conference against Racism, Racial Discrimination, Xenophobia and Related Intolerance of 31 August-7 September 2001. The Policy Recommendation was considered necessary in order to elaborate ECRI's constant recommendations to governments to adopt effective legislation in their national law, and ECRI saw this as an opportune time to further the international debate on these issues. Giancarlo Cardinale of the ECRI secretariat outlines the preparation of the Recommendation, which contains comprehensive key elements of national constitutional, civil, administrative and criminal law against racism and racial discrimination.

Parallel to the intergovernmental efforts in the framework of the Council of Europe, the long campaign to convince the European Union to extend its protection against discrimination (on the grounds of sex and nationality) to victims of racism culminated in the insertion of Article 13 into the EC Treaty under the 1997 Treaty of Amsterdam, in force since 1999, and the swift enactment of Community legislation to combat discrimination, namely Directive 2000/43/EC of 29 June 2000 implementing the principle of equal treatment of persons irrespective of racial or ethnic origin, and Directive 2000/78/EC of 27 November 2000 establishing a general framework for equal treatment in employment and occupation. The debates among the European Union institutions and between those institutions and civil society organisations, in particular the Starting Line group, which led to the developments at EU level, are discussed by Isabelle Chopin and Jan Niessen in Chapter 4.

In Chapter 5 Adam Tyson, who represented the European Commission in the negotiations leading to the adoption of the Racial Equality Directive, gives his account of the process, detailing the difficulties that some Member States had with individual provisions, largely based on the differing traditions Member States have had in dealing with questions of race and ethnicity. An explanation of the compromise reached to overcome these obstacles and secure unanimous agreement on the text of the Directive within 7 months – a record for Community law requiring substantive national legislative changes – follows.

In Chapter 6, Sejal Parmar reflects on the case law of the European Court of Justice in the field of sex equality which has articulated the principle of equal treatment, and its relevance for the interpretation and implementation of the Racial Equality Directive. While the latter goes beyond the scope of existing EC sex discrimination protection in several significant ways, the cross-fertilisation of concepts across the grounds of discrimination and the fact that the origins of and inspiration for the Racial Equality Directive lie in this body of law suggest that it is likely that the court will draw on these precedents as a model for the evolution of Community anti-discrimination law on other grounds. Nevertheless, the Court should, according to Parmar, also be open to influence from other sources, namely international human rights law instruments such as the International Convention on the Elimination of All Forms of Racial Discrimination.

In Chapter 7 Per Johansson summarises a series of reports produced in two research projects comparing national anti-discrimination law with the provisions of the Racial Equality Directive, the first initiated by the Migration Policy Group (MPG) and the European Monitoring Centre on Racism an Xenophobia in 1999 and the second undertaken in 2001 in the framework of a joint project of European Roma Rights Centre, Interights and MPG on the implementation of European anti-discrimination law. In all, the research covered twenty-six countries, fifteen EU Member States and eleven candidate countries, eight of which will become members of the EU in May 2004.

Part III seeks to analyse the recent developments at European level in the fight against racism and compare the policy and legal instruments emanating from the Council of Europe and the European Union (including Article 21(1) the EU Charter of Fundamental Rights and the proposed Framework Decision on racism and xenophobia). Mark Bell examines the efforts of both organisations to shape national legislation on racial discrimination and the approaches they have taken to this end. ECRI's model legislation goes much further than the EU instruments combined, yet it lacks the enforceability enjoyed by the EU guarantees. The EU legislation establishes strict minimum requirements, whereas ECRI purports to identify best practice to be taken up voluntarily by governments at a time when they are forced to change their laws to comply with EU obligations. To the extent that the EU and Council of Europe standards diverge, difficulties will inevitably arise, which, Bell suggests, should be overcome by accession of the EU to the ECHR.

In the final chapter, Ann Dummett provides a socio-political analysis of trends and development concerning racial and ethnic discrimination in twenty-six European states, based on the above-mentioned country reports. Dummett warns that variations in perception among the member States of what constitutes discrimination are likely to be problematic in the implementation of European standards. She calls upon governments to review their policies and practices overall for discriminatory aspects, citing immigration and asylum as typical examples of discriminatory policies.

The challenge for the years ahead is to find acceptance in European societies of the diversity to which it is now home. To secure success, the new European legal instruments to combat discrimination, which have rightly brought renewed hope to human rights advocates across the continent, must be accompanied by a change in mentality of all sectors of society and in the political will to eradicate discrimination.

Jan Niessen and Isabelle Chopin
Migration Policy Group

PART I

COUNCIL OF EUROPE ANTI-DISCRIMINATION STANDARDS

Janneke Gerards

1. THE APPLICATION OF ARTICLE 14 ECHR BY THE EUROPEAN COURT OF HUMAN RIGHTS

1. Introduction

The principle of equal treatment has always been of comparatively little significance to the case law of the European Court of Human Rights. Article 14, containing the non-discrimination clause, has frequently been described as a toothless provision, having little to offer to individual applicants.[1] Indeed, the Court only rarely applies the provision. In most cases, it first examines complaints about substantive rights protected by the Convention, after which a complaint about unequal treatment is often considered of insufficient importance to justify separate examination. Moreover, the Court hardly ever finds a violation of Article 14, except for those cases in which the discrimination is allegedly based on a 'suspect' ground: mostly, the Court finds that the situations presented to it are not 'analogous' or 'similar', or that the discrimination is objectively and reasonably justified.

It is also remarkable that the Court does not always deal with discrimination cases in a satisfactory manner. Although in most cases it carefully tests a discrimination complaint against Article 14, the Court's case-law shows a rather large amount of more or less unconvincing applications of the provision. A curious interpretation has, for example, been given in the recent *Fogarty* case, dealing with the invocation of sovereign immunity by the American embassy in an employment dispute.[2] The applicant, a former staff member of the embassy, considered the invocation unreasonable: in her opinion, successful invocation of

---

1 W. Kewenig, *Der Grundsatz der Nichtdiskriminierung im Völkerrecht der internationalen Handelsbeziehungen*, 1972, p. 106.

2 ECHR 21 November 2001, *European Human Rights Cases* 2002/4.

Jan Niessen, Isabelle Chopin (eds.), The Development of Legal Instruments..., *3-60*

state immunity prevented her from instituting proceedings against her employer, whereas access to court was not restricted to employees of other organizations. With respect to this submission, the Court considered the following:

> This immunity applies in relation to all such employment related disputes, irrespective of their subject matter and of the sex, nationality, and place of residence or other attributes of the complainant. It cannot therefore be said that the applicant was treated differently from any other person wishing to bring employment-related proceedings against an embassy, or that the restriction placed on her right to access to court was discriminatory. It follows that there has been no violation of Article 14 […].[3]

The Court found no discrimination in this case, apparently because every possible complainant – not only the applicant – would be affected by the restriction of access to court in employment related proceedings against the embassy. This reasoning is highly questionable, as would be clear if the complaint would have been based on a somewhat different set of facts. It would, for instance, be interesting to supplement the rule that no employment related proceedings could be brought against the US embassy with the hypothetical specification that this only applies to redheaded persons. In the approach chosen by the Court, such a specification would not constitute a violation of Article 14: the hypothetical rule would treat all redheaded persons wishing to institute proceedings against the embassy exactly alike, raising no problems at all from a formal equality point of view. It will however be evident that the hypothetical specification would render the rule completely arbitrary: a person's hair colour can hardly be considered of relevance for the possibility to institute employment proceedings.

Fortunately, Article 14 is not very often interpreted and applied in this unconvincing and unsatisfactory manner; in most cases, the interpretation is quite reasonable. This contribution will therefore mainly focus on the interpretation the Court usually gives to the non-discrimination provision and on the possible improvement of its interpretation methods. Such improvements would especially seem to be desirable with regard to the upcoming entry into force of Protocol No. 12, which will undoubtedly strengthen the significance of the non-discrimination principle to the European Convention of Human Rights.

Before elaborating on the methods used by the Court in interpreting Article 14, it may seem useful to provide some insight into the contents and meaning of Article 14 to enhance the appreciation and understanding of the Court's decision model. In section 2 of this contribution, attention will therefore be paid to several special characteristics of the provision, such as its accessory character and the grounds of discrimination listed in the article, and to the stance the

3 Paras 42-43.

Court has taken with respect to the distinction between formal and substantive equality and between direct and indirect discrimination. The decision model that is developed by the Court for the assessment of complaints about unequal treatment will be discussed subsequently in section 3. Section 4 will deal specifically with the way in which the Court has given effect to its margin of appreciation doctrine in discrimination cases. Finally, several proposals for amendment of the Court's doctrine will be put forward in section 5.

2. General Aspects of Article 14

2.1 The Accessory Character of Article 14

2.1.1 The Court's Approach to the Accessory Character

Article 14 of the European Convention on Human Rights provides the following

> The enjoyment of the rights and freedoms set forth in the Convention shall be secured without any discrimination on any ground such as sex, race, colour, language, religion, political or other opinion, national or social origin, association with a national minority, property, birth or other status.

As is apparent from this definition, the framers of the Convention did not have the intention to lay down a general and independent principle of equal treatment. The article is accessory in character and is, as such, primarily intended to guarantee effective exercise of the rights and freedoms protected by the Convention. As a consequence of the accessory character of the provision, complaints with respect to alleged violations of Article 14 would only be admissible if a sufficient relationship could be shown between the asserted discrimination and one of the rights or freedoms protected by the substantive provisions of the Convention. As a result, an individual applicant will always have to establish a clear connection between a substantive Convention provision to be able to successfully invoke the prohibition of discrimination.

Initially, the requirements regarding the connection between substantive Convention provisions and Article 14 were rather stringent. The European Commission on Human Rights adopted a strict approach, declaring complaints only admissible if it had also found a violation of the relevant substantive Convention provision.[4] As a result, the effectiveness of the prohibition on dis-

---

4 See e.g. Application 16/808, 8 March 1960, *Isop v. Austria*, Yearbook of the European Convention on Human Rights 5 (1962), p. 108: 'Whereas, in regard to the complaint that the said refusal constituted a violation of Article 14 of the Convention, it is to be observed that this Article, by its express terms, forbids discrimination only with regard to the enjoyment of the rights and freedoms guaranteed in the Convention; and whereas the Commission has already held above that such right is not violated in

crimination was limited: claims about a violation of Article 14 were almost never successful.

When the Court was offered the opportunity to decide on a discrimination case for the first time, namely in the *Belgian Linguistics* case (1968), it gave a somewhat more flexible interpretation to the necessity of a connection with a substantive provision: according to the Court's decision in the *Belgian Linguistics* case, a discrimination complaint may also be admissible if a substantive provision is not violated.[5] Some proof of a connection with a substantive provision is however still required. Usually, the Court determines the applicability of Article 14 on the basis of considerations such as the following

> According to the Court's established case law, Article 14 complements the other substantive provisions of the Convention and the Protocols. It has no independent existence, since it has effect solely in relation to 'the enjoyment of the rights and freedoms' safeguarded by those provisions. Although the application of Article 14 does not necessarily presuppose a breach of those provisions – and to this extent it is autonomous – there can be no room for its application unless the facts at issue *fall within the ambit* of one or more of the latter. (para. 71, emphasis added) [6]

Thus, it would appear to be sufficient that the applicant shows that the constellation of facts on which the discrimination claim is based may also be brought under the ambit of one of the substantive Convention provisions.[7]

---

the present case; whereas it follows that Article 14 of the Convention has no application in the circumstances of the present case.'

5 ECHR 23 July 1968, *Belgian Linguistics case*, Series A, vol. 6, para. 9.

6 ECHR 28 May 1985, *Abdulaziz*, Series A, vol. 94. The requirements in this judgment seem to be somewhat less stringent than in earlier cases. In the *Schmidt and Dahlström* case, decided some ten years earlier, the Court still demanded a discrimination 'linked to the exercise of a right guaranteed' (ECHR 6 February 1976, Series A, vol. 21). In the *Marckx* case, the Court already seemed to weaken this requirement to some extent: for the complaint to be admissible, it then only required that the discrimination 'comes within the sphere' of a substantive Convention provision (ECHR 13 June 1979, Series A, vol. 31). In 1983, the Court used the formula cited in the main text for the first time, namely in the *Van der Mussele* case (ECHR 23 November 1983, Series A, vol. 70); since then, this formula forms part of the Court's well established case-law (see e.g. ECHR 27 June 2000, *Cha'are Shalom Ve Tsedek*, EHRC 2000/66, para. 86). See K.J. Partsch, 'Discrimination', in: Macdonald, Matscher and Petzold (eds.), *The European System for the Protection of Human Rights*, London 1993, pp. 582-583.

7 This criterion is not very clear, and the Court has not offered any further indications as to the way in which it should be applied. From the case-law it has however been clear that the criterion is easily met: there are but few cases in which the Court

2.1.2 *Consequences of the Accessory Character*

Although the Court's flexible approach to the accessory character of Article 14 renders it comparatively easy to show a sufficient connection with a substantive provision, the accessory character does still have problematic consequences. In many cases, a rather technical construction is required to bring an alleged discrimination under the scope of both Article 14 and a substantive provision. An example of such a construction may be found in the *Thlimmenos* case,[8] in which the applicant complained about the refusal to appoint him to the post of a chartered accountant because of a former conviction for insubordination. The applicant's complaint focused on the distinction that was made on the ground of his

---

was unable to bring a discrimination complaint under the ambit of a substantive Convention provision. Lack of a sufficient connection seemed to be found only if the discrimination concerned a substantive provision that was not accepted by the State or with respect to which the State made a reservation (F. Matscher, 'Betrachtungen über das Diskriminierungsverbot (Art. 14 EMRK) nach der neueren Praxis der Strassburger Instanzen', in: Adamovich and Pernthaler (eds.), *Auf dem Weg zur Menschenwürde und Gerechtigkeit*, Vienna 1980, p. 637). Furthermore, a connection is absent if the fundamental right concerned is not clearly safeguarded by the Convention, such as would be the case for the right to access to work or the right to medical treatment. However, it must be remarked that recent case law seems to indicate that the Court has somewhat sharpened the criteria a discrimination has to meet in order to be admissible. An example of this is the Court's judgment in *Prince Hans-Adam II of Liechenstein v. Germany* (ECHR 12 July 2001, *European Human Rights Cases* 2001/64). With respect to the complaint about an alleged infringement of the right to property (Article 1 of the First Protocol), the Court found no violation, as, according to the Court's well-established case-law, is not necessary for the applicability of Article 14. With respect to the applicant's discrimination claim, the Court however stated that '[...] the facts of which the applicant complained under Article 1 of Protocol No. 1 [...] did not amount to an interference with any of his rights under that provision. He cannot therefore claim that in these respects he had been discriminated against in the enjoyment of his property rights' (para. 92). This conclusion is not really comprehensible against the background to the aforementioned case-law: Article 1 of the First Protocol might not have been violated, but the Court had found the provision to be applicable to the facts of the case. It therefore only had to examine whether the discrimination complaint related to the same complex of facts that was relevant to the claim under Article 1 First Protocol. It is difficult to predict how the Court will deal with its earlier, flexible approach in the future and whether the *Prince Hans-Adam* case must be regarded as a deliberate departure to this approach. It does not seem to be unimaginable that the case constitutes an exception, as it concerned difficult and sensitive political and policy matters. Recent cases seem to affirm this reading of the case, as the Court in those cases does not formulate stringent requirements with respect to the need to show a connection with a substantive provision. See e.g. ECHR 4 June 2002, *Wessels-Bergervoet*, *European Human Rights Cases* 2002/60 and ECHR 11 June 2002, *Willis*, *European Human Rights Cases* 2002/62.

8 ECHR 6 April 2000, *European Human Rights Cases* 2000/45.

status as a convicted person. It is almost impossible to bring such a distinction under the scope of one of the substantive Convention provisions, but the Court was nevertheless of the opinion that it was desirable to examine the Article 14 complaint. In order to do this, it had to opt for a somewhat artificial construction. The Court first observed that the applicant had actually been convicted because of a religiously inspired refusal to wear a military uniform, and therefore concluded that, in essence, the case showed a substantive distinction based on religion: erroneously, no distinction was made in the relevant legislation between persons who were convicted of offences committed exclusively because of their religious beliefs and persons that were convicted of other offences. Seen in that perspective, the Court accepted that the set of facts fell within the ambit of a Convention provision, namely Article 9 (protecting freedom of religion), leading it to the conclusion that the Article 14 complaint could be examined in substance.[9]

It might be argued that an application with constructions of this kind can hardly be objected against, even though the constructions sometimes seem a bit far-fetched. A more problematic consequence of the accessory character is, however, the fact that it prevents the Court from examining a wide variety of discrimination claims. The Court is particularly limited in the examination of distinctions that infringe social or economic rights, as the Court only rarely finds that these rights fall under the scope of the Convention.[10] As a result, complaints about unequal treatment with respect to such issues as access to employment, vocational training or social security will often be declared inadmissible, even if the distinction is allegedly based on suspect grounds such as race, nationality or sex.[11] For that reason, the choice for an independent prohibition of discrimination, such as is contained in Protocol No. 12, may certainly be considered desirable.

9 Paras 41 and 42.

10 The accessory character may also have restricting effects in cases concerning other rights. See further K. Kerdel, 'Meer gelijkheid in de bescherming tegen discriminatie? Protocol 12 bij het EVRM', *Nemesis* 2001, p. 43, who gives the example of a difference in treatment with respect to conditions for entry to the judicial profession.

11 Cf. Harris/O'Boyle/Warbrick, *Law of the European Convention on Human Rights*, London 1995, p. 464 and 486 and Strasser, 'Remedies against racial discrimination and other forms of racism, xenophobia or intolerance under the ECHR', in: Woltjer and De Beert (eds.), *Juridische middelen ter bestrijding van rassendiscriminatie en racial gemotiveerde geweldpleging*, Leiden 1996, p. 41. Restrictions may also be found in other cases. In the *Botta* case, the Court for instance found that the right of a disabled person to have access to the beach during his vacation concerns very broad and undefined interpersonal relationships and therefore does not fall under the scope of protection of Article 8. For that reason, the Court also found Article 14 to be inapplicable (ECHR 24 February 1998, Reports 1998-I, paras 35, 39 and 40).

One last important consequence of the accessory character of Article 14 is the fact that the Court almost never gives an actual, substantive assessment of a discrimination complaint. In the large majority of cases, the complaint concerns unequal treatment with respect to the exercise of a right or freedom protected by the Convention. As the Court always starts its examination of a complaint with the assessment of the alleged violation of the substantive Convention provisions, it will often already consider certain aspects of the difference in treatment in that context. In those cases, the Court almost always concludes that separate examination of the Article 14 complaint is superfluous or otherwise unnecessary.[12] Presently, the Court only seems to examine a complaint about an alleged violation of Article 14 if no violation of a substantive provision has been found; if the discrimination complaint concerns an aspect of the case that is clearly distinct from the complaint raised under a substantive provision; or if the discrimination complaint concerns a similar aspect of the case, but raises interesting questions from a legal point of view.[13]

2.2 *Grounds of Discrimination; Requirement of a Distinction Based on Personal Characteristics*

The formulation of Article 14 makes clear that the list of discrimination grounds contained in the Article is not exhaustive.[14] As a result, it is possible in theory to

12 In the *Airey* case the Court stated: 'If the Court does not find a separate breach of one of those Articles [substantive provisions, JHG] that has been invoked both on its own and together with Article 14, it must also examine the case under the latter Article. On the other hand, such an examination is not generally required when the Court finds a violation of the former Article taken alone. The position is otherwise if a clear inequality of treatment in the enjoyment of the right in question is a fundamental aspect of the case [...]' (ECHR 9 October 1979, *Airey*, Series A, vol. 32, para. 30).

13 It is not entirely clear when the Court deems the Article 14 complaint a fundamental aspect of the case. The Court seems to use this argument especially when it feels reluctant to express its opinion about the acceptability of a difference in treatment, for instance because the case concerns sensitive issues (as in the cases with regard to unequal treatment of homosexuals; see e.g. ECHR 22 October 1981, *Dudgeon*, Series A, vol. 45, para. 69), or because it then would have to deal with difficult problems of justification (such as in cases in which a difference in treatment instinctively seems justified, but it is difficult to find objective arguments supporting this feeling). See also Harris/O'Boyle/Warbrick 1995, n. 11 above, pp. 468-469 and Matscher 1980, n. 7 above, p. 638.

14 The Court explicitly affirmed this in the *Engel* case (ECHR 23 November 1976, Series A, vol. 22), in which it stated that: 'the list set out in that provision [Article 14, JHG] is illustrative and not exhaustive, as is shown by the words 'any grounds such as' (in French 'notamment')' (para. 72).

bring every imaginable inequality in treatment before the Court, as long as the requirement of connexity is met: there is no need for the applicant to show that the alleged discrimination is based on one of the grounds explicitly mentioned in Article 14.[15]

However, the *Kjeldsen* case, decided by the Court in 1976, clearly shows that the possibilities for bringing complaints about unequal treatment are not unlimited.[16] In this case, the Court pointed out that Article 14 only prohibits discriminatory treatment 'having as its basis a personal characteristic ('status') by which persons or groups of persons are distinguishable from each other' (para. 56). However, it appears from later case law that the *Kjeldsen* requirement is interpreted very broadly and, moreover, that it is not consistently applied. In the *Lithgow* case,[17] for example, a complaint was made about an inequality in the calculation of the amount of financial compensation that was awarded to the applicant company after it had been nationalized. In calculating the amount of compensation, the national authorities valued some companies by reference to their assets, while other companies (such as the applicant's) were valued by reference to their earnings. Though this distinction can hardly be found to be based on a personal characteristic, however broad the interpretation that is given to this notion, the Court examined the complaint under Article 14 and found the discrimination to be objectively justified.[18]

Notwithstanding cases such as *Lithgow*, a number of recent Turkish cases seem to show that the Court has not completely abolished the *Kjeldsen* require-

15 As is apparent from the *Rasmussen* case (ECHR 28 November 1984, Series A, vol. 87), a clear characterization of the ground of discrimination is indeed often missing. This case concerned a difference in procedural rules with respect to paternity proceedings: the 'father' could only institute such proceeding within a certain period after the birth of the child, whereas a similar restriction was not provided for the mother. Although it is easy to characterize this difference in treatment as a discrimination on grounds of sex, the Court ruled the following: 'For the purposes of Article 14, the Court [...] finds that there was a difference of treatment as between Mr. Rasmussen and his former wife as regards the possibility of instituting proceedings to contest the former's paternity. There is no call to determine on what ground this difference was based, the list of grounds appearing in Article 14 not being exhaustive.' (para. 34)

16 ECHR 7 December 1976, Series A, vol. 23.

17 ECHR 22 May 1984, Series A, vol. 102.

18 Likewise, the fact that the discrimination did not seem to be based on a personal characteristic did not prevent the Court from examination. See e.g. *Fredin*, in which the applicants claimed that their permit to exploit a gravel pit was revoked, while other companies were allowed to continue their activities. The Court examined the merits of their complaints, although it was clear that the decision was mainly inspired by environmental considerations and no personal characteristics of the applicants were involved (ECHR 18 February 1991, Series A, vol. 192). Cf. also the *Building Societies* case (ECHR 23 October 1997, Reports 1997, VII).

ment. The applicants in these cases complained about the fact that Turkish criminal procedural rules offered better protection to persons suspected of 'ordinary' offences than to persons suspected of specific, mainly terrorist, offences. With respect to this submission, the Court observed the following

> The Court notes that in principle the aim [of the distinct procedural rules, JHG] is to penalise people who commit terrorist offences and that anyone convicted under that law will be treated less favourably with regard to automatic parole than persons convicted under the ordinary law. It deduces from that fact that the distinction is made not between different groups of people, but between different types of offence, according to the legislature's view of their gravity. The Court sees no ground for concluding that that practice amounts to a form of "discrimination" that is contrary to the Convention.[19]

Apparently, for Article 14 to be applicable, the Court still requires some connection between the ground of discrimination and a characteristic of a person or group.

2.3 Direct and Indirect Discrimination; Formal and Substantive Equality

2.3.1 Direct and indirect discrimination

Equal protection doctrine usually distinguishes between the notions of direct and indirect discrimination. This distinction is particularly important if an equality provision only prohibits discriminations based on specific, exhaustively listed grounds or characteristics (e.g. race or gender). In that situation, there will be direct discrimination where discrimination is actually and directly based on one of these grounds. Indirect discrimination will be found if a direct classification or distinction, based on 'neutral', not explicitly prohibited grounds, has the actual effect of distinguishing on the basis of such a ground. For instance, a statutory rule providing that part time workers will not be awarded an end-of-year bonus distinguishes directly on the basis of working time, which could be regarded as a neutral and relatively unproblematic ground. However, it is statistically proven that most part time workers are women, which implies that the disadvantage created by the statutory rule will affect far more women than men. Having regard to the actual result of the measure, it could therefore be concluded that the measure discriminates on basis of gender. For that reason, the relevant measure could be found unacceptable when tested against an equal-

---

19 ECHR 8 July 1999, *Gerger*, not published, para. 69. See also ECHR 17 October 2000, *Mutlu and Yildiz*, not published. The Court has also stated that there is no discrimination based on personal characteristics if the difference in treatment is caused by differences in regional or geographical characteristics; see ECHR 6 June 2000, *Magee*, *European Human Rights Cases* 2000/63, para. 19.

ity provision that only prohibits discrimination based on gender, even though it does not explicitly discriminate on that ground.

As the prohibition of discrimination in Article 14 is not limited to an exhaustively listed number of grounds, there is, in principle, no need for the use of the concept of indirect discrimination: it is possible to challenge any inequality in treatment, on whatever ground it is based. Nonetheless it may be useful to the applicant to invoke the concept, as the Court scrutinizes some cases of discrimination more strictly than others. A violation of the equality provision will be, for example, more easily found where the applicant is able to show that the alleged discrimination is based on a suspect ground, such as gender (in which case a strict test will be applied), rather than in cases in which a classification, apparently based on a neutral ground such as working time, is challenged directly (and the Court will exercise more restraint).

Initially, the Court did not seem to recognize the concept of indirect discrimination,[20] but more recent cases show a new and different approach. This may be illustrated by the recent *Kelly* case regarding outbursts of violence in Northern Ireland.[21] The applicants alleged that the great majority of the persons who had been injured or killed as a result of actions of the security forces were Catholics; Protestants almost never appeared to be victims of these acts. According to the applicants, the use of violence by the security forces therefore constituted an indirect discrimination based on religion, a ground that normally effects a strict test. The Court considered the following

> Where a general policy or measure has disproportionately prejudicial effects on a particular group, it is not excluded that this may be considered as discriminatory notwithstanding that it is not specifically aimed or directed at that group. However, even though statistically it appears that the majority of people shot by the security forces were from the Catholic or nationalist community, the Court does not consider that statistics can in themselves disclose a practice, which could be classified as discriminatory within the meaning of Article 14. There is no evidence before the Court, which could entitle it to conclude that any of those killings [...] involved the unlawful or excessive use of force by members of the security forces. (para. 148)

These considerations show that the Court recognizes the concept of indirect discrimination at least in principle, but do also show that the number of successful indirect discrimination complaints will be extremely limited, as the Court formulates strict requirements with respect to the burden of proof that the

20 Cf. Harris/O'Boyle/Warbrick 1995, p. 477 and see e.g. ECHR 25 May 1985, *Abdulaziz*, Series A, vol. 94, para. 85.

21 ECHR 4 May 2001, *European Human Rights Cases* 2001/40.

applicant will have to meet. It does not appear to be sufficient that the applicant shows a clear disproportionate disadvantage of the relevant measure for a vulnerable or especially protected group: some additional evidence or proof seems to be required. Unfortunately, the Court does not provide any information as to the nature of this additional evidence. From the cited consideration it might be inferred that it is necessary to show that the exercise of authority, resulting in a disproportionate disadvantage for a special group, is illegitimate in itself. As a result of such a requirement, measures will be tested against Article 14 only if they actually aim at reaching discriminatory effects. In that interpretation, unintentional discriminatory effects are unproblematic, even if they are especially harmful to the group that is disadvantaged by them. However, the Court's ruling in the *Kelly* case is not very clear on this point; further case law is awaited before actual conclusions may be drawn with respect to the Court's approach in scrutinizing indirect discrimination.

2.3.2 Formal and Substantive Discrimination

Next to the distinction between direct and indirect discrimination, equality doctrine usually also distinguishes between formal and substantive discrimination. The Court's stance with respect to this distinction has long been unclear, which is also caused by the fact that the Court has been confronted only rarely with complaints about equal treatment of unequal cases (substantive discrimination).[22] Recently, in its *Thlimmenos* case,[23] the Court has however explicitly accepted that not only formal discrimination (unequal treatment of equal cases), but also substantive discrimination falls within the scope of Article 14. The *Thlimmenos* case concerned a legislative provision stipulating that persons who had been convicted of a felony could not be appointed as a chartered accountant.

22 It may be inferred from a 1996 case, *Stubbings*, that the Court at first did not feel inclined to recognize the concept of substantive equality (ECHR 22 October 1996, Reports 1996-IV). In this case, the Court had to pronounce itself on a complaint of several British women who had been the victim of sexual abuse during their childhood. At an advanced age, they experienced severe psychological problems, but only realized that there might be a connection with the childhood abuse much later. When the complainants commenced proceedings to obtain compensation for the damage for the alleged assaults, their claims were dismissed as time-barred: according to UK law, personal injury proceedings had to be instituted within six years from the eighteenth birthday of the victim. The applicants claimed that the uniformity of the time limit violated Article 14, arguing that there existed clear differences between the specific character of the psychological injury that they had suffered and other cases of intentionally caused injury. The Court reached a different conclusion: 'The Court observes [...] that as between the applicant and victims of other forms of deliberate wrongdoing with different psychological after-effects, there was no disparity in treatment, because the same rules of limitation are applied to each group.' (para. 73)

23 ECHR 6 April 2000, *European Human Rights Cases* 2000/45.

The applicant argued that this legislative provision did not sufficiently respect the diversity in degree and character of possible offences (he himself had been convicted because of his refusal to wear a military uniform, which he did not consider of relevance for the professional and ethical standards he would have to meet as a chartered accountant), and therefore contained a substantive discrimination that could not be held compatible with Article 14. As to this submission, the Court observed the following:

> The Court has so far considered that the right under Article 14 not to be discriminated against in the enjoyment of the rights guaranteed under the Convention is violated when States treat differently persons in analogous situations without providing an objective and reasonable justification. However, the Court considers that this is not the only facet of the prohibition of discrimination under Article 14. The right not to be discriminated against in the enjoyment of the rights guaranteed under the Convention is also violated when States without an objective and reasonable justification fail to treat differently persons whose situations are significantly different. (para. 44)[24]

Subsequently the Court applied the justification test it has developed for the examination of complaints about formal discrimination. Hereinafter, it will therefore be assumed that the Court's decision model is applicable in cases of both formal and substantive discrimination.

3. The Court's Decision Model

3.1 Development, Contents and Application of the Court's Decision Model

In the first judgment ever rendered by the Court with respect to Article 14, the *Belgian Linguistics* case,[25] the Court pronounced itself upon several fundamental issues of interpretation and application of this provision. The Court not only gave its opinion about the accessory character of the prohibition of discrimination (discussed in the above), but also elaborated several methods that may be used in examining discrimination cases. In its judgment, the Court developed a decision model that it has used consistently in all later cases concerning the prohibition of discrimination. It therefore seems useful to cite the most important passage of the Court's judgment in its entirety:

> It is important [...] to look for the criteria which enable a determination to be made as to whether or not a given difference in treatment, concerning of course

24 The Court affirmed this judgment in ECHR 18 January 2001, *Jane Smith, European Human Rights Cases* 2001/19, para. 138.

25 ECHR 23 July 1968, Series A, vol. 6.

> one of the rights and freedoms set forth in the Convention, contravenes Article 14. On this question the Court, following the principles, which may be extracted, from the legal practice of a large number of democratic States, holds that the principle of equality of treatment is violated if the distinction has no objective and reasonable justification. The existence of such a justification must be assessed in relation to the aim and effects of the measure under consideration, regard being had to the principles which normally prevail in democratic societies. A difference of treatment in the exercise of a right laid down in the Convention must not only pursue a legitimate aim: Article 14 is likewise violated when it is clearly established that there is no reasonable relationship of proportionality between the means employed and the aim sought to be realised. (p. 34)

In this passage, it is significant that the Court only pays attention to the *justification* of an alleged discrimination, whereas a justification test can only be applied if it is clear that the Court is presented with actual inequality in treatment: there is no need to look for a justification if the applicant is clearly not treated differently from another person or group.[26] This means that the justification test would normally constitute only the second step in the examination of a discrimination complaint: first, a court will have to determine whether there is an actual case of unequal treatment. Apparently, the Court initially experienced some difficulties in applying this 'first phase test': in most cases, it simply assumed the presence of an inequality in treatment and immediately assessed the arguments advanced as a justification by the respondent government.[27] It was only in the

26 By contrast, the European Commission for Human Rights, which was authorized under the old Convention to give a substantive opinion of the case before putting it before the Court, and whose opinions often formed an important source of inspiration to the Court, did indeed consistently apply a first phase test: the Commission always started its examination with an assessment of the comparability of the cases placed before it. See e.g. the *Grandrath* case, in which the Commission observed that 'the notion of discrimination between individuals implies a comparison between two or more different groups or categories of individuals and the finding that one group is treated differently from – and less favourably than – another group or category' (Appl. 2299/64, *Grandrath v. Austria*, Yearbook of the European Convention on Human Rights 10 (1967), p. 694); cf. Partsch 1993, p. 585. Alike, a comparability test is also visible in the *Belgian Linguistics* case. In giving its opinion with regard to the first of the six specific Article 14 complaints, the Court stated that 'Article 14 does not prohibit distinctions in treatment which are founded on an objective assessment of essentially different factual circumstances [...]' (p. 44). This statement does however not influence the Court's methodology: the contested difference in treatment itself is tested in accordance with the cited decision model.

27 An illustration of this approach is visible in the *Engel* case (ECHR 23 November 1976, Series A, vol. 22), dealing with a difference in treatment between army officers of different ranks with respect to the execution of disciplinary penalties and sanctions.

Marckx case,[28] decided in 1979, that the Court added a real first phase test to its decision model, ruling that the respondent government only has to advance a justification if the applicant has shown that the cases presented to the Court are sufficiently comparable or analogous: 'Article 14 safeguards individuals, *placed in similar situations*, from any discrimination in the enjoyment of the rights and freedoms set forth in the other provisions.' (para. 32, emphasis added)

It is apparent from many cases decided after *Marckx* that the Court considers this 'comparability test' a fixed and important element in its decision model. After *Marckx*, the Court's decision model can therefore be defined as follows:[29]

1. Is the applicant placed in a similar or analogous position as the person or group he refers to?
   If no: The difference in treatment is acceptable;
   If yes:
2. Does the distinction have an objective and reasonable justification?
   - Does the difference in treatment pursue a legitimate aim?
   - Is there a reasonable relationship of proportionality between the means employed and the aim sought to be realised?[30]

After having determined that the complaint concerned a difference in treatment based on rank, it expressed the following opinion: 'The hierarchical structure inherent in armies entails differentiation according to rank. Corresponding to the various ranks are differing responsibilities which in their turn justify certain inequalities of treatment.' This consideration shows a combination of the first and the second phase of the test, in that the incomparability or dissimilarity of the cases is considered a justification for the difference in treatment. This combination may cause problems with respect to the onus of proof, as it is exactly the sharp division between the first and the second testing phase that makes it possible to apportion the burden of proof between both parties: the state only needs to advance arguments in justification of its distinction if the applicant has sufficiently proven that there is sufficient cause for that.

28 ECHR 13 June 1979, *Marckx*, Series A, vol. 31.

29 This is a well established caselaw. See e.g. ECHR 18 February 1991, *Fredin*, Series A, vol. 192, para. 60, ECHR 23 June 1993, *Hoffmann*, Series A, vol. 255-C, ECHR 22 October 1996, *Stubbings*, Reports 1996-IV, para. 72, ECHR 23 October 1997, *Building Societies*, Reports 1997-VII, ECHR 29 April 1999, *Chassagnou*, Reports 1999-III, para. 91, ECHR 21 December 1999, *Salgueiro da Silva Mouta*, *European Human Rights Cases* 2000/16, para. 26, ECHR 1 February 2000, *Mazurek*, *European Human Rights Cases* 2000/25, para. 46, ECHR 6 April 2000, *Thlimmenos*, *European Human Rights Cases* 2000/45, para. 19, ECHR 11 January 2001, *P.M. v. Italy*, not yet published, para. 53, ECHR 18 January 2001, *Chapman*, not yet published, para. 129, ECHR 28 June 2001, *VGT Verein gegen Tierfabriken*, *European Human Rights Cases* 2001/55, para. 86, ECHR 11 October 2001, *Sahin*, *European Human Rights Cases* 2001/81, para. 56 and ECHR 16 October 2001, *Eliazer*, *European Human Rights Cases* 2001/82, para. 40.

30 Some authors have given a different interpretation to the decision model that has been developed in the *Belgian Linguistics* case. Heringa has, for instance, stated that the requirement for an objective and reasonable justification must be regarded as a

As is apparent from this reproduction of the Court's decision model, the Court only deems it necessary to examine the arguments advanced as a justification if it is clear that the applicant is placed in a similar or analogous position as the person or group he compares himself to. If the cases presented to the Court are not sufficiently comparable, the Court will not address the issue on whether the discrimination may be found unjustified for other reasons, such as a lack of proportionality between the differences in situation and the difference in treatment.[31] However, as soon as the Court reaches the conclusion that the applicant is placed in a situation similar to the person or group he compares himself to, the Court will always examine the arguments the Government advances to justify the difference in treatment. The second part of the Court's decision model consists of two criteria, elaborating and detailing the justification test. The criteria are cumulative in character: a distinction will be consistent with the equality principle only if it pursues a legitimate aim and stands in a reasonable (in the Court's terminology: proportional) relationship to this aim.[32] Thus, if the Court finds that the difference in treatment serves a legitimate aim, it is not possible to reject the discrimination claim on that basis in this situation, it is always necessary to also assess the reasonableness of the means (the distinction) that is used to reach this aim.

Though the foregoing would seem to follow clearly from the cases cited above, the Court's case law shows that the Court often misapplies its own decision model and is not always consistent in its interpretation of the various testing criteria. In many cases the Court does not examine whether the proportionality requirement has been met, even though it has concluded that a legitimate aim was pursued.[33] In other cases, the Court does not pay any attention

separate requirement, next to the requirements of a legitimate aim and a reasonable relationship of proportionality (Heringa, 'Discriminatieverbod', in: Heringa, Schokkenbroek and Van der Velde, *EVRM Rechtspraak & Commentaar*, Den Haag 1998, p. 3.14-5; idem McKean, *Equality and discrimination under international law*, 1995, p. 221). Gomien, Harris and Zwaak have given a third possible interpretation: they argue that a discrimination is unacceptable if 'the distinction does not have an aim, that is, it has no objective and reasonable justification having regard to the aim and effects of the measure under consideration' (*Law and practice of the European Convention on Human Rights and the European Social Charter*, Strasbourg 1996, p. 350). However, the interpretation in that an objective and reasonable justification is present is clear when the difference in treatment pursues a legitimate aim and there exists a reasonable relationship of proportionality that seems to be most in line with the Court's case law.

31 See for an application ECHR 18 December 1986, *Johnston*, Series A, vol. 112.

32 See for an application ECHR 23 October 1990, *Darby*, Series A, vol. 187, paras 33-34. Cf. also Partsch 1993, n. 6 above, p. 590 and Helfer, 'Note: Finding a consensus on equality: the homosexual age of consent and the European Convention on Human Rights', *New York University Law Review* 1044 (1990), p. 1067.

33 See e.g. ECHR 22 May 1986, *Lithgow*, Series A, vol. 102 (para. 181) and ECHR 2 March 1987, *Monnell and Morris*, Series A, vol. 115 (paras 73 and 75).

to the presence of a legitimate aim or the relationship between means and ends, but only generally considers whether the difference in treatment can be thought to be objectively justified.[34] Remarkable is also that the function of the comparability test for the examination of discrimination claims remains unclear: an assessment of similarity or comparability is often omitted[35] and in some cases, elements of comparability are mixed with the examination of the justification.[36] However, it must be admitted that the Court mostly applies the decision model reproduced above, quite diligently assessing whether the different criteria are met. For that reason, it seems useful to elaborate on the manner in which the Court applies the criteria contained in its model.

---

34 In *Kamasinski* the Court observed: 'in so far as any difference exists between defendants in civil actions and defendants to civil claims in criminal proceedings, the interests of the proper administration of justice provide an objective and reasonable justification [...]' (ECHR 19 December 1989, Series A, vol. 168, § 93; § 100 also provides an example). It may be inferred indeed from the cited passage that the Court thinks that the conditions of a legitimate aim and a reasonable relationship of proportionality are fulfilled, but it does not apply these elements explicitly. The same goes for the *Moustaquim* case, in which the Court again ruled that the discrimination was objectively and reasonably justified without testing against the separate criteria of the decision model (ECHR 18 February 1991, Series A, vol. 193). Only if the Court refers to its opinion regarding a complaint under one of the substantive provisions, such summary reasoning might be considered. See for an example of that approach ECHR 18 January 2001, *Jane Smith, European Human Rights Cases* 2001/19, para. 138.

35 See e.g. ECHR 29 November 1991, *Pine Valley Developments*, Series A, vol. 222, § 64, ECHR 21 November 1994, *The Holy Monasteries*, Series A, vol. 301-A, para. 92 and ECHR 29 April 1999, *Chassagnou*, Reports 1999-III, para. 92. The comparability test is sometimes absent in the usual definition of the decision model, without there being any good reason for that; see e.g. ECHR 3 October 2000, *Camp and Bourimi, European Human Rights Cases* 2000/82, para. 13. Remarkable are also the judgments in which the Court does not examine whether the *cases* presented to the court show relevant differences, but whether they are differently *treated*; see e.g. ECHR 23 June 1993, *Hoffmann*, Series A, vol. 255-C, paras 31-33 and ECHR 21 December 1999, *Salgueiro da Silva Mouta, European Human Rights Cases* 2000/16, paras 26-28. Several specific situations in which a comparability test is usually left away will be discussed separately in paragraph 2.2.2.

36 See e.g. ECHR 29 February 1988, *Bouamar*, Series A, vol. 129: '[...][A difference of treatment] stems from the protective – not punitive – nature of the procedure applicable to juveniles in Belgium. In the Court's view, there is *accordingly* an objective and reasonable justification for the difference in treatment' (para. 67, emphasis added). A like approach was chosen in ECHR 18 February 1991, *Moustaquim*, Series A, vol. 193, para. 49.

3.2 The First Phase of the Court's Test: Comparability

3.2.1 Criteria Used by the Court in Determining Comparability

It has been shown in the foregoing that an examination of the reasons that are advanced as a justification for a difference in treatment is, according to the Court in its *Marckx* case,[37] only necessary if the persons or groups of persons that are differently treated are placed in an 'analogous' or 'similar' position.[38] In *Marckx*, the Court regrettably did not clearly indicate how this analogy or similarity is to be determined.[39] Later case law also lacks clarity in this respect: the Court does not seem very much inclined to offer national authorities and courts general and comprehensible standards for the application of the comparability test.

A representative example of the approach usually adopted by the Court may be found in the *Van der Mussele* case.[40] The applicant in this case was a Belgian lawyer who was still in training. In his capacity as a pupil *avocat*, he was obliged to grant legal assistance and advice free of charge to indigent people who could not afford to pay for regular legal services ('pro Deo' assistance). He felt disadvantaged by this obligation, especially because the State did accord remuneration to judges and registrars and paid the emoluments of interpreters in pro Deo cases. Furthermore, the applicant felt that he received less favourable treatment than medical practitioners or dentists, who were not required to provide their services free of charge to indigent persons. The Court, however, did not find any discrimination contrary to Article 14 in this case

> Article 14 safeguards individuals, placed in analogous situations, from discrimination. Yet between the Bar and the various professions cited by the applicant, including even the judicial and Para judicial professions, there exist fundamental differences [...], namely differences as to legal status, conditions for entry to the profession, the nature of the functions involved, the manner of exercise of those functions, etc. The evidence before the Court does not disclose any similarity between the disparate situations in question: each one is characterised by a corpus of rights and obligations of which it would be artificial to isolate one specific aspect. (para. 46)

Although the facts of this case offered sufficient opportunity to develop criteria or standards for the determination of comparability, the Court did not make

37 ECHR 13 June 1979, Series A, vol. 31

38 No substantial difference seems to exist between the terms 'analogous' and 'similar'; the Court uses both terms indiscriminately.

39 The omission of the comparability test in cases about specific differentiation criteria will be discussed later on.

40 ECHR 23 November 1983, Series A, vol. 70.

very good use of it, only stating that the cases brought forward by the applicant were ruled by a set of rights and obligations that differed in important respects from the situation of pro Deo lawyers.[41] This approach is problematic in that it potentially enables the Court to find about every difference in treatment in conformity with Article 14. It is important to note that it is possible to find differences between persons, cases or situations in each case presented to the Court, as all cases are always both comparable and incomparable in certain respects. Pertinent is therefore not whether the cases presented show some differences, but whether the observed differences are actually relevant in the light of the purpose of the distinction. For that reason, it is only possible for the Court to express a reasoned opinion about the comparability of the cases presented to it by determining what differences are of real importance to the comparison and by clearly pointing out *why* the observed differences are relevant. In doing so, it is essential for the Court to determine a clear and inherently legitimate standard of comparison.

In the cited passage from the *Van der Mussele* case, such careful determination cannot be recognized. Indeed the Court mentions several respects in which the various professions differ, such as differences in legal status and conditions for entry to the profession, yet fails to observe why these differences are relevant to the assessment of the contested difference in treatment.[42] Furthermore, it is

41 See also Harris/O'Boyle/Warbrick 1995, n. 11 above, p. 474, stating that the Court's reasoning is cursory. Especially one reference of the Court, omitted in the citation in the main text, to the Commissions examination of the evidence is inconsequential, as the Commission paid hardly any attention to the evidence.

42 This is a recurring defect in the Court's judgments; see also ECHR 18 February 1991, *Fredin*, Series A, vol. 192, in which the Court was asked for its opinion about the closure of a gravel pit, allegedly inspired by considerations of environmental protection. Fredin observed that only his pit had been closed down, while other pits caused comparable environmental damage, and therefore alleged a violation Article 14. The Court gave the following opinion: '[…] the Court has to presume that the applicants' pit is the only one to have been closed […]. However, this is not sufficient to support a finding that the applicants' situation can be considered similar to that of other ongoing businesses which have not been closed. The Court perceives no reason why it should assess the evidence otherwise than did the Commission and accordingly holds that no issue of discrimination contrary to Article 14 arises' (para. 61). The Commission's report was however very short: the Commission only stated that a report that had been put forward by the applicants showed that the applicants were the only gravel pit owners whose permission for exploitation of the pit was withdrawn. In the Commission's opinion, the applicant did advance insufficient evidence to prove comparability, which led to the conclusion that comparability could not be demonstrated (see ECRM 6 November 1989, *Fredin*, Series B, vol. 182, paras 75 and 77). The Commission did however not formulate a clear standard of comparison; for that reason, the Court could not have sufficed with the cited passage in giving a sound opinion about the comparability.

not apparent from the Court's opinion what source it has used in determining its chosen standard of comparison, which may lead to the insertion of hardly discernible and verifiable subjective elements in the Court's reasoning.

Regrettably, the reasoning in the *Van der Mussele* case is not very exceptional. Defects, sometimes of a quite serious nature, may also be discerned in many other cases in which the comparability test is applied. Even though the Court often states that two cases or situations are similar (or dissimilar), it only rarely points out why this is the case, thus obscuring the factors that are relevant in deciding the comparability issue.[43] Problematic is also the lack of clarity as to

43 In *Moustaquim*, concerning a difference in treatment of Belgians and foreigners with respect to the possibility of deportation for reasons of criminal behaviour, the Court confined itself to the single observation that 'in the instant case the applicant cannot be compared to Belgian juvenile delinquents' (ECHR 18 February 1991, Series A, vol. 193, para. 49). Sound reasoning is also lacking in the *Observer and Guardian* case. This case concerned a publication ban with respect to a certain law suit. The applicants instituted proceedings against the ban, arguing that they were treated disadvantageously in comparison to foreign newspapers: from lack of jurisdiction, the ban could not be outstretched to those newspapers. The Court observed: 'If and in so far as foreign newspapers were subject to the same restrictions as Observer and Guardian, there was no difference of treatment. If and in so far as they were not, this was because they were not subject to the jurisdiction of the English courts and hence were not in a situation similar to that of the *Observer* and *Guardian*' (ECHR 26 November 1991, Series A, vol. 216, para. 73). This reasoning is deficient in that respect that the applicants did indeed recognize the lack of jurisdiction; this even constituted one of the main reasons to complain about the ban. For that matter, the Court does usually not advance better or stronger arguments in support of the conclusion that two cases *are* comparable; see e.g. ECHR 23 October 1990, *Darby*, Series A, vol. 187, para. 32. In recent judgments, the Court's reasoning is sometimes more convincing. In the *Building Societies* case it paid, for instance, much attention to the factual circumstances that led it to the conclusion that the applicants were dissimilarly placed than the persons with whom they compared themselves to (ECHR 23 October 1997, *Building Societies*, Reports 1997-VII, para. 89). More careful reasoning is sometimes also realized by a reference to the opinion with respect to the alleged violation of a substantive provision (see e.g. ECHR 16 October 2001, *Eliazer*, *European Human Rights Cases* 2001/82, para. 41). Special care in determining comparability may also be found in ECHR 22 October 1996, *Stubbings*, Reports 1996-IV, para. 73 and ECHR 18 February 1999, *Larkos*, Reports 1999-I, para. 30. However, these cases do not seem to reflect an actual new approach: even in recent cases, the Court regtlarly states without any further explanation that the cases presented to it are not sufficiently comparable. An example is ECHR 28 June 2001, *VGT Verein gegen Tierfabriken*, *European Human Rights Cases* 2001/55. The case concerned the prohibition of a television commercial directed against bio-industry that was inspired by the commercial's political character; advertisements of the meat industry were however not prohibited. The Court observed that '[i]n the present case, the Court notes the decision of the Federal Court of 20 August 1997 according to which promotions of the meat industry were economic in nature in

the proof of comparability the Court requires. Even though the Court has ruled in several cases that the applicant's discrimination complaint was insufficiently supported by evidence, it has never clearly indicated what kind of evidence *would* have sufficed.[44] Such lack of clarity is clearly not desirable, having regard to the importance of legal certainty and the need for individual applicants to be able to evaluate the usefulness of instituting a discrimination complaint.

3.2.2 *Omission of the Comparability Test in Specific Cases*

As has been stated above, the Court developed only few criteria for the determination of comparability. In addition to that, the Court seems to be quite inconsistent in the application of the test: though the test officially constitutes an important element of the Court's decision model, no attention is paid to it in a relatively large amount of cases.[45] In other cases the test is mentioned indeed, yet not applied in substance: the Court often seems to assume that the cases presented to it are sufficiently comparable and switches immediately to the examination of the justification. Two categories of cases in which comparability is often assumed will hereinafter be discussed in more detail.

a. Suspect Classifications

It is well established in the case law of the Court that distinctions or classifications that are based on specific grounds of differentiation, such as nationality or gender, must be considered 'suspect'. Such classifications will be scrutinized much more carefully than usual and will hardly ever be found to be objectively justified.[46] With respect to suspect classifications, the Court pays little attention to the test of comparability. In some cases the test is mentioned indeed,

---

that they aimed at increasing the turnover, whereas the applicant association's commercial, exhorting reduced meat consumption, was directed against industrial animal production and related to animal protection. As a result, the applicant association and the meat industry cannot be considered to be 'placed in comparable situations' as their commercials differed in their aims' (paras 87-88). Thus, the Court indicated the existence of differences between the commercials with respect to their purposes, but it did not explain why these differences ought to have relevance in deciding the case before it. See also ECHR 29 April 1999, *Chassagnou*, Reports 1999-III, para. 120 and ECHR 11 January 2001, *P.M. v. Italy*, not yet published, para. 54.

44 See e.g. the already cited *Fredin* case, ECHR 18 February 1991, Series A, vol. 192, para. 61; cf. also ECHR 23 September 1982, *Sporrong and Lönnroth*, Series A, vol. 52, para. 77.

45 The comparability test is also sometimes absent in the usual definition of the decision model, that is cited in about every discrimination case; the reason for this omission remains unclear. See e.g. ECHR 29 November 1991, *Pine Valley Developments*, Series A, vol. 222, para. 64 and ECHR 3 October 2000, *Camp and Bourimi*, *European Human Rights Cases* 2000/82, para. 13.

46 See further paragraph 4.

yet a substantive application of the test is mostly omitted: in most cases, the Court simply seems to assume that the cases presented to it are sufficiently and relevantly comparable.[47] The Court itself has never given any reasons for the omission, but it seems possible to find an explanation in the character of the relevant grounds of differentiation.[48] As will be discussed in more detail in section 4 of this contribution, the Court has only accepted the 'suspectness' of a limited amount of grounds, namely nationality,[49] illegitimate birth,[50] religion,[51]

47 The deviation is also clear from the way in which the decision model is defined. As has been explained, the Court usually mentions the comparability requirement, but this element is missing in cases about suspect classifications. See the above cited *Abdulaziz* case and e.g. ECHR 11 October 2001, *Sahin, European Human Rights Cases* 2001/81, para. 56.

48 Kewenig has given yet another explanation, stating that there are strong indications of comparability if the ground on which the alleged discrimination is based is explicitly mentioned in an equality provision (1972, p. 75). For instance, if a Treaty, constitution or statute would explicitly prohibit discrimination based on sex, this implies that man and woman are probably placed in a similar position. This explanation does however not seem very suitable for Convention purposes, as Article 14 does only give a list of examples of prohibited criteria of differentiation; this makes it difficult to attach more weight to the grounds listed in the Article itself than to grounds not mentioned therein. This might be illustrated by the fact that the Court has explicitly recognized homosexual orientation as a suspect ground of discrimination, even though this ground is not explicitly mentioned in the text of Article 14 (see ECHR 21 December 1999, *Salgueiro da Silva Mouta, European Human Rights Cases* 2000/16).

49 ECHR 16 September 1996, *Gaygusuz*, Reports 1996-IV.

50 ECHR 13 June 1979, *Marckx*, Series A, vol. 31 (not yet mentioning the 'very weighty reasons'-formula, but showing a clearly intensified review), ECHR 28 October 1986, *Inze*, Series A, vol. 126, ECHR 1 February 2000, *Mazurek, European Human Rights Cases* 2000/25, para. 49, ECHR 3 October 2000, *Camp and Bourimi, European Human Rights Cases* 2000/82 and ECHR 11 October 2001, *Sahin, European Human Rights Cases* 2001/81.

51 ECHR 23 June 1993, *Hoffmann*, Series A, vol. 255-C and ECHR 21 December 1999, *Salgueiro da Silva Mouta, EHRC* 2000/16; in these cases the Court did not use the very weighty reasons formula, but applies a very strict test. In both cases the Court does seem willing to pay attention to the similarity of the cases placed before it (see para. 31 respectively para. 28), but its test boils down to answering the question whether there is an impairment of individual interests that is essentially caused by the applicants religion respectively homosexuality. In the *Thlimmenos* case (ECHR 6 April 2000, *European Human Rights Cases* 2000/45), also concerning discrimination based on religion, the comparability test is also not visible. This omission is the more remarkable in this case, as the Court did not apply a very weighty reasons test. Furthermore, the case concerned substantive inequality, a situation in which the Court requires the situations to be 'significantly different'. After such a statement, it might be expected that the Court at least pay some attention to the comparability test.

gender or sex[52] and sexual orientation.[53] These grounds all relate to personal characteristics that (almost) never bear on someone's daily social behaviour or position. Therefore, these characteristics are only very rarely considered as constituting an acceptable basis for distinction.[54] Seen against this background, it is not surprising that the Court assumes comparability as soon as it is clear that a difference in treatment is based on a suspect ground: indeed, differences in sex, religion, etc., will almost never be relevant from a legal point of view, which has as a result that persons of unequal birth, religion, etc. will mostly be 'placed in a similar situation'.

However, some differences between the groups concerned may be considered of relevance, even though the differences relate to unchangeable or mostly irrelevant personal characteristics. Certain biological differences, such as those relating to pregnancy, may have as a consequence that men and women are to be considered incomparable, even though a distinction based on biological differences constitutes discrimination on the suspect ground of sex. Likewise, religious differences may sometimes be relevant, for example in defining health requirements with respect to food. As comparability is no longer self-evident in cases concerning these issues, the Court in these cases seems to pay more attention to the comparability test than is usual.[55] The same goes for suspect

---

52 ECHR 28 May 1985, *Abdulaziz*, Series A, vol. 94, ECHR 24 June 1993, *Schuler-Zgraggen*, Series A, vol. 263, ECHR 22 February 1994, *Burghartz*, Series A, vol. 280-B, ECHR 18 July 1994, *Karlheinz Schmidt*, Series A, vol. 291-B, ECHR 21 February 1997, *Van Raalte*, Reports 1997-I and ECHR 27 March 1998, *Petrovic*, Reports 1998-II.

53 ECHR 21 December 1999, *Salgueiro da Silva Mouta*, *European Human Rights Cases* 2000/16.

54 This does actually not form a good explanation for the choice to consider certain grounds suspect. Transsexuality, for instance, is another personal characteristic that in principle does not influence someone's daily social functioning, but discrimination based on this ground is not characterized as suspect (cf. ECHR 30 June 1998, *Sheffield and Horsham*, European Human Rights Reports 1998, 163). The characterization of a discrimination as suspect mainly seems to be inspired by other considerations and factors, such as the existence of a European consensus as to the suspectness. In paragraph 3.3.2 special attention will be paid to these factors.

55 Illustrative in this connection is the *Van Raalte* case (ECHR 21 February 1997, Reports 1997-I). The case concerned contributions under the Dutch Child Care Benefits Act. Payment of these contributions was mandatory to every citizen, whether or not the contributor would make use of the benefits flowing from the Act; only unmarried, childless women aged 45 or older were exempted from the obligations, as it is very improbable that women aged above 45 will get children: the legislator therefore deemed it unreasonable that this group would have to contribute to the costs of the Child Care Benefit System. For men aged above 45, there was no such exemption made, as men are able to beget children. In this situation, there was a bio-

classifications that are placed in a different context than is usual. An example of this is the *Gaygusuz* case,[56] concerning discrimination based on grounds of nationality. Normally, nationality cases trigger a very marginal test: these cases usually concern immigration policy, a field in which states are mostly accorded a wide margin of appreciation.[57] However, the discrimination at stake in the *Gaygusuz* case did not concern immigration, but was based on the context of social security: according to the relevant legislation, only Austrian employees (not migrants) were entitled to specific social security benefits. In this context, the Court considered nationality an irrelevant personal characteristic that ought not to have any influence on someone's rights, and therefore characterized the distinction as suspect. Notwithstanding this characterization, the Court paid explicit attention to the comparability of the presented cases, probably because of the fact that similarity was, against the background of the immigration cases, not completely self-evident.

b. Other Cases in Which Comparability Is Assumed

The Court has also omitted the comparability test in several cases concerning non-suspect classifications, apparently assuming that the cases put before it are sufficiently analogous. In some of these cases, this omission may be explained by the fact that a determination of comparability would imply an assessment of the same arguments and considerations as would be relevant to the application of the justification test; in those cases it is not really useful to give a separate ruling as to the similarity of the cases concerned.[58] In other cases, the assumption of comparability may find its explanation in considerations of procedural economy. For the Court it is sometimes easier to find a justification than to determine comparability, which may make it very efficient to skip the first phase test.[59] Finally,

---

logical difference between the sexes that could be reasonably considered relevant to the contested measures. The Court explicitly paid attention to the comparability test: 'At the time of the events complained of contributions under he general Child Care Benefits Act were levied from unmarried childless men aged 45 or over but not from unmarried childless women of the same age. This undoubtedly constitutes a 'difference in treatment' between persons in similar situations, based on gender. The factual difference between the two categories relied on by the Government, namely their respective biological possibilities to procreate, does not lead the Court to a different conclusion. It is precisely this difference which is at heart of the question whether the difference in treatment complained of can be justified.' (para. 40). Cf. also ECHR 27 March 1998, *Petrovic*, Reports 1998-II, para. 36.

56 ECHR 16 September 1996, *Gaygusuz*, Reports 1996-IV.

57 See further paragraph 3.2.5.

58 See explicitly e.g. ECHR 28 November 1984, *Rasmussen*, Series A, vol. 87, para. 37.

59 See e.g. ECHR 2 March 1987, *Monnell and Morris*, Series A, vol. 115, especially para. 73.

a comparability test is sometimes left out if the determination of comparability would necessitate careful examinations of national law: as can be explained from the Court's subsidiary position as an international court, the Court does not easily feel called upon to give such explanations.[60]

3.2.3 *Test of Disadvantage as an Alternative to the Comparability Test*

The case-law discussed in the above section shows that the Court only pronounces itself explicitly as to the comparability of the cases presented to it where there seem to exist actual reasons to doubt such comparability, or where the application of a comparability test seems to fit well into the outcome the Court favours. The omission of the comparability test in other cases may, however, lead to problematic consequences, as the lack of a first phase test will result in an immediate obligation for the state to advance an objective and reasonable justification. Due to the lack of a first phase test, such an obligation would even exist in cases in which it is evident that the interests of the applicant are not impaired by the difference in treatment at all. To avoid this negative consequence, the Court often applies an alternative test, especially in cases concerning allegedly suspect classifications. The respondent state is generally only put under the obligation of advancing a justification if it is sufficiently established that the applicant is actually disadvantaged by the difference in treatment and if the difference in treatment is really based on the alleged suspect ground.[61] Thus, the comparability test is sometimes replaced by a 'test of disadvantage'.

A clear example of an application of the test of disadvantage may be found in the *Buckley* case.[62] The applicant, a Gypsy, was allowed by national law to place a caravan on specifically assigned terrains, but not on a piece of land she owned. In her opinion, the relevant legislation discriminated on grounds of race, a ground that may easily be characterized as suspect. In practice, however, the applicant seemed to experience little disadvantage from the fact that she acted contrary to national law: in the period in which her caravan was standing on her

60 Cf. e.g. ECHR 19 December, *Kamasinski*, Series A, vol. 168.

61 The second requirement is visible in two judgments in which the Court had to express itself about the award of custody of a child after a divorce. In both cases the applicants argued that the judge had attached decisive value to a suspect criterion of differentiation, necessitating the Court to investigate whether this criterion had been decisive indeed. See ECHR 23 June 1993, *Hoffmann*, Series A, vol. 255-C, para. 33 and ECHR 21 December 1999, *Salgueiro da Silva Mouta*, *European Human Rights Cases* 2000/16, para. 28. The Court also carefully examines the presence of a disadvantage and the grounds on which it is based if the complaint concerns a substantive inequality allegedly based on a suspect ground; see e.g. ECHR 6 April 2000, *Thlimmenos*, *European Human Rights Cases* 2000/45, paras 16-17.

62 ECHR 25 September 1996, Reports 1996-IV.

piece of land, she only received two minor fines and was never threatened with removal. The Court therefore reached the following conclusion

> [...][I]t does not appear that the applicant was at any time penalised or subjected to any detrimental treatment for attempting to follow a traditional Gypsy life-style. In fact, it appears that the relevant national policy was aimed at enabling Gypsies to cater for their own needs. (para. 88)

As the applicant's case did not show any clear disadvantage caused by her race or Gypsy status, the Court found no reason to examine whether the difference in treatment was objectively justified. In this case, the test of disadvantage is clearly used as a first phase test, as is also the case in several other judgments with respect to suspect classifications.[63] The requirement of disadvantage seems

---

63 See e.g. ECHR 25 May 1985, *Abdulaziz*, Series A, vol. 94, para. 74 (discrimination on grounds of sex), ECHR 28 October 1987, *Inze*, Series A, vol. 126, para. 39 (discrimination on grounds of illegitimate birth), ECHR 25 November 1994, *Stjerna*, Series A, vol. 299-B, para. 51 (discrimination on grounds of illegitimate birth), ECHR 24 February 1995, *McMichael*, Series A, vol. 307-B, para. 96 (discrimination on grounds of legitimate fatherhood; a very weighty reasons test was not applied in this case, but it clearly concerned a suspect discrimination), ECHR 16 December 1997, *Canea Catholic Church*, Reports 1997-VII, para. 46 (discrimination on grounds of religion; again, the Court did not apply a very weighty reasons test, but it is clear that the case concerns a discrimination that has been considered suspect in other cases), ECHR 1 February 2000, *Mazurek*, *European Human Rights Cases* 2000/25, para. 45 (discrimination on grounds of illegitimate birth, a special case, because the Court applied a comparability test in addition to the test of disadvantage), ECHR 6 April 2000, *Thlimmenos*, *European Human Rights Cases* 2000/45, paras 16-17 (discrimination on grounds of religion; a thorough investigation was especially called for because the case concerned a substantive discrimination; formally, there was equality of treatment, which could raise doubts as to the presence of disadvantageous treatment), ECHR 13 July 2000, *Elsholz*, *European Human Rights Cases* 2000/73, paras 59-61, ECHR 3 October 2000, *Camp and Bourimi*, *European Human Rights Cases* 2000/82, para. 12, ECHR 11 October 2001, *Sahin*, *European Human Rights Cases* 2001/81, para. 55 and ECHR 21 November 2001, *Fogarty*, *European Human Rights Cases* 2002/4, para. 42 (in which the Court wrongfully found no disadvantage: see my case comment in *European Human Rights Cases* 2002/4). The test of disadvantage is however not always explicitly applied: the Court often just assumes that the contested measure causes an impairment of interests of a certain group (see e.g. ECHR 24 June 1993, *Schuler-Zgraggen*, Series A, vol. 263 and ECHR 22 February 1994, *Burghartz*, Series A, vol. 280-B). It is remarkable also that the Court sometimes applies the test of disadvantage outside the context of suspect classifications; see e.g. ECHR 2 March 1987, *Monnell en Morris*, Series A, vol. 115, para. 75. In these cases the Court's reasoning with respect to the test is mostly minimal: mostly the Court only states that the disadvantage must be sufficiently serious. Illustrative in this respect is

to be interpreted quite broadly in these cases; for example, the Court does not require any actual proof of detriment on the side of the applicant.[64] Apart from this, the Court has given almost no clarity as to the way in which the disadvantage criterion should be applied. It is for instance not entirely clear whether emotional, rather intangible, disadvantage, which may be caused by prejudice or gross stereotyping, would oblige the state to put forward a justification. Also, no indication has been given as to the exact nature of the evidence that would be necessary in order to prove disadvantage.

3.3 The Second Phase of the Test: Justification

3.3.1 Presence of a legitimate aim

If the Court has concluded that the cases presented to it are sufficiently comparable (or if it is sufficiently clear that the applicant has been disadvantaged by the alleged discrimination), it will move on to the assessment of the arguments that have been advanced in justification of the discrimination.

According to the Court's decision model, it will start its assessment with an examination of the aim the state pursues with the classification or distinction. In this context, it is of importance that the Court not only examines the aims that have been put forward by the respondent government, but sometimes also verifies whether there are other aims or goals that possibly, but implicitly, inspired the difference in treatment. This stricter supervision is sometimes necessary as the Court usually accepts even very general and broad aims, such as 'the interests of the child' or 'the protection of public health'.[65] For states it is relatively

the *Boyle & Rice* case, concerning a difference in prison regimes. Although the Court could imagine that it must be difficult for a prisoner to be replaced from a prison with a fairly flexible regime to a very strict prison, it concluded that '[...] it [is] evident that in principle the difference in treatment complained of does not raise an arguable issue of discrimination under Article 14' (ECHR 27 April 1988, Series A, vol. 131, para. 86).

64 Frowein/Peukert, *Europäische MenschenRechtsKonvention. EMRK-Kommentar*, Strasbourg 1996, p. 447. However, stringent requirements have to be met in proving that a disadvantage is actually based on a suspect ground. In the *Velikova* case (ECHR 18 May 2000, *European Human Rights Cases* 2000/57), for instance, the applicant claimed that she was discriminated against because of her ethnic origin. The Court in this case demanded that the applicant proved 'beyond reasonable doubt' that the disadvantage she allegedly suffered was actually based on this ground. The Court did not give reasons for this burden of proof and did not repeat this requirement in several later judgments. Further case-law therefore must be awaited to determine whether this requirement is applicable to other discrimination claims as well.

65 See further paragraph 2.3.2, in which the legitimacy of the aim pursued will be discussed in more detail. See also Sundberg-Weitman, stating that the international *bona fide*-principle implies that all aims must be justified to exclude unreasonable dif-

easy to invoke such, undoubtedly reasonable and legitimate aims to conceal other, less easily justifiable considerations that also inspired the classification.[66] An effective protection of fundamental rights certainly justifies such investigations into the existence of hidden motives.

In the first cases in which the Court had to express itself about Article 14 complaints, it consistently paid attention to the question whether the difference in treatment was inspired not only by the aims and goals put forward by the state, but eventually also by different, more implicit considerations.[67] More recently, however, the Court seems to have ceased to show interest in the possible discrepancy between the alleged and the actual purposes of a classification. Only in cases in which the applicants explicitly challenge the aims advanced by the state, the Court sometimes seems willing to pay attention to the determination of the exact purpose of the discrimination.[68] This approach does not seem unreasonable: even if the Court would have sufficient means at its disposal to search, of its own accord, for hidden motives, it would easily exceed the limits

---

ferences in treatment ('Legal tests for applying the European Convention on Human Rights and Freedoms in adjudicating on alleged discrimination', *Nordisk Tidsskrift for International Ret* 1980, pp. 50-51). She also points out another problem with respect to the aims of a difference in treatment, namely 'killing two birds with the same stone'. This problem arises if a difference in treatment is supported by several purposes on the same hierarchical level. According to Sundberg-Weitman, it is sufficient if at least one of these purposes is legitimate and would be strong enough to support the difference in treatment on its own (p. 52).

66 Cf. Harris/O'Boyle/Warbrick 1995, n. 11 above, p. 479. This problem arises especially in applying the second paragraph test of Articles 8-11: as it is fairly easy to justify a measure, using one of the broad and general aims listed in these Articles, applicants often state that the aim advanced is not the actual aim of the measure. The Court does however not seem inclined to carefully investigate the truthfulness of such claims. See Harris/O'Boyle/Warbrick 1995, n. 11 above, pp. 290 and 344.

67 ECHR 27 October 1975, *National Union of Belgian Police*, Series A, vol. 19: 'The Government has urged, that it wished to avoid 'trade union anarchy' [...]. This is a legitimate aim in itself and the Court has no reason to think that the Government had other and ill-intentioned designs.' See also ECHR 6 February 1976, *Swedish Engine Drivers' Union*, Series A, vol. 20, para. 46 and ECHR 6 February 1976, *Schmidt and Dahlström*, Series A, vol. 21, para. 40. Examples in which the Court did make use of another formula are ECHR 24 November 1986, *Gillow*, Series A, vol. 109, in which the Court found with regard to Article 8 para. 2 that the aim was justified, and continued to state: 'The Court does not find it to be established that the legislation pursued any other purpose' (para. 54) and ECHR 27 April 2000, *L./Finland*, not yet published, in which the Court observed that '[t]here is nothing to suggest that it was applied for any other purpose in the present case' (para. 108); idem in ECHR 27 April 2000, *K. and T./Finland, European Human Rights Cases* 2000/49, para. 134.

68 See e.g. ECHR 21 February 1986, *James and Others*, Series A, vol. 98, para. 48.

of its judicial powers by doing so in every case.[69] Furthermore, such an active position would hardly be reconcilable with the Court's subsidiary function: the Court is an international institution and will therefore have to exercise some restraint in assessing national acts and measures.[70] From the point of view of the protection of individual rights and interests, however, it would sometimes be desirable for the Court to show a little more activity, especially in cases in which states only have a limited margin of appreciation, and the respondent state has only advanced very general, abstract aims such as the 'interests of justice'[71] or the 'avoidance of administrative burdens'[72].[73]

It has been mentioned before that the Court only finds a difference in treatment of comparable cases acceptable if the aim pursued by the differential treatment is legitimate. Article 14, other than several substantive Convention provisions (e.g. Articles 8-11), does not contain an exhaustive list of aims and goals that can immediately be considered legitimate.[74] As a result, the amount of possible legitimate aims that can be advanced in justification of a discrimination is almost unlimited, which enables the Court to develop its own criteria to assess the reasonableness and legitimacy of the advanced aims and purposes.[75] Unfortunately, the Court has not made very good use of this opportunity, mostly examining the goals and aims on a case-by-case basis. It is also remarkable that the Court accepts the legitimacy of almost every aim presented to it, even wel-

69 Cf. Kewenig 1972, n. 1 above, p. 106.

70 See for this reason for restraint further paragraph 4.

71 ECHR 19 December 1989, *Kamasinski*, Series A, vol. 168, para. 93.

72 ECHR 21 February 1986, *James and Others*, Series A, vol. 98, para. 68.

73 Cf. Helfer 1990, n. 32 above, p. 1066.

74 This does not mean, however, that Article 14 leaves much more room than provisions such as Articles 8-11: the aims listed therein are formulated in such general terms that almost all imaginable and not completely arbitrary measures will serve at least one of them. See Loucaides, *Essays on the Developing Law of Human Rights*, London 1995, p. 189 and Harris/O'Boyle/Warbrick 1995, n. 11 above, p. 290. Cf. also Schokkenbroek, *Toetsing aan de vrijheidsrechten van het Europees Verdrag tot Bescherming van de Rechten van de Mens*, Diss. Leiden 1996, p. 184. The Court's reasoning in judgments relating to substantive Convention provisions is mostly more careful and comprehensive than the reasoning in Article 14 cases, which also seems true for the proportionality test. One good example of a better test with respect to the substantive provisions is the *Gillow* case, in which the Court found the aim to be justified indeed, yet gave sound reasons for this conclusion (ECHR 24 November 1986, Series A, vol. 109). The Court's purpose review is especially comprehensive and careful if the complaint concerns Article 1 First Protocol; see e.g. *James* (ECHR 21 February 1986, Series A, vol. 98, paras 47-49) and *Building Societies* (ECHR 23 October 1997, Reports 1997-VII, para. 81).

75 ECHR 23 July 1968, *Belgian Linguistics case*, Series A, vol. 6.

coming very general and abstract purposes and considerations: any specificity or actuality of the aim advanced does not seem to be required.[76]

However, it cannot be inferred from this restricted purpose review that Article 14 is a toothless provision, having no real importance. Especially with respect to suspect classifications, the aims pursued by the state must meet stringent requirements; the Court even demands that the discrimination be supported by 'very weighty reasons'.[77] This requirement does not however so much relate to the reasonableness and legitimacy of the aim itself, as it does to its weight. In many suspect discrimination cases the Court has found that the aim pursued is, in itself, not illegitimate, but is not sufficiently strong to justify the difference in treatment.[78] This implies that the Court in these cases actually applies a test of proportionality in the disguise of a purpose test: important is not the legitimacy of the aim itself, but the weight of the aim in relation to the interests impaired by the classification.

In testing suspect classifications, the Court makes use of the same casuistic approach as in examining 'regular' classifications, which makes it difficult to indicate what criteria and circumstances are most relevant in assessing the legitimacy of the aim. Only in its *Inze* case the Court did develop three criteria that are of a somewhat higher level of generality.[79] Firstly, it can be inferred from this case that the Court requires, with respect to suspect classifications, a sufficient level of specificity: general and abstract considerations do not seem acceptable as a justification. Secondly, the Court does not allow for classifications that are based

---

76 There is only one case in which the Court did not find a justification and which did not concern a suspect classification. In this case, the respondent state did not advance any justification at all, making the Court's decision quite evident (ECHR 23 October 1990, *Darby*, Series A, vol. 187, paras 33-34).

77 See also Helfer 1990, n. 32 above, p. 1067 and Van Dijk/Van Hoof, *Theory and Practice of the European Convention on Human Rights*, Deventer 1997, p. 727. It is possible to find examples of cases in which there was a suspect classification, but the Court still found a legitimate aim. This was the case in *McMichael* (ECHR 24 February 1995, Series A, vol. 307-B) (the specific circumstances of the case were explained, in which the interests of the child were very weighty indeed) and in *Petrovic* (ECHR 27 March 1998, Reports 1998-II). The latter case will be discussed later on in more detail, as it shows a curious application of the margin of appreciation doctrine. This deviation could also explain the shortness of the Court's reasoning.

78 An example may be found in the earlier mentioned *Abdulaziz* case (ECHR 28 May 1985, Series A, vol. 94, paras 78-79). Another example is the *Hoffmann* case, in which the Court also stated that the purpose (protection of the interests and health of a child) were legitimate in themselves, but could not justify a difference in treatment exclusively based on religion (ECHR 23 June 1993, Series A, vol. 255-C, paras 34 and 36); idem in ECHR 21 December 1999, *Salgueiro da Silva Mouta*, *European Human Rights Cases* 2000/16, paras 30 and 36. Cf. also Partsch 1995, p. 1054.

79 ECHR 28 October 1987, *Inze*, Series A, vol. 126.

exclusively on traditional notions. The underlying principle of this criterion is probably the fact that traditional opinions are often based on overbroad stereotypes or on prejudice against socially poorly accepted or integrated groups.[80] Thirdly, the purpose must meet an actual need, which means that the reason for the discrimination needs sufficient factual basis to be in conformity with Article 14.[81] These criteria would appear to be applicable in a large number of cases; it is therefore regrettable that the Court does not apply them more generally.

3.3.2 The Relationship between the Difference in Treatment and the Aim Pursued: Proportionality

According to the Court's decision model, the presence of a legitimate aim is not sufficient to find a difference in treatment consistent with the prohibition of discrimination: it is also necessary to establish the presence of a reasonable relationship of proportionality between the interests impaired by the distinction and the aims pursued therewith. Careful application of the proportionality requirement is of great importance to the Court's review of alleged discriminations, especially because, as has been shown above, the motive review test mostly constitutes a rather weak part of the Court's test and does not offer individual applicants much protection against unjustified or even arbitrary distinctions.

Unfortunately, the Court has been quite reluctant in giving a more detailed interpretation of the requirement of a 'reasonable relationship of proportional-

80 The Court expressed some doubts as to the legitimacy of traditional opinions as a justification before, namely in the *Marckx* case (ECHR 13 June 1979, Series A, vol. 31, para. 40). In later case-law the Court sometimes accepted that the purpose of protecting the 'traditional family' was justified in itself, but was not sufficiently weighty to support a difference in treatment based on a suspect ground; see ECHR 1 February 2000, *Mazurek*, *European Human Rights Cases* 2000/25, para. 50.

81 The requirement of the aim reflecting a concrete and factual situation may also be found in the *Karlheinz Schmidt* case (ECHR 18 July 1994, Series A, vol. 291-B). This case concerned the payment of a contribution to the fire department, which served as a financial compensation for the factual obligation to assist in the activities of the fire department. Women were excluded from this factual obligation and were also not obliged to pay a financial compensation. The exclusion of women from the obligation to assist the fire department in its activities was inspired by the desire to protect their health: the government based the difference in treatment on the physical and mental differences between women and men, making women less fit to extinguish fires and assist in other relevant activities. The Court observed that '[…] what is finally decisive in the present case is that the obligation to perform such service is exclusively one of law and theory. In view of the continuing existence of a sufficient number of volunteers, no male person is in fact obliged to serve in a fire brigade. The financial contribution has – not in law but in fact – lost its compensatory character and has become the only effective duty. In the imposition of a financial burden such as this, a difference of treatment on the ground of sex can hardly be justified' (para. 28).

ity'. As a result, it is not entirely clear whether the formula should be interpreted as constituting a proportionality test in the strict sense of the term, only leaving room for reviewing the balance of interests involved in making a distinction, or as constituting a proportionality review in the broad sense, which for example would also imply a test of appropriateness[82] or subsidiarity[83] of the distinction. The second interpretation does seem to be most consistent with the Court's case law, as the reasoning of many judgments can only be explained in terms of appropriateness, necessity or subsidiarity.

As will be discussed in more detail in section 4, the intensity of the Court's review of the relationship between a distinction and its aims is variable. As a rule, the Court seems to opt for a somewhat restricted review: as is clear from the model that is usually applied by the Court, a difference in treatment is justified as soon as a '*reasonable* relationship of proportionality' is present. In order to prove a violation of Article 14, it seems necessary for the applicant to show a clear lack of proportionality or even arbitrariness.[84]

The restraint exercised by the Court is not unreasonable, as the authority to strike a balance of interests primarily rests with the national authorities. The Court does supervise the exercise of this authority indeed, yet will take due distance in doing so, especially when a case concerns general rules that have been enacted by a national legislative body.[85] Even though the Court sometimes assesses the reasonableness of the relationship between the distinction and its aims very

---

82 Meaning that the Court will examine whether the difference in treatment forms a suitable means to achieve the aims pursued.

83 Meaning that no other, less burdensome or disadvantageous measures than the distinction made were available to achieve the aims pursued.

84 See Schokkenbroek 1996, n. 74 above, p. 37.

85 Frowein/Peukert 1996, n. 64 above, p. 452. According to Sundberg-Weitman, the proportionality test always infringes State sovereignty in an unacceptable way. In her opinion, such test may not be applied (1980, n. 65 above, p. 53). This statement does however seem too extreme. If an international court such as the Court would be unable to decide whether a national measure affects individual interests in an arbitrary or too far reaching manner, international protection would lose much of its power. Furthermore, the Court is the highest institution that is authorized to give an interpretation of the Convention; it would therefore seem strange if it would not have the possibility to examine what interests and rights are relevant in deciding whether a Convention provision is violated (Burke, 'Note: Secret Surveillance and the European Convention on Human Rights', *Stanford Law Review* 1981, p. 1133). Of course, the Court should exercise due restraint in reviewing national legislation. As Bossuyt has explained, the Court must therefore take account of its double subsidiary role: not only must it exercise an international court's restraint towards the national authorities, but must also take care of its relationship as a court towards a representative legislative body (Bossuyt, *L'Interdiction de la discrimination dans le droit international des droits de l'homme*, Brussels 1976, p. 83).

carefully,[86] namely in those cases in which it applies its strict 'very weighty reasons' test, the proportionality test is mostly marginal in character. The marginal or restricted character of the Court's review finds expression mostly in a general test of arbitrariness,[87] or even in the complete omission of a test of the relationship between the distinction and its aims.[88] The Court also shows restraint by its practice of giving only few arguments for its findings as to the proportionality of the distinction: in many cases it restricts itself to stating that there is a reasonable relationship between the difference in treatment and the aims pursued.[89]

In a limited number of cases the Court applies a more comprehensive and careful proportionality test, namely in cases concerning suspect classifications or cases in which the Court refers to its findings with respect to the infringement of substantive Convention provisions in applying the proportionality test. In those cases, the Court mostly pays explicit attention to elements such as appropriateness, necessity and proportionality in strict sense.

a. Appropriateness

If a discriminatory measure does not form an appropriate means to attain the aims pursued, while negatively affecting individual rights or interests, it cannot be considered desirable to maintain such a measure. In such circumstances, the national authorities may be expected to amend the measure, or to replace it by a more effective one. The Court seems to have adopted this reasoning in several of its judgments. An example of this may be found in the *Abdulaziz* case,[90] concerning a UK regulation regarding family reunion (the '1980 Rules'). The 1980 Rules made distinctions on basis of gender, by making it much more difficult for migrant women residing and working in the UK to obtain a family reunion permit than for men in a similar position. In its judgment, the Court stated the following: 'The Court accepts that the 1980 Rules [...] had, as the Government stated, the aim of advancing public tranquillity. However, it is not persuaded that this aim was served by the distinction drawn in those rules between husbands and wives.' (para. 81)

86 E.g. ECHR 27 October 1975, *National Union of Belgian Police*, Series A, vol. 19, para. 49.

87 See e.g. *Lithgow* (ECHR 8 July 1986, Series A, vol. 102, paras 181 and 183), *Kamasinski* (ECHR 19 December 1989, Series A, vol. 168, paras 93 and 100), *Moustaquim* (ECHR 18 February 1991, Series A, vol. 193, para. 49), *C. v. Belgium* (7 August 1996, Reports 1996-III) and *Building Societies* (ECHR 23 October 1997, Reports 1997-VII, para. 90). In these judgments the Court first stated that there was a legitimate aim and then immediately concluded that there was an objective and reasonable justification.

88 Cf. ECHR 22 October 1996, *Stubbings*, Reports 1996-IV.

89 E.g. ECHR 23 November 1976, *Engel and Others*, Series A, vol. 22, para. 72.

90 ECHR 25 May 1985, Series A, vol. 94

Although the Court gives a clear opinion as to the appropriateness of the contested regulation in the cited passage, it is remarkable that it does not give any arguments as an underpinning of its opinion: its findings as to the ineffectiveness of the 1980 Rules appear to be mainly based on subjective doubts and assumptions. Apparently, the Court did not feel the need to base its opinion on empirical or scientific evidence advanced by the parties to the case.

b. Necessity/Subsidiarity

The case-law with respect to the relationship between means and ends shows that the test normally used by the Court in applying the proportionality requirement of Article 14 is strongly comparable to the 'pressing social need' test that is applied with respect to several substantive Convention provisions, such as Articles 8-11.[91] Where a more intensive test is applied the Court often examines whether the difference in treatment may be considered 'necessary' in order to achieve the aims pursued.

An example of an application of the necessity test in the context of an Article 14 complaint may be found in the *Camp and Bourimi* case.[92] The case concerned problems with respect to rights of inheritance that arose when the biological father of a child born out of wedlock died before the child was born and before the father had the chance of legally recognizing it. By means of 'letters of legitimation' it appeared possible to obtain legal recognition of the family ties between the father and his child, but as a result of Dutch family law the child could not be regarded as a lawful heir. The Dutch government argued that the contested regulations were meant to ensure legal certainty and to protect the interests of third parties: other heirs should enjoy the certainty that they would not have to give up a lawful inheritance to descendants of the deceased who would unexpectedly turn up. The Court ruled as follows

> [...][W]hen it comes to the question of the proportionality of the means chosen to achieve this aim the Court observes that Sofian [the child concerned in the case, JHG] was not a descendant of whose existence the other heirs were unaware. Here, there is no indication that the exigencies of the situation required the level of protection that was afforded to [...] [applicant's] parents and siblings to the detriment of his son. The Court considers that in these circumstances Sofian's exclusion from his father's inheritance was disproportionate. (para. 15)

In this argumentation a necessity test can clearly be recognized, as the Court examines whether the difference in treatment was, in the concrete circumstances of the case, actually needed to achieve the aims pursued.

91 See ECHR 7 December 1976, Series A, vol. 24, para. 48.

92 ECHR 3 October 2000, *European Human Rights Cases* 2000/82.

In the context of the necessity test, the Court also often examines whether the aim pursued could have been attained by using less discriminatory or less disadvantageous means. An example of this 'subsidiarity test' may be found in the *Rasmussen* case,[93] concerning Danish statutory rules with respect to denial of paternity of a child born during marriage. In the interests of legal certainty and to protect the interests of the child, the husband could start paternity proceedings only within five years of the child's birth, but the statutory rules contained no such time limit for the mother. In Danish case law, however, a 'doctrine of acknowledgement' had been developed, according to which the right to institute paternity proceedings expired as soon as one of the spouses explicitly or implicitly recognized the husband as the father of the child. This doctrine was valid for both the husband and the wife and aimed, just as the statutory rules, at protecting the child against the burdens of legal paternity proceedings instituted years after its birth. In the opinion of the applicants, the existence of the doctrine proved that the aim of the statutory regulations could also have been reached without distinguishing on the basis of sex. The Court ruled as follows

> It is true that an equivalent result might have been obtained through the doctrine of acknowledgement, but [...] the competent authorities were entitled to think that as regards the husband the aim sought to be realised would be the most satisfactorily achieved by the enactment of a statutory rule, where as regards the mother it was sufficient to leave the matter to be decided by the Courts on a case-by-case basis. Accordingly, [...] the authorities [...] did not transgress the principle of proportionality. (para. 41)

Even though the Court applied a marginal test and did not find the difference in treatment in breach of the proportionality criterion, the cited considerations undoubtedly show an application of the subsidiarity test.

c. Proportionality in Strict Sense

The test of proportionality in strict sense constitutes an important element in the application of the substantive Convention provisions. In most cases, the Court's opinion about the balance of interests struck by the national authorities is even decisive for the outcome of the cases, especially where an intensive test is applied. This is different for the application of Article 14: in assessing the justification of an alleged discrimination, the Court only rarely gives a clear opinion about the balance of interests underlying the classification. The explanation for this difference would seem to be the same one as has earlier been given to explain other omissions in the Court's application of its decision model: the Court usually chooses to exercise restraint and prefers to leave the assessment of the reason-

93 ECHR 28 November 1984, Series A, vol. 87; cf. also Schokkenbroek 1996, n. 74 above, p. 200.

ableness of a balance of interests to the national authorities. Again, a different approach is often chosen if the Court opts for a more intensive test, for instance because it has to give its opinion about a suspect classification. As has been said before, such classifications may only be justified by very weighty reasons, which implies not only that the respondent government has to put forward objective and legitimate arguments, but also that these arguments must be important and convincing enough to support a very serious impairment of interests. In order to assess the quality and weight of the advanced justification, the Court will have to compare the weight of the interests served by the classification against the weight of the interests impaired by it. The very weighty reasons test therefore actually constitutes a proportionality test in strict sense.

A remark should be made in that the Court's Article 14 case law does not show many examples of suspect classification cases in which the Court does pay real attention to the proportionality test. In most cases, the Court is very brief in its reasoning, contenting itself with the statement that no objective and reasonable arguments may be found to justify the difference in treatment. Representative for the Court's approach are considerations such as the following, originating from the *Schuler-Zgraggen* case[94]

> [...] very weighty reasons have to be put forward before [...] a difference of treatment could be regarded as compatible with the Convention. The Court discerns no such reason in the instant case. It therefore concludes that for want of any reasonable and objective justification, there has been a breach of Article 14.[95]

Such extraordinarily brief reasoning does certainly not improve the controllability of the Court's conclusions or the clarity of the considerations underlying its findings. The lack of legal certainty that is caused by this way of reasoning seems to be compensated only to some extent by the very great predictability of the outcome of the very weighty reasons-test: where this test is applied, the Court almost never reached the conclusion that the difference in treatment is consistent with Article 14. Thus, if a distinction is based on suspect grounds, it is almost certain that it is not acceptable, notwithstanding any arguments that the respondent government might put forward to justify it. As a consequence, the accent of the test of suspect classifications has actually shifted from a substantive scrutiny of the difference in treatment to the determination of the applicability of the very weighty reasons test. In section 4 the factors determining this applicability will be explored in more detail.

94 ECHR 24 June 1993, Series A, vol. 263.

95 Para 67. A comparable approach may be found in *Gaygusuz* (ECHR 16 September 1996, Reports 1996-IV).

4. Intensity of the Court's Review: The Margin of Appreciation Doctrine and the Very Weighty Reasons Test

4.1 The Margin of Appreciation Doctrine

4.1.1 Contents of the Margin Appreciation Doctrine

The intensity of the Court's review is mainly determined by the well-known doctrine of the margin of appreciation. This doctrine is primarily developed in order to give the states some discretion to assess the necessity of measures they wish to take in fields that fall within the scope of the Convention. Only when the states transgress the limits of the margin of appreciation accorded to them will the Court conclude that they have acted in violation of the Convention.

The Court has made clear that attributing a margin of appreciation cannot be considered equivalent to the assumption that a state has acted in accordance with the Convention, which would imply that it would have to restrict itself to assessing whether the state has acted 'reasonably, carefully and in good faith'.[96] It is certainly not true that, as soon as a wide margin of appreciation is accorded, a state always enjoys the benefit of the doubt. Instead, the margin of appreciation doctrine should be regarded as a mechanism enabling the Court to determine the intensity of its review of national acts and measures.[97] The Court leaves room for discretion to the States which may be considered a voluntary restriction of its own judicial powers: in such cases the Court will refrain from far-reaching examinations of the details of an act or measure.[98] In the Court's case law, this starting point is mainly visible in the requirements a state has to meet in justifying an infringement of individual rights: if the State is accorded a wide margin of appreciation, the Court will only demand that it advances 'sufficient reasons' to justify the infringement, while the reasons will have to be 'sound' or 'pertinent' as soon as the margin of appreciation is, for some reason, more narrow.[99] The margin of appreciation doctrine may therefore be regarded as an instrument of differentiation in the intensity of the Court's review: in case of a wide margin, the national measures will be tested only marginally, but if the Court opts for a narrow margin, a much more intensive test will be applied.[100]

---

96 ECHR 29 March 1979, *Sunday Times*, Series A, vol. 30, para. 59; see also Schokkenbroek 1996, n. 74 above, p. 203. In the *Olsson* case, the Court expressed a reason for this point of view: whether a state has acted 'reasonably, carefully and in good faith' depends to a large extent on the subjective opinion of the state itself, while the Courts desires to use a more objective standard (ECHR 24 March 1988, Series A, vol. 130, para. 82).

97 Burke 1981, n. 84 above, p. 1132 and Schokkenbroek 1996, n. 74 above, p. 203.

98 See Alkema, 'Rechterlijk toezicht en de Europese vrijheidsrechten', in: *Vrijheid en Recht ('s Jacobbundel)*, Zwolle 1975, p. 8.

99 Velaers, *De beperkingen van de vrijheid van meningsuiting*, Antwerpen 1991, p. 355.

100 Macdonald, 'The Margin of Appreciation', in: Macdonald, Matscher and Petzold

4.1.2 Factors Determining the Margin of Appreciation

a. Common Ground Factor: Existence of a European Consensus

One of the most important factors determining de margin of appreciation that is left to the state is the existence of a 'common ground'. In a large number of cases the Court investigates whether there is a consensus between the various Member States of the Council of Europe with respect to the subject of the complaint it has to decide upon.[101] The main reason for such comparative research may be found in the fact that the national authorities are ultimately responsible for the implementation of the Convention. Would the Court show itself less inclined to take account of the ruling opinions and the case-law and statutory legislation on the national level, the eagerness of the states to effectively and

---

(eds.), *The European System for the Protection of Human Rights*, Dordrecht 1993, pp. 84-85: 'The margin of appreciation is really just the other side of the scope of review coin; it is the amount of latitude left to national authorities once the appropriate level of review has been decided on by the Court.' See also O'Donnell, 'The Margin of Appreciation Doctrine: Standards in the Jurisprudence of the European Court of Human Rights', *Human Rights Quarterly* 1982, p. 477. Schokkenbroek indicates that it is not entirely possible to regard the margin of appreciation and the intensity of the review as two sides of the same coin, especially because the margin of appreciation doctrine in some cases does not offer a convincing explanation for existing differences in the strictness of the test applied (1996, n. 74 above, p. 211). It is true indeed that in certain opinions of the Court a wide margin is left, yet a rather strict test is applied. This does not mean, however, that the margin of appreciation and the intensity of the review have to be regarded as different concepts: it also could seem to indicate that the Court's test is sometimes inaccurate and inconsistent.

101 The concept of the European consensus is not only used in determining the intensity of the review, but also functions as a method of interpretation. As such, it is particularly useful if the Court wants to give a new, far reaching or controversial to a Convention provision and seeks a legitimation for such interpretation, but also if the text of a certain provision is simply unclear and difficult to interpret. Examples of the use of the common ground argument as a method of interpretation may be found in ECHR 30 June 1993, *Sigurdur A. Sigurjónsson*, Series A, vol. 264, ECHR 24 June 1993, *Schuler-Zgraggen*, Series A, vol. 263, ECHR 16 December 1999, *V. v. UK, European Human Rights Cases* 2000/15, paras 73-77 and ECHR 11 July 2002, *Christine Goodwin/UK, European Human Rights Cases* 2002/74, paras 84-85. In this paragraph, no attention will be paid to the use of the common ground factor as a method of interpretation, which implies that questions as to compatibility of the consensus principle with other principles of Convention interpretation, e.g. autonomous or evolutive interpretation, will remain unanswered. See therefore extensively Heringa, 'Artikel 14 EVRM: een achtergestelde waarborg?', in: Heringa and Myer (eds.), *45 Jaar Europees Verdrag voor de Rechten van de Mens*, Leiden 1996, p. 108 ff. and Brems, 'The Margin of Appreciation Doctrine under the European Convention on Human Rights: Its Legitimacy in Theory and Application in Practice', *Zeitschrift für Ausländisches Recht und Völkerrecht* 1996, p. 304 ff.

swiftly execute the Court's judgments would probably diminish very strongly.[102] Also, the use of the consensus argument often renders a valuable justification for controversial judgments, and may render difficult decisions about sensitive issues, such as trans-sexuality or abortion, more acceptable.[103]

In the determination of the intensity of the review, the use of the common ground factor usually results in a less strict test if no or only little agreement is distinguished between the different states. If, on the other hand, a clear European consensus appears to exist, the intensity of the review depends on the character of the consensus. If the large majority of European states approves of a certain restriction of individual rights, the Court will mostly apply a marginal test, but it will intensify its review as soon as a restrictive act or measure appears to be generally condemned.[104]

Though the common ground principle would seem to constitute a useful and objective factor in determining the intensity of the Court's review, the practical application of the principle might raise some questions.[105] In the first place, it is very difficult to determine when a European consensus may be said to exist: the question might be asked whether it is necessary that there be absolute agreement, in the sense that every single European state cherishes the same opinion, or whether it is sufficient that only a small majority of states adopts a specific policy. Furthermore, it is uncertain to what extent it should be possible to take account of special circumstances or opinions in a state, especially when a case touches on controversial or ethically sensitive issues. Until now, the Court has not explicitly provided an answer to these questions, limiting itself to a case-by-case determination of the existence of a European consensus; unfortunately, this approach has

102 Academics have advanced the explanation that the fundamental rights protected by the Convention flow logically from the common heritage of the various states, making it difficult to understand the content of the Convention provisions without taking paying heed to the national legal systems (Brems 1996, n. 100 above, p. 300, Carozza, 'Propter honoris respectum: uses and misuses of comparative law in international human rights: some reflections on the jurisprudence of the European Court of Human Rights', *Notre Dame Law Review* 1998, p. 1226 and Heringa 1996, n. 100 above, p. 110). Although this argument may explain the use of the common ground factor in interpreting Convention provisions, it offers only a limited and partial explanation for the use of the factor in determining the amount of discretion left to the states.

103 Harris/O'Boyle/Warbrick 1995, n. 11 above, p. 296.

104 Cf. Heringa 1996, n. 100 above, p. 110.

105 Furthermore, the use of a European consensus as determinative factor for the intensity of the Court's review may be criticized, as it may lead to the development of a minimum standard of protection: fundamental rights will be protected only to the extent that is accepted by a majority of European states, even if a stronger protection would be desirable. This may be illustrated by the Court's case-law concerning trans-sexuality. See also Carozza 1998, n. 101 above, p. 1218 and 1228.

resulted in the lack of a clear and detailed doctrine.[106] Notable is also the regular absence of a thorough analysis of the statutory law and case law of the different states, which makes it difficult to determine what factors usually lead the Court to the conclusion of a lack or the presence of a common ground.[107] However, it may be inferred from the very limited number of cases in which the Court has found sufficient agreement between the national legislations that a consensus will not easily be found: as appears from its case-law, the Court has chosen a stringent approach, only intensifying its review if almost all states have adopted comparable measures or policies with respect to almost all aspects of the right concerned.[108]

One may ask whether such an approach does justice to the desire to protect individual and fundamental rights. For many states, the Court's judgments form important occasions to improve fundamental rights protection.[109] If the Court only accepts a narrower margin if there is a very high level of European consensus, the urge for innovation and improvement emanating from its case law will be rather limited. Conservative states, reluctant to implement the Convention, will probably be affirmed in their attitude by the Court's restraint, instead of being inspired to accept legislation that progressively safeguards individual and fundamental rights. As a consequence of the strict use of the common ground argument, there might be a risk that the Convention is degraded to a smallest common denominator of human rights protection.[110] To ensure actual and increasing protection of fundamental rights, the Court ought to act as a pioneer.[111] To leave a wide margin of appreciation to the states, even if there is a clearly visible development in the direction of a European consensus, cannot be reconciled with such a role.

---

106 Cf. Helfer, 'Consensus, Coherence and the European Convention on Human Rights', *Cornell International Law Journal* 1993, p. 140.

107 Cf. Helfer 1993, . 106 above, p. 154, Brems 1996, n. 100 above, p. 285 and Carozza 1998, n. 101 above, p. 1224. It is remarkable that the Court only rarely makes explicit what states it has involved in its examination or what methods of comparative research it uses.

108 Helfer 1993, n. 105 above, p. 142.

109 Cf. Tomuschat 1992, 'Europe – A common constitutional space', in: De Witte and Forder (eds.), *The Common Law of Europe and the future of legal education*, Deventer 1992, p. 136 ff., giving various examples of amendments the states have made in their legislation and policies in response to the Court's judgments.

110 Velaers 1991, n. 98 above, p. 365 and Carozza 1998, n. 101 above, pp. 1218 and 1228.

111 This could even be regarded as a constitutional responsibility of the judiciary: it is its duty to protect fundamental and individual rights, even if a parliamentary majority or, as in this case, a majority of states does not accept such protection (cf. Koopmans' nabeschouwing bij Wiarda, *3 Typen van rechtsvinding*, 4th Edition, Deventer 1999, p. 134).

b. The Better Placed Argument

The accordance of a wide margin of appreciation is also justified in many cases by the 'better placed argument': the Court often considers itself less able than the national authorities to evaluate local or national conditions and the need for the enactment of certain measures.[112] As is apparent from several judgments, the Court will, for instance, exercise restraint if the complaint concerns sanctions that have been imposed by a national court;[113] or if the infringement is caused by decisions that have been made in protection of the interests of a child, such as placement in a foster family. The better-placed argument also explains the Court's reservation in deciding on cases about Article 1 of the First Protocol (protection of property). The rights and interests involved in property cases are frequently of a socio-economic character, and measures affecting these rights are often highly political and complicated. In several of its judgments, the Court has therefore indicated that this kind of measures necessitates a wide margin of appreciation for the states,[114] especially where a complaint concerns control on the use of property,[115] planning and environmental rules and procedures,[116] or housing policies.[117]

c. The Character and Weight of the Aims Pursued

The Court has explicitly stated that the character and weight of the aims pursued may have some influence on the margin of appreciation that is left to the states.[118] The Court will, for instance, mostly exercise restraint if a measure affecting an individual right is taken in protection of national security, or if it is meant to protect sensitive moral or ethical values. In the first situation, the margin of appreciation will be wide because the states themselves are best able to evaluate the demands and needs involved in protecting national security.[119]

---

112 This factor is also applied by the Court as a general legitimation for its use of the margin of appreciation doctrine; see further supra paragraph 3.1.2.

113 E.g. ECHR 27 January 1987, *Weeks*, Series A, vol. 114, para. 50.

114 E.g. ECHR 21 February 1986, *James*, Series A, vol. 98, para. 46.

115 ECHR 18 February 1991, *Fredin*, Series A, vol. 192, para. 51.

116 ECHR 25 September 1996, *Buckley*, Reports 1996-IV, para. 75 and ECHR 18 January 2001, *Jane Smith, European Human Rights Cases* 2001/19, para. 99.

117 ECHR 19 December 1989, *Mellacher*, Series A, vol. 169, para. 45, ECHR 28 September 1995, *Spadea and Scalabrino*, Series A, vol. 315-B, para. 29 and ECHR 28 July 1999, *Immobiliare Saffi*, Reports 1999-V, para. 49. See also Ovey 1998, p. 12.

118 ECHR 26 April 1979, *Sunday Times I*, Series A, vol. 30, para. 59. See also ECHR 23 October 1986, *Gillow*, Series A, vol. 109, para. 55 and ECHR 26 March 1987, *Leander*, Series A, vol. 116, para. 59.

119 See e.g. the *Klass* case, concerning telephone tapping for purposes of criminal investigations. The Court postulated in its judgment the importance of a strict interpretation of Article 8 para. 2. 'Secret surveillance' – monitoring telephone calls, opening cor-

In the second example, the reason for restraint may be found in the fact that it is very difficult to give an objective assessment of the ruling values in a specific state at a certain point in time.

The examples make clear that the common ground and better-placed factors play an important role in determining the character and weight of the aims pursued. It might even be argued that the factor 'character and weight of the aims pursued' is no independent factor at all, but only forms a *specialis* of these more general factors.

d. Context of the Contested Measure

In a limited number of cases, the extent to which a margin of appreciation is left to the state is determined by the context in which the contested measure has been taken. This factor seems to play an important role in the case law concerning immigration policy. The Convention does not prevent states from taking regulative or restricting measures in this field, thus offering them a relatively large freedom of action.[120] The Court therefore deems it a primary task of the

respondence, etc. without the concerned person's knowledge – is only allowed if this is strictly necessary to conserve democratic interests. This reasoning would seem to indicate a very strict test, but the Court also expressed the opinion that the present threat posed to the democratic society by espionage and terrorism was such as to justify a large amount of discretion for the states to enable effective control. The actual test that was applied by the Court was therefore rather marginal: the Court restricted itself to assessing whether there existed sufficient procedural guarantees against abuse (ECHR 6 September 1978, Series A, vol. 28, paras 42, 48 en 49; see also Schokkenbroek 1996, pp. 94-95). In the same way the Court accepted the need to avoid violence and protect national security as a sufficient basis for the award of a wide margin of appreciation in recent cases against Turkey: '[...] where such remarks incite to violence against an individual, a public official or a sector of the population, the State authorities enjoy a wider margin of appreciation when examining the need for an interference with the freedom of expression' (ECHR 8 July 1999, *Ceylan*, Reports 1999-IV, para. 34; idem in ECHR 2 October 2001, *Stankov*, *European Human Rights Cases* 2001/84, para. 90); cf. also, outside the specific context of the Turkish cases, also ECHR 27 September 1999, *Lustig-Prean and Beckett*, *European Human Rights Cases* 1999/2, para. 82.

120 In the *Berrehab* case, the Court for instance observed: 'In determining whether an interference was 'necessary in a democratic society', the Court makes allowance for the margin of appreciation that is left to the Contracting States. In this connection, it accepts that the Convention does not in principle prohibit the Contracting States from regulating the entry and the length of stay of aliens' (ECHR 21 June 1988, Series A, vol. 138, para. 28; see also ECHR 28 May 1985, *Abdulaziz*, Series A, vol. 94, para. 67). Idem in ECHR 11 July 2000, *Ciliz*, *European Human Rights Cases* 2000/72, para. 66, which also shows that a wide margin is left in most immigration cases, but it still remains necessary for the states to guarantee sufficient procedural safeguards with respect to deportation. The presence of such procedural safeguards will normally be reviewed quite strictly, even though the underlying immigration policy itself will be tested only marginally.

national authorities to evaluate the necessity of statutory rules regulating such issues as the entrance of immigrants, family reunion or deportation.[121] Important is also that immigration policy is narrowly linked to state sovereignty, which is a reason in itself for an international institution such as the Court to take a restrained position. On the other hand, the Court will leave a much narrower margin of appreciation to the states and will often opt for a more intensive test as soon as measures that are disadvantageous to immigrants are not being taken within the context of immigration policy, but fall within other policy fields (such as social security).[122]

The Court not only leaves a wider margin of appreciation in cases concerning immigration issues, but it will also exercise restraint if the infringement is caused by the army or prison regulations: in both cases, the Court accepts that there exists a special situation that justifies different and often further reaching measures than would be acceptable in 'normal life'.[123] Finally, the Court has indicated that a wider margin of appreciation will be allowed if the applicant is a civil servant or police officer.[124]

e. The Character and Importance of the Affected Right: Fundamental Rights and Core Rights

Another factor that is of importance in determining the level of intensity of the review may be found in the character and importance of the right that has been infringed by the contested measure: if the right is fundamental in character, the Court will mostly apply a very strict test.[125] In determining whether or not a right is fundamental, the Court seems to take an objective notion of the weight of the right as a starting point, evaluating whether the right has, in itself, special value and may be objectively considered of special interest for the individual. It is not important whether the right is of any importance from the subjective point of view of the applicant party; this issue will only be relevant for the sub-

121 Cf. ECHR 7 August 1996, *C./Belgium*, Reports 1996-III.

122 ECHR 16 September 1996, *Gaygusuz*, Reports 1996-IV, para. 42.

123 E.g. ECHR 23 November 1992, *Hadjianastassiou*, Series A, vol. 252, para. 46 and ECHR 25 February 1983, *Silver*, Series A, vol. 61, para. 98.

124 ECHR 20 May 1999, *Rekvenyi*, Reports 1999-III, para. 43. According to the *Wille* case this is also relevant to members of the judiciary (ECHR 28 October 1999, *European Human Rights Cases* 1999/7, para. 64). See also ECHR 26 September 1995, *Vogt*, Series A, vol. 323, para. 53 and ECHR 2 September 1998, *Ahmed and Others*, Reports 1998-VI, para. 61.

125 ECHR 25 September 1996, *Buckley*, Reports 1996-IV, para. 74. This does however not say very much about the outcome of the case: in many cases in which a narrow margin of appreciation has been left to the states because a fundamental right has been infringed, the infringement is found to be sufficiently justified. Cf. O'Donnell 1982, n. 98 above, p. 484.

stantive assessment of the alleged violation, namely in the context of the test of proportionality in strict sense.[126]

Academics have sometimes criticized the role of the importance and fundamental character that the infringed right plays in deciding what amount of discretion should be left to the states, because every single right contained in the Convention must be considered of great importance to the individual; seen from that point of view, the margin of appreciation should always be very limited.[127] This criticism does not seem completely justified. Every fundamental right has different aspects, some of which can be considered 'core rights', being of greater importance to the individual than other more 'peripheral' aspects of the right. It is not unreasonable to apply a stricter test with respect to an alleged violation of a core right than a violation of a right that may be placed in the periphery of the relevant Convention right. Of course it must be admitted that it is very difficult to determine what aspects of a right should be characterized as belonging to the very essence of the right concerned.[128] The Court's case law contains several criteria that would appear useful in this respect. The Court seems to characterize aspects of Convention rights as core rights especially if they prove to be essential to the well functioning of a pluralistic and democratic society.[129] This is, for example, the case with press freedom, but not with expressions that are primarily commercial in character.[130] For Article 8, it also seems possible to

126 In very exceptional cases the Court does pay some attention to the importance of the right to the applicant concerned; see ECHR 26 March 1987, *Leander*, Series A, vol. 116.

127 See Schokkenbroek 1996, n. 74 above, p. 129 and Velaers 1991, n. 98 above, p. 334; the latter observes that there is no such thing as the 'essence of the right to freedom of expression'.

128 Cf. Burkens, *Algemene leerstukken van grondrechten naar Nederlands constitutioneel recht*, Zwolle 1989, p. 95.

129 This also goes for Article 9 of the Convention. See ECHR 25 May 1993, *Kokkinakis*, Series A, vol. 260-A, para. 31, ECHR 26 September 1996, *Manoussakis*, Reports 1996-I, para. 44 and (more implicitly) ECHR 14 December 1999, *Serif*, *European Human Rights Cases* 2000/14, para. 49.

130 In *markt intern Verlag* the Court for instance observed the following: '[...] the Contracting States have a certain margin of appreciation in assessing the existence and extent of the necessity of an interference [...]. Such a margin of appreciation is essential in commercial matters and, in particular, in an area as complex and fluctuating as that of unfair competition. Otherwise, the European Court of Human Rights would have to undertake a re-examination of the facts and all the circumstances of each case. The Court must confine its review to the question whether the measures taken on the national level are justifiable in principle and proportionate' (ECHR 25 October 1989, Series A, vol. 165, para. 33). It must however be remarked that the outcome of the case was supported by a minimal majority and all dissenting opinions were directed against the cited passage. In a later judgment, the Court nuanced its opinion

define a core right: according to the Court's case-law, the essence of this provision may be found in the protection of very intimate aspects of the private life of individual persons. As a general rule, it could therefore be inferred from the Court's case law that political rights and rights that are closely linked to human dignity belong to the core of the rights protected by the Convention.

f. The Character of the Infringement

Finally, the character of the infringement may influence the amount of discretion that is left to the states.[131] The Court has accepted the relevance of this factor in several cases, such as the *Lustig-Prean and Beckett* case.[132] The applicants in this case were working for the UK armed forces, but were dismissed from their functions when the army authorities discovered their homosexual orientation. The applicants felt especially harmed by the fact that the army authorities had been probing deeply in their private lives to assemble proof of their homosexuality. With regard to the margin of appreciation that was to be left to the UK in this case, the Court observed the following

> Concerning as it [the dismissal and the investigations that took place after suspicions were raised as to the applicant's sexual orientation, JHG] did a most intimate aspect of an individual's private life, particularly serious reasons by way of justification were required. In the case of the present applicants, the Court finds the interferences to have been especially grave for the following reasons. In the first place, the investigation process [...] was of an exceptionally intrusive character. [...] Secondly, the administrative discharge of the applicants had [...] a profound effect on their careers and prospects. [...] Thirdly, the absolute and general character of the policy, which led to the interferences in question, is striking.[133]

The application of the very strict test by the Court in this case does not only seem inspired by the fact that a core right had been affected, though that factor certainly did play a role as well, but also because of the seriousness and intrusive character of the infringement.[134]

---

by observing that the margin of appreciation will be narrower if an expression contributes to a public debate about an issue of general importance (ECHR 25 August 1998, *Hertel*, Reports 1998-VI, para. 47).

131 ECHR 26 March 1987, *Leander*, Series A, vol. 116, para. 59, emphasis added.

132 ECHR 27 September 1999, *European Human Rights Cases* 1999/2.

133 Paras 83, 84, 85, 86 and 98.

134 See for a comparable judgment ECHR 8 December 1999, *Freedom and Democracy Party (ÖZDEP)*, *European Human Rights Cases* 2000/12, para. 45 ('such drastic measures may be taken only in the most serious cases').

g. Balancing of Factors Determining the Margin of Appreciation

In most cases that are brought before the Court, several of the factors that have been discussed in the above are of relevance. If the various factors point in the same direction, this is not problematic at all: the factors then even reinforce each other. This is, for instance, the case if there is a European consensus, pointing in the direction of a strict test, while a fundamental core right of the applicant has been infringed; there are no special reasons to exercise restraint; and the Court is sufficiently able to evaluate the necessity of the infringement: in such a situation, it is clear that the margin of appreciation should be very narrow and that the Court is allowed to apply a strict test.[135]

A more problematic situation may arise if the various factors contradict each other. One may easily imagine a case in which the character of the aims pursued necessitate a wide margin, while the concerned measure affects fundamental core rights; or in which an individual right is seriously infringed, but the discrimination concerns a policy field in which the Court feels unable to pass a far reaching judgment. In such cases, the Court will have to balance all factors that are relevant in determining the amount of discretion that should be left to the state, carefully taking into account their relative weight.

Having regard for the importance of the intensity of the review for the assessment of an alleged violation and for the outcome of the case, it is very much desired that the Court gives careful argumentation for its balancing exercise and clearly indicates what value it attaches to the different factors that are relevant to the case before it. Unfortunately, a comprehensive argumentation for the choice of a certain level of review is often absent in the Court's judgments: mostly, the Court restricts itself to concluding that a wide or narrow margin of appreciation will be accorded to the state, only rarely explaining what arguments have inspired this choice.[136] However, an analysis of the relevant case law shows a certain pattern. In determining the intensity of the review, the importance of the affected right almost always seems to form the starting point of the Court's reasoning. If the right cannot be considered particularly fundamental or important, the Court will mostly leave a wide margin of appreciation to the state and will exercise much restraint in assessing the alleged violation. In these circumstances,

135 An example of a case in which all factors pointed in the same direction (namely a wide margin of appreciation) is ECHR 18 January 2001, *Jane Smith*, *European Human Rights Cases* 2001/19: the case concerned a policy field in which the states should be accorded a large discretion to take decisions (para. 99), while it appeared from an investigation by the Court that there was only limited consensus as to the question how problems as were relevant to the case were to be dealt with (paras 100-101). Furthermore, the Court observed that the applicant's rights and interests were not impaired in a very serious way (paras 104 and 110).

136 Cf. Harris/O'Boyle/Warbrick 1995, n. 11 above, p. 297 and O'Donnell 1982, n. 98 above, p. 479.

the margin of appreciation will only be narrowed if special factors emerge that convincingly plead for a stricter test.[137] If, on the other hand, the complaint concerns the infringement of a core right, the Court's test will mostly be very strict. Only very convincing factors may then lead to a lower level of scrutiny and may widen the margin of appreciation that is left to the state.

4.2 The Very Weighty Reasons Test

4.2.1 Translation of the Margin of Appreciation Doctrine into a Very Weighty Reasons Test

As early as in the *Belgian Linguistics* case, the Court has stated that the margin of appreciation doctrine is applicable in cases concerning discrimination; it was even in the context of an application of Article 14 that the Court ruled for the very first time that a certain amount of discretion should be left to the states to enable them to make choices and take measures in fields governed by the Convention.[138] In later case law, the Court has confirmed the applicability of the margin of appreciation doctrine time and again, referring to the various factors that have been described in the above. It is however interesting that the Court has sometimes given a special interpretation to the margin of appreciation doctrine in its case law regarding Article 14. The initial impetus to this interpretation may be found in the *Abdulaziz* case.[139] The case concerned employment issues and immigration policy, which are normally fields in which a wide margin of appreciation is left to the states. In this case however, the Court thought it decisive that the alleged discrimination was based on grounds of sex.

> Although the Contracting States enjoy a certain 'margin of appreciation' in assessing whether and to what extent differences in otherwise similar situations justify a different treatment, the scope of this margin will vary according to the circumstances, the subject matter and its background. As to the present matter, it can be said that the advancement of the sexes is today a major goal in the member States of the Council of Europe. This means that *very weighty reasons* would have to be advanced before a difference of treatment on the ground of sex could be regarded as compatible with the Convention. (para. 78, emphasis added)

According to this passage, a difference in treatment based on grounds of sex may only be justified by very weighty reasons. In practice, this means that the Court

137 Cf. O'Donnell 1982, n. 98 above, pp. 492-493.

138 ECHR 23 July 1968, Series A, vol. 6, para. 10; see also the citation in paragraph 3.1.1.

139 ECHR 25 May 1985, Series A, vol. 94.

strictly scrutinizes the arguments put forward by the respondent government, carefully examining whether they are of sufficient importance to support the classification. In these cases, the Court only rarely accepts a justification: the use of the 'very weighty reasons' terminology almost always implies the finding of a violation of Article 14. As a result, the possibility of the states to make a distinction on grounds of sex is extremely limited, which means that they are left with almost no margin of appreciation.

It is important to observe that the application of the very weighty reasons test in discrimination cases does not mean that the actual margin of appreciation doctrine has completely lost its relevance to the application of Article 14. If the Court does not use the very weighty reasons terminology, this does certainly not imply that a marginal, restricted test will be applied. In most Article 14 cases, the Court will simply make use of the factors that normally determine the amount of discretion that is to be left to the states. It is therefore possible that the Court applies a strict test in assessing an alleged discrimination, for instance if the discrimination affects fundamental rights such as the freedom of expression or the right to a home, even though no mention is made of the need to advance very weighty reasons.[140]

4.2.2 Criterion for the Applicability of the Very Weighty Reasons Test: Suspectness of the Discrimination

The ground on which the alleged discrimination is based determines the applicability of the very weighty reasons doctrine. As has been said before, the Court has characterized discriminations on certain personal or group characteristics as suspect.[141] The Court has not yet developed general criteria which could be helpful in deciding which discriminations should be regarded suspect, but it is clear that the very weighty reasons test is consistently applied to discriminations based on sex or gender, illegitimate birth, religion, nationality and sexual orientation.

a. Discrimination Based on Grounds of Sex or Gender

As is already evident from the before-cited *Abdulaziz* case, the very weighty reasons test is consistently applied to gender or sex discrimination.[142] In many

140 See e.g. ECHR 24 November 1986, *Gillow*, Series A, vol. 109.

141 It is important to note that the Court itself does not make use of the term 'suspect classifications'; it is only used here to clarify the Court's case-law regarding these classifications.

142 Further applications of the very weighty reasons test may be found in ECHR 24 June 1993, *Schuler-Zgraggen*, Series A, vol. 263, para. 67, ECHR 22 February 1994, *Burghartz*, Series A, vol. 280-B, para. 27 and ECHR 18 July 1994, *Karlheinz Schmidt*, Series A, vol. 291-B, para. 27. It is remarkable that the Court in the *Rasmussen* case (ECHR 28 November 1984, Series A, vol. 87) , that was decided just before the *Abdulaziz* case and also concerned discrimination on grounds of sex, did not deter-

of the cases concerning gender discrimination, the Court has given a clear argumentation for its choice for a strict test. Decisive value seems to be attached to the fact that all states that are members of the Council of Europe strive for equal rights for men and women, thus constituting a clear common ground condemning discrimination based on sex. It is remarkable that the common ground factor is, as yet, the only argument that has been advanced as a justification for the application of the very weighty reasons test: a more substantive or fundamental argumentation seems to be absent. No attention has been paid, for instance, to the fact that sex is an unchangeable, personal characteristic, or to the fact that sex is mostly irrelevant to the daily social functioning of the individual. Remarkable is also that no importance seems to be attached to the fact that most sex discrimination is based on overbroad generalizations or are the result of stereotyping or traditional opinions about role patterns, which could in themselves constitute an important and objective argument to intensify judicial scrutiny. The absence of such substantive arguments as a foundation for the choice of a very weighty reasons test may be deplored. The reason for that point of view has been given already: if the Court only applies an intensive test if a clear European consensus is visible, it deprives itself of the possibility to fulfil the role of a pioneer in the field of fundamental rights and of the means to actively contribute to the development of such consensus.[143]

---

mine the ground of discrimination; by leaving this question unanswered, the Court avoided the question on whether there was any reason to intensify the review. It is difficult to explain the difference between the cases, but some explanation may be found in the fact that the *Rasmussen* case concerned the controversial and sensitive issue of paternity proceedings; it might be understandable that the Court did not feel like giving a sweeping judgment about this issue (see Heringa 1998, n. 30 above, p. 3.14-11 and Merrills, *The Development of International Law by the European Court of Human Rights*, Manchester 1993, p. 172). It is also interesting to note that the Court does not take the 'congruence' of the discrimination into account in characterizing 'sex' as a suspect ground of discrimination. It has been argued by a Dutch academic, Van Maarseveen, that congruent discrimination (i.e. discrimination which is in accordance with the normal pattern of discrimination) must be scrutinized more strictly than discongruent discrimination (i.e. discrimination which deviates from the normal pattern). With respect to discrimination on grounds of sex, the normal pattern is that women are discriminated against much more often than men; accordingly, discrimination against women should be reviewed with much less restraint than discrimination against men (Van Maarseveen, *Discriminatie*, Alphen a/d Rijn 1990, pp. 28 and 31). It is apparent from cases such as *Karlheinz Schmidt* (ECHR 18 July 1994, Series A, vol. 291-B), *Burghartz* (ECHR 22 February 1994, Series A, vol. 280-B) and *Van Raalte* (ECHR 21 February 1997, Reports 1997-I), however, that the Court does not consider this factor of any relevance; cf. also Schokkenbroek 1998, p. 22.

143 Theoretically, the question about what the consequences would be when a once existent common ground would disappear may arise. Such disappearance would not diminish the importance of the substantive factors that support an intensive review

The very weighty reasons test is consistently applied to all discriminations based on grounds of sex. In two recent cases, however, the Court chose an approach that in some respects deviates from the *Abdulaziz* line of jurisprudence. In the first place, the *Van Raalte* case is of importance,[144] because of the choice the Court made in that case for a somewhat different, apparently stronger formulation of the test. The *Van Raalte* case concerned contributions under the Dutch Child Care Benefits Act. Payment of these contributions was mandatory to every citizen, whether or not the contributor would make use of the benefits flowing from the Act; only unmarried, childless women aged 45 and above were exempt from the obligations. The Court stated that very weighty reasons had to be advanced in justification of the gender discrimination resulting from the relevant provision. It went on, however, to state the following

> [W]hile Contracting States enjoy a certain margin of appreciation under the Convention as regards the introduction of exemptions to such contributory obligations, Article 14 requires that any such measure, in principle, apply even-handedly to both men and women unless *compelling reasons* have been adduced to justify a difference in treatment. (paras 41 and 42, emphasis added)

Apparently, not only very weighty, but even *compelling* reasons were needed in this case to justify the difference in treatment between men and women. It might be inferred from this formulation that the Court has sharpened its test, but it is as yet unclear whether it was indeed the Court's intention to do so.[145] This does not appear to be very probable, especially because the practical significance of sharpening the test will be very limited: the use of the very weighty reasons test itself already implies that the difference in treatment will almost always be found in violation of Article 14. Further case law is awaited to reveal the exact meaning of the *Van Raalte* case.

A second, more important deviation of the very weighty reasons formula may be found in the judgment that was rendered by the Court in the *Petrovic* case, concerning an Austrian act about parental leave.[146] The relevant provisions stipulated that both men and women could take up one year's parental leave after the birth of their child, but only women were eligible for a special parental leave allowance. According to the governing case law, such difference in treatment, based on grounds of sex, would be considered suspect and might be justi-

---

in certain cases, but in the present doctrine, it might justify a more marginal test. It is obvious that this is an undesirable consequence of the stance the Court has adopted.

144 ECHR 21 February 1997, Reports 1997-I.

145 Cf. Heringa/Woltjer, 'Gelijke behandeling in het sociale zekerheidsrecht: 'Straatsburg' scherpt de eisen aan', *Nederlands Juristenblad* 1997, p. 1713.

146 ECHR 27 March 1998, Reports 1998-II.

fied only by advancing very weighty reasons. In its judgment, the Court however considered the following

> It is true that the advancement of the equality of the sexes is today a major goal in the member States of the Council of Europe and very weighty reasons would be needed for such a difference in treatment to be regarded as compatible with the Convention. However, the Contracting States enjoy a certain margin of appreciation in assessing whether and to what extent differences in otherwise similar situations justify a different treatment in law. The scope of the margin of appreciation will vary according to the circumstances, the subject matter and its background; in this respect, one of the relevant factors may be the existence or non-existence of common ground between the laws of the Contracting States. It is clear that at the material time that is at the end of the 1980s there was no common standard in this field, as the majority of the Contracting States did not provide for parental leave allowances to be paid to fathers. (paras 37-39)

It would appear from this reasoning that the Court felt an urge to create some room for differentiation in the intensity of the scrutiny in sex discrimination cases. The starting point still seems to be that very weighty reasons are advanced to justify such discrimination, but in special circumstances the states may be accorded more discretion than usual. This would imply that the Court distances itself from the strict doctrine it adhered to until 1998, according to which all discrimination on grounds of sex is immediately suspect and must always be strictly scrutinized.

In itself, there is much to be said in favour of a more flexible approach. It is important to determine the suspectness of a ground of discrimination not in the abstract, but to give a concrete evaluation of the need for strict scrutiny in each individual case that is put before the Court. Such case-by-case determination of the level of intensity is of special significance if account is being taken not only of the common ground factor, but also of substantive factors, such as whether the difference is based on stereotypes or traditional role models; or whether the affected group suffers from a long history of discrimination: if it is clear that such factors do not play a role in a case brought before the Court, there is less reason to intensify the level of scrutiny.[147]

In the approach that has been chosen by the Court, the lack of a substantive foundation for the intensification of the level of scrutiny will, in the end, appear to be problematic. In the Court's opinion, only the existence of a European consensus is decisive, not the question of whether the difference in treatment is

147 It is obvious that it is also necessary to balance the different factors in cases such as these: even if a classification is not suspect, it is possible that there are other factors present in the case that would necessitate a more intensive review (such as the fact that a fundamental core right has been infringed by the classification).

based on an unchangeable, irrelevant personal characteristic or on traditional notions or gross stereotyping. With regard to parental leave allowances, and undoubtedly also other policy fields, many states have apparently chosen to grant these benefits only to women. The chances are considerable that this difference in treatment is inspired by the stereotypical notion that it is mostly the woman who makes use of the possibility of parental leave after the birth of her child, while the man immediately starts working again. It is highly questionable whether it is desirable to transform such notions into a justification for a marginal test, especially where a court that ought to be the leading authority in the field of fundamental rights protection applies such a test. For those reasons, it would be desirable for the Court to contemplate the advisability of its choice to take only the existence of a European consensus into account in deciding on the applicability of the very weighty reasons test.

b. Discrimination on the Basis of Illegitimate Birth

In its *Marckx* case,[148] decided in 1979, the Court already indicated that there exists a European consensus with respect to the desirability of granting equal rights to children born out of wedlock and their parents. In the *Marckx* case the Court did not yet mention the margin of appreciation doctrine or the necessity to advance very weighty reasons, but a strict test is already visible. In the *Inze* case, decided somewhat later, the Court explicitly confirmed the necessity of a stricter test.[149] The applicant in this case, an eldest child born out of wedlock, was not entitled to inherit his father's farm, as Austrian inheritance law gave priority to legitimate children. The Court found the following

> The question of equality between children born in and born out of wedlock as regards their civil rights is today given importance in the member States of the Council of Europe. This is shown by the 1975 European Convention on the Legal Status of Children born out of Wedlock, which is presently in force in respect of nine member States of the Council of Europe. The Republic of Austria ratified it on 28 May 1980 [...]. *Very weighty reasons* would accordingly have to be advanced before a difference of treatment could be regarded as compatible with the Convention. (para. 41, emphasis added)

Again, the existence of a common ground seems to be the only and decisive factor that determined the Court's choice for a very weighty reasons test. The same remarks that have been made in the above with respect to sex discrimination and these also apply to discrimination on the basis of illegitimate birth.[150]

---

148 ECHR 13 June 1979, Series A, vol. 31, para. 41.

149 ECHR 28 October 1987, Series A, vol. 126.

150 For discrimination on grounds of illegitimate birth, it is clear that the Court has con-

c. Discrimination on Grounds of Nationality

The Court also applies the very weighty reasons test with respect to discrimination based on nationality. It did so for the first time in the *Gaygusuz* case.[151] The applicant in this case resided and worked in Austria, but had the Turkish nationality. After having been disabled for a certain period, he requested, as a temporary provision, an advance to his pension, but his request was denied because he did not have the Austrian nationality. With respect to the intensity of the scrutiny, the Court stated the following

> [...] [T]he Contracting States enjoy a certain margin of appreciation in assessing whether and to what extent differences in otherwise similar situations justify a different treatment. However, very weighty reasons would have to be put forward before the Court could regard a difference of treatment based exclusively on the ground of nationality as compatible with the Convention. (para. 42)

It is remarkable that this conclusion is not supported by any substantive reasoning: the Court does not explain why an intensive test is necessary in cases about

---

sistently applied a very weighty reasons test; see e.g. ECHR 1 February 2000, *Mazurek*, *European Human Rights Cases* 2000/25, para. 49, ECHR 3 October 2000, *Camp and Bourimi*, *European Human Rights Cases* 2000/82 and ECHR 11 October 2001, *Sahin*, *European Human Rights Cases* 2001/81, para. 81. Only one deviation from this consistent application may be found, namely in the *McMichael* case (ECHR 24 February 1995, Series A, vol. 307-B). According to Scottish law, a father who had been married to the mother at the moment of the birth of his child was invested with parental authority; biological fathers could only obtain parental authority by filing an application with a court. This case clearly showed a difference in treatment of legitimate and illegitimate fathers, which should normally result in the application of a strict test. In this case, however, the Court did not refer to the margin of appreciation doctrine at all and concluded, after the application of an apparently marginal test, that the discrimination was objectively and reasonably justified. This judgment may only be explained by the fact that the case did not deal with a discrimination of illegitimate children, but of illegitimate fathers. With children, illegitimacy is an unchangeable characteristic, for which they cannot be held responsible (a factor the Court explicitly deemed of importance in the above mentioned *Mazurek* case). This is different for the case of illegitimate fathers, who may easily be able to change their status by officially recognizing the child. It might be argued that the Court considers this difference of importance, thereby implicitly recognizing that the changeability of the personal characteristic on which a discrimination is based may be of value for its characterization as suspect. However, it seems to appear from a later case, *Sahin* (ECHR 11 October 2001, *European Human Rights Cases* 2001/81, para. 57), that this argumentation may not be the main reason for the approach in *McMichael*: the *Sahin* case also concerned a discrimination against illegitimate fathers, which was strictly scrutinized by the Court by the application of a very weighty reasons test.

151 ECHR 16 September 1996, *Gaygusuz*, Reports 1996-IV.

discrimination on grounds of nationality and even refrains from referring to the existence of a European consensus. The lack of reasoning is all the more surprising as nationality is not always regarded as a suspect criterion for differentiation. The context of the difference in treatment appears to be of special interest in this regard: as has been explained earlier, the Court leaves a wide margin of appreciation to the state in most immigration cases (which almost inevitably result in discrimination on grounds of nationality), applying only a very marginal test.[152]

d. Discrimination on Grounds of Religion

As is apparent from its case law, the Court will apply a very intensive test if a complaint concerns difference in treatment based on religion. However, in the most important case in this respect, *Hoffmann*,[153] the Court did not use the very weighty reasons formula, but chose a somewhat different construction. In its judgment, the Court stated that '[n]otwithstanding any arguments to the contrary, a distinction based essentially on a difference in religion alone is not acceptable.' (para. 36)

It might be inferred from the *Hoffmann* case that it is not sufficient to advance very weighty reasons to justify a difference in treatment based on religion: from the cited consideration, it would appear that, in the Court's opinion, distinctions that are exclusively based on religion are not acceptable at all.[154] The Court does not give reasons for this opinion, which makes it difficult to understand why the Court would think that no distinctions based on religion, notwithstanding possible justification, could be considered compatible with Article 14. It is not very probable that the Court would really want to create a subcategory of 'very suspect classifications' within the category of suspect classifications. Such a subcategory would imply that the Court deems discriminations based on religion inherently unacceptable, while this would not be the case for discriminations that are exclusively based on illegitimate birth. It is unlikely that the Court would give such an important value judgment without giving further reasons,

152 It has been indicated above that this approach might be reasonable indeed, as the intensity of the scrutiny ought to be determined on a case-by-case basis. The suspectness of the ground of discrimination is only one (albeit very important) factor in the determination of the intensity of the review; other factors may be relevant as well. Therefore, the Court will always have to balance the suspectness and seriousness of the discrimination against factors that might justify a less intensive review (such as the better placed argument, the international law argument of subsidiarity or the context argument). It is problematic that the Court's choice for a certain level of scrutiny mostly lacks an adequate foundation, which makes it difficult to discover whether the balance that has been struck in a concrete case is sufficiently justified.

153 ECHR 23 June 1993, Series A, vol. 255-C.

154 Cf. Heringa 1998, p. 3.14-12.

and it is difficult to see how such distinction could be justified. Therefore, it must be assumed that the formula used by the Court in cases relating distinctions based on religion does not create a substantive deviation from the very weighty reasons doctrine. Also, it may be expected that the Court will accept the legitimacy of some differences in treatment based on religion if they are sufficiently justified by objective and reasonable arguments: in those circumstances, it might be argued that the difference in treatment is not essentially based on religion, but is also inspired by other considerations.[155]

e. Discrimination Based on Sexual Orientation

In the *Salgueiro da Silva Mouta* case,[156] the Court has expressed itself for the first time about a difference in treatment inspired by sexual orientation. The judgment concerned the question about whether, after a divorce, the custody of the child should be awarded to its father or to its mother. The judge in first instance expressed the opinion that the father and mother were equally able and loving parents, and, after careful consideration, awarded the custody to the father. The appeal judge, basing himself on nearly the same set of facts as the judge in first instance, reached the opposite conclusion. In his judgment, he seemed to attach much value to the fact that the father lived together with another man, with whom he also maintained a homosexual relationship. The Court found that the appeal judge's considerations regarding the father's homosexual relationship had been decisive for the outcome of the appeal case and that the award of custody to the mother therefore constituted a difference in treatment that was essentially based on the applicant's homosexual orientation. As to the reasonableness of this difference in treatment, the Court expressed the following opinion

> Force est donc de constater, au vu de ce qui précède, que la cour d'appel a opéré une distinction dictée par des considérations tenant à l'orientation sexuelle du requerrant, distinction qu'on ne saurait tolérer d'après la Convention. Dès lors, la Cour ne peut conclure à l'existence d'un rapport raisonnable de proportionnalité entre les moyens employés et le but visés [...]. (para. 36)

155 This conclusion is supported by the *Thlimmenos* case, concerning a substantive discrimination based on grounds of religion (ECHR 6 April 2000, *European Human Rights Cases* 2000/45). For unknown reasons, the Court did not apply a very weighty reasons test in that case (which can only be explained by the substantive character of the discrimination), but a regular justification test. Although the Court did not come to the conclusion that the equal treatment was sufficiently justified and did not seem to apply a very strict test, this case clearly shows that the Court is willing to apply a regular justification test even in cases concerning discrimination on grounds of religion.

156 ECHR 21 December 1999, *European Human Rights Cases* 2000/16.

The formula used in this case is strongly comparable to the above-mentioned *Hoffman* case. Again, the Court unfortunately did not express any reasons for its findings and conclusions, thereby obscuring the factors that led it to accept homosexual orientation as a suspect ground of discrimination and that led to the conclusion that even that a difference in treatment exclusively based on that ground can never be found to be compatible with Article 14.

5. Conclusion

In the foregoing, it has been explained how the European Court handles cases concerning Article 14 and in what way it has interpreted this provision. It has been made clear that the Court did develop an elaborate decision model, yet it does not always apply this model in a diligent and comprehensive manner.

In the first place, the Court's use of the comparability test may be criticized. As has been shown, the Court almost never clearly indicates how this test should be applied, obscuring the way in which it reaches the conclusion that two cases, persons or situations are placed in a similar or in a dissimilar position. This lack of clarity does not improve the verifiability or the acceptability of the Court's judgments with respect to Article 14. Furthermore, it should be mentioned that the use of a comparability test itself does not always lead to desirable results. The Court starts from the opinion that, as soon as it is clear that two persons or cases are placed in a different position, any difference in treatment of those persons or cases will be acceptable: as is apparent from the Court's decision model and case-law, a justification is only required in case of difference in treatment of persons who are placed in an analogous situation. In taking this point of departure, the Court passes by the fact that not every unequal treatment of unequal cases can be considered reasonable. It is quite imaginable that a specific difference in treatment does not stand in a proportionate relationship to the differences shown by the cases placed before the Court, as may be illustrated by the example of a criminal code providing that manslaughter will be punished with two years imprisonment, while the sanction for murder is the death penalty. Furthermore, it is possible that the difference in treatment does not constitute an effective or suitable means to attain the aims that are pursued in making it. If such difference in treatment does negatively affect individual rights or interests, it is not reasonable to sustain it, even if the cases presented to the Court are not entirely comparable. It is of importance that the Court itself seems to recognize that the application of a comparability test is not always useful or necessary. It has been shown that the test is omitted in quite a number of cases, because of the overlap the application of the test would cause with the substantive justification test. Although such omission is not at all unreasonable or even desirable, it might cause problems relating to the burden of proof: if no first phase test is applied, the respondent government will always be required to advance objective and reasonable arguments for its distinction, even if there were no good reason to put the state under such an obligation. For the respondent government, the lack of a first phase test has another disadvantage as well: in the absence of such a test it often will not be entirely clear about what kind difference in treatment the applicant exactly complains about, making it difficult for the state to focus its defence in the second phase.

For the above mentioned reasons, it might be better for the Court to replace its comparability test for a test of disadvantage, such as it already applies in cases regarding allegedly suspect discriminations. The test of disadvantage has the advantage that it is relatively easily to apply and guarantees a large measure of objectivity. In using the comparability test, the Court relatively often formulates a standard of comparison itself, not referring to the legal framework in which the difference in treatment should be placed or to the aims pursued by the distinction, or even confines itself to stating, without any further argumentation, that the cases placed before it are comparable or incomparable. In applying the test of disadvantage, it is much more difficult to render badly reasoned or subjective judgments, as it is almost impossible to say something about the disadvantage the applicant has suffered without referring to objective and verifiable facts.

If the Court chooses to apply the test of disadvantage structurally as a first phase test, it is necessary that it add some detail to the test it presently uses. To warrant the selective character of the test, it is important that it should not be too easy to prove disadvantageous treatment. One useful additional element might be to require the applicant to show that he is actually and demonstrably affected in his interests by the difference in treatment. This would not be the case, for instance, if the disadvantage he allegedly suffers is compensated by other measures or acts, or if the applicant seems to be disadvantaged at first sight, but not if the facts of the case are investigated in more detail. Furthermore, it is essential that the disadvantage suffered is sufficiently objective in character and relates to interests that are legally recognized and protected: there is no need for the state to advance a justification for a disadvantage that is purely subjectively experienced by the applicant. This does not mean that immaterial disadvantages will never call for a justification: such disadvantage may cause serious impairments of interests, for example where the applicant is the victim of stigmatisation. In such cases, however, the burden of proof for the applicant will be heavy, and the Court might be required to give elaborate, careful and comprehensive reasons for the conclusions it reaches.

The justification test developed by the Court looks attractive and complete on paper, making it all the more regrettable that it is only rarely applied in a comprehensive and diligent manner. It is very much desired that the Court, in every single case put before it, should examine in a much more structured and careful way whether the difference in treatment meets all the requirements formulated in the decision model. The exact contents of the test to be applied by the Court could be made somewhat dependent on the chosen level of intensity of the review, i.e. the extent to which a margin of appreciation is left to the respondent state. If a very weighty reasons test was chosen, the Court for instance could be expected to carefully probe into the actual considerations inspiring discrimination, in order to formulate stringent requirements as to the legitimacy of those considerations and to rigorously examine whether the distinction forms an effective means to attain the aims pursued, whether the aims could not have been achieved by other, less disadvantageous or less discriminatory measures, and whether the balance of interests underlying the distinction may be considered sufficiently reasonable. Is the test more restrained or marginal in character, as will often be the case in complaints concerning socio-economic issues, the demands might be much lower. In those cases, it would for instance be up to the applicant to demonstrate that one of the requirements formulated in the decision model is not properly fulfilled. However, even in applying a marginal test, the Court's reasoning still ought to be elaborate and convincing, and should not be restricted to the single statement that the difference in treatment is objectively and reasonably justified.

The intensity of the Court's review of national measures depends on a large number of factors. Although the Court has carefully and convincingly described these factors in its case-law, it is regrettable that it has never made clear how these factors should be balanced in a concrete situation. This may be problematic in cases where the various factors point in different directions, for instance in a case where a socio-economic measure infringes a fundamental right that belongs to the core of one of the Convention provisions. The Court's non-discrimination jurisprudence is somewhat clearer on this point, as it is clear that a very strict test will always be applied if it has been shown that the alleged discrimination is based on suspectness ground. The suspectness, for its part, seems to be determined primarily by the existence of a common ground condemning the use of the discrimination ground concerned. However, it has already been explained that this approach shows some defects: it might be better if other factors rather than the incidental existence or non-existence of a European consensus could also be of influence in the determination of the intensity of the review.

In this respect, a decisive and general criterion for intensifying the test may be found in the probability that the difference in treatment is inspired by faulty or discriminatory considerations, i.e. whether it is likely that the political-democratic process of decision making did not function in a satisfactory, neutral and objective manner. As soon as that is the case, it is essential for the Court to demand a strong and convincing explanation for the impairment of interests that is the result of such decision-making and to leave a narrow margin of appreciation to the state. On the contrary, as long as there is no reason to doubt the neutrality and objectivity of the national decision making process, the Court will have to keep a certain distance, not only because of its position as an international court, but also because the primary responsibility to take measures that affect citizen's lives and interests lies with political and representative organs; such measures are to be reviewed by the judiciary only with due restraint.

It is possible to define various factors in which an indication of the malfunctioning of the political-democratic process may be found and that are relevant to discrimination cases put before the Court. If a difference in treatment is based on an unchangeable personal or group characteristic, or on a characteristic that is normally irrelevant for someone's daily social functioning, or if it is relatively generally accepted that it is not reasonable to use a specific characteristic as a basis for differentiation (the common ground argument), there will be good reason for the Court to carefully examine the reasons that inspired the contested distinction. This is even more so if the group that is disadvantaged by the difference in treatment is the victim of prejudice or if the general attitude towards that group is determined by hostility or gross stereotyping; if the group has a longstanding history of discrimination and stigmatisation; or if the group has only weak political representation (rendering it difficult to influence the decision making process). Furthermore, there may be reason to doubt the fair and objective functioning of the democratic process if the difference in treatment affects fundamental core rights; or if the impairment of interests caused by the distinction is irreversible or very serious. In those cases, there is good reason for the Court to apply a strict justification test.

As has been said before, a less demanding test is called for if there are no objective factors that may raise doubts as to the neutrality and fairness of the democratic process. Moreover, in some cases there may be special reasons for the exercise of judicial restraint. If the Court is presented with a case concerning a distinction that is embedded in very complex socio-economic legislation; if there is no or almost no common ground as to the interests served by the distinction (such as is the case with relation to the protection of morals); if the distinction is made in special emergency circumstances or in a situation deviating from normal life (such as is the case for army or prison regulations); or if the difference in treatment touches a policy field that is closely linked to state sovereignty (such as is the case with respect to immigration matters), the Court will have to restrict itself to a global and marginal test of the justification that has been advanced by the respondent state.

If the Court would consistently apply a test of disadvantage, followed by an elaborate justification test, while carefully using a single level of intensity that is in itself sufficiently reasonable, the application and interpretation of Article 14 would be much improved, thus enhancing the acceptability and verifiability of the Court's conclusions. Eventually, such improvement would result in a more important role for the non-discrimination principle in Convention law than has been the case until now. Taking into account the impending entry of Protocol 12 into force, the existence of an independent non-discrimination provision may be of great importance.

Jeroen Schokkenbroek[1]

2. A NEW EUROPEAN STANDARD AGAINST DISCRIMINATION: NEGOTIATING PROTOCOL NO. 12 TO THE EUROPEAN CONVENTION ON HUMAN RIGHTS

1. Introduction

On 26 June 2000, the Committee of Ministers of the Council of Europe adopted Protocol No. 12 to the European Convention on Human Rights (ECHR), providing for a general prohibition of discrimination. The Protocol was opened for signature by the (currently 45) member States of the Council of Europe on 4 November 2000 in Rome, on the occasion of the 50th anniversary of the ECHR. To date, the Protocol has been signed by 32 member States, five of which have ratified it. The Protocol has not yet entered into force since, under its Article 5, paragraph 1, entry into force requires ten ratifications.

The adoption of Protocol No. 12 is the result of several years of intergovernmental work in the 1990s, notably by the Steering Committee for Human Rights (CDDH). That Committee, composed of senior officials of all member States (usually from ministries of foreign affairs or of justice), is the competent intergovernmental body to prepare new human rights instruments for adoption by the Committee of Ministers. Most of the work of the CDDH is, in turn, prepared in one of its subcommittees. In the case of instruments providing for further substantive human rights guarantees, the Committee of Experts for the

1 Head of the Human Rights Law and Policy Division of the Directorate General of Human Rights, Council of Europe. Any views expressed in this contribution are entirely personal and do not necessarily reflect the position of the Council of Europe.

Jan Niessen, Isabelle Chopin (eds.), The Development of Legal Instruments..., *61-79*

Development of Human Rights is the competent subcommittee. It was this committee that carried out most of the preparatory work for Protocol No. 12.

This contribution aims to provide an overview of the genesis of Protocol No. 12, with special emphasis on some aspects of its drafting history which may shed light on the intended content and scope of the non-discrimination provision contained in Article 1 of the Protocol. Indeed, during the preparatory work on the Protocol, some issues proved to be quite controversial and it would appear that the structure and content of the non-discrimination norm that was finally adopted can only be properly understood having regard to the choices made and compromises reached during the drafting process. These issues will be analysed further below (in section 3), but first a broad overview of the various stages in the genesis of the Protocol will be given.

2. Background and Drafting History of Protocol No. 12

The "Prehistory": The Period up to 1993

In a way, the background and history of Protocol No. 12 began already in 1950 with the adoption of the ECHR itself. In the words of its preamble, the governments adopting the ECHR were resolved "to take the first steps for the collective enforcement of certain of the rights stated in the Universal Declaration [of Human Rights of 1948]". Even a superficial comparison between the two texts shows that in matters of equality and non-discrimination, the ECHR standard was less ambitious than the one contained in the Universal Declaration. Article 14, ECHR, provides: "The enjoyment of the rights and freedoms set forth in this Convention shall be secured without discrimination on any ground such as sex, race, colour, language, religion, political or other opinion, national or social origin, association with a national minority, property, birth or other status." Put briefly, this provision does not contain a free-standing prohibition of discrimination. This has been confirmed in constant case-law of the European Court of Human Rights (hereinafter: the Court) according to which Article 14 applies only where the case presents a nexus with another right or freedom guaranteed by the ECHR. In the terms used by the Court, "there can be room for the application of Article 14 if the facts of the case fall within the ambit of one or more of the other substantive provisions of the Convention or its Protocols."[2]

Thus, the drafters of Article 14 sought inspiration in the non-autonomous Article 2 of the Universal Declaration (see also the later Article 2 of the International Covenant on Civil and Political Rights), not in the broader provision of Article 7 of the same Declaration (which was the model for the subsequent Article 26 of the Covenant), guaranteeing equality before the law, equal protection of the law as well as a general non-discrimination principle. The reasons

---

2 See, for example, *Inze v. Austria*, judgment of 28 October 1987, Series A Vol. 126, § 36.

why a more restrictive approach was followed in Article 14 do not appear clearly from the *travaux préparatoires* of the ECHR, but it has been suggested that, as a matter of international law, the principles of equality and of non-discrimination were still very much in their infancy at the time the ECHR was drafted and indeed for a considerable period of time thereafter. For example, it was certainly not self-evident at the time that any guarantee of equality and non-discrimination would extend to non-nationals. Neither was it clear then that not every difference of treatment amounted to a discrimination.[3]

The possibility of extending the scope of Article 14 has been considered on several occasions in the past, both by the Parliamentary Assembly and by intergovernmental committees of experts.[4] As early as 1960, the Assembly proposed that a provision on equality before the law be included in the Convention (Recommendation 234). The Committee of Experts on Human Rights, however, took the view that such a provision should not be inserted in the draft text of Protocol No. 4 to the ECHR, the main argument being that the notion of equality before the law was subject to a "wide variety of judicial interpretations". The Committee also rejected the idea of including a more limited right to equality "in the application of the law", considering that such a right could be deduced from existing provisions of the ECHR (Articles 6 and 14), that it, too, might be open to "dangerous legal interpretations" and that the nature of the supervision exercised by the control organs of the ECHR raised "delicate questions".

The question also came up in the context of an examination of the co-existence of the UN Covenants and the ECHR. When examining Article 26 of the Covenant on Civil and Political Rights (CCPR), the Committee of Experts again stressed the implementation difficulties that were likely to arise if the principles of equality before the law and of equal protection of the law were inserted in the ECHR, particularly if this implied an obligation for States to enact legislation to ensure equality in a broad sense, i.e. that the law should be the same for everyone. On the other hand, the Committee felt that no such difficulties arose if equality before the law involved a requirement of equality but not identity of treatment as regards the conditions under which the law was to be applied.

The Parliamentary Assembly, however, did not give up in the face of such intergovernmental reluctance. In Recommendation 583 (1970) it again made the proposal that a Protocol to the ECHR be drawn up securing "equal treatment of persons in the enforcement of the law" and prohibiting discrimination in the

---

3 These examples are given by F. Edel, Le protocole no. 12 à la Convention européenne des droits de l'homme, in: *Europe des libertés* 2001, pp. 11-16 (11-12), citing a 1959 report by Horst Lannung, Chairman of the Legal Affairs Committee of the Parliamentary Assembly of the Council of Europe (doc. 1057, pp. 12-13).

4 The following text draws on Council of Europe document CDDH (82) 38 Addendum II of 14 December 1982, giving (in paragraphs 15 – 20) a historical overview of previous attemps to strengthen the non-discimination guarantee in the ECHR.

exercise of certain rights. The Committee of Experts again rejected this. The next attempt by the Assembly seemed to have better chances of success. Recommendation 683 (1972) proposed to secure in a protocol to the ECHR equal treatment of persons in the enforcement of the law as well as an enforceable right not to be unfairly discriminated against in respect of access to employment and housing. These ideas were taken up by the Committee of Experts in 1974 and lead to further study of the question of equality of treatment (non-discrimination), in particular equality of treatment between women and men, in the context of its general work programme. In 1977, the majority of a subcommittee of experts mandated to examine a possible extension of the list of rights in the ECHR was of the opinion that the right to equality before the law and the equal protection of the law was a fundamental right and was in favour of including a right along the lines of the first sentence of Article 26 CCPR ("All persons are equal before the law and are entitled without any discrimination to the equal protection of the law.").

Notwithstanding the majority position of its subcommittee, the Steering Committee for Human Rights decided in 1977 not to retain this right in its list of rights to be included in a future additional Protocol to the ECHR. This was to become Protocol No. 7 to the ECHR of 22 November 1984, the purpose of which was precisely to add to the ECHR certain CCPR rights not yet included in the original text of the ECHR or in that of the two earlier additional Protocols, Protocol No. 1 of 1952 and Protocol No. 4 of 1963.

However, the issue returned to the Council of Europe's intergovernmental agenda quite soon, as part of the follow-up to two important texts adopted by the Committee of Ministers. In the Declaration on Human Rights of 27 April 1978, the Committee of Ministers decided to give priority to exploring the possibility of extending the list of rights of the individual, notably in the social, economic and cultural fields, "which should be protected by European Conventions or any other appropriate means". And in the Declaration on Intolerance – A Threat to Democracy of 14 May 1981, the conviction was expressed that tolerance and respect for the dignity and intrinsic equality of all human beings are the very basis of a democratic and pluralistic society and the decision taken to initiate a "study of legal instruments applicable in the matter with a view to their reinforcement where appropriate".

In a report of December 1982, the Steering Committee for Human Rights took stock of previous work on the question and presented its views as to the direction of future work that could be undertaken. It recognised that "there are certain limitations in the scope of protection afforded against discriminatory measures under Article 14 which are inherent in the wording of this Article and which would seem to leave little room for the further development of the case law of the European Commission and Court of Human Rights: a discriminatory measure would not as such be in violation of the European Convention on Human Rights unless it could be shown that it affects negatively the enjoyment of a right or freedom set forth therein."[5] The CDDH considered that the question of the possible extension of Article 14, ECHR, should be studied further. However, it also pointed out that the limitations in the protection afforded by that Article would be reduced if new rights were added to the ECHR, since Article 14 would apply in relation to such rights. More generally, the CDDH stated that, in the light of previous work on the issues of equality and non-discrimination, "the prospects of succeeding in elaborating a general clause on equality before the law and the equal protection of the law, or a similar general clause on equality between women and men, do not seem high." The CDDH therefore suggested that the question of equality might be approached on a sectoral basis. It referred to a provision it had already drafted for inclusion in a future additional Protocol to the ECHR, which provided that spouses shall enjoy equality of rights and responsibilities of a private law character between them, and in relation to their children, as to marriage, during marriage and in the event of its dissolution. It felt that this approach could be extended through the possible inclusion of provisions granting equality in certain sectors, such as employment.[6] It agreed to pursue this question in the context of ongoing work on extending ECHR rights.

While the provision on equality between spouses was in fact adopted as Article 5 of Protocol No. 7 to the ECHR in 1984, work carried out in the 1980s on extending the list of ECHR rights by adding rights in the social, economic and cultural fields did not yield concrete results. It would go far beyond the scope of the present contribution to give details, but two main reasons for this lack of success were, on the one hand, difficulties in identifying rights that were capable of sufficiently precise definition to be judicially enforceable (cf. the judicial nature of the ECHR control system) and, on the other, the requirement that any such rights should be "new" rights, i.e. rights not yet protected by one of the existing ECHR provisions (rights not capable of being deduced from them in a dynamic – evolutive interpretation by the European Court of Human Rights).[7] In the end, following a Ministerial Conference held in Turin in October 1991, it was decided to insert new rights into the European Social Charter.[8]

5 *Ibidem*, § 11.

6 *Ibidem*, §§ 24-25.

7 The attempts to insert social, economic and cultural rights into the ECHR system are discussed at length in K. Berchtold, Council of Europe activities in the field of economic, social and cultural rights, in: F. Matscher (ed.), *The Implementation of Economic and Social Rights*, Engel Verlag 1991, pp. 355 – 370. As Berchtold records (at p. 367), two sectoral equality rights had been identified for possible inclusion in the ECHR system: the right of men and women to equal pay for work of equal value and the right of men and women to equality of rights with regard to employment and occupation.

8 This ultimately resulted in the Revised Social Charter of 3 May 1996, updating the rights of the 1961 Charter and adding new rights to it.

In other words, by 1991, the prospects for strengthening the ECHR protection of equality and against discrimination appeared to be at an all-time low. All attempts made since 1960 had clearly failed. However, the international context was slowly changing, in particular as a result of worrying increases in manifestations of racism in the 1990s, which also affected the work and the political priorities of the Council of Europe from 1993 onwards.

The Vienna Summit (1993) and the Proposals by the ECRI[9]

At the first ever Summit meeting of the Heads of State and Government of the member States of the Council of Europe (Vienna, October 1993), a Declaration and a Plan Of Action were adopted which express concern about growing manifestations of racism, xenophobia, anti-Semitism and intolerance in Europe. Among the measures agreed on were a pan-European awareness-raising campaign against these evils (the "All Different-All Equal" campaign) but also the creation of a new European expert body: the European Commission against Racism and Intolerance (ECRI). One of the many tasks given to ECRI was to study international legal instruments with a view to their reinforcement where appropriate.[10]

Having studied all existing international human rights instruments which deal with discrimination issues, ECRI submitted its findings to the Committee of Ministers. It considered that the protection offered by the ECHR from racial discrimination should be strengthened by means of an additional protocol containing a general clause against racial discrimination. ECRI drew attention to the fact that the ECHR's main provision in the field of non-discrimination is Article 14, which prohibits discrimination with regard to the enjoyment of the rights and freedoms set forth in the Convention. This clause, therefore, has no independent existence. Its protection does not extend to areas not covered by the substantive rights laid down in the ECHR and its Protocols. According to ECRI, this accessory nature of Article 14 might explain why the Strasbourg case-law on racial discrimination was somewhat sparse; so far, the European Court of Human Rights had not found any violation of that provision as a result of racial

9 The following sections are based on parts of an earlier article, written before the adoption of Protocol No. 12 to the ECHR: see J. Schokkenbroek, Towards a Stronger European Protection against Discrimination: The Preparation of a new Additional Protocol to the European Convention on Human Rights, in: Gay Moon (ed.), *Race Discrimination: Developing and Using a New European Legal Framework*, Oxford 2000, pp. 29 – 37.

10 ECRI also conducts country-by-country reviews, draws up country-specific or general policy recommendations, etc.
More information on ECRI and its activities can be obtained from its website (*www.coe.int, see under Human Rights/combating racism.*).

discrimination. In this respect, it was noted that the European Convention was lagging behind other international instruments in the matter of non-discrimination (especially those adopted in the framework of the United Nations).

ECRI was convinced that the establishment of a right to protection from racial discrimination as a fundamental human right would be a significant step to combat the manifest violations of human rights which result from racism and xenophobia. It emphasised that discriminatory attitudes and racist violence are currently spreading in many European countries and observed that the resurgence of racist ideologies and religious intolerance is adding to daily tension in our societies with an attempt to legitimise discrimination.

In proposing a new protocol, ECRI recognised that the law alone cannot eliminate racism in its many forms vis-à-vis various groups, but it stressed also that efforts to promote racial justice couldn't succeed without the law.

ECRI proposed the following outline of a possible non-discrimination provision:

1. Everyone shall be protected against discrimination on the grounds of race, colour, language, religion or national or ethnic origin.
2. This provision shall not exclude distinctions made by a State between citizens and non-citizens which are applied in accordance with law and justified in a democratic society.

In the light of ECRI's proposals, the Committee of Ministers decided in December 1995 to instruct the CDDH to "examine the advisability and feasibility of a legal instrument against racism and intolerance taking account of ECRI's reasoned report on the reinforcement of the non-discrimination clause of the ECHR". It should be noted that these terms of reference do not refer specifically to a draft protocol to the ECHR but to "a legal instrument" in general terms. This indicates that, at a political level, the advisability of adopting an ECHR protocol on the matter was by no means generally accepted yet.

By that time, the CDDH had already been seized of another dossier: the question of equality between women and men as a fundamental human right. It is to this matter that we shall now turn.

The Work of the Steering Committee for Equality between Women and Men (CDEG)

For several years the intergovernmental committee competent in matters of equality between women and men (CDEG) had been examining the possibility of including in the ECHR system a substantive right of women and men to equality.

The CDEG had also noted the weakness of Article 14 of the ECHR in that it did not provide legal protection for equality between women and men as an autonomous fundamental right. There is no protection against discrimination on the ground of sex in the application of rights not guaranteed by the ECHR, since the latter does not recognise the right of women and men to equality as such.

According to the CDEG, a further weakness concerned the legal and conceptual approach to sex discrimination. Article 14 equated all unlawful discrimination grounds, such as race, colour, religion, language, political opinion and sex and placed them on the same footing. This method was felt to be inappropriate, since the experience and practice of anti-discrimination legislation showed that, in cases of discrimination on the grounds of sex, sex is a characteristic of another order – which could be termed structural. All other grounds of discrimination (race, colour, origin, religion, language, political opinion, etc.) are experienced by a gendered subject, and therefore a gendered legal subject. Inequalities that have arisen on the ground of sex cannot be eradicated by treating sex as a variable subject, which has only to be eliminated for an abstract equality between asexual legal subjects to be achieved. That would be to misunderstand the importance of the gendered division of tasks, roles, resources and powers between women and men, which is constructed and maintained by society on the basis of biological sex differences. The difference between the sexes is a permanent characteristic of the human race, and respect for the human person demands that the sexual duality of legal subjects be recognised. This recognition means taking account of the way in which "gender" structures law and the organisation of social, economic, political, private and cultural relationships.

On the basis of this approach, the CDEG suggested the following outline of a possible provision for a new protocol to the ECHR

> The right of women and men to equality is guaranteed in all areas of life in society [in accordance with respect for the liberty and dignity of the human being].
>
> Public authorities shall take steps to ensure the effective enjoyment of the right of women and men to equality [introducing, if necessary, all appropriate measures to secure the full development and advancement of women].
>
> The exercise of this right shall not prevent the High Contracting Parties from providing for such special rights or regimes for women, as are prescribed by law and are necessary in a democratic society.

The Committee of Ministers referred the CDEG proposals to the CDDH. The CDDH had serious difficulties in accepting the idea that gender-based discrimination should be treated separately in a distinct additional protocol to the ECHR. Apart from the question of the precise wording suggested by the CDEG, there was widespread criticism of giving such "separate treatment" to gender equality: this was felt to sit ill with one of the basic tenets of international human rights law: the principle of universality. It was argued that this principle militated against singling out, in a separate protocol to the ECHR, any one specific ground of discrimination. This observation is interesting in the light of the CDDH's earlier attempts (in the 1980s, see above) to follow a "sectoral" approach to equality in any new ECHR provisions. It seems safe to assume that this new attitude of the CDDH was, at least in part, inspired by the failure of that older approach.

The Next Stage: Convergence of the 'Anti-Racism' and 'Equality-between-Women-and-Men Strands

An important stage was reached in October 1996, when the CDDH had before it both the ECRI and the CDEG proposals. It decided to recommend to the Committee of Ministers that the possibility of standard-setting solutions to the question of equality between women and men be explored further, but not in the form of a specific draft protocol to the ECHR. This approach was subsequently endorsed by the Committee of Ministers. At the same meeting, the CDDH instructed one of its subordinate bodies, the Committee of Experts for the Development of Human Rights (DH-DEV), to examine the question of a possible legal instrument against racism and intolerance and mentioned some options to be examined in this regard: an additional protocol to the ECHR based on ECRI's proposal, an additional protocol which would broaden, in a general fashion, the field of application of Article 14, a (framework or other) Convention, a recommendation from the Committee of Ministers to governments of member States or other measures.

Throughout 1997, the DH-DEV and the CDDH worked on these two questions. During this work, the conclusion was drawn quite rapidly that the best way forward on both questions was to examine the possibility of drawing up an additional protocol to the ECHR containing a general prohibition of discrimination, which would contain a non-exhaustive list of discrimination grounds. Other types of legal instruments were also considered (especially a European (Framework) Convention against racism or a recommendation of the Committee of Ministers) but they were not supported by a majority of experts for various reasons. It was felt that an anti-racism Convention would offer no added value in comparison with the UN Convention on the Elimination of All Forms of Racial Discrimination (CERD), and the supervisory machinery which could be envisaged for such a Convention would be less effective than the ECHR control mechanism and contribute to the proliferation of international mechanisms in the human rights field. More generally, both a recommendation and a Convention were considered to be too weak an instrument.

In October 1997, the CDDH discussed the question of the advisability and feasibility of an additional protocol to the ECHR broadening, in a general fashion, the field of application of Article 14 ECHR. It had before it several text variants for a provision prohibiting discrimination which had been prepared by the DH-DEV.

In the debate, some experts warned against rushing into the adoption of an additional protocol. They feared that empowering the Court to interpret an autonomous non-discrimination provision might lead to unpredictable case-law covering a wider range of areas. They also warned against the possibility of considerable horizontal effects (i.e. legal effects on relations between private persons) of such a provision and wondered whether such a protocol was the best way to combat discrimination. One expert preferred to wait and see how the new single Court of Human Rights would manage with its impressive workload before adopting an additional protocol in this field.[11]

Others thought that the time was now ripe for filling a clear lacuna in the human rights protection offered by the ECHR. This step was a necessary and important one in terms of progress in the protection of human rights at the European level and had been thoroughly discussed on several occasions over a long period of time. They felt that one should not exaggerate certain fears, since the Court had so far shown a fairly prudent and consistent approach to the interpretation of Article 14, recognising a margin of appreciation for States Parties. Furthermore, certain of the text variants which were before the CDDH contained limitations of the possible horizontal effects. It was observed that the new Court would have to find ways to manage its workload anyway, irrespective of whether the additional protocol would be adopted or not.

After these discussions, the CDDH voted in favour of elaborating an additional protocol to the ECHR broadening, in a general fashion, the field of application of Article 14 of the Convention. It therefore advised the Committee of Ministers of its opinion that such a protocol was advisable and feasible, both as a standard-setting solution regarding equality between women and men and as a legal instrument against racism and intolerance. It suggested that the key provision of the protocol would contain a non-exhaustive list of discrimination grounds and be worded along the following lines

> The enjoyment of any right set forth by law shall be secured without discrimination on any ground such as sex, race, colour, language, religion, political or other opinion, national or social origin, association with a national minority, property, birth or other status. No one shall be discriminated against by a public authority on any ground such as those mentioned in the first sentence of this provision.

However, the CDDH added that this wording could be improved and that it would have to be examined whether an equality clause would be inserted in the provision or whether a reference in the preamble would suffice. It would also

11 Protocol No. 11 to the ECHR, which established a permanent European Court of Human Rights replacing the previous two-tier structure (Court and Commission), entered into force on 1 November 1998.

have to be examined whether a clause expressly allowing for positive measures should be added to the provision.

On the basis of this report of the CDDH, the Committee of Ministers decided in March 1998 to instruct the Steering Committee to draft such a protocol to the ECHR and to clarify, through the preparation of a draft explanatory report, the precise nature and scope of the undertakings of the Parties to such a protocol.

By the summer of 1999, the preparatory work had reached the stage where it was possible for the CDDH to present a draft text to the Committee of Ministers and to ask for its transmission to the European Court of Human Rights and the Parliamentary Assembly for opinion. The Committee of Ministers decided accordingly and the draft Protocol No. 12 to the ECHR and its draft Explanatory Report were published as a Parliamentary Assembly document.[12] The Court welcomed the draft protocol as providing a clear legal basis for the examination of discrimination issues not covered by Article 14 but signalled that its entry into force would generate a significant number of additional individual applications, which would require additional resources for the Court.[13] The Assembly regretted the absence of a separate clause containing the principle of equality between women and men; it also proposed to include "sexual orientation" in the list of discrimination grounds of the Protocol.[14] The CDDH examined these opinions and finalised the draft Protocol at a special meeting in March 2000. As stated in the introduction above, the Committee of Ministers adopted Protocol No. 12 on 26 June 2000, and opened it for signature in Rome on 4 November 2000.[15]

3. Some Comments on the Content of Protocol No. 12

The main operative provision of the Protocol is Article 1, which reads as follows:

> Article 1 – General prohibition of discrimination
>
> 1. The enjoyment of any right set forth by law shall be secured without discrimination on any ground such as sex, race, colour, religion, political or

12 See Document 8490 of 2 September 1999.

13 The Court's opinion, adopted on 6 December 1999, was published as Parliamentary Assembly Document 8608 of 5 January 2000.

14 See the Report of the Committee on Legal Affairs and Human Rights of 14 January 2000, doc. 8614 (rapporteur: E. Jurgens).

15 The text of the Protocol (ETS 177), the Explanatory report, and up-to-date information on ratifications and signatures are available through the Council of Europe's treaty database (http://conventions.coe.int).

other opinion, national or social origin, association with a national minority, property, birth or other status.

2. No one shall be discriminated against by any public authority on any ground such as those mentioned in paragraph 1.

Apart from a minor technical change, this wording is identical to that of the earlier draft of October 1997 (see above). It will be clear that the CDDH had decided not to include an equality clause in the operative part of the Protocol; the same is true for an explicit provision allowing positive measures. In fact, it was agreed, by way of compromise, to address these matters in the three recitals of the preamble, which provides

> Having regard to the fundamental principle according to which all persons are equal before the law and are entitled to the equal protection of the law;
>
> Being resolved to take further steps to promote the equality of all persons through the collective enforcement of a general prohibition of discrimination by means of the Convention for the Protection of Human Rights and Fundamental Freedoms signed at Rome on 4 November 1950 (hereinafter referred to as "the Convention");
>
> Reaffirming that the principle of non-discrimination does not prevent States Parties from taking measures in order to promote full and effective equality, provided that there is an objective and reasonable justification for those measures (...)

The last recital makes it absolutely clear that "positive measures" that seek to promote equality will not be prohibited by the Protocol, provided that they do not constitute discrimination towards persons or groups not covered by such measures.[16] In other words there must be a justification for such measures (usually the existence of de facto inequalities and the fact that there are disadvantaged groups) and those measures should be proportionate to the legitimate aim which they pursue. This is spelled out in paragraph 16 of the Explanatory Report, which also explains why the Protocol does not contain an operative provision obliging States to adopt such positive measures. Such a programmatic obligation would sit ill with the whole nature of the Convention and its (judicial)

---

16 It is therefore odd that some governments have explained their hesitations towards the Protocol by referring to their concern that it does not exempt positive discrimination; see, as concerns the United Kingdom, G. Moon, The Draft Discrimination Protocol to the European Convention on Human Rights: A Progress Report, *European Human Rights Law Review* [2000], pp. 49-53 (at p. 53).

control system, which are based on the collective guarantee of individual rights that are formulated in terms sufficiently specific to be justiciable.

The Explanatory Report offers further clarifications on the drafters' intentions as concerns the scope and nature of the undertakings laid down in the Protocol. Here, only some of the most important issues will be discussed: first of all, the question of the scope of protection offered by the Protocol and, linked to that, the question of positive obligations which might flow from Article 1.[17]

It goes without saying that *the scope of protection from discrimination* which the Protocol aims to offer extends beyond the current guarantee of Article 14 of the Convention. The purpose is to offer a general prohibition of discrimination in the form of an independent, free-standing guarantee. It is recalled that Article 14 prohibits discrimination only with regard to the "enjoyment of the rights and freedoms" of the ECHR. The report specifies that the protocol's additional protection in comparison with Article 14 concerns, in particular, cases where a person is discriminated against:

(i) in the enjoyment of any right specifically granted to an individual under national law;

(ii) in the enjoyment of a right which may be inferred from a clear obligation of a public authority under national law, i.e. where a public authority is obliged by national law to behave in a particular manner;

(iii) by a public authority in the exercise of discretionary power (e.g. granting certain subsidies);

(iv) by any other act or omission by a public authority (e.g. behaviour of law enforcement officers when controlling a riot).

The report states that the drafters considered it unnecessary to specify which of these four elements are covered by the first paragraph of Article 1 and which by the second. Both paragraphs are complementary and their combined effect is that all four elements are covered by Article 1. This may seem an unnecessarily cumbersome way of drafting, but the reasons for this have everything to do with the scope of positive obligations that may flow from the new provisions. They will be explained below in that context.

For the rest, the Protocol follows closely the model of the existing Article 14. This was a deliberate choice:

---

17 The following comments draw, in particular, on the Explanatory report and on the Final Activity Report of the CDDH to the Committee of Ministers (document CDDH (97) 41 Addendum of 28 October 1997).

- The list of discrimination grounds is identical to that in Article 14. In particular, it was decided not to take up the Parliamentary Assembly's suggestion to include "sexual orientation" in the list: this was considered to be unnecessary because the list was non-exhaustive (cf. the Court's judgment of 21 December 1999 in the case of *Salgueira da Silva Mouta v. Portugal*, which makes it clear that discrimination on that ground is already prohibited under the identical open-ended list of Article 14, ECHR) and because inclusion of any particular additional ground might give rise to unwarranted *a contrario* interpretations as concerns grounds not so included;[18]
- As was stated above, it was decided not to include a provision on the right to equality before the law or to equal protection of the law in the operative part of the Protocol (as guaranteed, for example, by Article 26 of the CCPR). The Explanatory Report, however, reduces the importance of this omission somewhat by stating, in paragraph 15, that the equality principle "does not appear *explicitly*" in the text of Article 1 of the Protocol (emphasis added) and by stressing that the two principles are closely intertwined, giving examples of references by the Court to the principle of equality;
- The drafters refer to the Court's consistent case-law on the notion of discrimination, no departure from that case-law is envisaged;
- The drafters refrained from introducing a restriction clause, for example concerning distinctions based on nationality. Depending on its wording, such a clause might have contained either a blanket restriction, exempting all distinctions based on nationality from the scope of the non-discrimination provision, or a qualified restriction, such as the one that had been proposed

18 This argument shows that the drafters, in line with Article 14 ECHR but contrary to the views of the Parliamentary Assembly, did not want to establish any sort of hierarchy between grounds explicitly mentioned and those not so mentioned in the protocol. Some experts had in fact even indicated that if the list of grounds was to be updated at all, they would wish to remove the term "race" from that list (arguing that the use of this term was no longer in line with present-day scientific views since all human beings belonged to the human race!) and to add "disability" to the list (see document CDDH (97) 41 Addendum, § 20). The DH-DEV preferred to stick to the existing list of grounds appearing in Article 14. The decision not to modify the list of grounds appearing in Article 14 may be criticised (cf., apart from the Assembly's opinion, also N. Frangakis, The prohibition of discrimination in the case-law of the European Court of Human Rights, and Protocol No; 12 to the European Convention on Human Rights, in M. Gavouneli and V. Kyriakopoulos (eds.), *Olympia II: Human Rights in the 21st Century*, Athens/ Komotini 2002, p. 153-177 (170). However, there is little doubt in the mind of the present author that the *legal* – as opposed to purely political – significance of refusing to add grounds to a non-exhaustive list is nil, and that, had the debate been fully opened on possible changes to the list of grounds, it would have led to a considerable delay in the drafting of the Protocol and possibly even to failure to adopt a text.

by ECRI (see section 2 above). The majority of the DH-DEV was against a restriction clause, considering that it was not necessary given that not every distinction amounts to discrimination. This point is explained with some emphasis in paragraph 19 of the Explanatory Report, referring also to the margin of appreciation. Indeed, a restriction clause would have been most unfortunate, given the general nature of the principle of non-discrimination and the fact that the very notion of discrimination already permits justified distinctions that are proportionate and have a legitimate aim;

It was also decided not to make Article 16 ECHR applicable to this Protocol. Article 16 allows States Parties to impose restrictions on the political activity of aliens, notwithstanding Articles 10, 11 and 14, ECHR. Paragraph 32 of the Explanatory report does not state the reasons for this choice, but, during its drafting work, the DH-DEV had expressed serious doubts as to the need to make Article 16 applicable in relation to the new Protocol. Article 16 has so far hardly ever been applied by the European Court of Human Rights[19] and it seemed inappropriate to revive and even expand the principle of Article 16 now, having regard also to the origins of the drafting work on a new instrument against racism and intolerance. The DH-DEV did recognise that this choice meant that, for all practical purposes, Article 16 would become obsolete in relation to Article 14 ECHR in respect of the States Parties to Protocol No. 12.

The wording of the two paragraphs of Article 1 reflects a delicate compromise, or, to use the words of the explanatory report, a "balanced approach" regarding *the question of positive obligations*. This refers to obligations of States, over and above their basic obligation to refrain from performing any discriminatory act (the "negative obligation"), to take active steps to prevent or remedy discrimination, including discrimination between private persons (horizontal effects, or *Drittwirkung*).

The question of positive obligations was undoubtedly the most controversial one during the negotiations. It certainly influenced the decision not to include an explicit operative provision on equality in the protocol (as mentioned above, the compromise was to refer to the equality principle in the preamble): some experts feared that such a significant departure from the wording of Article 14, ECHR, might lead to unpredictable developments in the case-law of the Court. But it was also central to the discussions on the precise wording of the future non-discrimination provision. The DH-DEV had, in fact, identified and retained three different variants for that provision, which in its view represented different degrees of positive obligations for the States Parties.

---

19 Note the rather dismissive manner in which the Court rejected the argument drawn from Article 16 by the French government in the *Piermont v. France* judgment of 27 April 1995, Series A Vol. 314.

While all variants contained an open-ended list of discrimination grounds identical to the list in Article 14, *variant 1* began with the phrase: "No one shall be discriminated on any ground such as ...". This was considered to be the most far-reaching variant, allowing for substantial positive obligations since its wording did not distinguish between public authorities and private actors as being the source of the discrimination. A *second variant* opened with the phrase "The enjoyment of any right set forth by law shall be secured without discrimination on any ground such as ...". This variant obviously appealed to those who wished that the Protocol would depart as little as possible from Article 14. However, it was considered by many experts to be too restrictive and even problematic from a purely legal point of view. It was questionable whether such a provision would really give rise to an autonomous non-discrimination guarantee, since it referred to "any right set forth by law". For example, it was highly uncertain whether discrimination in fact (e.g. factual behaviour of law enforcement officials, etc.) would be fully prohibited by such a text; the same problem existed with regard to the exercise of discretionary power by public authorities (see the above comments on the scope of protection of the Protocol, categories (iv) and (iii), respectively. Those experts also feared that the Court would be drawn into delicate and complicated assessments as to whether an individual application concerned an alleged discrimination in the enjoyment of a "right set forth by law". They referred to the rather complicated case-law of the Strasbourg Court on the notions of "right" and "civil rights and obligations" in Article 6 § 1, ECHR (conditioning the right of access to court). It was considered to be an open question to what extent the word "law" would have an autonomous meaning; there was a risk that such a formula could give rise to different levels of protection in different States Parties, depending on whether a given subject-matter would or would not be recognised as a "right" by national law. Interestingly, however, the DH-DEV rejected a proposal to modify this formula by substituting the term "national law" for the term "law". One of the reasons was that this might have long-term implications for the Court's interpretation of the term "law" elsewhere in the Convention.

In the end, it was a *third variant* that obtained most support, both in the DH-DEV and in the CDDH. It consisted of the second variant, but expanded with a second sentence beginning with the words: "No one shall be discriminated against by a public authority on any ground such as ... ". This was, in essence, the text ultimately retained for Protocol No. 12. This second sentence sought to avoid the restrictive effects or uncertainties attached to the second variant (those linked to the use of the formula "any right set forth by law" – see above), without opening the door to possible positive obligations (including indirect horizontal effects) as widely as variant 1 would have done. The use of the term "public authority" clearly seeks to limit horizontal effects, without excluding them altogether. In particular, the view was expressed that national courts and even legislatures would be covered by the notion of "public authority". On this point, the

Explanatory report indeed confirms (in paragraph 30) that all such authorities are covered, as is the case under the Court's interpretation of the same term in Article 8 § 2 and Article 10 § 1 of the ECHR.

Notwithstanding a certain lack of elegance in its wording, this third variant ultimately acquired the strongest support because it reflected best the consensus that had been achieved as to the scope of protection that the drafters wished to attach to the Protocol: a truly general prohibition of discrimination (see the above-mentioned points (i) to (iv)). In particular, the Court will not be required to make difficult assessments as to whether or not an applicant complaining of discrimination can rely on a "right set forth by law" (the first paragraph of Article 1 of the Protocol); it will be sufficient to argue, under the second paragraph, that the discrimination complained of was the result of an act or omission of a "public authority" within the meaning of the second paragraph. From this perspective, the added value of first paragraph resides in the fact that it more readily attracts positive obligations ("shall be secured").

More generally, the question remains as to the extent of positive obligations intended by the drafters of Protocol No. 12. Paragraph 24 of the Explanatory report states that, while such positive obligations cannot be excluded altogether, the prime objective of Article 1 is to embody a negative obligation for the Parties: the obligation not to discriminate against individuals. The report explains that an additional protocol to the ECHR, which typically contains justiciable individual rights formulated in concise provisions, would not be a suitable instrument for defining the various elements of such a wide-ranging positive obligation. Reference is made to the detailed rules of already existing instruments against discrimination such as the United Nations Convention for the Elimination of All Forms of Racial Discrimination (CERD) and the United Nations Convention on the Elimination of All Forms of Discrimination against Women (CEDAW). At the same time, the report recognises that the duty to "secure" without discrimination the enjoyment of any right set fort by law (see the first paragraph of Article 1) could entail positive obligations, for example in cases where there is a clear lacuna in domestic law protection from discrimination. However, the report goes on to say (paragraph 27) that the extent of any such positive obligations under Article 1 is likely to be limited: it refers to two textual elements which seek to limit possible horizontal effects. The first paragraph is circumscribed by the reference to "any right set forth by law" whereas the second prohibits discrimination by a "public authority".

On this basis, the Explanatory report concludes that any positive obligations in the area of relations between private persons would concern, at the most, relations in the public sphere normally regulated by law, for which the State has a certain responsibility, such as arbitrary denial of access to work, access to restaurants or to other services, etc. Purely private matters would not be affected. Regulation of such matters would be likely to interfere with the right to respect for private and family life and other rights guaranteed by Article 8 of the Convention.

4. Final Comments

While the Protocol may seem a fairly modest extension of the ECHR guarantees, certainly when compared to Article 26 of the Covenant on Civil and Political Rights, it should be borne in mind that observance of the new provision will be subject to judicial control by the European Court of Human Rights. One might add that the Protocol will be directly applicable by domestic courts in almost all States Parties.[20] In fact, there is little doubt that it was precisely this feature of supranational judicial control, not the substantive norm as such (cf. Article 26 CCPR, by which virtually all States concerned are already bound) which made negotiations during the preparation of the Protocol so difficult and which indeed led to the failure of the earlier attempts to include a free-standing provision on equality and non-discrimination in the ECHR system. During the negotiations on the Protocol, delegations of the member States were keenly aware that, ultimately, it will be for the Court to interpret its Article 1 and to define gradually through the case-law the scope of the obligations that flow from it. This point should not be exaggerated, however. Some degree of vagueness is inherent in the wording of most provisions guaranteeing fundamental rights and freedoms, whether in a constitutional bill of rights or in a human rights treaty. Indeed, the ECHR contains quite a few of such provisions, and it would have been inappropriate to apply higher standards of precision in respect of the new Protocol.

The adoption of the Protocol reveals a broad political acceptance of the fact that the persistence of discrimination in our European societies and the emergence of new manifestations of discriminatory attitudes warrant a reinforcement of the protection which the ECHR offers against human rights violations in this field. Certainly, one should not expect the Protocol to be or to become a panacea for all forms of discrimination that may occur in society. It should be remembered that the European Convention imposes obligations on States, not on private persons as such. The whole logic of the collective enforcement mechanism – through complaints against States Parties – is based on this premise. But the new protocol does provide an important basic safeguard, affirm that discrimination is nothing less than a human rights violation, and equip the European Court of Human Rights with a legal tool enabling it to address certain forms of discrimination for which the States Parties may be held accountable but which are not yet prohibited by the rather limited provision of Article 14.

20 To date, only Ireland has not yet given domestic effect to the ECHR in its legal order. However, legislation to that effect was recently adopted in Parliament and is expected to enter into force by the end of 2003.

The many signatures of the new Protocol at the European Ministerial Conference on Human Rights in Rome in November 2000 heralded a significant improvement in the European system for the protection of Human Rights and were as such an excellent way to celebrate the 50th anniversary of the Convention. The next steps, which should be pursued vigorously, are ratification and entry into force of the Protocol. It seems reasonable to expect that the number of ten ratifications required for entry into force will be reached within the next two years. Of course, the Court was right in pointing out that Protocol 12 will increase the Court's workload in the future. However, the current overburdening of the Court by a steadily increasing number of individual applications must be recognised as a serious problem in its own right, one that is not related to the question of the substantive guarantees offered by the Convention. It should be stressed that, fortunately, the aforementioned Ministerial Conference has politically accepted that the question of the Court's caseload constitutes a serious and urgent problem. Work has since been started to identify both short- and medium-term solutions for tackling this issue, and it is most likely that this will lead to future reform of the control mechanism established by the ECHR.[21]

21 See, *inter alia*, Resolution No. 1 adopted at the Ministerial Conference and the recent decision of the Committee of Ministers (November 2002) to instruct the CDDH to present a coherent set of concrete proposals for reform by April 2003. The CDDH report and subsequent developments can be found at www.coe.int (click on Human Rights, then on ECHR Reform).

Giancarlo Cardinale[1]

3. THE PREPARATION OF ECRI GENERAL POLICY RECOMMENDATION No 7 ON NATIONAL LEGISLATION TO COMBAT RACISM AND RACIAL DISCRIMINATION

1. Introduction

The background to ECRI's decision to prepare a general policy recommendation on national legislation to combat racism and racial discrimination includes two main aspects. Firstly, the need to follow-up the conclusions of the European Conference against Racism[2] and the World Conference against Racism, Racial Discrimination, Xenophobia and Related Intolerance,[3] the final documents of which stress the essential role of effective national legislation in these areas. Secondly, in its country-specific reports, ECRI consistently recommends to governments the adoption of effective legislation in the different branches of the law. The need was therefore felt to provide member States of the Council of Europe with more guidance as to what ECRI meant by such a recommendation. In preparing its general policy recommendation No. 7, moreover, ECRI also wished to contribute to the international debate on these issues, and in particular to provide a set of suggestions at a time when a number of member States of the Council of Europe are engaged in the process of reviewing their legislation with a view to meeting the standards contained in the Directives based on Article 13

1 ECRI Secretariat. Views expressed here are purely personal to the author.

2 European Conference against Racism – European Contribution to the World Conference Against Racism, Racial Discrimination, Xenophobia and Related Intolerance, Strasbourg, 11-13 October 2000.

3 World Conference Against Racism, Racial Discrimination, Xenophobia and Related Intolerance, Durban, 31 August-7 September 2001.

Jan Niessen, Isabelle Chopin (eds.), The Development of Legal Instruments..., *81-92*

of the Amsterdam Treaty.[4] In this respect, ECRI's suggestions appear all the more useful as they aim to extend the protection against racism and racial discrimination further than existing international standards. The adoption of an approach which advocates higher standards of protection was naturally facilitated by the fact that ECRI is a body composed of independent members, whose recommendations are not subject to negotiations reflecting national interests and are not legally-binding, and whose mandate is wide and not hampered by strict rules concerning competence.

ECRI entrusted the main responsibility for the preparation of this general policy recommendation to an *ad hoc* working group composed of some of its members. The group's work was reviewed at regular intervals by ECRI's plenary meetings, during which fundamental decisions on the scope of the recommendation and its content were taken. A pivotal role in shaping the recommendation was also played by non-governmental organisations, national specialised bodies in the field of combating racism and racial discrimination and other relevant interlocutors, who were invited by ECRI to give their contribution to the recommendation in writing and, for a number of them, orally during a hearing.

ECRI had initially envisaged a recommendation focusing exclusively on civil and administrative law provisions against racial discrimination. As work progressed, however, the view prevailed, advocated notably by those members of ECRI who were more familiar with legal approaches to discrimination favouring recourse to criminal law, that the recommendation should not limit itself to civil and administrative law provisions, but should also detail relevant constitutional and criminal law provisions. Moreover, from the start, a considerable number of ECRI members had argued that the preparation of a recommendation focusing exclusively on racial discrimination could be wrongly interpreted as indicating that ECRI attributed more importance to combating racial discrimination than other aspects of racism (such as racially-motivated offences, racist expressions and racist organisations). In order to meet this concern, it was proposed that ECRI's recommendation on national legislation against racial discrimination be the first of a series of recommendations which would subsequently include, at least, a recommendation on racially-motivated offences, one on racist expressions and one on racist organisations, each one of these covering all branches of the law. Finally, however, it was felt that one single recommendation covering both racial discrimination and the other aspects of the fight against racism would ensure better internal coherence and reflect more accurately ECRI's view

4 Directive 2000/43/EC of the Council of the European Union implementing the principle of equal treatment between persons irrespective of racial or ethnic origin, and Directive 2000/78/EC of the Council of the European Union establishing a general framework for equal treatment in employment and occupation. The deadlines for Member States of the EU to comply with the Directives 2000/43/EC and 2000/78/EC are 19 July 2003 and 2 December 2003 respectively.

that all these areas deserve equally urgent attention by the national legislator. This choice was consciously made in spite of its time implications: in fact, the final adoption of ECRI general policy recommendation n°7 did not take place until December 2002, i.e. almost 21 months after the initial decision to undertake this project, a considerably longer time than that needed for the preparation of any other ECRI general policy recommendation.[5]

ECRI general policy recommendation No. 7 (hereinafter: the Recommendation) contains the elements that ECRI considers to be key to effective national legislation against racism and racial discrimination. Some ECRI members supported the idea that ECRI should recommend to member States the adoption of a single comprehensive body of legislation, as this would secure gains in terms of visibility, awareness among the legal community and society in general of the legislation and, ultimately, effectiveness. However, the prevailing view was that a single act would be at variance with the legal tradition of many countries and that the Recommendation should be an instrument compatible with the different existing legal traditions, which may favour an approach whereby the relevant provisions are scattered throughout the legal system of a particular country. During the discussions, it was also emphasised that the concepts of racism and racial discrimination vary over time, and that the fight against racial discrimination is increasingly seen as part of a more general fight against all types of discrimination. Thus, while the scope of the Recommendation is limited by ECRI's mandate, the key components contained therein might be included in broader legislation encompassing the fight against racism and racial discrimination.[6] For example, when adopting legal measures against discrimination, member States might prohibit, alongside racial discrimination, other forms of discrimination such as those based on gender, sexual orientation, disability, political or other opinion, social origin, property, birth or other status.

In preparing the Recommendation, ECRI drew inspiration from national legislation and existing international standards, in particular: the International Convention on the Elimination of All Forms of Racial Discrimination (ICERD); Article 14 of the European Convention on Human Rights (ECHR); Protocol 12 to the ECHR; the Directives based on Article 13 of the Amsterdam Treaty; and the proposal of the EC Commission for a Council Framework Decision on combating racism and xenophobia. However, as mentioned above, in many aspects, the Recommendation goes further than existing international standards. Amongst the most significant additions are: the inclusion of nationality (meaning citizenship of a country), religion and language among the criteria that identify persons and groups of persons enjoying protection against

5 ECRI general policy recommendations 1 to 6 can be found in: Compilation of ECRI general policy recommendations, CRI (2001) 7 (Council of Europe, Strasbourg, January 2001).

6 The Recommendation, Explanatory Memorandum, para. 4.

racism and racial discrimination; the application of the prohibition of discrimination to a very broad range of areas, including the activities of the police and border control officials; the attribution of more extensive powers to the national specialised bodies to combat racism and racial discrimination; and the establishment of a positive duty on public authorities to promote equality and to prevent discrimination in carrying out their functions.

This paper attempts to describe the path, including supporting arguments and alternative options, which led ECRI to formulate these and other proposals contained in the Recommendation. Some of the arguments and options are obviously similar to those advanced by stakeholders in the preparation of the other instruments mentioned above. The author would like to emphasise that the paper will focus exclusively on racial discrimination and will not extend to other aspects of the fight against racism, such as racially-motivated offences, racist expression and racist organisations, which are equally covered by the Recommendation. The structure of the paper follows that of the Recommendation, which starts with the definitions of racism and racial discrimination, goes on to detail the provisions by branch of the law – constitutional, civil and administrative and criminal – and concludes with an outline of some common provisions applicable to all branches of the law.

2. Definitions

2.1 A Wide Notion of Racism and Racial Discrimination

The definitions of racism and racial discrimination contained in the Recommendation cover behaviour based on different grounds. Such grounds include those usually referred to in other national and international instruments against racism and racial discrimination, such as race and national or ethnic origin, but also language, religion and nationality (meaning citizenship of a country). A certain number of ECRI members expressed the view that the definitions of racism and racial discrimination should be confined to behaviour based on race and national or ethnic origin and that for behaviour based on language, religion and nationality the notion of 'related intolerance' should be used instead.[7]

---

7 A preliminary debate was held concerning the acceptability of the use of the word 'race', which, according to some views, could imply recognition by ECRI of the existence of different human races, a postulate of all racist theories. However, two main considerations worked in favour of maintaining the use of the word 'race' in the Recommendation: first, the fact that removing 'race' from the grounds covered by an instrument aimed at combating *rac*ism and *rac*ial discrimination and maintaining only the other grounds would cause confusion. A second consideration was that the Recommendation should give priority to ensuring as effective a protection as possible to victims of racism and racial discrimination, and that, in the day-to-day reality

One of the arguments put forward in favour of the wider notion of racism and racial discrimination is based on ECRI's mandate – which is to combat racism, antisemitism, xenophobia and intolerance – and the way in which ECRI has interpreted this mandate. The concepts of racism, antisemitism, xenophobia and intolerance vary over time and, since the beginning of its work, ECRI has interpreted its mandate as combating violence, discrimination, prejudice and disadvantage faced by persons or groups of persons, notably on grounds of race, colour, language, religion, nationality and national or ethnic origin. ECRI considered that racism and racial discrimination are phenomena targeting all persons and groups of persons covered by its mandate and that, as a result, the notions of racism and racial discrimination in the Recommendation should cover conduct connected with grounds such as nationality, religion and language. By the same token, however, those who favoured a more restrictive notion of racism and racial discrimination noted that the mandate of ECRI expressly refers to 'intolerance' alongside 'racism'. The view prevailed, however, that were the notions of racism and racial discrimination confined only to behaviour based on race and national or ethnic origin, they would fail to encompass numerous and important manifestations of racism and racial discrimination taking place in European societies today. Moreover, based on its country-specific monitoring activities covering all member States of the Council of Europe, ECRI considered that nowadays racist and racially-discriminatory conduct is in many cases based on a mix of grounds, which often include nationality, language and religion and that, as a result, it is not possible in the day-to-day reality of the situation to keep these grounds separate from one another. It was felt that ECRI's role as a moral authority against racism in Europe conferred on it the responsibility of advocating national legislation which offers adequate protection against all contemporary manifestations of racism and racial discrimination.

It should be noted, however, that ECRI does not necessarily require that member States adopt such a wide notion of racism and racial discrimination in their domestic legislation. As concerns racism, the definition is only given for the purposes of the Recommendation. As for racial discrimination, what ECRI recommends is that the legal provisions against discrimination adopted by the member States cover discrimination on all the grounds mentioned by ECRI and not that they necessarily define such discrimination as 'racial' discrimination.

---

of the situation, such victims include people generally and erroneously perceived as belonging to 'another race'. The solution found was therefore to maintain the use of the term 'race' but to include the following footnote:

> 'Since all human beings belong to the same species, ECRI rejects theories based on the existence of different «races». However, in this Recommendation ECRI uses this term in order to ensure that those persons who are generally and erroneously perceived as belonging to «another race» are not excluded from the protection provided for by the legislation'.

2.2 *Definition of Direct Racial Discrimination*

The definitions of direct and indirect racial discrimination contained in the Recommendation draw inspiration from the case law of the European Court of Human Rights, which utilises the notion of unjustified differential treatment to define discrimination. According to this approach, discrimination occurs when differential treatment has no objective and reasonable justification, i.e. when it has no legitimate aim or when there is no reasonable relationship of proportionality between the means employed and the aim sought to be realised. ECRI has chosen to maintain this approach for both direct and indirect discrimination. During the discussions, however, the view was expressed that the legitimate aim and proportionality test should be confined to instances of indirect discrimination only, and that the definition of direct racial discrimination should not contain such a test. Accordingly, cases in which direct differential treatment were to be allowed should be provided for as specific exceptions. This approach, based on the case law of the European Court of Justice in the field of gender discrimination, is the approach reflected in the Directives of Article 13 of the Amsterdam Treaty.

The reasons why ECRI chose to maintain the legitimate aim and proportionality test for direct discrimination are mainly linked to the grounds covered by the Recommendation. While Directive 2000/43/EC covers discrimination on the basis of race and ethnic origin, ECRI's Recommendation covers discrimination on the basis of race, colour, language, religion, nationality and national or ethnic origin. Direct differential treatment on the basis of race and ethnic origin can be justified in a very limited number of cases and it is therefore possible to list these as specific exceptions, as the Directive does in Article 4 (genuine and determining occupational requirements). However, the number of cases in which direct differential treatment on the basis of language, nationality and even religion may be justified is considerably greater. ECRI found it therefore impractical to make an exhaustive list of such cases. Hence, the need to resort to a general clause, the legitimate aim and proportionality test, which would, in practice, help distinguish between justified and unjustified direct differential treatment. However, aware of the risk that such a test might be interpreted too loosely by national jurisdictions – thereby allowing for differential treatment on any of the grounds mentioned to be considered lawful in a greater number of cases than justified – ECRI chose to add in its Explanatory Memorandum a reference to the need to interpret such a test as restrictively as possible.[8]

It should also be borne in mind that the Recommendation applies to a very wide range of areas. Therefore, even when compared with Directive 2000/78/EC which deals with a broader range of grounds (religion or belief, disability,

8 The Recommendation, Explanatory Memorandum, para. 8.

age and sexual orientation) and which still provides for specific exceptions where direct differential treatment is permitted, ECRI's approach of applying the legitimate aim and proportionality test to all cases of discrimination still appears justified, as Directive 2000/78/EC only covers the field of employment and occupation.

2.3 Definition of Indirect Racial Discrimination

The notion of indirect discrimination requires a comparison between the impact of a provision, criterion or practice on different groups of persons. ECRI's main concern in defining indirect racial discrimination was to avoid that such comparison should necessarily take place on the basis of statistical evidence, as is the case when notions such as 'proportion of the members of one group' are used to define indirect discrimination. ECRI's view was that the need to resort to statistical evidence to this effect would render a finding of indirect racial discrimination impossible in many cases, as collection of data on some of the grounds covered by the Recommendation is not carried out – or is, in fact, illegal – in many member States of the Council of Europe. ECRI therefore opted for a more neutral wording by which indirect racial discrimination is deemed to occur 'where an apparently neutral factor such as a provision, criterion or practice cannot be as easily complied with by, or disadvantages, persons belonging to a group designated by a ground such as race, colour, language, religion, nationality or national or ethnic origin'. As mentioned above, the legitimate aim and proportionality test also applies to cases of indirect discrimination.

3. Constitutional Law Provisions

ECRI considered it to be essential that constitutions provide a solid legal basis against discrimination. It therefore recommended that they enshrine: the principle of equal treatment – which is understood as encompassing the principle of equality of all persons before the law; the commitment of the State to promote equality – which provides a constitutional basis for the adoption of temporary special measures (see paragraph 4.1); and the individual right to be free from discrimination on grounds such as race, colour, language, religion, nationality or national or ethnic origin. In consideration of the wide range of areas covered, and notably nationality, ECRI recognised that constitutions may provide that exceptions to the principle of equal treatment may be established, but only under two conditions: that they are established by law and that they do not constitute discrimination. In accordance with the proposed definition of discrimination, this last condition is satisfied only if the differential treatment has an objective and reasonable justification.

4. Civil and Administrative Law Provisions

The general approach followed by ECRI is to recommend that member States tackle racial discrimination through civil and administrative means. In addition, member States should use criminal law provisions in certain cases (see Section 5). Thus, most of the civil and administrative law section of the Recommendation is devoted to provisions against discrimination.

4.1 Temporary Special Measures

In order to allow for measures aimed at overcoming situations of disadvantage experienced by persons designated by the enumerated grounds, the Recommendation stipulates that national legislation should provide that the maintenance or adoption of such measures does not contravene the prohibition of discrimination. It was felt within ECRI that more clarity was needed on what these measures, defined as temporary special measures, included. Thus, the Recommendation specifies that such measures do not only include measures aimed at facilitating the full participation, in all fields of life, of persons designated by the enumerated grounds – an example of which would be the organisation of a recruitment campaign by the police designed so as to encourage in particular applications from members of certain ethnic groups under-represented within the police. Temporary special measures also include measures designed to compensate for disadvantages suffered by persons designated by the enumerated grounds – for instance, a factory owner with no employees from a certain ethnic group among his managerial staff but many employees from that ethnic group on the assembly line, could lawfully organise training courses for workers from that ethnic group seeking promotion.

4.2 Acts to Be Considered as Forms of Discrimination

The Recommendation enumerates certain acts, which should be considered by national legislation as forms of discrimination.[9] In theory, it would be possible to cover these types of conduct using the proposed definitions of discrimination and the general legal principles. However, ECRI's country-specific monitoring mechanism made it aware of how, in practice, these acts often tend to be overlooked or excluded from the scope of application of the legislation. Thus, to ensure the effectiveness of the legislation, ECRI opted for the specific enumeration of certain acts as forms of discrimination. These acts include, among others: segregation, announced intention to discriminate and inciting another to discriminate. By including segregation, ECRI intended to address practices

9 The Recommendation, para. 6.

such as separation of children of certain ethnic background, notably Roma, from children of other ethnic backgrounds in schools. It should be noted that, in accordance with the proposed definition of discrimination, for segregation to occur, it is not necessary that the treatment of the separated group be less favourable, but only that separation lack an objective and reasonable justification. Announced intention to discriminate covers conduct such as placing discriminatory advertisements. Its explicit mention as a form of discrimination aims at ensuring that action can be taken against the discriminator even in the absence of a specific victim. For instance, an employment advertisement indicating that Roma need not apply should fall within the scope of the legislation, even if no Roma has actually applied. While the inclusion of instructions to discriminate among the acts to be considered as forms of discrimination did not give rise to an extensive debate within ECRI, the inclusion of incitement to discriminate was agreed only after two preliminary questions had been clarified. Firstly, that the difference between instructing and inciting lay in the relationship of authority which, in case of instructions, exists between the person instructing and the person instructed. Second, that incitement to discriminate should not be confused with *public* incitement to discrimination, hatred and violence, which the Recommendation covers in its criminal law section.[10]

In earlier drafts, harassment also appeared among the acts to be considered as forms of discrimination, as in Directive 2000/43/EC. However, at a later stage the view prevailed that, in order to try and limit the notion of discrimination as much as possible to that of differential treatment *stricto sensu*, harassment related to one of the enumerated grounds should be prohibited as such, and not as a form of discrimination. The definition of harassment, which is heavily based on the definition contained in the Directive, makes clear that the responsibility of persons other than the material author of the harassment is limited to situations where these persons have clearly failed to take reasonable action to avoid the creation of an environment of the type described.

4.3 Fields of Application

According to the Recommendation, the personal and material scope of the prohibition of discrimination is practically unlimited. The prohibition of discrimination applies to all public authorities and to all persons, be they natural or legal persons, whether they act in the public or in the private sector. It also applies to all areas, although the Recommendation enumerates a number of them for illustrative purposes. From the outset of its work on the Recommendation, ECRI felt that it was particularly important to ensure that the activities of the police and other law enforcement officials, border control officials, the army

10 The Recommendation, para. 18 a).

and prison personnel be covered by the prohibition of discrimination. These areas are therefore mentioned explicitly (as a part of 'public services'). Based on its country-specific monitoring work, moreover, ECRI considered that a further guarantee of effectiveness needed in this area is the attribution to one or more independent bodies of the investigations of alleged acts of discrimination committed by members of the police, border control officials, members of the army and prison personnel.[11]

4.4 *Positive Duty on Public Authorities*

It is somewhat natural that an instrument focusing on legal provisions against discrimination takes a marked remedial approach to the phenomenon of discrimination. At different stages of the work on the Recommendation, however, it was stressed that such a remedial approach should be complemented by an approach oriented towards prevention of discrimination through the promotion of equality and awareness raising. The recommendation to place public authorities under a statutory duty to promote equality and to prevent discrimination in carrying out their functions reflects precisely this approach. The main hesitations in this respect concerned the vagueness of the content of such a duty and its enforceability. ECRI addressed the first aspect by recommending that the obligations incumbent on public authorities under this duty, including the elaboration and implementation of equality programmes, should be spelled out as clearly as possible in the law, although it appeared clear that a greater level of precision could be attained through further regulations. As concerns enforceability, ECRI envisages a pivotal role for the national specialised bodies, whose action should not be limited to guidance, but should include the possibility of initiating proceedings in the case of a public authority's failure to comply with the duty.

5. Criminal Law Provisions against Discrimination

Although most of the anti-discrimination provisions are to be found in the section of the Recommendation devoted to civil and administrative law, ECRI chose to recommend that member States resort to criminal law sanctions for certain cases of discrimination. These are cases of racial discrimination in the exercise of one's public office or occupation.[12] The obvious idea behind this choice is that criminal sanctions should be limited to areas characterised by a certain public dimension, whereas racially-discriminatory behaviour taking place within the private sphere should be exempted from criminal sanctions and

11 The Recommendation, para. 28.

12 The Recommendation, Explanatory Memorandum, para. 18 h).

remedied exclusively through civil and administrative means. Thus, for instance, racial discrimination when renting a flat could be subject to criminal sanctions if committed by a letting agency, whereas only civil and administrative means should be available against a private individual who discriminated in renting his or her flat.

To some extent, such a solution constitutes a compromise between those ECRI members who favoured a wider application of criminal law sanctions to cases of racial discrimination and those who supported the idea that discrimination should be tackled exclusively by civil and administrative means. Two main arguments were used in favour of the latter view. Firstly, that the introduction of criminal law provisions against racial discrimination in long-established national systems based on civil anti-discrimination provisions was likely to disturb the delicate balance attained through many years of experience in the area of civil anti-discrimination litigation. The second argument was that criminal law provisions against discrimination could have a counterproductive effect if not adequately applied, which is often the case due to the difficulties encountered in proving racial discrimination at the level required by criminal law. However, the symbolic value of criminal law sanctions – which mark society's rejection of racial discrimination – and their dissuasive effect were considered powerful arguments that warranted recourse, at least in some circumstances, to criminal law.

6. Common Provisions

6.1 National Specialised Bodies

The establishment of national specialised bodies to combat racism and racial discrimination has always been one of ECRI's priorities. This is reflected in the fact that ECRI devoted the second in its series of general policy recommendations to this issue. This recommendation contains ECRI's position on the statute of such a body, the forms it might take, its responsibilities, administration and style of operation. As a result, the question of the provisions to be included in the Recommendation concerning the establishment of national specialised bodies did not give rise to much debate. However, taking into account the provisions contained in Article 13 of Directive 2000/43/EC – which require the establishment of bodies that provide independent assistance to victims of discrimination, conduct independent surveys and publish independent reports and recommendations – ECRI considered that it was useful to emphasise the need for the body itself, and not just its functions, to be independent. According to its general policy recommendation n°2, to which the Recommendation explicitly refers, independence of the specialised body implies, among other things: clear terms of reference setting out provisions for appointment of members and providing appropriate safeguards against arbitrary dismissal or non-renewal of appointments; provision of sufficient funds to carry out functions and responsibility effectively; annual approval of the funding by the parliament; guarantee of the ability to manage resources, appoint staff and express views without interference from the State; and discussion on the performance of the body in Parliament. As concerns the functions of the national specialised bodies, it was ECRI's intention to push for more competences to be attributed to such bodies, notably as concerns investigative powers, which may result, where appropriate, in legal proceedings. Adjudication of complaints of racial discrimination is one more function included by ECRI general policy recommendation n°2 in the list of responsibilities which can be attributed to national specialised bodies. In view of the need to separate adjudicating functions from functions of legal assistance and investigation, ECRI chose to suggest in the Recommendation that a separate body could be entrusted with the adjudication of complaints of racial discrimination through legally binding decisions, within the limits prescribed by the law.

6.2 Who Can Bring Judicial Proceedings

The main issue of ECRI's debate around the entitlement to bring judicial proceedings was the possibility for associations, trade unions and other legal entities with a legitimate interest in combating racial discrimination to file complaints even if a specific victim is not referred to. Hesitations in this respect were connected to the fact that such a mechanism is not known in many legal systems within the member States of the Council of Europe. However, the proposal was retained in view of two main considerations. First, it was noted that such a possibility would help in cases where victims are afraid of retaliatory measures and in cases of discrimination affecting many persons where consent cannot be obtained from everybody. Second, the possibility for organisations to file complaints without referring to a specific victim would help combating structural forms of discrimination and allow for interests that individual victims do not pursue before the courts to be represented jointly.

PART II

EUROPEAN UNION ANTI-DISCRIMINATION LEGISLATIVE MEASURES

Jan Niessen and Isabelle Chopin

4. THE STARTING LINE AND THE RACIAL EQUALITY DIRECTIVE

The adoption of the Racial Equality Directive and the Employment Equality Directive[1] marked the end of years of debates on whether to enact Community legislation to combat discrimination on grounds of racial, ethnic or national origin and of pressure for such legislation from civil society on European institutions and individual Member States. This chapter looks back at these debates among European institutions and between these institutions and civil society organisations, highlighting in particular the role of the Starting Line.[2]

1. Parliamentary Reports

In the early 1980s, the Council of Ministers re-launched the idea of the internal market and gave the European Commission the mandate to design a strategy as

1 Council Directive 2000/43/EC of 29 June 2000 implementing the principle of equal treatment between persons irrespective of racial and ethnic origin (OJ L 180,19/07/2000) and Council Directive 2000/78/EC of 27 November 2000 establishing a general framework for equal treatment in employment and occupation (OJ L 303, 2/12/2000).

2 Without claiming that the Starting Line coalition was the sole and most important player, it is a widely recognised fact that this coalition played a crucial role in the design and adoption of Community anti-discrimination legislation by making its own legislative proposals and stimulating co-operation among stakeholders in a Europe-wide campaign. This can be evidenced by the European Parliament's many references to the Starting Line (see further in this chapter). Also European Commission officials expressed on many occasions their appreciation of the Starting Line. For the most recent example, see Barbara Nolan, The Directive on racial discrimination: history, innovative features and some practical examples from experience at the national level. Paper presented at the Danish EU Presidency Conference on the Implementation of the anti-discrimination directives into national law (Copenhagen, 14-15 November 2002).

Jan Niessen, Isabelle Chopin (eds.), The Development of Legal Instruments..., *95-110*

to how to complete it.[3] This primarily economic programme, known as the '1992 operation', also offered opportunities to move social issues (including equality and anti-discrimination) up on the European policy agenda.

Of the European institutions, it was the European Parliament that initiated the debates on anti-discrimination in 1984 by creating a Parliamentary Enquiry Committee to look into the rise of fascism and racism in Europe. In 1985 this Committee presented a very complete report that became known as the Evrigenis Report.[4] The report 'lays emphasis on the fundamental importance of defending a democratic and pluralistic European society and respecting the dignity of men and women whatever their race, sexual orientation, religion, nationality or ethnic origin'.[5] It stated that

> An effort must be made to define more broadly Community powers and responsibilities in the area of race relations by applying a teleological interpretation of the Treaties, on the basis, inter alia, of seeking the useful effect of the relevant provisions and of the European Community's implicit powers (…) and, if necessary, by revision of the Treaties.[6]

This report was followed in 1986 by the first common declaration of the European institutions condemning all forms of intolerance, warning about the dangers of racism and insisting on the need to prevent all forms of discrimination.[7] The 1989 Community Charter of the Fundamental Social Rights of Workers mentioned the importance of combating every form of discrimination including discrimination on the grounds of sex, colour, race, opinion and belief.[8] A 1990 Council resolution promised the Union would act 'clearly and unambiguously to counter the growth of racism and xenophobia'.[9] In 1991, the European

3 See for this period in the European Union's history, Bino Olivi, L'Europe difficile. Histoire politiques de la Communauté européenne (Paris, 1998).

4 European Parliament, Committee of Inquiry into the Rise of Fascism and Racism in Europe, reports on the findings of the inquiry, European Parliament, December 1985.

5 European Parliament, Resolution on the rise of fascism and racism in Europe, adopted on 16 January 1986. OJ No. C36, 17.2.1986.

6 European Parliament, Committee of Inquiry into the Rise of Fascism and Racism in Europe, Report on the findings of the inquiry, (December 1985), page 96, point 319 (j).

7 European Parliament, Council and Commission, Declaration against Racism and Xenophobia (OJ C 158, 25/06/1986).

8 European Commission, Community Charter of the Fundamental Social Rights of Workers. Office for Public Publications of the European Communities, Luxembourg, 1990.

9 Council Resolution on the fight against racism and xenophobia (OJ C157/1, 27/05/1990).

Parliament published a second report on the issue.[10] The report, which became known as the Ford Report, showed that there were many expressions of racial discrimination requiring different approaches to eliminate it, that no Member State was free from this disease and that there were very active racist organisations at work in Europe, many of them working together transnationally.

Both the Evrigenis Report and the Ford Report, but not the Joint Declaration, called for the adoption of European legislative measures.[11] The Council of Ministers and the European Commission were of the opinion that the European Treaties did not provide a legal basis for the European institutions to act on racial discrimination, a *conditio sine qua non* for any action at the Community level, let alone to enact anti-discrimination legislation. The European Parliament and the two parliamentary rapporteurs maintained that whether or not the European institutions were competent to take legal and other measures was more a matter of political will than of a strict interpretation of the European Treaties. The Rapporteurs referred to Article 235 (now Article 308) of the EC-Treaty, which could very well provide the necessary basis to act on racial discrimination. This article states that where the Treaties do not provide the legal basis for action, action may be taken as long as it is necessary for the attainment, in the course of the operation of the common market, of one of the objectives of the Community, and by unanimous vote in the Council. Apparently, not all Member States, nor the European Commission, considered the fight against racial discrimination with legal and other means to be one of the objectives of the European Community.

2. The Drafting of the Starting Line

The two parliamentary reports were well received by the NGO community. A few organisations took the matter a step further and drafted their own proposal for European anti-discrimination legislation. The proposal was given the name 'the Starting Line'.[12] An initiative of the Churches' Commission for Migrants

---

10 European Parliament, Committee of Inquiry into the Rise of Fascism and Racism in Europe, Report on the findings of the inquiry, European Parliament, Report drawn up on behalf of the Committee of Inquiry into Racism and Xenophobia (Ford Report) (1991) 97-98. The Ford report was based on research undertaken by, among others, Antonio Cruz, editor of the Migration News Sheet (providing country by country information on expressions of racial discrimination), Jan Niessen (providing a general overview) and Searchlight (providing information on extremist right-wing organisations).

11 The Economic and Social Committee also recommended the adoption or strengthening of national and European anti-discrimination legislation. See its 1988 Opinion on the Proposal for a Council Resolution on the fight against racism and xenophobia.

12 The group of drafters included experts in (international) law, activists and a former senior civil servant of the European Commission from Belgium, France, Germany, Italy, the Netherlands and the United Kingdom. The Starting Line. A proposal for

in Europe, the British Commission for Racial Equality and the Dutch National Bureau against Racism, in 1991, these organisations formed an informal group, the Starting Line Group, which was in the following years to be joined by such organisations as the Commissioner for Foreigners of the Berlin Senate, the Belgian Centre for Equal Opportunities and Opposition to Racism, the Dutch Centre for Foreigners, and European organisation such as Caritas Europa, the European Jewish Information Centre and the European Anti-Poverty Network.[13] These organisations were convinced of the necessity and urgency of fighting racism across the European Union. They may, on the basis of their respective mandates, have had differing views on how to combat discrimination generally and implement different strategies, but they agreed on the essential and critical role of anti-discrimination legislation.

There are good reasons for why Community legislation was proposed. First, the level of protection against racial and ethnic discrimination varied considerably in the Member States thus creating in the European Union a situation of unequal protection against it.[14] In the early 1990s, most Member States had constitutional equality and anti-discrimination provisions, and some had more specific anti-discrimination or equality provisions included within their civil, administrative or penal system. However, only six countries, namely Austria, Belgium, France, the Netherlands, Sweden and the United Kingdom, had at that time specific and more elaborated legislation against racism.[15] Nevertheless, the scope and implementation of these diverse pieces of legislation or provisions varied from one country to another.[16] A Community measure would not

---

a draft Council Directive concerning the elimination of racial discrimination (April, 1993). This publication was translated into all the languages of the then twelve Member States and published in a format that made photocopying of the document easy. The proposal was reproduced in Ann Dummett, The Starting Line: a proposal for a draft Council Directive concerning the elimination of racial discrimination; New Community Vol. 20 (3) pp 530-538.

13 A few other organisations joined the network for a certain period of time, among them the French Consultative Commission on Human Rights and the European Migrants' Forum.

14 "Measure for Measure, A Comparative Analysis of Measures to Combat Racial Discrimination in the Member Countries of the European Community", by Ian Forbes and Geoffrey Mead, Equal Opportunities Studies Group, (University of Southampton, Research Series N 1992).

15 European Commission against Racism and Intolerance (ECRI), "Legal measures to combat racism and intolerance in the Member States of the Council of Europe", report prepared by the Swiss Institute of Comparative Law, March 1995.

16 Commission of the European Communities, Legal measures to combat racism and xenophobia. Comparative assessment of the legal instruments implemented in the various Member States to combat all forms of discrimination, racism and xenophobia and incitement to hatred and racial violence (December 1992).

only oblige Member States without legislation to put it in place[17] but also set minimum standards applicable across the expanding European Union. Second, the drafters of the Starting Line maintained that different levels of protection against discrimination in various Member States and a lack of protection in a significant number of Member States could amount to an infringement of free movement rights. Citizens would be less inclined to exercise their free movement right and actually prevented from doing so if they were not sufficiently protected against discrimination. In other words, the drafters linked their proposal to the Community programme to complete the internal market, which aimed to remove obstacles to the freedom of movement of goods, services, capital and persons. This link, together with the reference to Article 235, gave the proposal a solid basis in Community law and the drafters hoped that it would convince the European Commission to use its exclusive right of legislative initiative. It was also used to convince governments to actively support a Commission initiative.[18] Third, as a matter of principle the drafters wanted to elaborate the Union's human rights commitments which were common to all Member States and to expand Community gender equality legislation to race, ethnicity and nationality. Therefore, the wording and certain concepts of the Starting Line were borrowed from international human rights standards[19] and Community gender equality standards. By taking this line, the Starting Line was not entirely locked into the common market logic and appealed to overall human rights and equality commitments.

In terms of the type of legal measure, the drafters preferred a directive. A directive defines the goals to be achieved, but leaves considerable freedom to the Member States to incorporate these goals into national law. A directive sets minimum standards allowing Member States not only to tailor these standards to fit in with their national traditions, law and practices, but also to go beyond these standards and offer more protection than the minimum standards required. Transposing European measures into national law would engage national parliaments and all stakeholders in an ongoing debate on anti-discrimination

17 This was in particular important for those Member States where it was not even considered necessary to adopt anti-discrimination legislation, for example Greece and Germany.

18 It was meant in particular to convince the governments of those Member States where anti-discrimination legislation was already in place but who failed to see that the Community action was needed to protect their citizens' free movement rights. This was the case, for example, of the United Kingdom and Sweden after its accession in 1995. Once convinced, such countries could play a leading role in preparing a favourable climate within the Council of Ministers for a Commission initiative.

19 Use was made in particular of the International Convention on the Elimination of all forms of Racial Discrimination. Ireland was the only country that had not ratified this Convention. It did so in December 2000.

policies and practices. These factors would greatly enhance the effectiveness of anti-discrimination legislation.

The Starting Line proposed that Member States be required to adopt legal measures to prohibit direct and indirect discrimination on the grounds of race, colour, descent, nationality, national or ethnic origin in different fields such as the exercise of a professional activity, social security, health and welfare benefits, education, vocational guidance and training, housing, provision of goods, facilities and services, participation in social, cultural, religious and public life. Sanctions were foreseen for authors of racial discrimination, as was compensation for victims. The proposal contained provisions on the presumption of discrimination and the sharing of the burden of proof. It prohibited racist and xenophobic propaganda and insult, and incitement to racial discrimination, hatred or violence. It advocated outlawing organisations promoting such propaganda as well as withholding support by public institutions of racist organisations.[20]

3. The Campaign

The Starting Line Group made its proposal public in 1992, just before the Edinburgh European Council. This may have inspired the Council's adoption of a Declaration on Racism and Xenophobia, which mentioned education and national legal measures as means to combat racial discrimination. The Group subsequently launched a campaign to rally support for the Starting Line among non-governmental and governmental actors at national and European level, eventually leading to 400 organisations throughout the European Union supporting the Starting Line proposal.

The European Parliament expressed its support for the Starting Line proposal on a number of occasions. In the 1993 Resolution on Racism and Xenophobia, it '...call[ed] on the Commission to draw up as a matter of urgency a directive laying down measures to strengthen the legal instruments existing in this field in the Member States, using the document entitled "the Starting Line"...'.[21]

In the 1994 Resolution on Racism, Xenophobia and Anti-Semitism, the European Parliament reiterated its demand, and

> ...repeat[ed] once more its request to the Commission to draw up as a matter of urgency a directive laying down measures to reinforce the relevant legal instru-

---

20 For a more detailed analysis of the Starting Line proposal, see Isabelle Chopin, The Starting Line Group: A harmonised approach to fight racism and to promote equal treatment. In: European Journal of Migration and Law (Vol.1 No.1 1999, 111-129).

21 European Parliament, Resolution on Racism and Xenophobia, 2 December 1993, PE 177.105.

ments in the Member States, using the document "the Starting Line" as a basis and taking into account Parliament's guidelines for anti-racist policy...[22]

In the 1995 Resolution on Racism, Xenophobia and Anti-Semitism, the European Parliament 'call[ed] once more upon the Commission to submit a proposal for an anti-discrimination directive as a matter of urgency...'.[23]

The vast majority of the Member States were, on the contrary, not willing to consider the adoption of Community anti-discrimination legislation. At best they preferred intergovernmental co-operation on the matter. At the EU Corfu Summit in June 1994 the decision was made to create the Consultative Commission on Racism and Xenophobia, whose mandate was to make 'recommendations on co-operation between governments and the various social bodies in favour of encouraging tolerance and understanding of foreigners' and to 'develop a global strategy at the Union level aimed at combating acts of racist and xenophobic violence'.[24]

The European Commission was divided over whether or not the Treaty provided the necessary legal basis for granting it the authority to act on racial issues. Waiting for more favourable times, the European Commission preferred not to use its right of legislative initiative, but to prepare other initiatives. In 1995, the Commission adopted a Communication on Racism, Xenophobia and Anti-Semitism[25] and a proposal for a Council Decision designating 1997 as European Year Against Racism.[26]

Because of this situation and in view of the Intergovernmental Conference (IGC) announced in 1991 to take place in 1996, the Starting Line Group decided to adapt its strategy. It drafted a proposal for an amendment to the Treaty to the effect that the European institutions would have the powers to act, on the basis of a qualified majority and by using the co-decision procedure, on racial, ethnic and religious discrimination. In addition, the proposal, that was given the name the Starting Point, proposed adding to the list of the European Community objectives the elimination of discrimination against persons or groups of persons, whether citizens of the European Union or not, on the grounds of

22 European Parliament, Resolution on Racism, Xenophobia and Anti-Semitism, 27 October 1994 PE 184.353.

23 European Parliament, Resolution on Racism, Xenophobia and Anti-Semitism, 26 October 1995.

24 Presidency Conclusions, European Council at Corfu, 24-25 June 1994.

25 European Commission, Communication on Racism, Xenophobia and Anti-Semitism. Commission Communication COM(95) 653 final.

26 European Commission, Proposal for a Council decision designating 1997 as European Year against Racism, Brussels, 13 December 1995, COM (95) 653. The proposal was adopted by the Council of Ministers 23/07/1996 C237.

race, colour, religion, or national, social or ethnic origin, and the promotion of harmonious relations between such persons or groups of persons.

The European Parliament and the European Commission also referred to the IGC. The European Parliament 'recommend[ed] that the Commission should introduce a proposal for an anti-discrimination directive…' and 'insists that after the revision of the treaties, the European Community should be entrusted with clear competencies which empower it to take action'.[27] In its 1994 White Paper on Social Policy, the Commission argued that with a new Treaty revision 'serious consideration must be given to the introduction of a specific reference to combating discrimination on the grounds of race [and] religion…'.[28] Even the Consultative Commission on Racism and Xenophobia, initially not willing to consider Community legislative action, expressed itself in favour of a Treaty amendment that would provide for Community competence to take action against discrimination based on race, ethnic origin or religion, and legislation was to be regarded as an essential element in any effective European strategy aimed at combating racism and xenophobia.[29]

The Starting Line Group stepped up its campaign and focussed its attention on the national level by convening a series of consultations in the Member States so as to gain support for both the Starting Line and the Starting Point proposals. Seminars were organised and national conferences attended resulting in a greater awareness among the NGO community of opportunities the IGC offered for the insertion of an anti-discrimination clause into the EC Treaty and the subsequent adoption of Community anti-discrimination legislation. An international conference was held in Amsterdam in early 1997 at a crucial moment.[30] The Irish government, which had prepared a proposal for a new text of a new Treaty that included an anti-discrimination article, had handed over the EU Presidency to the Dutch government for the final stages of the IGC. The conference included an extensive exchange with representatives of the Dutch government and the presentation of an overview of the positions taken by individual governments on matters related to anti-discrimination, migration and asylum.[31] The conference

27 European Parliament, Resolution on Racism, Xenophobia and Anti-Semitism, 27 April 1995.

28 European Commission, White Paper on Social Policy (COM (94) 333).

29 Consultative Commission on Racism and Xenophobia, Final report from the Consultative Commission on Racism and Xenophobia to the General Affairs Council/ European Council, Brussels, 28 May 1996, 6871/1/96, Raxen 18.

30 The conference was the initiative of the Dutch Standing Committee on international immigration, asylum and criminal law asylum and jointly organised with the Migration Policy Group.

31 Simon Hix and Jan Niessen prepared the overview. See Reconsidering European migration policies. The 1996 Intergovernmental Conference and the reform of the

designed a strategy to keep anti-discrimination on the IGC agenda and to press individual governments to vote in favour of the inclusion of an anti-discrimination clause in the EC Treaty.

4. Article 13 and the New Starting Line

The ICG was concluded with the adoption of the Amsterdam Treaty in June 1997. This Treaty inserted an anti-discrimination article into the EC Treaty (Article 13). Article 13 has no direct effect. Appropriate action may be taken on the basis of Article 13 requiring a proposal from the Commission to be approved with the unanimous support of the Council after consultation with the European Parliament. Furthermore, the scope of measures taken on the basis of Article 13 is limited to the fields regulated by Community law. Nevertheless, the revised EC Treaty provided the European institutions with new significant powers to act on discrimination based on sex, racial or ethnic origin, religion or belief, disability, age or sexual orientation.

In the light of the Treaty changes, the Starting Line Group revised its proposal for a directive. Since nationality was regrettably not included in Article 13, the new Starting Line addressed only discrimination on the basis of race or ethnicity and religion or belief. To deal with the position of third-country nationals, two additional but separate proposals were drafted on equal treatment of third-country nationals. These proposals were based on two other amendments of the EC Treaty, namely the new Title IV (equal treatment of third-country nationals) and the new Article 137 (4) (employment conditions for third-country nationals legally residing in the Member States).[32] More so than was the case with the old Starting Line, the wording of the new Starting Line was very similar to existing Community legislation against gender discrimination, in particular with regard to the principles of direct and indirect discrimination and the sharing of the burden of proof.[33]

Maastricht Treaty (Migration Policy Group, Churches' Commission for Migrants in Europe and the Starting Line Group, 1996).

32 These two proposals were later elaborated in the Amsterdam Proposals on immigration and asylum of which at least three pertain to equal treatment of third-country nationals. Immigration Law Practitioners' Association and Migration Policy Group, The ILPA/MPG proposed Directives on immigration and asylum. Prepared by Steve Peers (reader at the University of Essex) for ILPA and MPG (Brussels/London, 2000). Available electronically at www.migpolgroup.com.

33 Isabelle Chopin and Jan Niessen (eds.), Proposals for legislative measures to combat racism and to promote equal rights in the European Union (Brussels/London 1998). This joint publication of the British Commission for Racial Equality and the Starting Line Group was also translated into French.

The new Starting Line offered protection against direct and indirect discrimination and victimisation. The field of application covered the exercise of a professional activity, access to employment, working conditions (including dismissal), vocational guidance and vocational training, social security, health and welfare benefits, education, housing, provision of goods and services, and the participation in political, economic, social, cultural and religious life. This covered more than what is regulated by Community law, but the drafters still wanted very much to elaborate and expand the Union's commitments to human rights and equality. The proposal contained an exemption clause, allowed positive action and divided the burden of proof more equally among victims and perpetrators. It also prohibited incitement or pressure to racial or religious discrimination and any organisation that promotes such incitement or pressure. Also prohibited was any act or practice by a public authority or public institution of racial or religious discrimination against persons, groups of persons or institutions. Finally, the proposal provided for appropriate and effective judicial remedies, the creation of independent bodies, co-operation and consultation with NGOs and a reporting mechanism on the implementation of the Directive.

5. Engaging More Stakeholders

The new Starting Line was officially presented at the UK Presidency Conference on Combating Racism (Manchester, 1998). At this conference the European Commission repeated what it had announced at the end of the 1997 European Year against Racism: that it would propose an anti-discrimination directive as soon as the Amsterdam Treaty entered into force. Less sure of the position of the Member States, the Starting Line Group held, in the course of 1998, a series of interviews with officials of all Member States. The interviews made many senior policy-makers aware of the anti-discrimination clause in the revised EC Treaty. It also took stock of the political will among the Member States to support future legislative initiatives.[34] From these interviews it became clear that Community anti-discrimination legislation was not a high priority for the Member States. It was even unlikely that a few Member States would take the lead in pressing for or strongly supporting a Commission initiative to that effect. Even countries with anti-discrimination legislation in place were reluctant if not hostile[35] to Community legislative initiatives in this field.

It was therefore felt necessary to engage more stakeholders in national and European debates. Using the momentum created by the European Year against

34 Isabelle Chopin, Article 13: a new challenge for European institutions (Migration Policy Group, January 1999). This work was co-sponsored by the Dutch Ministry of Interior.

35 This was the case in the United Kingdom and Sweden.

Racism, the Starting Line Group again focused the discussion on the adoption of Community anti-discrimination legislation as a critical means to combat racism. It circulated the new Starting Line and again organised and attended seminars and conferences across the Union. At European level special attention was given to the position of employers who, together with trade unions, carry much weight in the Brussels corridors of power. Employers' organisations could very well oppose anti-discrimination legislation out of fear of the introduction of a European type of affirmative action, which in Europe is wrongly equated with a quota system. In addition, employers could also try and play legislative measures off against employers' voluntary action, clearly preferring voluntary to legislative action. A Transatlantic Dialogue was organised which attempted to clarify Canadian and US policies and practices for a European private and public sector audience. An important conclusion of this meeting was that legislation and voluntary action are complementary strategies. There is no effective voluntary action by employers when no legislative framework exists, whereas legislation without voluntary action would probably result in a purely legal and minimalist approach to combating racism.[36]

During 1998, when it became very clear that the European Commission, supported by the European Parliament, would indeed 'take appropriate action' and propose an anti-discrimination directive, a study project was designed to compare the existing legislation in the Member States with the new Starting Line and, once presented by the European Commission, the official proposal for a directive. If such a directive was adopted it would have to be transposed into the laws of the Member States and the research would show what adaptations of national law would need to be made in order to comply with an anti-discrimination directive.[37]

36 Lori Lindburg, European and North American approaches to the employment integration of immigrants and ethnic minorities. Voluntary versus legislative measures (Migration Policy Group, 1998).

37 The Migration Policy Group, in its capacity as secretariat of the Starting Line Group, made a first research proposal and discussed it with the European Commission. MPG decided, however, to develop the project together with the newly created European Monitoring Centre on Racism and Xenophobia (EUMC). The EUMC made the report on the research's first phase available electronically. See, Isabelle Chopin and Jan Niessen (eds.), Research on national and European legislation combating racism. Joint project of the Migration Policy Group and the European Monitoring Centre on Racism and Xenophobia; Project period 1 May 1999-31 January 2000. The second phase of the project was completed in 2002 (see footnote 43).

6. The Racial Equality Directive

The Amsterdam Treaty entered into force on 1 May 1999 and by the end of the year the Commission had presented its proposals for two directives.[38] Clearly, after many years of consultations with the Member States, the European Parliament, the social partners and NGOs on how to best combat racism in Europe, the European Commission, once given the necessary powers, needed little time to formulate and present its proposals. The proposal for a Council Directive implementing the principle of equal treatment between persons irrespective of racial or ethnic origin (or the Racial Equality Directive) provided protection against discrimination on grounds of racial and ethnic origin in (self-) employment and occupation, vocational training, employment and working conditions, membership of and involvement in professional organisations, social protection, social advantages, education and access to and supply of services. It defined and prohibited direct and indirect discrimination, harassment and victimisation, introduced the sharing of the burden of proof in cases of racial and ethnic discrimination, and provided procedures and mechanisms for the protection of victims of discrimination (including the establishment of an independent body). The proposal for a Council Directive establishing a general framework for equal treatment in employment and occupation (or the Employment Equality Directive) provided protection against discrimination on grounds of religion or belief, disability, age or sexual orientation in (self-) employment and occupation, vocational training, employment and working conditions, membership of and involvement in professional organisations. It introduced the same definitions of discrimination and protection against discrimination as the Racial Equality Directive (except for the establishment of an independent body). The Starting Line Group welcomed the legislative proposals as very important instruments for the fight against all forms of discrimination across the European Union. The Group compared the Racial Equality Directive with its own proposal and concluded that there were more similarities than differences between the two proposals.[39] It was therefore decided to press for the adoption of the Commission's proposal. This strategy was based on three considerations.

---

38 Proposal for a Council Directive implementing the principle of equal treatment between persons irrespective of racial and ethnic origin (COM (1999) 566 final) and Proposal for a Council Directive establishing a general framework for equal treatment in employment and occupation (COM (1999) 565 final). The Commission also presented a proposal for an Action Programme: Proposal for a Council Decision establishing a Community Action Programme to combat discrimination 2001-2006 (COM (1999) 567 final).

39 For a detailed analysis, see Isabelle Chopin, Possible Harmonisation of anti-discrimination legislation in the European Union. European and non-governmental proposals. In: European Journal of Migration and Law (Vol. II No.3-4 2000, 413-444).

First, on the basis of the interviews with senior policy-makers, the Starting Line Group had come to the conclusion that it was unlikely that the Member States would adopt a proposal that offered more protection than that of the Commission. On the contrary, Member States would probably try to water it down. Therefore, the proposal for a Racial Equality Directive needed to be presented to Member States as an acceptable compromise compared with the Starting Line, as long as the essential elements of the proposal were maintained in the negotiations within the Council of Ministers. In other words, the Starting Line Group should not ask for the best but for the second best and concentrate their activities not on pressing the European Commission to produce a better text, but rather on putting the Member States under pressure to accept the Commission's proposal.

Second, years of campaigning for the Starting Line and also the European Year against Racism had created a more favourable climate for the adoption of Community anti-discrimination legislation, but political climates can change rapidly. Therefore, the Commission's proposal had to be adopted as soon as possible and ideally within one year (meaning in the year 2000). Since its adoption required the unanimous approval of the Member States, any opposition from a Member State with regard to the scope, definitions or specific articles of the proposed Racial Equality Directive had to be countered. Although the negotiations were held behind closed doors, from the conversations with negotiators from some Member States it became more or less clear which obstacles were being put up and by which Member State. This led to some targeted responses at national level by the Starting Line Group.

Thirdly, the Starting Line Group, and no doubt also others such as the European Commission, estimated that the 'Austrian situation' could play in favour of a rapid adoption of the proposal. The inclusion of an extreme right-wing party in that country's government led to strong protests from governments of the other Member States. The Austrian government would probably not dare to oppose the proposed directive out of fear that this would cement the mistrust of the other 14 Member States of Austria as far as human rights commitments were concerned. At the same time, the Starting Line Group was ready to name and shame other governments if they opposed the adoption of the proposed directive. This strategy could only be applied as long as the 14 Member States kept their pressure on Austria and the Starting Line Group estimated that this would probably not last longer than one year.

Apart from the possible obstacles Member States were putting in the way,[40] there were two other impediments that could endanger the adoption of the proposed directive. The first was of the Commission's own making. From the outset

40 See Adam Tyson's contribution to this book: "The Negotiating of the European Community Directive on Racial Discrimination," p. 111-130.

the Commission presented its two legislative proposals as a package that had to be adopted in its entirety. There was quite some support for this approach from the side of governments, the European Parliament and some NGOs. The Starting Line Group, on the contrary, took the position that the two proposals should be adopted one by one, starting with the Racial Equality Directive. It was clear from the beginning that the Employment Equality Directive, given the many and considerably different grounds of discrimination it covers, would require much more debate and negotiation. The delay this would cause could very well work against the adoption of the Racial Equality Directive given the fact that the pressure on Austria was expected to come to an end within one year. It could not even be excluded that this was precisely the purpose of those Member States that wanted to deal first with the Employment Equality Directive (among them Portugal and France, holding the EU Presidency during the year 2000), or of those MEPs who kept requesting the adoption of the whole package. Fortunately, the European Commission changed its position and started to work first towards the adoption of the Racial Equality Directive.

The second problem was the position of the European Parliament that had to deliver its Opinion on the two proposals. Strangely enough, the European Parliament did not seem to be in a hurry to prepare these Opinions. It appointed rapporteurs rather late in the day and long after the Economic and Social Committee[41] and the Committee of the Regions had done so. Whereas the European Commission and the Council of Ministers were trying to get a political agreement on the Racial Equality Directive before the end of the Portuguese Presidency (June 2000), the European Parliament did not want to discuss the reports on the proposals prepared by its own Committees in a plenary session before the summer.[42] That indeed would have led to a delay with potentially very negative consequences for its adoption. The European Parliament felt that they were pressured by the European Commission and the European Council and claimed that they needed more time and suggested that they organise hearings in order to form its Opinion. Many organisations (probably including the European Commission) made clear that after years of discussions and the adoption of Resolutions seeking legislative measures (along the lines of the Starting Line) it was now time to act expeditiously. Under considerable pressure, the European Parliament agreed to deliver its Opinion on the Racial Equality Directive indeed before the summer.

41 Mr Sukdev Sharma was appointed as the European Economic and Social Committee's rapporteur. The Starting Line Group's secretariat worked closely together with Mr Sharma and the Starting Line Group's director acted as expert advisor to Mr Sharma.

42 The Starting Line Group's secretariat worked closely together with the various rapporteurs.

It should be noted that in the Commission's original proposal, no clause pertaining to consultations with NGOs was included. However, civil society pressure on the Commission and cooperation with the European Parliament rapporteurs secured the adoption of a provision to this end.

7. The Transposition

The Racial Equality Directive was adopted in June 2000 and the Employment Equality Directive in November 2000. Within a period of three years, Member States (and candidate countries upon accession) must ensure that their legislation implements the principles laid down in the Racial Equality Directive. Consequently, the debates would shift to the national level as governments and non-governmental actors took stock of what needed to be done in order to comply with the two Directives.[43] The European Commission would play a facilitating role in the transposition process, establishing working parties of representatives of Member States' ministries responsible for the transposition. It also created groups of independent experts to monitor and advise the Commission on the transposition.[44]

The Starting Line Group considered its mission accomplished and as its final activity published recommendations for the transposition[45] and organised a number of informal meetings with Brussels-based European networks of non-

43 For this exercise the second series of country reports could be used since they compared national legislation with the requirements of the Racial Equality Directive and the Employment Equality Directive as far as religious discrimination is concerned. See, Isabelle Chopin and Jan Niessen, Anti-discrimination legislation in EU Member States. A comparison of national anti-discrimination legislation on the grounds of racial or ethnic, religion or belief with the Council Directives. The reports are available electronically from the European Monitoring Centre on Racism and Xenophobia in English and French and each individual report in the language of the respective Member State (www. eumc.eu.int). Similar reports on eleven candidate countries were produced by the Migration Policy Group, the European Roma Rights Centre and Interights (available at www.migpolgroup.com). All these reports are summarised by Per Johannson in Chapter 8: "Comparing National and Community Anti-Discrimination Law" of this book.

44 One of them was formed and is managed by the Migration Policy Group and deals with discrimination on grounds of race or ethnicity and religion and belief. Other independent experts groups are dealing with sexual orientation and disability.

45 Isabelle Chopin and Jan Niessen (eds.), The Starting Line and the incorporation of the Racial Equality Directive into the national laws of the EU Member States and Accession States. With a preface by Odile Quintin, Director General, DG Employment and Social Affairs (Brussels/London, 2001). This was again a joint publication of the Commission for Racial Equality and the Starting Line Group.

governmental actors that were key for the monitoring and influencing of the transposition process.[46]

Although the adopted Racial Equality Directive did not provide the maximum legal protection against discrimination the Starting Line had called for, it nevertheless set high minimum standards. The Starting Line Group wanted to avoid that non-governmental actors continue to push for the adoption of a European legal instrument that was much more in line with the Starting Line. It had taken many years to adopt the directive and the Starting Line Group estimated that it was unrealistic to expect that in the near future the adopted directive would be amended and improved. Therefore, recommendations were made to link anti-discrimination work more with the unfolding EU Social Policy Agenda and the European Employment Strategy.[47] For the next three years the focus had to be on the transposition and in that process there would be possibilities to gain back some of the lost terrain. As is the case with all Community policies, the Racial Equality Directive is the result of negotiations between the Council of Ministers, the European Parliament and the European Commission, and therefore a compromise. Consequently, there could be instances that individual Member States would be willing to go further on certain provisions of the Directive and adopt new legislation or adapt existing legislation more in line with what the Starting Line had proposed. The Directive itself leaves the possibility of offering higher levels of protection than the required minimum standards. With this in mind, the Starting Line was compared with the Racial Equality Directive on the basis of which precise recommendations were made as to which issues needed to be taken up in the transposition debates at national level.[48]

With these recommendations the Starting Line Group discontinued its activities.

---

46 In particular co-operation on the transposition was established between the secretariat of the Starting Line Group and the newly created European Network against Racism, leading among other things to an action handbook. See, Isabelle Chopin, Campaign against racism and xenophobia: from a legislative perspective at European level (European Network against Racism, November 1999). This publication is also available in French and German.

47 Jan Niessen, The further development of European anti-discrimination policies. In: Isabelle Chopin and Jan Niessen (eds.), The Starting Line and the incorporation of the Racial Equality Directive into the national laws of the EU Member States and Accession States (Brussels/London, 2001).

48 Mark Bell, Meeting the challenge? A comparison between the EU Race Directive and the Starting Line. In: Isabelle Chopin and Jan Niessen (eds.), *The Starting Line and the incorporation of the Racial Equality Directive into the national laws of the EU Member States and Accession States* (Brussels/London, 2001).

Adam Tyson

5. THE NEGOTIATION OF THE EUROPEAN COMMUNITY DIRECTIVE ON RACIAL DISCRIMINATION[1]

1. Introduction

On 29 June 2000, the Council of Ministers of the European Union adopted a directive on the implementation of the principle of equal treatment between persons irrespective of racial or ethnic origin.[2] The Directive was published in the Official Journal of the European Communities and entered into force on 19 July 2000. The Member States have had three years, until 19 July 2003, in which to introduce the national laws and arrangements necessary to meet the standards contained in the directive.

The Directive is the result of a long campaign over many years by a range of non-governmental organisations, most notably the Starting Line Group, the European Parliament and the European Commission. It was made possible by a change to the European Community Treaty agreed by Heads of State and Government at the conclusion of the Intergovernmental Conference at Amsterdam in June 1997, when they decided to introduce a new Article into the Treaty. This new Article, later numbered Article 13, enables the Council of Ministers to take action to combat discrimination on a range of grounds: sex, racial and ethnic origin, religion and belief, disability, age and sexual orientation. Article

---

1 European Commission. Views expressed here are purely personal to the author. Revised version of article "The Negotiating of the European Community Directive on Racial Discrimination" in European Journal of Migration and Law 3: 199-229, 2001.

2 Council Directive 2000/43/EC of 29 June 2000 implementing the principle of equal treatment between persons irrespective of racial or ethnic origin (OJ L 180 of 19/07/2000, pp. 22-26).

Jan Niessen, Isabelle Chopin (eds.), The Development of Legal Instruments..., *111-130*

13 entered into force with the rest of the Treaty of Amsterdam on 1 May 1999, following ratification by all the Member States.

The Commission made a package of proposals to implement the new Article 13 on 25 November 1999. The package consisted of two proposals for directives and a separate proposal for an accompanying action programme to provide financial support to trans-national activities to combat discrimination. The draft directives concerned, first, the prohibition of racial and ethnic discrimination in employment and some other areas of everyday life and, second, the prohibition of discrimination on other grounds, but only in the employment field. In its accompanying Communication (COM (1999) 564 final of 25 November 1999), the Commission argued that it believed that there was a political consensus among the Governments of the Member States to combat discrimination on grounds of racial and ethnic origin in a wider range of areas than on other grounds, largely because of the national experience of legislation against this form of discrimination and because of the existence of more evidence of racial discrimination in these areas. The action programme was intended, among other things, to examine the need for and the effectiveness of legislation prohibiting discrimination on other grounds in the wider areas covered by the racial discrimination directive.

The Commission's proposal for a directive was based heavily on the framework of legislation already in place at Community level on gender equality. The gender equality framework is contained in a variety of legal and declaratory texts. The legal provisions lay down general principles and set a minimum standard which national legislators must respect in creating their own frameworks, going into further detail where necessary. The proposal for a directive on racial and ethnic discrimination maintains the approach based on setting general objectives and minimum standards. In doing so, it draws its inspiration not only from the legally binding texts in the gender field but also from pieces of soft law in the field, such as the resolutions and recommendations on sexual harassment. In addition, it includes concepts found in international instruments and in the national legislation of some states.

The directive was negotiated and adopted by the Council in seven months from the date of its proposal by the Commission.[3] This is a record for the adoption of a piece of Community law requiring substantial legislative changes at national level and it might, on the face of it, suggest that the Governments of the Member States had little difficulty with the Commission's original proposal.

---

3 The second Directive (Council Directive 2000/78/EC establishing a general framework for equal treatment in employment and occupation) was adopted by the Council on 27 November 2000 and was published in the Official Journal on 3 December 2000 (OJ L 303 of 3/12/2000, pp. 16-22). Many of the solutions agreed in the negotiations on the Racial Discrimination Directive were applied *mutatis mutandis* to the Employment Equality Directive.

In fact, though no Member State was opposed in principle to the idea of Community law on racial discrimination, a number of Governments had serious difficulties with particular points.

To try to shed some light on the intentions of the legislator in adopting the various provisions of the directive, this paper will examine the positions taken by Member States in the negotiations. Though the paper will not name individual countries, the author hopes that it will assist organisations wishing to follow the process of transposition of the directive into national law. The paper examines each of the main provisions of the directive in turn and tries to explain why changes were made to the Commission's original proposal, presenting the author's understanding of the national concerns about each as they were presented in the negotiations in the Council of Ministers. The final text of the Directive is reproduced as an annex to the paper.

2. A Conundrum: How to Speak About 'Race' in a Directive Which Fights Racism

Article 13 of the Treaty, the legal base of the Directive, empowers the Council to combat discrimination on grounds of 'racial or ethnic origin'. In some language versions, this is rendered as 'race or ethnic origin'. The Commission repeated the Treaty language in the different language versions in its proposal for the Directive.

It soon became apparent in the negotiations that a number of Member States were unhappy with the language used in the directive to refer to racial and ethnic origin. This revealed philosophical differences between the Member States as to whether it was possible even to refer to 'racial origin' or 'race'. The argument that this was simply a repetition of Treaty language did not satisfy those delegations, even though the same language had been agreed by Heads of State and Government only two years previously without any discussion of this point. For some Member States, the mention of 'race' or 'racial origin' was tantamount to accepting racist theories that alleged the existence of separate human races. For others, this was accepted language used to discuss issues related to racism and in no way suggested an acceptance of such theories. Indeed, for some, it was important to use the word 'race' (rather than relying solely on ethnic origin) in order to be clear that the directive was combating 'racism'. A number of attempts were made to compromise on this point: one was to repeat the wording of the legislation of one Member State, which referred to the 'supposed' racial origin of the victim of discrimination. However this proposal was rejected as it might have narrowed the impact of the Directive: it suggested, in some language versions at least, that to succeed in a case of alleged discrimination, the court would need to be convinced that the author of the discrimination had had in his or her mind at the time of the alleged discrimination an idea (or supposition) about the racial origin of the victim. This could be difficult to prove and could limit the concept of discrimination to situations where the action concerned was deemed to have a discriminatory purpose rather than simply a discriminatory effect.

The final compromise, therefore, was the addition of a recital which declares that the Community deplores theories based on the alleged existence of separate human races and that the use of the term 'racial origin' (or 'race' in other language versions) in no way implies an acceptance of such theories.

3. Know Your Enemy: How to Define Discrimination (Article 2)

For legislation against discrimination to be effective, it needs to contain clear definitions of the type of action or behaviour, which is to be prohibited. The Commission had proposed definitions of the two forms of discrimination commonly found in national and international discrimination law: direct and indirect. In addition, the Commission had proposed that harassment on racial or ethnic grounds should be deemed to be discrimination and subject to the same rights of redress and sanctions. The definition of direct discrimination was taken almost verbatim from the precedent in Council Directive 97/80/EC on the shift of the burden of proof in sex discrimination cases. This was therefore familiar to the Member States and caused no difficulty in the negotiation. However, the Commission's proposal for the definition of indirect discrimination did not follow the precedent of Directive 97/80/EC and caused some concern to a number of Member States.

The definition of indirect discrimination in Community law on sex discrimination contained in Directive 97/80/EC was based on the case law of the European Court of Justice.[4] Under that definition, an apparently neutral provision, criterion or practice which disadvantages a substantially higher proportion of the members of one sex, which is not appropriate and necessary and which is not justifiable by objective factors unrelated to sex will be held to be discriminatory. To make this finding, the Court must therefore be convinced that a particular provision, criterion or practice will affect a greater *proportion* of one sex than the other if applied to each as a group. On occasions, this can be difficult to demonstrate and, in the case of new areas of law, which have not previously been tested, it can require considerable research and statistical work involving extremely lengthy proceedings. However, the requirement itself is not usually impossible to fulfil, because all Member States collect statistical information broken down by gender to some degree and because it is commonplace to record the gender breakdown of employees and job applicants. But the same cannot be said of discrimination on grounds of racial and ethnic origin. Only a small minority of the Member States record ethnic data

4 Note that the definition of indirect indiscrimination on grounds of gender has since been brought into line with that on grounds of racial and ethnic origin by Council Directive/2002/73/EC (OJ L 269, 05/10/2002, pp. 15-20).

through censuses, for example, while in others it is unlawful to record the ethnic origin of individuals as it is seen either to be an infringement of personal privacy or as a racist act in itself. This latter case is often a reaction to the experience of holding ethnic data during the 1930s and 1940s, which facilitated the identification of Jews and others for transportation to the concentration camps. As a result, opposition to the collection of ethnic data is widespread across society, including among anti-racist NGOs, in Member States, which have had this experience.

The Commission therefore proposed a definition of indirect discrimination which did not rely on the test of disproportion, but rather drew its inspiration from the case-law of the European Court of Justice in judgements on the free movement of workers and, in particular, the O'Flynn case.[5] This proposal allowed the court or other competent body to judge whether an apparently neutral provision, criterion or practice was likely to disadvantage an individual belonging to a particular racial or ethnic group. This would remove the (largely impossible) burden of providing statistical proof in a case of alleged indirect discrimination and so facilitate the case for the complainant, relying instead on the judgement of the court as to whether a provision would amount to indirect discrimination unless it could be objectively justified.

Nevertheless, some Member States wanted to retain the definition used in the Burden of Proof Directive. This group included, understandably, Member States, which regularly gather racial and ethnic data, as they argued that complainants would have no more difficulty than was already the case in sex discrimination cases. But it also included Member States, which wanted on principle to maintain the parallels between this Directive and the Community's existing gender discrimination framework. In particular, they were reluctant to agree to a definition, which apparently made it easier to win a case of racial discrimination than a case of gender discrimination. At the same time, some of the Member States which were strongly opposed to the collection of ethnic data also felt that the definition proposed by the Commission ('a provision, criterion or practice which [was] likely to put [certain] persons at a disadvantage') was too wide and would make it too difficult for a respondent to defend a case, particularly when linked with the proposed shift in the burden of proof (see below).

As a result of these positions, splits developed in the Council working group, with camps holding seemingly irreconcilable views on how to define indirect discrimination. Nevertheless, a compromise was eventually reached, combining elements necessary to satisfy both camps. The resulting text was designed both to tighten the definition proposed by the Commission (changing the notion of 'likely to put at a disadvantage' to 'would put at a disadvantage') and to allow, but not oblige, Member States to require the presentation of statistical data to

5 Case C-237/94.

demonstrate a disproportionate impact on different groups if they wished to do so. The final text, therefore, makes clear that

> Indirect discrimination shall be taken to occur where an apparently neutral provision, criterion or practice would put persons of a racial or ethnic origin at a particular disadvantage compared with other persons, unless that provision, criterion or practice is objectively justified by a legitimate aim and the means of achieving that aim are appropriate and necessary.

While the accompanying recital clarifies that

> The appreciation of the facts from which it may be inferred that there has been direct or indirect discrimination is a matter for national judicial or other competent bodies, in accordance with rules of national law or practice. Such rules may provide in particular for indirect discrimination to be established by any means including on the basis of statistical evidence.

The somewhat empty formulation 'persons of a racial or ethnic origin' results from the unease of some Member States in referring to 'persons of a particular racial or ethnic origin', linked to their refusal to accept the notion of racial origin in itself (cf. reference above).

In practice, this means that different tests of indirect discrimination may be applied in different Member States, depending on their traditions and, in particular, the acceptability of ethnic monitoring and the collation of related statistics. However, the use of the word 'would' implies that all Member States will have to provide for the use of hypothetical comparators in the demonstration of indirect discrimination.

4. How to Define Racial Harassment (Article 2.3)

The concept of harassment had already been dealt with in Community texts in the field of gender discrimination, though only through soft law.[6] The Commission believed that it was now important to provide legal redress against discrimination and drew both on previous Community texts and on the practice in some Member States of deeming harassment to be discrimination, giving the same

6 Council Resolution of 29 May 1990 on the protection of the dignity of men and women at work (OJ C 157, 27/06/1990, pp. 3-4); Commission Recommendation 92/131/EEC of 27 November 1991 on the protection of the dignity of women and men at work (OJ L 049, 24/02/1992, pp. 1-8); Council Declaration of 19 December 1991 on the implementation of the Commission Recommendation on the protection of the dignity of women and men at work, including the code of practice to combat sexual harassment (OJ C 027, 04/02/92, p. 1).

rights of protection to victims. While all Member States agreed in principle with the proposal that harassment should fall under the scope of the directive, three difficulties arose in the discussions. First, where the legislation of some Member States already dealt with sexual harassment, it provided protection only in cases where the harassment was carried out with the purpose of obtaining sexual favours in return for some professional advantage (or absence of disadvantage). Those Member States were therefore uneasy with the idea that harassment could also extend to situations, which had the effect, but not necessarily the purpose of creating a hostile etc environment, fearing an extra burden on, in particular, employers. Second, a group of Member States wished to be able to limit the responsibility of employers to situations for which they were clearly responsible and to absolve them from responsibility for behaviour over which they had no control. Third, while some Member States were content to cover harassment between employees in the workplace, they were less willing to extend the protection to areas outside of employment and, in particular, to education and access to goods and services. In the last case, they questioned the responsibility of, for example, schools for conduct between pupils and of shops etc for the behaviour of customers.

It is clear from the Commission's explanatory memorandum to the proposals that the intention behind the provision was that it should deal with behaviour of a serious and usually repeated nature (it is unlikely (though not impossible), for example, that an isolated incident could create the kind of environment described by the Directive). To underline this point, some Member States argued for, and secured, additions to the list of adjectives, which describe the environment created by harassment so that the final text reads

> Harassment shall be deemed to be discrimination within the meaning of paragraph 1, when an unwanted conduct related to racial or ethnic origin takes place with the purpose or effect of violating the dignity of a person and of creating an intimidating, hostile, degrading, humiliating or offensive environment.

The clear link to the creation of an environment and the apparent strengthening of the nature of the environment to some extent persuaded Member States that they could limit the responsibility of employers to situations where they had clearly been negligent in not taking reasonable action to prevent the existence of an environment of the type described by the directive. It also persuaded them that they could accept the coverage of behaviour, which had the purpose or effect of violating the dignity of a person. However, it was not sufficient to give some Member States the assurance they needed and so the Council agreed to add a further sentence to the provision: 'In this context, the concept of harassment may be defined in accordance with the national laws and practice of the Member States'.

With these additions, the Council agreed that the concept of harassment should be applicable to all the fields falling within the material scope of the Directive. The final text, therefore, appears to allow Member States to define harassment in the way they wish, as long as it covers, at the very least, situations falling within the material scope of the Directive in which the dignity of a person is violated (whether intentionally or not) and in which an environment which can be described by at least one of the adjectives in the list has been created.

5. How to Deal with Incitement (Article 2.4)

In its consideration of the Commission's proposal, the European Parliament was concerned to ensure that incitement to racial violence or hatred was also covered by the proposal. In the Commission's view, this was not possible for two reasons: first, wider questions of racism and xenophobia (as opposed to racial and ethnic discrimination) fall more properly under Article 29 of the Treaty on European Union rather than under Article 13 of the Treaty establishing the European Community; second, to be consistent with the definition of discrimination in the Directive, it is necessary to prove that an individual has suffered a particular disadvantage as a result of the discriminatory act, which is not always so in cases of incitement. The Commission accepted, however, that it should be possible to cover incitement or instructions to discriminate where a potential victim would be put at a disadvantage if the incitement or instruction were to lead to a discriminatory act. It therefore amended its original proposal following the European Parliament's opinion to the effect that incitement or instructions to discriminate (for example by an employer to his or her personnel manager or to an employment agency) should be deemed to be discrimination for the purposes of the Directive and should therefore lead to the same protection for victims. Though some Member States were uneasy with this notion, others argued that it was essential to provide protection against such pressure to discriminate and so the point was included. However, some Member States argued that incitement, whether to racial hatred or violence on the one hand or to racial discrimination on the other, was a criminal act and should therefore be dealt with under the Treaty on European Union, rather than under Article 13 of the European Community Treaty. This interpretation was rejected by the Commission, maintaining that criminal aspects of discrimination fall clearly under the Community Treaty, but the Council nevertheless amended the term from 'incitement' to 'instruction'. This is clearly a narrower term than 'incitement', implying some hierarchical relationship between the parties, but nevertheless covers implicit as well as explicit instructions.

6. Who Should Be Protected against Discrimination and in Which Fields (Article 3)

As was to be expected, the material scope of the directive proposed by the Commission was the source of much discussion in the negotiations, though ultimately relatively little was changed. The introductory sentence was expanded to meet the European Parliament's wish to clarify intentions already contained in the Commission's proposal, in particular to emphasise the application to both legal and natural persons and public bodies. The coverage of legal persons caused difficulties for some Member States, where the legal system does not provide for access to the Courts for the legal person itself in discrimination cases, but only of representatives of such legal persons who could show that they themselves had suffered some disadvantage as a result of the discrimination against the legal person. For this reason, a clarifying recital was added to enable Member States to continue with this system

> It is important to protect all natural persons against discrimination on grounds of racial or ethnic origin. Member States should also provide, where appropriate and in accordance with their national traditions and practice, protection for legal persons where they suffer discrimination on grounds of the racial or ethnic origin of their members.

There was little discussion of the employment-related areas in which the prohibition of discrimination should apply, with all Member States accepting the application to various aspects of employment (the European Parliament sought and secured the application to practical work experience), despite some concern (though final acquiescence) from Member States with a long tradition of not interfering in the affairs of the social partners about the application of the directive to the membership of and involvement in organisations of workers or employers. The areas outside of the employment field were a greater cause for concern for a number of Member States. While they had no difficulty with making clear that the term 'social protection' included healthcare as well as social security, there was some discussion about the interpretation of the concept of 'social advantages'. The Commission indicated in its Explanatory Memorandum that, in the context of Regulation (EEC) No 1612/68 on freedom of movement for migrant workers, the European Court of Justice had defined social advantages as benefits of an economic or cultural nature which are granted within the Member States either by public authorities or private organisations. The same concept was to be applied in this case. Some Member States questioned the applicability of a concept, which had been developed in the field of free movement to situations, which were purely internal to a State and were concerned as to how they would transpose the term into national law. Ultimately, however, those Member States accepted that the prohibition of discrimination should apply to social advantages, even if the precise extent of the term was not clear and that it would be likely to develop over time.

The application of the Directive to the field of education was also questioned by some delegations, though principally in an attempt to limit what they regarded as a possible extension of Community competence into this field. The Commission had already recognised the limitations on Community competence by repeating in its proposal the condition included in Article 149 of the European Community Treaty that the Directive should fully respect the responsibility of the Member States for the content of teaching and the organisation of education systems and their cultural and linguistic diversity. Some Member States felt, however, that this addition, rather than being helpful, created an *a contrario* argument that all aspects of education other than the content of teaching, the organisation of education systems and their cultural and linguistic diversity fell within Community competence. To avoid this impression, those Member States preferred to delete the quotation from Article 149.

The coverage of goods and services created perhaps the greatest difficulty for Member States in this context. Some noted that Community competence in the field of goods and services was principally limited to trans-national situations and that services were defined by Article 50 of the Treaty as being 'normally provided for remuneration, insofar as they are not governed by the provisions relating to freedom of movement for goods, capital and persons'. Some delegations insisted that the directive should not cover situations such as a person privately selling a bicycle to a neighbour, renting a holiday home to a friend or even to the choice of tenants in an apartment block, while others insisted that there was no reason to exempt such situations. This problem was not solved until it was discussed by Deputy Ambassadors in the Committee of Permanent Representatives (COREPER), when agreement was reached by limiting the application to those goods and services 'which are available to the public'. There was then no difficulty in securing the clarification that housing also fell under the definition of goods and services. This clarification clearly indicates that the intention of the legislator in this case is to go beyond the narrow, trans-national definition of Community competence in the field of goods and services.

7. How to Preserve Differences of Treatment Based on Nationality (Article 3.2)

The discussion of the material scope also prompted Member States to raise the question of the overlap between discrimination on grounds of racial or ethnic origin and differences of treatment based on nationality. To deal with this point, the Commission's original proposal contained the express statement in the recitals that, although the directive applied to nationals of third countries, it did not prevent differences of treatment based on nationality. The Explanatory Memorandum recognised that nationality is dealt with not by Article 13 TEC, but by separate Articles of the Treaty (in particular Articles 12 and 39) and by existing secondary legislation. While in general Member States welcomed this (wanting in particular to maintain differences in their social protection systems with respect to the rights of non-EU nationals), the non-application to differences of treatment based on nationality was seen by some in the European Parliament and in civil society as one of the major weaknesses in the directive (and perhaps in the design of Article 13 itself). While the Commission's recognition of the limitation of the directive to the Article 13 grounds was welcomed by Member States, some felt that it was not sufficient to preserve certain aspects of their systems and, in particular, those dealing with immigration and asylum. Those countries argued, for example, that it was an essential part of the asylum system to draw differences based on ethnic origin where asylum seekers were persecuted in their country of origin precisely on the basis of their ethnic origin.

The Commission argued that there was no need for concern on this point as admission policies were not included in the material scope of the directive and therefore that the directive did not apply to these situations. However, the delegations feared that other differences of rights (such as access to social benefits or to employment), which often flowed from the immigration status, which was awarded to such asylum seekers, might be covered. The Commission's assurances that such differences would be attributable to immigration status and not to racial or ethnic origin did not convince the delegations which continued to insist on a specific exclusion of such situations. This exclusion was finally agreed with the addition of a second paragraph to Article 3

> This Directive does not cover difference of treatment based on nationality and is without prejudice to provisions and conditions relating to the entry into and residence of third-country nationals and stateless persons on the territory of Member States, and to any treatment, which arises from the legal status of the third-country nationals and stateless persons concerned.

And a reinforcement of the accompanying recital

> This prohibition of discrimination should also apply to nationals of third countries, but does not cover differences of treatment based on nationality and is without prejudice to provisions governing the entry and residence of third-country nationals and their access to employment and to occupation.

There is no particular significance in the inclusion of the reference to stateless persons in the body of the text but not in the recital, though it can be argued that the recital indicates that the reference in the article to 'any treatment which arises from the legal status of the third-country nationals and stateless persons concerned' might be interpreted as being restricted principally to situations related to access to the labour market.

8. How to Legitimate Exceptions to the Prohibition on Differences of Treatment for Particular Jobs (Article 4)

The Commission had proposed that there should be extremely limited exceptions to the prohibition of differences of treatment to take account of the desirability, for very particular posts, of using ethnic origin as a determining factor. Such could be the case in casting an actor/actress for a role based on historical fact, where the ethnic origin of the actor was important in creating an impression of authenticity (for example a slave in the American South). The Commission underlined that it had taken a slightly different approach from the one adopted in the case of the 1976 Equal Treatment Directive, which allowed Member States to designate particular activities as being exempt from the prohibition on discrimination. The new proposal required every post for which the exemption was sought to be judged on its particular merits, so that it would no longer be possible, for example, to have a blanket exemption for actors or photographic models.

This proposal for an exemption from the general prohibition of discrimination was extremely important for Member States which already provided for such exceptions in their national legislation, but was strongly opposed by others which saw such an explicit exemption as a legalisation of discrimination (and which had no need of such an exemption in their law to enable them to permit such differences), even though the exemption remained purely an option for Member States. In addition, the term used by the Commission – 'genuine occupational qualifications' – which had been taken from the national law of some Member States, was confusing to others (and created even more difficulties in translation). The stand off was resolved by tightening the conditions under which the exemption may be employed. This included an insistence that the requirement should be both genuine and <u>determining</u> and that the objective of the difference of treatment should be legitimate and the requirement itself proportionate. Finally, the Council agreed that Member States, which made use of this option, should inform the Commission on its use in the context of the regular reports, which they are required to provide under Article 17. Both ideas were taken from the 1976 Equal Treatment Directive (where the reporting requirement at least is perhaps easier to fulfil, as that allows the Member States to report simply on the list of activities which were exempted under national legislation rather than giving a description of how the exemption has been used in practice, as is implied by the Directive under consideration here).

9. How to Allow for – But Not Require – Positive Action (Article 5)

Just as positive action is permitted in the field of gender equality to overcome disadvantages suffered by one sex or the other, the Commission considered that the same latitude should be provided to Member States which wished to allow or encourage positive action to overcome disadvantages linked to racial or ethnic origin. The Member States were broadly in agreement with this point, wishing only to ensure that the language in the directive was as close as possible to that already found in Article 141 of the EC Treaty. However, a number of questions arose as to whether limits to positive action in the gender field set by the European Court in cases such as Kalanke, Marschall, Badeck and Abrahamsson[7] would also apply to equal treatment irrespective of racial or ethnic origin. This point of course remains to be tested. However, it is already clear that the same basic principles underlying the use of positive action to overcome the effects of gender discrimination can also be applied in the case of racial or ethnic discrimination – that is in particular that the positive action should be limited in time to the period necessary to overcome the disadvantage being targeted and that it should be sufficiently flexible to allow exceptions in particular cases.

10. How to Secure the Complainant's Right to Redress (Article 7)

The principal element in the provisions on the defence of rights – providing individuals with a means of redress for alleged discrimination – was uncontroversial in the Council. Codifying the case-law of the European Court of Justice in gender equality cases, the proposal also gave a right to redress for discrimination which takes place even after the (e.g. employment) relationship has ended (making it possible to take action in the case of discriminatory references provided by a former employer, for example).

The Commission proposal allowed for either administrative or judicial procedures to be used, which provoked some discussion as to whether administrative procedures really provided sufficient protection. The Commission's position was that such procedures had proved extremely effective in some Member States and that the key test of their effectiveness was in the enforceability of any decisions (the test laid down in the directive itself when it speaks of the 'enforcement of obligations under this directive'). A Member State which chose to use administrative procedures which did not in themselves lead to legally enforceable decisions would have to ensure that an enforceable method could be applied in the event of either side not agreeing to abide by the decision of the administrative body.

The new element in this provision was the obligation on Member States to ensure that associations, organisations or other legal entities should have the right to pursue the procedures for redress on behalf of the complainant with his or her approval. Some groups in the European Parliament in particular wanted to see this as a provision requiring the possibility of class actions, while some

7 Kalanke C-450/93; Marschall C-409/95; Badeck C-158/97; Abrahamsson C-407/98.

Member States were strongly opposed to class actions as they were not foreseen in their own judicial systems. For some Member States, it was even difficult to accept that an organisation or association should act in its own name on behalf of an identified victim, though they could accept that such organisations should be able to support a victim, including by providing them with legal counsel to fight a case. In the Commission's view, the precise status of such an organisation before the court is less important than the access to support from a respected organisation, which greatly influences the ability of a complainant to win a case. In that light, the Commission was content to allow the Member States to define the nature of organisations which should have such rights (i.e. those 'which have, in accordance with the criteria laid down by their national law, a legitimate interest in ensuring that the provisions of this Directive are complied with') and to allow Member States to decide whether such organisations should be empowered to act on their own behalf or only in support of a particular complainant.

Finally, the Member States wished to clarify that national time limit within which cases must be submitted to the court or other body would not be affected by the Directive. This was accepted, while respecting the conditions laid down by the European Court of Justice in Emmott[8] (i.e. that the limits must not be less favourable than those relating to similar actions of a domestic nature nor framed so as to render virtually impossible the exercise of rights conferred by Community law).

A question which has since arisen in relation to the procedures to be used to provide redress for complainants concerns the choice of civil or administrative procedures on the one hand and criminal procedures on the other. While the Directive leaves the Member States free to choose whichever approach fits with their traditions and practices, some commentators have questioned whether it is in practice possible to use criminal procedures to deal with cases of alleged *indirect* discrimination. This is because it is usual in criminal proceedings to have to prove *intent* on the part of the defendant to commit a criminal act, whereas indirect discrimination may by its very nature be unintentional (the application of a dress code for employees may not be intended to disadvantage a particular racial or ethnic group, for example, but may do so in practice). The criminal law may therefore be unsuited to dealing with cases of indirect discrimination.

11. How to Share the Burden of Proof (Article 8)

The Commission's proposal suggested that, in civil and administrative (but not in criminal) cases, the burden of proving a case of discrimination should be shared between the complainant and the respondent so that, once a complainant makes out a *prima facie* case, the responsibility of proving that no discrimination had

8 Emmott C-208/90.

taken place should be for the respondent. The proposal was based heavily on the model agreed in gender discrimination cases which had already been dealt with in Directive 97/80 EC and with which Member States were familiar. The Commission's proposal for the new directive omitted only the option not to apply the shift of the burden of proof to cases in which it is for the court or competent body to investigate the facts of the case (a provision introduced by the Council in Directive 97/80 and which remains unclear in its meaning) and adding the clarification that the shift of the burden of proof applies also to cases where the complainant is represented or supported by an organisation or association etc. The Council quickly restored the optional exemption omitted from the Commission's proposal.

Because of the existence of the precedent, there was relatively little difficulty with this point in the Council insofar as it applied to allegations of discrimination in the labour market area, though there was some opposition from certain groups in the European Parliament. However, its extension into areas such as access to goods and services and education was a novelty for many Member States and thus met with some resistance.

In the labour market, the two parties to a case (of whatever nature) are considered to be of unequal power, with the employer being considerably stronger than the employee. It was considered natural therefore to shift the burden of proof once an initial case had been presented to the court in order to redress the balance of power between the parties. Some Member States argued, however, that this imbalance did not exist between the parties involved in the provision of goods and services and therefore that it was not appropriate to shift the burden of proof. It may also have been that while some Member States were content to apply the shift to their labour courts, where it could be contained, they were more reluctant to extend it to their civil courts which dealt with cases concerning goods and services (and, of course, a wide range of other issues not dealt with by the directive but to which the concept might spread through custom and practice).

The Commission argued, however, that the basic principles concerned in cases both inside and outside the employment field were precisely the same. The reason for shifting the burden of proof was that the party, which was alleged, to have discriminated was the only one, which held the information about how the allegedly discriminatory decision was arrived at. So it was for the employer to prove that an appointment or promotion was based on grounds related to the particular post in question and not related to racial or ethnic origin, just as it was for the provider of a good or a service to prove that the refusal to provide it (or the application of a condition which made it disadvantageous for the complainant to make use of an offer) was based on grounds unrelated to racial or ethnic origin. On this basis (and with the adaptation made to the reference to the provision of and access to goods and services in Article 3 – see above), the

Council accepted that the shift of the burden of proof should apply to all the areas within the material scope.

12. How to Protect People against Retaliation (Article 9)

To make sure that people have the confidence to make a complaint, they need to know that they will not suffer reprisals by the respondent to the case. There was no controversy surrounding this provision in the Council, with the only amendment being made to some language versions to make clear that the protections apply not only to victims of discrimination but also to others who may support a complainant by acting as witnesses etc.

13. How to Make Sure People Know Their Rights and Obligations (Article 10)

For any law to be effective, people need to know about it. The provisions on the dissemination of information were drawn largely from the 1976 Equal Treatment Directive and to that extent provoked little discussion. However, some Member States felt that the article infringed their rights under the principle of subsidiarity as to how to achieve the objectives of the directive and to that extent they sought and secured the deletion of the second paragraph of the Commission's proposal calling on them to provide information to competent public authorities on the measures taken to implement the directive.

In its amended proposal subsequent to the opinions of the European Parliament, the Committee of the Regions and the Economic and Social Committee, the Commission suggested that this provision should also be used as the vehicle for ensuring that racial or ethnic discrimination was not disguised as a difference of treatment based on nationality in an attempt to avoid the application of the directive (see point 7 above). This would to some extent have filled the gap in the directive left by its inability to prohibit discrimination based directly on nationality. However, the Council rejected this proposal. The remaining provision therefore simply puts a general obligation on the Member States to provide information about the provisions they adopt to 'the persons concerned' (clearly a very broad concept, which includes the public authorities deleted from the article by the Council) through measures they feel to be appropriate.

14. How to Encourage the Prevention of Discrimination in the Workplace through Social Dialogue (Article 11)

It is traditional for Community Directives in the social field to allow Member States to implement them through collective agreements between the social partners rather than through legislation, on the condition that such agreements provide equivalent legally enforceable rights and that they cover the entire target group. In this case, the Commission wished to highlight the importance of involving the social partners in the implementation process, as their action can have a considerable impact on the prevention of discrimination in the workplace. For that reason, the Commission brought this provision out of its more usual position in the final provisions on implementation (Article 16), to give it more prominence as a separate article in the text. At the same time, the Commission proposed a more promotional role for the Member States to encourage the social partners to become involved in fighting discrimination.

This proposal caused difficulties for some Member States because it was not as clear a statement of the power to implement the directive through collective agreements as had been found in earlier texts; because it seemed to require Government interference in the affairs of the social partners; and because it appeared to require Member States which were not used to social dialogue arrangements to introduce them. The last of the three problems was the most difficult to resolve (the first two being addressed respectively by the re-introduction of the standard text in the implementing article in addition to the social dialogue article and by adding a clear statement of respect for the autonomy of the social partners). The third problem was finally resolved by making the second paragraph (requiring the encouragement of agreements laying down anti-discrimination rules) apply only where it was consistent with Member States' national traditions and practices.

Both the original proposal and the text adopted by the Council are largely exhortatory provisions which leave to the Member States the judgement as to what is an 'adequate' measure to promote social dialogue or encourage the conclusion of agreements. It is difficult to imagine that there will be many challenges to Member States' implementation of this point, but it is likely to be used as a lever by social partner organisations for the opening up of negotiations. Moreover, the Commission will expect Member States to report on the steps they have taken to promote a dialogue with and between social partner organisations and will itself report in turn to the European Parliament.

15. How to Provoke a Wider Public Debate (Article 12)

The European Parliament voted to extend the arrangements for social dialogue to non-governmental organisations, which are particularly active in the fight against racism. The Commission accepted this in its amended proposal, believing that an encouragement to involve NGOs in the development of national policies would be likely to improve the effectiveness of those policies and help to raise awareness of the issues by provoking a public debate. The Council agreed to take the concept over in its final text. Although this is again a largely declaratory provision, it is nevertheless an important signal to Governments that they should involve non-governmental organisations in consultations about the implementation of the directive and in promoting the principle of equal treatment more widely. Again, the Commission will expect Member States to report on the steps they have taken to promote dialogue with civil society organisations on the implementation of the racial equality framework and will itself report to the European Parliament.

16. How to Encourage the Member States to Establish Bodies for the Promotion of Equal Treatment (Article 13)

The Commission proposed that all Member States should establish an independent body or bodies for the promotion of equal treatment on the grounds that such bodies can make a major contribution to the ability of victims to fight discrimination and that they play a significant role in raising awareness about the issue in society more widely. They also have the ability to de-politicise the question, allowing the formation of a common ground, which straddles political parties.

There was a good deal of concern about this proposal, not only from those Member States which were unfamiliar with such bodies, but also from some of those which had a long history of working with them, principally on the grounds that the proposal overstepped the line between setting objectives and telling Member States how to achieve them (so contravening the principle of subsidiarity). Others questioned what was meant by 'independence' and the potential impact on their national budgets. Long discussions followed about the impact on independence of financing from the Government or from Parliament, about the ability of the Government or an individual Minister to nominate members of a board or commission and about the precise tasks with which the bodies should be entrusted. Those Member States, which already had such bodies, gave brief presentations of their roles and responsibilities and in this way, the negotiations shifted from the level of principle (should they be included in the directive or not) to the detail (how should they be best described).

To avoid the question of what was meant by independence, the Commission proposed that, while the ideal situation was that the body should have its basis in a law passed by Parliament with its financing guaranteed at a level which allowed it to perform its essential tasks, the key test was that it should be able to organise its everyday work free from the interference of outside parties. It should be able to act independently in providing assistance to victims, conducting surveys and publishing reports and recommendations. The Council agreed to this approach and amended the proposal accordingly. This leaves many questions – about the precise legal status and financing for example – to be resolved at the level of national implementation, but it preserves the notion of the independence of the functions of the body (or bodies in Member States which may wish to have a series of structures for different territorial entities). As a minimum the Member

States must ensure that the body has sufficient resources to carry out the basic tasks allotted to it by the directive.[9]

17. How to Correct Existing Discriminatory Provisions (Article 14)

The Commission had proposed that all existing laws, regulations and administrative provisions contrary to the principle of equal treatment should be abolished and that, at the same time, any terms in individual or collective contracts should be declared null and void. This latter point created difficulty for some Member States, which argued that it was not possible to ensure that the many thousands of collective agreements in force were discrimination-proofed. The Commission proposed and secured, therefore, a system which allowed such provisions to be declared null and void once they were spotted or challenged.

18. How to Fix Appropriate Sanctions for Discriminatory Acts (Article 15)

As part of the effort to use the directive as a means of prevention, as well as of repression, of discrimination, the Commission proposed a provision on the sanctions, which should be fixed for contraventions of the principle of equal treatment. The proposal was a standard text in proposals in the social field, though the Council's standard reaction in previous negotiations had been to delete it. However, in this case and to the surprise of some, Member States, which had previously been opposed to equivalent articles suggested that the fight against racism was so important that they could now accept it. The Directive requires, therefore, that Member States introduce sanctions for the breach of the principle of equal treatment, which are 'effective, proportionate and dissuasive'. The main addition to the Commission's text is that sanctions may take the form of the payment of compensation to the victim.

19. Conclusion

It will be no easy matter to replicate the conditions which led to the rapid and successful conclusion of these negotiations, if only because so many of them were outside the control of any one of the parties to the process. The strong co-operation between the Commission, Council and European Parliament played an important role and the mobilisation of civil society to give a final push after

9 The Commission has since published a study on the roles and responsibilities of 21 specialised bodies to promote equality within the Member States of the EU. See http://europa.eu.int/comm/employment_social/fundamental_rights/prog/studies_en.htm.

so many years of pressure was certainly important in maintaining the momentum when it was needed most.

Despite the difficulties described above, the Council showed considerable will to reach agreement. It became clear at the informal meeting of Ministers for Employment and Social Affairs in Lisbon in February 2000 that this political will would be given extra impetus by the reaction of the 14 Heads of State and Government to the inclusion in the new Austrian Government of the Freedom Party of Jörg Haider. The subsequent decision of the European Parliament to speed up the adoption of its opinion on the Directive on racial and ethnic discrimination while leaving the other parts of the Article 13 package for later in the year also played its part in convincing the Presidency, and in its turn the Council, to relinquish its tactic of dealing in parallel with both this directive and its sister directive dealing with other grounds of discrimination in employment. This enabled the Council to concentrate its efforts on this directive in the first instance, undoubtedly removing some of the complications in the negotiations by allowing problems to be solved one at a time in a narrower context. In doing so, the Directive paved the way for the adoption of the Employment Equality Directive (Council Directive 2000/78/EC – q.v.) and the later revision of the legislation on gender equality in the employment field (Council Directive 2002/73/EC – q.v.).

Sejal Parmar

6. THE EUROPEAN COURT OF JUSTICE AND ANTI-DISCRIMINATION LAW: SOME REFLECTIONS ON THE EXPERIENCE OF GENDER EQUALITY JURISPRUDENCE FOR THE FUTURE INTERPRETATION OF THE RACIAL EQUALITY DIRECTIVE

1. Introduction

As the 'opening shot' of the EU's new anti-discrimination regime, Directive 2000/43/EC or the Racial Equality Directive is a pioneering piece of legislation.[1] Adopted on 29 June 2000, the Racial Equality Directive is the first piece of legislation taken under Article 13 EC[2] and should have been transposed into the national legal systems of the Member States by 19 July 2003, an implementation deadline earlier than the Framework Employment Directive or the Equal Treatment (Amendment) Directive.[3] It is broader in scope than either of these two later initiatives, outlawing racial discrimination in such diverse and important

1 Directive 2000/43/EC implementing the principle of equal treatment between persons irrespective of racial or ethnic origin OJ 2000, L 180/22.

2 Article 13 EC states: 'Without prejudice to the other provisions of this Treaty and within the limits of the powers conferred by it upon the Community, the Council, acting unanimously on a proposal from the Commission and after consulting the European Parliament, may take appropriate action to combat discrimination based on sex, racial or ethnic origin, religion or belief, disability, age or sexual orientation'.

3 Directive 2000/78/EC of November 2000 establishing a general framework for equal treatment in employment and occupation [2000] OJ L 303/16. Directive 2002/73/EC of 23 September 2002 amending Council Directive 76/207/EEC on the implementation of the principle of equal treatment for men and women as regards access to employment, vocational training and promotion, and working conditions [2002] OJ L 269/15.

Jan Niessen, Isabelle Chopin (eds.), The Development of Legal Instruments..., *131-154*

areas of social life as healthcare, education and housing. In one sweep, therefore, the Racial Equality Directive establishes and elevates the protection afforded to racial and ethnic origin above the other grounds of discrimination, including sex,[4] so that racial equality now perches at the pinnacle of a 'hierarchy of equalities' protected under EU law.[5] It is significant in its timing, coming into effect during a period of constitutional debate within the Union[6] and preceding the EU eastward enlargement that should bring to the fore a new range of minority issues.[7] And it also heralds a 'new era' of equality law in Europe alongside the new Protocol 12 of the ECHR, which is discussed in the subsequent chapters of this volume.[8]

But how far is the Racial Equality Directive truly a fresh start and a break from the past? Whilst race equality *legislation* seems a totally new venture for the Union, there remain connections between the Directive and established EU law through the basic, overarching principle of equal treatment that the Court of Justice has articulated in the field of gender equality. The Court has long been a key institu-

4 L. Waddington and M. Bell, 'More Equal than Others: Distinguishing European Union Equality Directives', (2001) 38 *Common Market Law Review* 587, 610. Flynn notes the 'special position' of gender discrimination within the Community's social policy to date in L. Flynn, 'The Implications of Article 13 EC – After Amsterdam, will some forms of discrimination be more equal than others', (1999) 36 *Common Market Law Review* 1127. See also S. Fredman, 'Equality: A New Generation', (2001) 30 *Industrial Law Journal* 145 at 158.

5 Under the Equal Treatment (Amendment) Directive, protection against discrimination on the grounds of gender remains limited to the fields of employment and occupation, and some aspects of social security. Discrimination on the grounds of age, religion, sexual orientation and disability is only prohibited in the sphere of employment. Moreover, Waddington and Bell have argued that the other grounds of discrimination in the Framework Employment Directive are the 'poor relations', and between these an 'internal hierarchy also exists, with age discrimination very firmly at the top of the heap'. See above at 610. However, such a hierarchy is the result of practical realities and it is difficult to justify on the basis of human rights and equality before the law.

6 See the website of the Convention. http://european-convention.eu.int/bienvenue.asp?lang=EN&Content=

7 The UN Development Programme Report released on Thursday, 16 January 2003, urges a new strategy to aid the Roma in Europe. See the report at http://www.ocean.sk/undp/. See also General Recommendation XXVII of the International Committee on the Elimination of Racial Discrimination on discrimination against Roma. For further information on the situation of the Roma see *Roma Rights Quarterly*, the quarterly newsletter of the European Roma Rights Center. According to the ERRC, the number of Roma in Europe is between 6.1-8.6 million whereas official figures suggest that the number lies between 2.3-2.6 million, most of whom reside in states looking to accede to the EU i.e. Bulgaria, the Czech Republic, Estonia, Hungary, Latvia, Lithuania, Poland, Romania, Slovakia and Slovenia and Turkey.

8 See S. Fredman, 'Equality: A New Generation', above at n. 4.

tional actor in developing the principles of equal pay and equal treatment of men and women under Articles 141 EC (ex Article 119 EC) and Article 137 (ex Article 118) and numerous directives.[9] On this basis, one may assume that the Court shall proceed in the same manner in the field of racial equality by embracing its function as interpreter of Treaty provisions and legislation on the principle of equal treatment irrespective of racial or ethnic origin. In adjudicating issues arising under the Racial Equality Directive, however, how far might the Court rely upon its old case law in the gender equality field? This chapter seeks to uncover some of the links between these two aspects of EU anti-discrimination law by explaining the specific relevance of the Court of Justice's previous jurisprudence in the field of gender equality for the interpretation of the Racial Equality Directive.[10]

2. The General Relevance of the EU Gender 'Experience'

Although it is the Community's first attempt at enacting a race relations law, its innovative quality and far-reaching nature have earned the Racial Equality Directive the label 'the most wide-sweeping equal opportunities legislation in the Community's history'.[11] The reasons for such a view are quickly apparent even from a cursory reading. Notably, the Directive provides for protection against racial discrimination, which is defined broadly to encompass the practice of harassment. The Directive is also broad in material scope covering the fields of employment and occupation, but also spheres such as social protection, education, access to goods and services including housing. Moreover, the Directive allows organisations with a 'legitimate' interest to support individual complainants in bringing cases under the legislation, while it requires Member States to establish a body/bodies for the promotion of equal treatment. In all these ways, the Directive goes beyond the level of protection guaranteed under gender equality legislation and jurisprudence to date. It might even be argued that the Directive presents such a radical progression from the parameters previously established in the field of EU sex equality law that the interpretation of the former has nothing or little to gain from a reflection on the latter.

---

9 Directive 75/117 [1975] OJ L45 (pay); Directive 76/207 [1976] OJ L39/40 (equal treatment); Directive 86/613 [1986] OJ L359/56 (self-employed); Directive 96/34 [1996] OJ 145/4 (parental leave); Directive 92/85 [1992] OJ L348/1 (concerning pregnancy).

10 See E. Guild, 'Article 13: The European Commission's Anti-Discrimination Proposals', (2000) 29 *Industrial Law Journal* 79; E. Guild, 'The EC Directive on race discrimination: surprises, possibilities and limitations', (2000) 29 *Industrial Law Journal* 416; L. Waddington and M. Bell, 'More Equal than Others: Distinguishing European Union Equality Directives', above at n. 4; D. Schiek, 'A new framework on equal treatment of persons in EC law', (2002) 8 *European Law Journal* 290.

11 D. Chalmers, 'The Mistakes of the Good European?', in S. Fredman (ed), *Discrimination and Human Rights: The Case of Racism* (Oxford: Oxford, 2001) 193, 194-6.

Yet one cannot dismiss the influence of the backdrop of the principle of equality between men and women that has been enshrined in Article 141 EC (ex Article 119 EC) from the beginning of the Community[12] and which, over the years, has developed into a core feature of the Community's social policy. The linkages with the history of sex equality law appear unavoidable for several reasons. First, there are the reasons related to the *origins* of the legislation. Though the initiative advances the EU's anti-discrimination approach in various ways, many of the provisions of the Racial Equality Directive derive from the sex equality field. The gender equality 'roots' of the Directive are felt in the substantive provisions, which shall be discussed below, but can be most clearly detected in the original Commission Proposal[13] and the Communication from the Commission on certain measures to combat discrimination that accompanied the 'Commission's Equality Package'.[14] These indicate the Commission's impulse towards ensuring consistency between racial or ethnic origin on the one hand, and gender on the other, as grounds of discrimination protected by EU law. The original Commission proposal, for example, emphasises that the definition of the principle of equal treatment in the Racial Equality Directive was intended to be consistent with the definition provided by the Equal Treatment Directive[15] and the Burden of Proof Directive[16] and with the case law of the Court of Justice on indirect discrimination.[17] In terms of material scope, the scope of application to the employment field was intended to be identical to the Equal Treatment Directive, and the original provision on genuine occupational qualifications is based on a similar provision in the Equal Treatment Directive. The Communication emphasises that in developing its package of proposals the Commission drew inspiration from the Community's 'long-standing commitment towards equal opportunities and equal treatment between women and men'[18] and the 'experience in the field of

---

12 C. Barnard, 'The Economic Objectives of Article 119', in D. O'Keeffe and T. Hervey (eds), *Sex Equality Law in the European Union* (Chichester: Wiley, 1996).

13 Proposal for a Council Directive implementing the principle of equal treatment between persons irrespective of racial or ethnic origin, COM (1999) 566 final 25.11.1999. This document also views the Community as a 'strong defender of the human rights of women and girls', recognising that 'discrimination on the grounds of racial or ethnic origin may affect women and men differently' (at 5).

14 Communication from the Commission to the Council, the European Parliament, the Economic and Social Committee and the Committee of Regions on certain measures to combat discrimination, COM (1999) 564 final.

15 Directive 76/207/EEC above at n. 9.

16 Directive 97/80/EC above at n. 9 .

17 The Commission Proposal highlighted in particular the judgement in Case C-237/94, *O'Flynn v Adjudication Officer* [1996] ECR 2417.

18 Communication above at n. 14 at 4.

gender discrimination'.[19] And in 'formulating these proposals', the original Commission also claims to have taken special account of past 'experience of fighting discrimination on grounds of sex' embodied in Equal Treatment and Burden of Proof Directives, but also in jurisprudence. Although the Commission Proposal was amended in the subsequent negotiation process, the impression left by gender equality law remains strong.

The second reason for emphasising the links between EU racial and gender equality law concerns the 'evolution of a multi-faceted EU anti-discrimination law'.[20] Since the coming into effect of Article 13 EC, the field of anti-discrimination law has been one of energetic legislative activity on the part of the Community institutions, not only regarding racial discrimination but also with the subsequent Framework Employment Directive and Council Decision establishing an Action Programme[21] in 2000, and the new Equal Treatment (Amendment) Directive that was adopted in September 2002. Gender equality legislation and jurisprudence influenced the drafting of the Racial Equality Directive and are likely to have a bearing on its interpretation. At the same time, the Racial Equality Directive appears to have, in turn, influenced the drafting of the new Equal Treatment (Amendment) Directive.[22] For instance, the latter has borrowed the new model of indirect discrimination used in the former.[23] There now seems to be a *reflexive cross-fertilisation* process between EU race and gender equality law in particular, in which legislative definitions are borrowed, adapted and integrated. Whilst this process may be extended to involve further legislation emanating from the Community institutions under Article 13 EC against discrimination on other grounds, because of greater political agreement on combating racial and sex discrimination, there will be arguably most room for mutual influence between EU race and gender equality law.

19 The Communication goes on to single out 'the policies which promote of equal treatment and positive action remedies enacted by Member States to compensate for structural inequalities' Communication above at n. 14 at 7.

20 See D. Schiek, 'A new framework on equal treatment of persons in EC law' above at n. 10 at 294.

21 Council Decision 2000/750/EC of 27 November 2000 establishing a Community action programme to combat discrimination (2001-2006) [2000] OJ L 303/23.

22 For details of similarities between the two Directives and the Framework Employment Directive see D. Schiek, 'A New Framework on Equal Treatment of Persons in EC Law' above at n. 10, 294-302.

23 The definition which is discussed below states: 'indirect discrimination shall be taken to occur where an apparently neutral provision, criterion or practice would put persons of a racial or ethnic origin at a particular disadvantage compared with other persons, unless that provision, criterion or practice is objectively justified by a legitimate aim and the means of achieving that aim are appropriate and necessary.'

Third, given that gender equality law was a source of inspiration for the Racial Equality Directive, Community institutions may well reflect more generally upon the 'experience' of EU gender equality jurisprudence in the future interpretation and implementation of its provisions. Recital 14 of the Directive asserts that in 'implementing the principle of equal treatment irrespective of racial or ethnic origin, the Community should, in accordance with Article 3(2) of the EC Treaty, aim to eliminate inequalities, and to promote equality between men and women, especially since women are often the victims of multiple discrimination'. And although the Programme of Action, which is designed to complement the two 2000 directives (the Racial Equality Directive and the Framework Employment Directive), does not address sex discrimination directly, the Commission is committed to ensuring that the gender perspective is effectively included in all actions and activities addressed in the programme to combat all other grounds of discrimination under Article 2 and 3 EC. Flynn previously noted 'the special position of gender discrimination within the Community's social policy to date', claiming that, 'whether in terms of institutional experience, expertise of the personnel in the institutions, or resources, it is highly probable that the measures used to address sex discrimination in the past will be treated as models in relation to other new protected statuses under Article 13 EC'.[24] One area in which the EU gender equality policies may influence the realm of racial equality policy is the 'soft-law' approach of 'mainstreaming' to the combat discrimination on racial or ethnic grounds.[25] The aim of this approach would be to 'mainstream' racial and ethnic equality across all EU policies and activities.

In this light, it is likely that the Court of Justice shall draw upon its own gender equality jurisprudence as a 'model', which it would regard as comprising of the most immediate and pertinent of precedents.[26] As a mark of its institutional support for the legislation, it may in its early case law declare that the general principle of equal treatment on the grounds of racial and ethnic origin, is a fundamental one in the Community legal order. This affirmation of the principle of equal treatment on the grounds of racial or ethnic origin would

24 Flynn above at n. 4 at 1140.

25 See the 1996 Communication on mainstreaming, COM (96)67 and the follow-up document COM (1998)122. More specific examples include the policy of mainstreaming gender equality in EC development co-operation, COM(2001) 295 and mainstreaming in the structural funds, COM(2001)539. For commentary see M. Pollack and E. Hafnor-Burton, 'Mainstreaming Gender in the EU' (2000), 7 *Journal of European Public Policy* 432 and S. Mazey, *Gender Mainstreaming in the EU: Principles and Practice* (Kogan Page, 2001).

26 Other potential points of reference include the approaches of Member States' laws and court decisions, the jurisprudence of the European Court of Human Rights and the decisions of the International Committee on the Elimination of Racial Discrimination.

be in keeping with the Court's established gender equality case law.[27] Given the human rights underpinnings of the Racial Equality Directive indicated in Recital 3,[28] the Court of Justice may well go beyond this broad pronouncement and echo the judgement of *Defrenne III.* In this decision, which was followed in the cases of *P v. S*[29] and *Schröder,*[30] the Court first ruled that the elimination of sex discrimination was one of the fundamental personal human rights, which must be protected within Community law.[31]

The following parts of this chapter examine the Racial Equality Directive in closer detail and highlight judicial decisions from the gender equality field that the Court *may* consider relevant in it pronouncements on the Directive. Given that it is impossible to know the first issues to be decided by the Court at this stage, the following sections are somewhat speculative in nature.

3. 'Racial or Ethnic Origin'

The Racial Equality Directive does not define 'race' or 'racial or ethnic origin', but rather the concept of discrimination on grounds of racial or ethnic origin.[32] In practice, however, discrimination related to race or ethnicity can persist under different guises.[33] As reports of racist incidents in the aftermath of '9/11' have indicated, the factors leading to so-called 'racial discrimination' are frequently tightly bound to other factors, such as religion or belief and nationality. Whilst

---

27 Cases 20/71, *Sabbatini* [1972] ECR 345; 21/74 *Airola* [1972] ECR 221; 75, 117/82, *Razzouk and Beydoun* v. *Commission* [1984] ECR 1509.

28 That recital states:

> 'The right to equality before the law and protection against discrimination for all persons constitutes a universal right recognised by the Universal Declaration of Human Rights, the United Nations Convention on the Elimination of all forms of Discrimination Against Women, the International Convention on the Elimination of all forms of Racial Discrimination and the United Nations Covenants on Civil and Political and Economic, Social and Cultural Rights and by the European Convention for the Protection of Fundamental Freedoms, to which all Member States are signatories'.

29 Case C-13/94, *P* v. *S and Cornwall County Council* [1996] ECR 2143, para. 19.

30 C-50/96, *Deutsche Telekom* v. *Schröder* [2000] ECR I-743, para. 56.

31 Case 149/77, *Defrenne* v. *Sabena* [1978] ECR 1365, paras. 26-27.

32 See also the International Convention on the Elimination of all forms of Racial Discrimination, which in Article 1 refrains from defining race.

33 The Human Rights Watch World Report for 2001 states: 'racism blights the lives of groups defined primarily by ethnicity, caste, or an identity shaped by *religion*' (emphasis added). *Human Rights Watch World Report 2001* http://www.hrw.org/wr2k1/special/racism.htm

the Directive appears to apply to third country nationals,[34] it goes on to exclude distinctions based on nationality even though the causes of racial discrimination and xenophobia are inextricably linked.[35] It also overlooks the interstices between race and religion as factors of discrimination.

Given the its generally conservative approach towards the definition of 'sex' in gender equality case law, however, the Court is likely to define the scope of 'racial or ethnic origin' restrictively. Following *P* v. *S*, a case concerning discrimination against transsexuals under Directive 76/207, it appeared that the idea of 'sex equality' would be granted a broad interpretation. Although the Court of Justice ruled in the case that sex discrimination under the Directive included discrimination arising from gender reassignment, in *Grant* the Court decided that the prohibition on discrimination on grounds of sex within Article 141 EC (ex Article 119 EC) did not cover discrimination on grounds of sexual orientation. The Court's restrictive approach to the notion of sex equality, which was reaffirmed in *Grant* in *D* v. *Council,*[36] is likely to be similarly applied in respect of 'racial equality'. Strong reasons do indeed exist for the exclusion of religious discrimination from the scope of the Racial Equality Directive: Article 13 EC expressly demarcates 'racial and ethnic origin' and 'religion or belief' as distinct grounds of discrimination that the Community may take action against; the Framework Employment Directive forbids discrimination on the grounds of religion within its terms whilst the Racial Equality Directive only refers to 'racial and ethnic origin'.

It is argued that in implementing the Racial Equality Directive, greater attention ought to be paid to the 'real-life' connections between different kinds of discrimination, in particular race and religion, through, for example, the concept of multiple discrimination. Simply because the discrimination in question is based on religion does not prevent it also being based on racial or ethnic origin and therefore falling within the scope of the Directive.[37] Hopes for a more inclusive definition of racial discrimination also rest with national law. Article 6(2) provides that 'under no circumstances' shall implementation of the Racial Equality Directive result in a reduction in the level of protection already afforded under national law. For example, UK courts have been more open to recognising the nexus between discrimination on the grounds of religion and race. Although the UK's Race Relations Act excludes religion from its prohibited grounds of

34 Article 3(1) on Scope states:' . . . this Directive applies to all persons'. See also C-230/97 *Awoyemi* [1998] ECR I-6781.

35 Article 3(2). Third country nationals are only protected if the difference in treatment is not related to provisions governing their entry and residence.

36 Case C-249/96, *Grant* v. *South-West Trains* [1998] ECR I-621. For comments, See M. Bell, (1999) 5 *European Law Journal* 63; C. Barnard, (1998) 57 *Cambridge Law Journal* 352.

37 E. Guild, 'The EC Directive on Race Discrimination: Surprises, Possibilities and Limitations', (2000) 29 *Industrial Law Journal* 416, 419.

discrimination, religious groups who have framed their arguments on racial or ethnic grounds have sometimes been successful in making their claims under its provisions.[38]

4. Scope

The Racial Equality Directive covers the four employment related fields covered by the Framework Employment Directive: conditions for access to employment, to self-employment and to occupation, including selection criteria and recruitment conditions, including promotion; access to all levels of vocational guidance, vocational training advanced vocational training and retraining, including practical work experience; employment and working conditions, including dismissals and pay; membership of an involvement in an organisation of workers or employers, or any organisation whose members carry on a particular profession, including the benefits provided by such organisations.[39] These same areas are also covered in the gender equality field by the new Equal Treatment (Amendment) Directive.[40] There is a developed jurisprudence on the principles of equal pay and equal treatment, which should be relevant for the Court of Justice's future judgements of the Racial Equality Directive.

The Court shall presumably interpret the idea of pay very broadly under the Racial Equality Directive as it has in the field of gender equality. Article 141 EC (ex Article 119 EC) has been granted a wide interpretation in cases such as *Garland*, in which travel benefits conferred in respect of employment, even after retirement and irrespective of any specific contractual obligation, were held to constitute pay.[41] In *Kowalska* the equal pay principle in Article 141 EC was held to cover a severance grant,[42] whilst in *Seymour Smith* the Court decided that compensation for unfair dismissal was pay since it was designed to replace pay to which the employee would have been entitled had she not been unfairly dismissed.[43] The Court has also held that the rules governing the system of salary-

38 The UK courts have accepted some of these categorisations and have extended the Act's protection to certain religious groups. The UK Courts have adopted a 'distinct community' test which allows high degree of self-identification and a concept of ethnic origin that is defined by virtue of behaviour which the individual could change. See *Mandla* v. *Dowell Lee* [1983] 2 AC 548.

39 Racial Equality Directive, Articles 3(1)(a)-(d).

40 Equal Treatment (Amendment) Directive, Article 3(1)(a)-(d).

41 In the particular case, these travel facilities for spouses and dependent children. Case C 12/81, *Garland* v. *British Rail Engineering Ltd.* [1982] ECR 359. See also Case C-249/96, *Grant* v. *South West Trains* above at n. 36.

42 Case C- 33/89, *Kowalska* v. *Freie und Hansestadt Hamburg* [1990] 2591.

43 Case C-167/97, *Seymour-Smith and Perez* [1999] ECR I-623.

classification into grades,[44] severance benefits, including statutory redundancy payments,[45] and statutory sick payments constitute pay.[46] In *Bötel,*[47] *Lewark*[48] and *Freers*[49] the Court ruled that statutorily required compensation payments to workers attending training courses which gave them the knowledge required for working on staff councils would constitute pay. Whilst the Court of Justice determined that statutory pension benefits would not be considered 'pay' in *Defrenne I,*[50] in *Bilka* the Court held that the benefits paid to employees under occupational pension schemes may constitute pay in certain circumstances.[51] In that case, the pension scheme was (1) contractual in nature; (2) not governed by statute but by the agreement between employer and employee, and (3) not financed in part by the public authorities but entirely by the employer.[52] In the important decision of *Barber*, the Court of Justice was asked whether contracted-out occupational pension schemes constituted pay.[53] Reflecting on its own reasoning in *Bilka*, the Court held that such schemes were covered by the equal pay principle. Article 141 EC (ex Article 119 EC) may be invoked against the employer or the trustees of the pension scheme, not just by an employee under that scheme, but also by the employees' dependents.[54] The Court drew

---

44 Case C-184/89, *Nimz* v. *Freie und Hansestadt Hamburg* [1991] ECR I-297.

45 Case C- 262/88, *Barber* v. *Guardian Royal Exchange* [1990] ECR 1989.

46 Case 171/88, *Rinner-Kühn* v. *FWW Spezial-Gebäudereinigung GmbH* [1989] ECR 2743.

47 Case C-360/90, *Arbeiterwohlfahrt der Stadt Berlin* v. *Bötel* [1992] ECR 3589.

48 Case C-457/93, *Kuratorium für Dialyse un Nierentransplantation* v. *Lewark* [1996] ECR I-243.

49 Case C-278/93, *Freers und Speckman* v. *Deutsche Bundespost* [1996] ECR I-1165.

50 Case 80/70, *Defrenne* v. *Belgium* [1971] ECR 445, paras. 6-10.

51 Case C-170/84, *Bilka-Kaufhaus GmbH* v. *Karin Weber von Hartz* [1986] ECR 1607.

52 The fact that the employer chose to arrange the particular scheme in question in a manner which corresponded to the statutory social security scheme was held to be irrelevant. Later, the Court has also held that the fact that affiliation to an occupational pension scheme was made compulsory by legislation for employees was irrelevant to the application of Article 141 EC (ex 119 EC). Case C-435/93, *Dietz* v. *Stichting Thuiszorg Rotterdam* [1996] ECR I-5223.

53 In *Moroni* the Court held that sums paid out under a supplementary pension scheme also constituted pay. Case C-110-91, *Moroni* v. *Collo* ECR I-6591.

54 Case C-200/91, *Coloroll Pension Trustees Ltd.* v. *James Richards Russell* [1994] ECR I-4389, 17-19; Case C-379/99, *Pensionskasse für die Angestellten der Barner Ersatzkasse* v. *Menauer* [2001] ECR I-7275. See also *Ten Oever*, in which the Court ruled that Article 141 EC (ex Article 119 EC) covered pensionable benefits payable to the employee but also the employee's survivor, such as a widow. Case C- 109/91, *Ten Oever* v. *Stichting Bedrijfspensioenfonds voor het Glazenwassers-en Schoonmaakbedrijf* [1993] ECR I-4879.

back from its position somewhat in the cases of *Coloroll* and *Neath*[55] concerning payments by an employer to a contracted-out occupational pension scheme (rather than payments to an employee, as in *Barber*) which were denied the status of 'pay' under Article 141 EC (ex Article 119 EC).

The Racial Equality Directive may have most impact and present the more interesting decisions under the legislation in cases arising from situations outside the context of the workplace. After all, the Directive has been lauded partly because of its broad scope which goes far beyond the realm of employment and occupation and sees the Community making full use of the competence provided by Article 13 EC to act 'within the limits of the powers conferred by [the Treaty] upon the Community'. Apart from the sphere of employment and occupation, which has been traditionally the focus for the EU's gender equality law, the Directive covers a range of fields social protection including social security and healthcare, social advantages, education, access to and supply of public goods and services including housing.[56] Most of these fields are completely new areas of attention for the Community's anti-discrimination law and, therefore, have not been discussed in the case law.[57]

Social security, however, has been examined in jurisprudence concerning Directive 79/7 on statutory social security. Social security must be strictly employment-related according to *Achterberg-te Riele*, in which the Court ruled that persons who give up work for a reason other than one of the five listed in the Directive (sickness, invalidity, old age, accidents at work and occupational diseases or unemployment), such as to look after children, fall outside the scope of the Directive.[58] The Court went further in *Johnson I*, deciding that in order to be covered by the Directive, the person in question must have also either given up employment or been obliged to give up seeking employment at the time of materialisation of one of the reasons in the Directive.[59] Various benefits have been held to be outside the material scope of the Directive by the Court, such as

---

55 Case C-152/91, *Neath* v. *Hugh Steeper Ltd* [1993] ECR I-6935.

56 Racial Equality Directive, Articles 3(1)(e)-(h).

57 The new Equal Treatment (Amendment) Directive only covers employment and occupation, so gender is now second in the hierarchy of grounds of discrimination protected under EU law.

58 Directive 79/7 [1979] OJ L6/24. Cases 48, 106 and 107/88, *Achterberg-te Riele* v. *Sociale Versekeringsbank, Amsterdam* [1989] ECR 1963.

59 Case C-31/90, *Johnson* v. *Chief Adjudication Office* [1991] ECR I-3723, 12-23. See also Case C-77/95, *Züchner* v. *Handelskrankenkasse (Ersatzkass) Bremen* [1996] ECR I-5689. See the Court's more generous case law also: Cases C-317/93, *Inge Nolte* v. *Landesversicherungsanstalt Hannover* [1995] ECR I-4625 and C-444/93, *Megner and Scheffel* v. *Innungskrankenkasse Vorderpfalz, now Innungskrankenkasse Rheinhessen-Pfalz* [1995] ECR I-4741.

housing benefit,[60] income support or supplementary allowance,[61] child benefit,[62] travel concessions on public transport for pensioners.[63] The Court has rejected the argument that Directive could be extend to cover measures of 'social protection'[64] going beyond social security proper. On the other hand, national health prescription exemptions for old-age pensioners,[65] winter fuel payment[66] have been held to fall within the scope of the Directive.

5. Concepts of Discrimination

The Racial Equality Directive explicitly prohibits three different forms of discrimination – direct discrimination, indirect discrimination, and harassment. Once again the Racial Equality Directive embarks upon extending the principle of equal treatment to areas beyond the established confines of EU gender equality law, fields in which there is no Court of Justice jurisprudence. Significantly, the Directive is the first occasion on which harassment has been outlawed under EU law. Similar provisions exist in the Framework Employment Directive and the Equal Treatment (Amendment) Directive that have been adopted in its wake.[67] Before the adoption of the Racial Equality Directive there was also no *legislative* definition of direct discrimination in EU law and indirect discrimination was only defined in legislation as late as 1997.[68] Consequently, the Court has been forced to play an important role in 'filling in the gaps' of gender equality legislation by shedding light on the meaning of the concepts of indirect and direct discrimination.

---

60 Case C-243/90, *R.* v. *Secretary of State for Social Security, ex part Smithson* [1992] ECR I-467.

61 Cases C-63-64/91, *Jackson* v. *Chief Adjudication Officer* [1992] ECR I-4737.

62 Cases C-245/94 & C-312/94, *Hoever and Zachow* v. *Land Nordrhein Westfalen* [1996] ECR I-4895.

63 Case C-228/94, *Atkins* v. *Wrekin District Council and Department of Transport* [1996] ECR I-3633.

64 See *Atkins* above.

65 Case C-137/94, *R.* v. *Secretary of State for Health, ex. p. Richardson* [1995] ECR I-3407.

66 Case C-382/98, *R.* v. *Secretary of State for Health, ex. p. Taylor* [1999] ECR I-8955..

67 The Employment Framework Directive, Article 2(2)(3). The Equal Treatment (Amendment) Directive also contains a definition of discrimination that encompasses harassment and sexual harassment in Article 2(2).

68 Under the Burden of Proof Directive 97/80/EC [1997] OJ14/6.

5.1 Direct Discrimination

Article 2(2)(a) of the Racial Equality Directive states: 'direct discrimination shall be taken to occur where one person is treated less favourably than another is, has been or would be treated in a comparable situation on grounds of racial or ethnic origin'.[69] The Court of Justice, in the *Defrenne II* decision, confirmed that Article 119 EC (now Article 141 EC) could have direct effect in a case of clear and direct pay discrimination.[70] Examples of such unjustified practices would include discrimination within legislation or collective labour agreements which 'may be detected on a purely legal analysis of the situation' or situations in which persons of different racial or ethnic groups received 'unequal pay for equal work carried out in the same establishment or service'.[71]

For the purposes of practical application of the Racial Equality Directive, the most significant aspect of this definition are the words 'comparable situation'. Given the absence of legislative guidance on the meaning of this phrase, the Court of Justice has had to explain its implications. But the identification of a suitably positioned comparator has been frequently problematic under sex discrimination case law.[72] The Court has sometimes appeared inconsistent, allowing comparisons to be made between a woman and a man who previously performed the same job[73] whilst rejecting reference to hypothetical comparators outside the scope of discrimination on the grounds of pregnancy.[74] It remains to be seen whether the Court maintains a similarly inconsistent approach in the field of racial equality. The fact that the Racial Equality Directive refers to one person being treated less favourably than 'another ... would *be*' (emphasis added) suggests that references to hypothetical comparators shall be allowed by the Court. If so, Waddington and Bell argue that 'this will not only raise interesting questions concerning interpretation and application, but also result in greater protection from direct discrimination' on grounds of racial and ethnic origin than currently exists with regard to sex discrimination.[75]

---

69 Framework Employment Directive and the Equal Treatment (Amendment) Directive.

70 Case 43/75, *Defrenne* v. *Sabena*, [1976] ECR 455, 18.

71 In *Dekker*, the Court held that a refusal of employment on the grounds of pregnancy could be regarded as direct sex discrimination since only women could be refused employment on this reason. Case C-177/88, *Dekker* v. *Stichting Vormingscentrum voor Jong Volwassenen*, [1990] ECR I-3941. See especially paragraph 10.

72 See E. Ellis, *EC Sex Equality Law* (Oxford: Clarendon, 1998).

73 Case 129/80, *MacCarthys Ltd.* v. *Smith*, [1980] ECR 1275.

74 *MacCarthys*, above; Case C-200/91, *Coloroll* v. *Russel*, [1994] ECR I-4398.

75 See Waddington and Bell above at n. 4 at 592.

5.2 Indirect Discrimination

In defining indirect discrimination, Article 2(2) of the Racial Equality Directive states that it 'shall be taken to occur where an apparently neutral provision, criterion or practice would put persons of a racial or ethnic origin at a particular disadvantage compared with other persons'. Under the Racial Equality Directive 'a provision, criterion or practice' is not deemed indirect discrimination if it 'is objectively justified by a legitimate aim and the means of achieving that aim are appropriate and necessary'. Before the adoption of a legislative definition of indirect discrimination first contained within the Burden of Proof Directive, the Court of Justice was left to elaborate the concept in the context of a number of sex discrimination cases. The approach of the Court heavily influenced the subsequent legislative definition. Given that the two concepts appear more interrelated in the case law, this section shall examine the Court's determination of indirect discrimination and its approach to objective justification.

The idea of *indirect* sex discrimination was developed in *Jenkins*[76] and then *Bilka-Kaufhaus,*[77] cases which involved part-time workers, mainly women, who were paid a lower hourly rate than full-time workers. The Court held that if proportionately more women work part-time, the exclusion of those part-time workers would be indirectly discriminatory and contrary to Article 141 EC where that exclusion could not be justified by factors unrelated to any discrimination on grounds of sex.[78] Following this gender equality case law there would be also no need to establish an intention to discriminate on the grounds of racial or ethnic origin the part of an employer.[79]

---

76 Despite the rulings in *Defrenne II* and *Macarthys* indicating that Article 141 EC could not have direct effect where discrimination was indirect, subsequent case law has indicated that the existence of indirect discrimination does not preclude the direct effect of the Article, when such discrimination can be identified on a 'purely legal analysis' without the need for further legislation. Case 96/80, *Jenkins* v. *Kingsgate (Clothing Productions) Ltd.* [1981] ECR 911; Case 129/79, *Macarthys Ltd.* v. *Smith* [1980] ECR 1275, 14-15.

77 Case 170/84, *Bilka-Kaufhaus* v. *Weber von Hartz*, [1986] ECR 1607.

78 In contrast, the *Enderby* case shows the problem of establishing *indirect* discrimination by demonstrating that the professions which are predominantly female is undervalued in comparison to the professions which are predominantly male. The hurdles are, arguably, even more difficult in a case of indirect racial discrimination where the 'male norm' of gender equality jurisprudence, is replaced by a 'white norm'. Case 127/92, *Enderby* v. *Frenchay Health Authority and the Secretary of State for Health* [1993] ECR 5535, see in particular 15-18; see also Case C-400/93, *Royal Copenhagen* [1995] ECR I-1275.

79 See paragraph 36 of *Bilka* case above at n. 77.

5.2.1 Disadvantageous impact

In determining whether a particular practice or provision has a disadvantageous or 'unfavourable' impact the Court has often required thorough statistical evidence in the gender equality field. This has proved problematic at times and has denied indirect discrimination on grounds of insufficient statistics.[80] In *Seymour-Smith*, for example, the Court held that 'the national court must verify whether the statistics available indicate that a considerably smaller percentage of women than men is able to fulfil the requirement impose by that measure'.[81] In contrast, in *Schnorbus*, the Court ruled that it was not necessary to rely on such statistical evidence.[82] The 1997 Burden of Proof Directive, which applied exclusively in the field of gender discrimination, also included a legislative definition of indirect discrimination that moved away from the statistics based approach.[83]

The Racial Equality Directive withdraws further from a reliance on statistics within the case law by defining racial discrimination as a provision, criterion or practice that 'would put persons of a racial or ethnic origin at a *particular* disadvantage compared with other persons'. In doing so, the drafters of the legislation have followed the approach of the Court in the free movement of persons case *O'Flynn.*[84] In *O'Flynn* the Court held that a rule was indirectly discriminatory where it was intrinsically liable to affect migrant workers more than their national counterparts and if there was a risk that it would place migrant workers at a particular disadvantage. The Court emphasised that it is not necessary to find that the measure did in practice affect a substantially higher proportion of migrant workers, as long as it was *liable* to have such an effect. The test for establishing indirect racial discrimination is easier to satisfy than the previous test for indirect sex discrimination because the burden of proof for establishing the necessary level of adverse treatment seems to be simpler to meet. Therefore, in demonstrating a case of indirect racial discrimination no statistical evidence is needed to show that other persons from racial or ethnic groups have also been discriminated against.

The shift, however, has not been wholly welcomed. Barnard and Hepple, for instance, argue that the result of the approach embodied within the Racial Equality Directive is that the individualistic, formal equality elements of indi-

80 Case C-189/91, *Kirsammer Hack*, ECR 1993, I-6215.

81 Case C-167/97, *R.* v. *Secretary of State for Employment, ex parte Seymour Smith*, [1999] ECR I-623, 65.

82 Case C-79/99, *Schnorbus* v. *Land Hessen* [2000] ECR I-10997.

83 Article 2(2) states: 'For the purposes of equal treatment ... indirect discrimination shall exist where an apparently neutral provision, criterion or practice disadvantages a substantially higher proportion of the members of one sex unless that provision, criterion or practice is appropriate and necessary and can be justified by objective factors unrelated to sex'.

84 Case C-237/94, *O'Flynn* v. *Adjudication Officer* [1996] ECR I-2617, 2639.

rect discrimination are retained.[85] As long as a *particular individual* is put at a disadvantage on racial grounds compared to individuals of a different group, the principle of indirect discrimination under the Directive is satisfied regardless of the impact on the group *as a whole*.[86] It is the individual who continues to bear the burden of bringing a case and the remedy is by way of individual compensation, rather than a 'direct requirement of restructuring'.[87] Moreover, the Directive shows an attachment to the use of statistical evidence through deference to national 'judicial or other competent bodies' concerning the 'appreciation of facts from which it may be inferred that there has been direct or indirect discrimination'. Recital 15 also asserts that national law or practice 'may provide in particular for indirect discrimination to be established by any means including on the basis of statistical evidence'.[88]

5.2.2 Objective justification

Although the scope of an 'objective justification' in the field of gender equality remains unclear, the Court of Justice, who has often left it up to national courts to decide whether a discriminatory practice is justified, has given some guidance. The case law indicates the Court's position that an authority must demonstrate that any discrimination which does occur is effective in achieving a legitimate purpose and goes no further than is necessary to achieve that aim. In paragraph 36 of the judgement in the *Bilka* case, concerning eligibility of part-time workers for an occupational pension scheme, the Court formulated a proportionality test for indirect discrimination. An instance of indirect discrimination can be justified if: (1) the measure answers a 'real need' of the employer; (2) the measure is 'appropriate' to achieve its intended objectives; and (3) the measures are 'necessary' to achieve those objectives.[89] This test was mirrored in *Rinner-Kühn* in which the Court applied a similar test[90] and suggested that 'social policy' might

85 C. Barnard and B. Hepple, 'Substantive Equality', (2000) 59 Cambridge Law Journal 562, 568. See Fredman, above at n. 4 at 165.

86 See Fredman, above at n. 4 at 165.

87 Fredman states these constraints, alongside the 'inevitability of statistical tangles in at least some cases, mean that indirect discrimination as a concept will inevitably play a minor role in bringing about change'. Above at n. 4 at 165

88 See Recital 15 of the Racial Equality Directive and Recital 16 of the Framework Employment Directive and Recital 10 of the proposed the Equal Treatment (Amendment) Directive.

89 See *Bilka* above at n. 77 para. 36.

90 Indirect discrimination was held to exist if (1) the measure was a 'necessary aim' of social policy; (2) the measure was 'suitable' as a means of achieving its aims; (3) the measure was 'requisite'. See also Case 184/89, *Nimz* v. *Freie und Hansestadt Hamburg* above at n. 44.

constitute good grounds for discrimination.[91] What other kinds of discrimination have been considered 'objectively justified' by the Court? In *Nimz*, the greater experience of full-time workers was held to be insufficient as a justification.[92] However, criteria such as mobility, training and length of service, which could disadvantage women, have been held to be valid objective justifications.[93] But *Hill and Stapleton*, a case concerning discrimination against job-sharers who were predominantly women, seems to indicate that the Court is applying a higher standard of scrutiny when the 'objective justification' exception is raised by Member States. In that case the Court ruled that such indirect discrimination could not be justified by economic considerations only.[94]

Despite the influence of the Burden of Proof Directive, the Racial Equality Directive's emphasis on a standard of proportionality arguably draws much more on gender equality case law. Given the similarities in the provisions of the 2000 Directives and the Equal Treatment (Amendment) Directive on indirect discrimination, it seems likely that the Court of Justice shall develop a common standard of 'objective justification' that proceeds from the base of gender equality jurisprudence.

5.3 Harassment

As indicated earlier, harassment is a new area of legislative activity for the Community. Harassment is defined in Article 2(3) of the Racial Equality Directive, which states that it 'shall be deemed to be discrimination ... when an unwanted conduct related to racial or ethnic origin takes place with the purpose or effect of violating the dignity of a person and of creating an intimidating, hostile,

91 In *Rinner-Kühn*, the Court found provisions of national legislation indirectly discriminatory. Although these provisions could have been objectively justified, the justification offered was inadequate according to the Court which followed the *Bilka* approach. Case 171/88, *Rinner-Kühn v. FWW Spezial-Gebäudereinigung GmbH* above at n. 46. See also Case C-457/93, *Kuratorium für Dialyse un Nierentransplantation* v. *Lewark* [1996] ECR I-243; Case C-278/93, *Freers und Speckman* v. *Deutsche Bundespost* [1996] ECR I-1165; Case 80/70, *Defrenne* v. *Belgium* [1971] ECR 445, paras. 6-10.

92 Case C-184/89, *Nimz* v. *Freie und Hansestadt Hamburg* above at n. 44 at paras. 13-14.

93 Case 109/88, *Danfoss* [1989] ECR 3199.

94 Case C-243/95, *Hill and Stapleton* v. *Revenue Commissioners* [1998] ECR I-3739. The relative ease with which the commercial objectives of an undertaking or employer can defeat a claim of indirect discrimination has been criticised by one commentator. See for an example Case C-189/91, *Kirschammer-Hack* v. *Sidal* [1993] ECR I-6185 and T. Hervey, 'Small Business Exclusion in German Dismissal Law', (1994) *Industrial Law Journal* 267.

degrading, humiliating or offensive environment.' This inclusion of harassment as a form of discrimination should be welcomed. But the provision goes to state that 'the concept of harassment may be defined in accordance with the national laws and practice of the Member States'. In doing so, the possible application of the provision is constrained. As Waddington and Bell point out, 'it would logically imply that those aspects of harassment which are not defined in Article 2(3) remain a matter for national law; for example, the liability of employers, schools, universities, hospitals, landlords for failing to prevent harassment'.[95] The Court may be called upon to determine the scope of this provision, but in the absense of earlier gender equality precedents.

6. Exceptions to the Principle of Equality

6.1 Genuine Occupational Qualifications

The Racial Directive Equality provides for differences treatment based on a relevant occupational requirement.[96] Under the heading, 'genuine and determining occupational requirements', the Directive states that '... Member States may provide that a difference of treatment which is based on a characteristic related to racial or ethnic origin shall not constitute discrimination where ... such a characteristic constitutes a genuine and determining occupational requirement, provided that the objective is legitimate and the requirement is proportionate'.[97] The newer definition of occupational requirement contained in the Racial Equality Directive follows the proportionality principle read into the Equal Treatment Directive by the Court. In particular, the Court in *Johnston* required the derogation from the fundamental principle of equality had to be construed narrowly, that '... derogations remain within the limits of what is appropriate and necessary for achieving the aim in view'.[98]

6.2 Positive Action

The Racial Equal Directive adopts a permissive approach to positive action policies: it does not require the imposition of positive duties, but they are allowed under its terms.[99] Article 5 therefore states: 'With a view to ensuring full equality

95 Waddington and Bell, above at n. 4 at 595.

96 See also Articles 4-6 of the Framework Employment Directive.

97 Racial Equality Directive Article 4. Article 4(1) of the Framework Employment Directive contains a similar provision.

98 Case 222/84, *Johnston* v. *Chief Constable of the Royal Ulster Constabulary*, [1986] ECR 1651, paragraph 38.

99 See S. Fredman, 'Reverse Discrimination in EU Law: A Critical Analysis' in J. Shaw

in practice, the principle of equal treatment shall not prevent any Member State from maintaining or adopting specific measures to prevent or compensate for disadvantages linked to racial or ethnic origin'.

The scope of positive action in EU law has sparked a lively debate in recent years, even with a handful of cases on the issue.[100] Following the 1997 Equal Treatment Directive, which first provided an exception for positive action measures,[101] the Court considered the meaning and scope of this provision in several high-profile cases.[102] In *Kalanke*, its most controversial decision,[103] the Court stressed that 'as a derogation from an individual right laid down in the Directive' the exception for positive action measures 'must be interpreted strictly'.[104]

The Treaty of Amsterdam inserted a new provision on positive action into Article 141 EC (ex Article 119 EC) which states: 'with a view to ensuring full equality in practice between men and women in working life, the principle of equal treatment shall not prevent any Member State from maintaining or adopting measures providing specific advantages in order to make it easier for the under-represented sex to pursue a vocational activity or to prevent or compensate for disadvantages in professional careers'. Whilst this provides a broader formulation than the terms of the Equal Treatment Directive, the Court's initial interpretation of Article 141(4) EC suggests that it does not significantly increase the scope for positive action.[105] Since *Kalanke*, the Court has maintained that it will not accept positive action schemes that produce 'equal results' through automatic mechanisms at the *selection stage*. The Court permits, however, a wide range of positive action measures including strict quotas, before

(ed), *Social Law and Policy in an Evolving European Union* (Oxford: Hart, 2000) 171; S. Fredman, Women and the Law (Oxford, Clarendon Press, 1997) ch. 8.

100 See among others, G. Mancini and S. O'Leary, 'The new frontiers of sex equality law in the European Union', 24 (1999) *European Law Review* 331.

101 Article 2(4) states: 'this Directive shall be without prejudice to measures to promote equal opportunity to men and women, in particular by removing existing inequalities which affect women's opportunities . . .'

102 Case-450/93, *Kalanke* v. *Freie Bremen*, [1995] ECR I-3069; C-409/97, *Marschall* v. *Land Nordrhein-Westfalen*, [1997] ECR I-6363; C-158/97, *Badeck* v. *Hessicher Ministerpräsident* [1999] ECR I-1875; C-407/98, *Abrahamsson and Anderson* v. *Fogelqvist* [2000] ECR I-5539.

103 S. Dagmar, (1996) 25 *Industrial Law Journal* 239; S. Moore (1996) 21 *European Law Review*; A. Peters (1996) 2 *European Law Journal* 177; S. Prechal (1996) *Common Market Law Review* 45; D. Schiek (1996) 25 *Industrial Law Journal* 239; L. Senden (1996) 59 *Modern Law Review* 876; S. Fredman (1997) 113 *Law Quarterly Review* 575. See also the Commission's own communication on the interpretation of the Court COM (96)88.

104 *Kalanke* above at n. 102 at para. 8.

105 See *Abrahamsson* above at n. 102. 64.

the point of employment selection. In *Badeck*, for instance, the Court was prepared to accept measures, which imposed a strict quota reserving at least 50% of training places for women, and requiring at least 50% of all candidates invited to interview to be women.[106] Moreover, the Court has not rejected all forms of positive action at the point of selection, but simply requires that such schemes are flexible in nature and guarantee an objective and individual assessment of all candidates.[107]

Whilst the Racial Equality Directive's positive action provisions are viewed as essential for the attainment of 'full equality in practice', Member States are left to determine whether they wish to strive for substantive equality through these schemes. Although the text of the Directive closely follows that found in Article 141(4) EC, it omits the most progressive aspect of that Treaty provision, the possibility of conferring 'specific advantages in order to make it easier for the under-represented sex to pursue a vocational activity'. Waddington and Bell note, therefore, that 'if anything, Article 5 of the Race Directive is more restrictive than Article 141(4) EC.' Notwithstanding, it is speculated that the EU approach for positive action under the Racial Equality Directive shall not differ substantially from the current approach of the Court as indicated in *Abrahammson.*[108] On the one hand, the Court may well extend these general principles on gender-based positive action policies to race-based positive action policies for two main reasons: firstly because the amendment to Article 141(4) EC was not followed by a new approach start on positive action in Community law by the Court, but rather an assimilation of Article 141(4) EC within the principles already established through its existing case law; and secondly because the Framework Employment Directive and the Equal Treatment (Amendment) Directive) contain only slightly different provisions on positive action and the Court would be expected to follow a similar approach in respect of positive action policies promoting equal treatment on all the Article 13 EC grounds of discrimination. It will be interesting to see how the Court deals with the particular issue of race and ethnicity when adjudicating on race-based positive action policies. Given the limited nature of the jurisprudence on gender-based positive action schemes, the first conflicts arising out of positive action schemes employed in the field of racial and ethnicity discrimination are likely be different to those discussed by the case law so far. It might be asked, however, how far the Court would be willing to extend its principles on gender-based positive action policies to training schemes, similar to the one in *Badeck*, which exclusively provided for persons of a particular ethnic origin. One might argue that complexities of different kinds

106 *Badeck* at n. 102, paras. 55 and 63.

107 Case C-409/95, *Marschall* above at n. 102, para. 35. The Court distinguished *Kalanke* from the *Marschall* case by reference to its so-called 'savings clause'.

108 Above at n. 102.

of discrimination merit different types of positive action programmes, adjusted to the particular social context within which the protected group finds itself. It is predicted, however, that the Court shall aim to maintain an 'equality among equalities' as far as possible and refrain from applying such a variable approach within the framework of EU anti-discrimination law.

7. Victimisation

The Racial Equality Directive obliges Member States to 'introduce into their national legal systems such measures as are necessary to protect individuals from any adverse treatment or adverse consequence as a reaction to a complaint or to proceedings aimed at enforcing compliance with the principle of equal treatment'.[109] Though the Racial Equality Directive appears to have gone beyond the notion of victimisation under the Equal Treatment Directive, it must be noted that the Court of Justice expanded its meaning under that Directive in *Coote*.[110] In this case, the Court took a more teleological view of the Directive and held that fear of victimisation 'might deter workers who considered themselves victims of discrimination from pursuing their claims ... and would consequently ... seriously ... jeopardise implementation of the aim pursued by the Directive'. The Court's more purposeful approach through its reference to the aim of the Directive allows a broader conceptualisation of victimisation and is one that should be applied under the Racial Equality Directive.[111] This gender equality case law on victimisation is particular instructive for the interpretation of the Directive, for it implies, that protection from victimisation extends beyond a situation in which a worker is dismissed following a complaint.

8. Enforcement

The Racial Equality Directive goes beyond the framework established by sex equality legislation law with some innovative mechanisms of enforcement.[112] In

109 Article 9 Racial Equality Directive.

110 The case concerned a woman who had sued her employer following her dismissal for being pregnant. After the unfair dismissal proceedings were completed (check), the employer refused to give her a reference and Mrs Coote sued again for victimisation. At first instance, the industrial tribunal held that s. 6 of the UK's Sex Discrimination Act only applied to persons currently employed by the defendant, and since Mrs Coote no longer worked for the defendant she was denied the protection of the Act. Case C-185/97, *Coote* v. *Granada Hospitality Ltd.* [1998] ECR I-5199.

111 See M. Connolly, 'Discrimination Law: Victimisation', (2002) *Industrial Law Journal* 161.

112 J. Blom, B. Fitzpatrick, J. Gregory, R Knegt and U. O'Hare, *The Utilisation of Sex Equality Litigation in the Member States of the European Community* V/782/96-EN 25-6 (Brussels: European Commission, 1996).

particular, the Directive recognises the need to provide better support to individual litigants by encouraging the participation of relevant associations. It provides for organisations 'with a legitimate interest', a criterion to be determined by national law, to 'engage, either on behalf or in support of the complainant, with his or her approval, in any judicial and/or administrative procedure provided for the enforcement of obligations under this Directive'.[113] In contrast to the Framework Employment Directive, the Racial Equality Directive also requires Member States to establish 'a body or bodies for the promotion of equal treatment'.[114] These bodies are required to be able to provide 'independent assistance to victims of discrimination in pursuing their complaints', conduct 'independent surveys concerning discrimination' and publish independent reports and recommendations on issues relating to discrimination.[115]

The Racial Equality Directive also permits a reversal in the burden of proof under certain circumstances in racial discrimination cases. Article 8(1) of the Racial Equality Directive states that 'Member States shall take such measures as are necessary, in accordance with their national judicial systems, to ensure that, when persons who consider themselves wronged because of the principle of equal treatment has not applied to them establish, before a court or other competent authority, facts from which it may be presumed that there has been direct or indirect discrimination, it shall be for the respondent to prove that there has been no breach of the principle of equal treatment'.[116] Even though the 1997 Burden of Proof Directive was the basis for the burden of proof provisions in the Racial Equality Directive, the underlying principles on the burden of proof can be traced to cases such as *Enderby* in which the Court stated that 'where there is a prima facie case of discrimination, it is for the employer to show that there are objective reasons for the difference in pay'.[117]

The Racial Equality Directive also specifies certain principles that must be used in national remedies in discrimination, although the detailed application

113 Article 7(2) Racial Equality Directive; Article 9(2) of the Framework Employment Directive contains an identical provision.

114 Article 13(1) Racial Equality Directive.

115 Article 13(2) Racial Equality Directive. Equality agencies have been part of the anti-discrimination strategy of a several EU Member States, such as the UK, Ireland, the Netherlands and Sweden.

116 A similar provision exists in Article 10 of the Framework Employment Directive.

117 The Court went on to observe in the same, paragraph 18 of the judgement that '[w]orkers would be unable to enforce the principle of equal pay before national courts if evidence of a prima facie case of discrimination did not shift to the employer the onus of showing that the pay differential is not in fact discriminatory'. C-127/92, *Enderby* v *Frenchay Health Authority and Secretary of State for Health*, [1993] ECR I-5535. See also C-109/88, *Handels-og Kontorfunktionaerernes forund i Danmark* v. *Danfoss*, [1989] ECR 3199,

of these provisions is left up to national discretion. According to Article 15 of the Racial Equality Directive, sanctions 'which may comprise the payment of compensation to a victim, must be effective, proportionate and dissuasive'. Although the Equal Treatment Directive does not specify any details on sanctions for breach of its obligations, in a series of cases the Court has applied the general principle of effective judicial protection in order to establish minimum standards in national remedies for sex discrimination cases.[118] It is noted that the Equal Treatment (Amendment) Directive offers a more detailed provision on sanctions, one that goes further than that contained within the Racial Equality Directive. The provision on ensuring 'real and effective compensation or reparation ... for the loss or damage sustained ... as a result of discrimination'[119] appears to codify in legislation the principles established in the Court, most notably in *Marschall (no. 2)*. Whilst the Commission may have considered it too daring to extend more detailed principles expounded in gender equality case law to the Racial Equality Directive, they shall have a bearing on the future interpretation of the Racial Equality Directive in any event given the emerging process of cross-fertilisation between gender and racial discrimination law. The 'shared commitment' to 'effective, proportionate and dissuasive' sanctions for each of the directives 'implies that the Court should demand equivalent standards in the remedies provided for each ground of discrimination'.[120]

9. Concluding Comments: Emerging from the Past Influence of Gender Equality

The judicial approach towards cases arising under the Directive will involve an interweaving of principles evolved previously within the field of gender equality in employment and occupation (such as those on positive action and indirect discrimination) with the Directive's own provisions. It is submitted, however, that the Court should also look to alternative points of reference besides its own jurisprudence, given the broad scope of the Directive beyond the employment-related focus of gender equality law. In particular, international human rights law should be cemented as a source of inspiration for EU law through decisions under the Racial Equality Directive. There is already a growing normative influence of human rights discourse through the EU Charter of Fundamental Rights that has been already felt in policy proposals and statements emanating from the Community institutions, the European Ombudsman, the opinions of

118 Case C-271/91, *Marschall* v. *Southampton and South-West Hampshire Area Health Authority*, [1993] ECR I-4367; Case C-180/95, *Draehmpaehl* v. *Urania Immobilienservice*, [1997] ECR I-2195.

119 Equal Treatment (Amendment) Directive Article 6(2).

120 Waddington and Bell above at n. 4 at 609.

the Court of First Instance[121] and various Advocates-General,[122] and the draft Treaty establishing a Constitution for Europe. The Court should draw on the Charter's equality provision,[123] but also international instruments such as the International Convention on the Elimination of Racial Discrimination, whose normative influence is after all recognised in the Racial Equality Directive. It is submitted that the cross-fertilisation process between the EU's different anti-discrimination measures and the Court's gender equality case law can only be truly progressive if the Court, when shaping the contours and determining the limits of this new area of anti-discrimination law is also open to such influences.

121 Case T-54/99, *Max.mobil Telekommunikation Service GmbH v Commission*, [2002] ECR II-313, paras 48, 57. In T-112/98, *Mannesmannroehren-Werke AG v Commission,* [2001] ECR II-729, the plaintiff invoked the Charter but the CFI dismissed the argument on the basis that the contested measure had been adopted before the Charter was proclaimed, paras 15, 76.

122 See AG Tizzano in C-173/99, *BECTU*, [2001] ECR I-4881; AG Mischo in C-122P & 125/99P, *D.*v *Council* [2000] ECR I-4319; AG Jacobs in C-270/99 P, *Z* v *Parliament*, [2001] ECR I-9197 and C-50/00 P, *Unión de Pequeños Agricultores* v. *Council*, [2002] ECR I-6677; AG Geelhoed in C-413/99, *Baumbast* [2002] ECR I-7091; AG Léger in C-353/99 P, *Council* v. *Hautala*, [2001] ECR I-9565; AG Stix-Hackl in C-60/00, *Carpenter* [2002] ECR I-6279.

123 Article 20.

Per Johansson

7. COMPARING NATIONAL AND COMMUNITY ANTI-DISCRIMINATION LAW

This chapter summarises a series of reports produced in two research projects. The first project started in 1999 and was initiated by the Migration Policy Group and carried out together with the European Monitoring Centre on Racism and Xenophobia.[1] The second project was carried out in the framework of a joint project of the Migration Policy Group, Interights and the European Roma Rights Centre on the implementation of European anti-discrimination law.[2] The two projects compared national anti-discrimination legislation on the grounds of racial or ethnic origin, religion or belief with Council Directive 2000/43/EC of 29 June 2000 implementing the principle of equal treatment between persons irrespective of racial or ethnic origin (Racial Equality Directive). The first project looked at the current 15 EU Member States, whereas the second project

1 This research project was carried out in two phases. The European Monitoring Centre on Racism and Xenophobia (EUMC) made the report on the first phase available electronically. See, Isabelle Chopin and Jan Niessen (eds), Research on national and European legislation combating racism. Joint project of the Migration Policy Group and the European Monitoring Centre on Racism and Xenophobia; Project period 1 May 1999 -31 January 2000. The second phase of the project was completed in 2002. For the second phase see Isabelle Chopin and Jan Niessen, Anti-discrimination legislation in EU Member States. A comparison of national anti-discrimination legislation on the grounds of racial or ethnic, religion or belief with the Council Directives. European Monitoring Centre on Racism and Xenophobia. The reports are available electronically (www.eumc.eu.int) in English and French and each individual report in the language of the respective Member State.

2 'Implementing European Anti-Discrimination Law', 2001-2003. The reports on the eleven candidate countries included in the research project are available from the website of the Migration Policy Group (www.migpolgroup.com): Bulgaria, Czech Republic, Estonia, Hungary, Latvia, Lithuania, Poland, Romania, Slovakia, Slovenia, and Turkey.

Jan Niessen, Isabelle Chopin (eds.), The Development of Legal Instruments..., *155-209*

looked also at 11 candidate countries. The research was based on a format and research questions concerning provisions in the Racial Equality Directive. In this chapter these questions will be reproduced followed by a summary of the 26 country reports.

1. The Legal Framework

Is there any legal framework at national level that puts into effect the principle of equal treatment, or that is designed to combat discrimination on the basis of racial or ethnic origin and/or on the basis of religion or belief? If so, what is the nature of this framework?

In the 26 European countries that are part of this study, the legal framework for combating discrimination on the grounds of racial or ethnic origin and on the basis of religion or belief, is constituted in a variety of ways, comprising provisions found in some or all constitutional law, criminal law, civil law, administrative law and international law. The following attempts to give the reader an overview of where anti-discrimination provisions can be found in the different legal systems.

1.1 Constitutional provisions

In most European States, the Constitution, at least to some extent, guarantees equal treatment and prohibits discrimination on grounds including racial or ethnic origin, nationality and religion or belief.[3] Exceptions are the Czech Republic, Denmark, and the United Kingdom (where there is no written constitution). While the Danish Constitution contains no prohibition or definition of

3 In Austria see Article 7 of the Austrian Federal Constitution, Article 2 of the Basic Law, Article 1 of the Constitutional Law on the Elimination of all Forms of Racial Discrimination 1993, and Articles 63 and 67 of the Treaty of St Germain; in Belgium Articles 10, 11 and 191 of the Constitution; in Bulgaria Article 6 of the Constitution; in Estonia Articles 9 and 12 of the Constitution; in Finland Chapter 1, section 1, Chapter 2, Section 6 of the Constitution; in France the preamble and Article 1 of the Constitution; in Germany Articles 3.1 and 3.3 of the Basic Law; in Greece Article 5.2 of the Constitution; in Hungary Article 70/A of the Constitution; in Ireland Articles 40.1, 40.3.1, 40.3.2 and 44.3.3 of the Constitution; in Italy Article 3 of the Constitution; in Latvia Article 91 of the Constitution; in Lithuania Article 29 of the Constitution; in the Netherlands Article 1 of the Constitution; in Poland Articles 13, 32.2, 33, 35, 53, 54.1, 58.1 and 60 of the Constitution; in Portugal Articles 1, 13, 15, 58, 59, and 60 of the Constitution; in Romania Articles 4(2) and 16 of the Constitution; in Slovakia Articles 7.5, 12, 34, 35, and 46 of the Constitution; in Slovenia Articles 14, 15 and 63 of the Constitution; in Spain Articles 1.1, 9.2, 10.1, 13.1 and 14 of the Constitution; in Sweden Chapter 2, Article 15 of the Constitution; in Turkey Article 10 of the Constitution.

racial discrimination, there are several provisions that prohibit discrimination on the grounds of faith or descent.[4] The aim of the reference to descent is said to be to tackle racial discrimination. Although the Constitution of the Czech Republic does not have a general anti-discrimination clause, it has proclaimed its Charter of Fundamental Rights and Basic Freedoms, which contains such a clause, to be part of the Constitutional order.[5] In Luxembourg the Constitution only goes so far as to explicitly guarantee aliens the protection accorded to persons and their property, and thus represents only a weak safeguard against discriminatory practices.[6]

The Constitution of a State can be said to be a compilation of goals and guarantees for a certain standard of rights and freedoms that the state sets up for its citizens and the people living within its geographical borders. In most states an individual cannot derive his or her rights directly from the constitution and call upon them in a court of law or any other administrative procedure. Rather, the goals and freedoms set out in the constitution are concretised in provisions of criminal, civil and administrative law. In order to be able to apply the rights and freedoms set out in the constitution, an individual must be able to point to a provision of criminal, civil, or administrative law and rely on a court of law or an administrative unit to apply it in such a way that the individual will be compensated for the wrong that s/he has suffered. Thus it is very important that relevant provisions exist in laws other than the constitution, and that there are relevant remedies available for individuals that have been wronged in a way that is not acceptable in a democratic state. In criminal law the state draws a line between what society will and will not accept, before punishing the perpetrator of a certain act within the system of penal sanctions. The aim of civil law, on the other hand, is to repair damage that has been caused to an individual by somebody acting against the will of society.

1.2 Criminal law provisions

Criminal law provisions on discrimination that explicitly refer to the prohibition of discrimination on grounds including racial or ethnic origin are in place in the majority of the European States.[7] Those that do not possess such explicit

4 Articles 67, 70 and 71 of the Constitution.

5 Article 6 of the Constitution.

6 Article 111 of the Constitution.

7 In Austria Article IX(1) no 3 of the Introductory Provisions to the Code of Administrative Procedure (Penal Administrative Law), §283, §321and §33Z5 of the Penal Code; in Belgium the Law of 30 July 1981 on the prevention of certain acts inspired by racism or xenophobia; in Bulgaria Articles 162, 163, 164 and 172 of the Criminal Code and Articles 10(1), (2) and 439b(1) of the Criminal Procedure Code; in the Czech Republic Criminal Code (Law 140/1961) §196, §198, §198a, §219, §221, §259,

criminal law provisions are Germany, Latvia, Poland and Slovakia. Religious discrimination is explicitly included in legislation in some countries, and in those in which it is not, its inclusion is often implicit.

In Belgium,[8] Denmark[9] and Sweden,[10] specific anti-discrimination penal law prohibits racial and/or religious discrimination, and specifies penal sanctions for the discriminatory practices listed therein.

The dissemination of expression of racial prejudice is prohibited in Denmark,[11] Italy[12] and Spain.[13] The Criminal Codes of Austria,[14] the Czech Republic[15] and Spain[16] provide that where an offence is committed for racist and xenophobic reasons, these shall be considered to be aggravating factors in determining the sentence. The crime of genocide is explicitly prohibited in Estonia,[17] Portugal,[18] Slovenia[19] and Spain,[20] and the crimes of genocide and apartheid

---

§260, §261, §263; in Denmark the Act on Prohibition against Differential Treatment on Grounds of Race etc. and section 266b Criminal Code; in Estonia Articles 61 and 72 of the Criminal Code; in Finland Chapter 11, Section 9 of the Penal Code; in France Articles 121.2, 225.1, 225.2, 225.4, 226.19, 226.24, and 432.7 New Penal Code; in Greece Law 927/1979; in Hungary Articles 155, 157, 174/B and 269 of the Penal Code; in Ireland the Prohibition of Incitement to Hatred Act 1989; in Italy Article 1 of Act no 205 of 1993; in Lithuania Articles 72 of the Criminal Code and 169 of the new Criminal Code; in Luxembourg Article 454 of the Penal Code; in the Netherlands 90quater, 137(c–g) and 429quater of the Criminal Code; in Portugal Articles 239, 240, 251and 252 of the Penal Code; Romania Articles 247 and 317 of the Criminal Code; in Slovenia Articles 141, 300 and 373 of the Criminal Code; in Spain Articles 22.4, 510.1, 510.2, 511.1, 512, 515 and 607.2 of the Penal Code; in Sweden Chapter 16, Article 9 of the Criminal Code and Act on measures against ethnic discrimination in working life in 1999:130; in Turkey Articles 175, 176, 179.2 and 312.2 of the Criminal Code, in the UK the Public Order Act 1986 and Part II of the Crime and Disorder Act 1998.

8 The Law of 30 July 1981 on the prevention of certain acts inspired by racism or xenophobia, M.B., 8 August 1981, 1 April 1994 (M.B. 14 May 1994) and 7 May 1999 (M.B. 25 June 1999).

9 The Act on Prohibition against Differential Treatment on Grounds of Race etc.

10 Act on measures against ethnic discrimination in working life in 1999:130.

11 Section 266 b of the Danish Criminal Code.

12 Article 1 of Act no 205 of 1993.

13 Article 510.2 of the Penal Code.

14 Paragraph 33Z5 of the Penal Code.

15 Law No 140/1961 of the Coll., the Criminal Code, as Subsequently Amended.

16 Article 22.4 of the Penal Code (L.O 10/1995, 23 November).

17 Section 1 of Article 61of the Criminal Code.

18 Article 239 of the Penal Code.

19 Official Gazette n. 63/94 and 23/99, Article 373.

20 Article 607.2 of the Penal Code.

are condemned through criminal law in Bulgaria[21] and Hungary.[22] In Austria[23] criminal law condemns acts committed within the context of neo-nazi ideology. Similarly in Belgium,[24] there is a Law punishing the denial, reduction, justification or approval of genocide perpetrated by the German National Socialist Regime during the Second World War.

Incitement to hatred on the grounds of nationality, race or religion is condemned in Austria,[25] Belgium,[26] Bulgaria,[27] Ireland,[28] Italy,[29] Hungary,[30] Estonia,[31] the Netherlands,[32] Romania,[33] Spain,[34] Slovenia,[35] Turkey,[36] and the UK.[37]

In Portugal[38] and Spain[39] the respective penal codes prohibit racial or religious discrimination perpetrated through the establishment of, or participation in, organisations with the objective of inciting violence, hatred and discrimination. In Turkey, there are also provisions forbidding various criminal acts based on religion.[40] Insulting language is prohibited in the criminal codes of Austria[41]

---

21 Criminal Code, Section III, Liquidation of Groups of the Population (Genocide) and Apartheid, Article 416. (1)(Amended – SG, No 153/1998).

22 Article 155 (Genocide) and Article 157 (Apartheid) of Act IV of 1978 on the Criminal Code.

23 Paragraph 3 of the Constitutional Act Prohibiting the National Socialist German Workers' Party (StGBl 13/1945 and Article IX(1) par.4 of the Introductory Provisions to the Code of Administrative Procedure (EGVG).

24 M.B., 30 March 1995, err. 22 April 1995.

25 Paragraph 283 of the Penal Code.

26 Article 1(1) of the Law of 30 July 1981 on the prevention of certain acts inspired by racism or xenophobia.

27 Article 162 of the Criminal Code.

28 Prohibition of Incitement to Hatred Act 1989.

29 Article 1 of Act no 205 of 1993.

30 Article 269 of the Penal Code.

31 Article 72(1) of the Criminal Code.

32 Articles 137c and 137d of the Criminal Code.

33 Article 317 of the Penal Code.

34 Article 510.1 of the Penal Code.

35 Article 63 of the Constitution.

36 Article 312/2 of the Criminal Code (No 765), amended on the 06.02.2002 in accordance with Turkey's national programme for the European Union Association.

37 Part III of the Public Order Act 1986.

38 Article 240 of the Penal Code.

39 Article 510.1 of the Penal Code.

40 Articles 175 and 176 of the Criminal Code.

41 Paragraph 283 of the Penal Code.

and Portugal.[42] While in Austria it is prohibited generally, including on racial and religious grounds, in Portugal it is prohibited when based on grounds of religion or acts of worship.

1.3 Civil law provisions

Specific anti-discrimination civil legislation has been enacted in Ireland,[43] the Netherlands,[44] Portugal,[45] Romania[46] and the UK.[47] Civil Code provisions relevant to the fight against racial or religious discrimination are identifiable in the following European States: the Czech Republic,[48] Hungary,[49] Greece,[50] the Netherlands,[51] Slovakia[52] and Spain.[53]

Austria,[54] Bulgaria,[55] the Czech Republic,[56] Denmark,[57] Finland,[58] France,[59]

---

42 Article 252 of the Penal Code.

43 Employment Equality Act 1998 (EEA), Equal Status Act 2000 (ESA).

44 Equal Treatment Act of March 1994.

45 The Anti-Discrimination Law, Law 134/99, 28 August.

46 Ordinance 137/2000 on the prevention and punishment of all forms of discrimination.

47 Race Relations Act 1976 (as amended by the Race Relations (Amendment) Act 2000) and the Race Relations (Northern Ireland) Order 1997.

48 Law No 40/1964 of the Coll., the Civil Code, as subsequently amended; Article 2 of the Civil Code Law No 99/1963 of the Coll., the Civil Procedure Code, as subsequently amended: no express mention of racial or ethnic discrimination, but general protection.

49 Articles 76 and 84 of the Civil Code.

50 Article 57 in conjunction with Article 4 of the Civil Code.

51 Article 162, book 6 of the New Civil Code: discrimination can constitute a wrongful act under the provision on tort.

52 Section 2 of Act No 40/1964 Coll., Civil Code as subsequently amended.

53 Article 27 of the Civil Code.

54 §33 ABGB, JGS Nr. 946/1811.

55 Promulgated 1986, last amended 31 March 2001, DV 26/1.04.1986 and 27/4.04.1986, amended DV 25/ 16.03.2001, entered into force 31.03.2001; Articles 8 and 243.

56 Article 1 of Law No167/1999 of the Coll., Law on Employment; Article 1 of Law No 65/1965 of the Coll., the Labour Code, as subsequently amended. Relevant amendment was published as the Law No 155/2000. of the Coll.; Resolution No 461/2000 of the Coll.

57 Act on prohibition against differential treatment at the labour market etc. (1996).

58 Employment Contracts Act Chapter 2, Section 2.

59 Articles L122–45 and L122–35 of the Labour Code.

Germany,[60] Hungary,[61] Ireland,[62] Italy,[63] Latvia,[64] Poland,[65] Slovakia[66] and Sweden[67] all have labour law that prohibits racial or religious discrimination in all aspects regarding working relationships.

There is legislation guaranteeing the principle of equality for members of minorities in the Czech Republic,[68] Hungary,[69] Latvia[70] and Lithuania.[71] In other States minority rights may be guaranteed by means of the direct application of international conventions to which they are signatory (e.g. Bulgaria has ratified the Framework Convention for the Protection of National Minorities which is directly applicable). In Austria,[72] the Czech Republic[73] and Slovenia,[74] legislation on associations prohibits associations that aim to deny or limit the individual, political or other rights of citizens resulting in racial, religious and other types of discrimination. In addition, Austria[75] and the Czech Republic[76] also have a Law on Assembly prohibiting the assembling of persons with the aim of encouraging the denial or restriction of the rights of citizens in a discriminatory manner. The Law on Political parties in Austria,[77] the Czech Repub-

60 Works Constitution Act.

61 Article 5 of Act XXII of 1992 on the Labour Code.

62 Employment Equality Act 1998.

63 Act No 286 of 1998 regulating immigration and the legal condition of foreigners; 1970 Worker's Act (20 May).

64 Article 7 of the Labour Law, replaced by Article 1 of the Labour Code from 1 June 2002.

65 Article 11 of the Labour Code.

66 Article 3 Labour Code, Section 112 Employment Act, Article 1 of new Labour Code in force from 1 April 2002.

67 Act on measures against ethnic discrimination in working life in 1999:130.

68 Law No 273/2001 of the Coll., Law on the Rights of Members of National Minorities and on Amendments to Certain Laws; Article 3.

69 Articles 3 and 4 of the Minorities Act.

70 Law on the unrestricted development and right to cultural autonomy of Latvia's nationalities and ethnic groups.

71 Law on Ethnic Minorities of the Republic of Lithuania.

72 §6(1) Associations Act.

73 Law No 84/1990 of the Coll., the Law on the Right to Association, as Subsequently Amended; Article 8.

74 The Associations Act, Official Gazette RS, No 60/95 and 49/98.

75 §§ 13 (1) and 18 Law on Assemblies.

76 Law No 84/1990 of the Coll., the Law on the Right to Assembly, as Subsequently Amended; Article 10.

77 § 1 Law on Political Parties

lic,[78] Lithuania,[79] Portugal[80] and Slovenia[81] prohibits neo-nazi and other parties propagating inequality and discrimination. In Turkey, legislation regulating political parties prohibits political parties that have purposes that go against the principle of equality of all individuals without any discrimination before the law, irrespective of language, race, colour, sex, political opinion, philosophical belief, religion, denomination, or similar consideration.[82]

Legislation on the protection of personal data prohibits the collection and processing of data that refers to an individual's race and religion without that person's consent in the Czech Republic,[83] Denmark,[84] Greece,[85] Italy,[86] Latvia,[87] Poland,[88] Portugal,[89] Slovakia[90] and Sweden.[91] In France, the Penal Code contains such a prohibition.[92] Similarly, Bulgaria has the Statistics Act[93] and the Census Act[94] stipulating that statistical and census data referring to an individual's race or religion shall be collected only with the consent of the individual.[95]

---

78 Law No 424/1991 of the Coll., the Law on Association in Political Parties and Political Movements, as Subsequently Amended; Article 4.

79 The law on Political parties and Political organisations.

80 Law 62/78, 6 October.

81 The Political Parties Act, Official Gazette RS, No 62/94.

82 Article 83 of the Act on Political Parties (No 2820).

83 Law 101/2000 of the Coll., the Law on the Protection of Personal Data and on Amendment to Certain Laws, as Subsequently Amended; Articles 4 and 9.

84 Article 7, Act on the treatment of information concerning individuals.

85 Article 2b Law 2472 on the protection of personal data, JO 50/A, 10 April 1997.

86 Data protection Act (No 675), 25 December 1996.

87 Personal Data Protection Law.

88 Article 27.1, Act on protection of Personal Data.

89 Law 67/98, 26 October, Law on the protection of personal data.

90 Act No 52/1998 Coll. on the Protection of Personal Data in Informative Systems.

91 Personal Data Act (SFS 1998: 204).

92 Article 226–19.

93 Promulgated in 1999, last amended April 2001.

94 Promulgated 2000.

95 All countries covered by this analysis are signatories of the 1981 Council of Europe Convention for the Protection of Individuals with regard to Automatic Processing of Personal Data (ratified by all but Bulgaria and Turkey), which lays down in Article 6 that 'personal data revealing racial origin, political opinions or religious or other beliefs, as well as personal data concerning health or sexual life, may not be processed automatically unless domestic law provides appropriate safeguards'. Additionally, EU Member States are bound by Directive 95/46/EC of the European Parliament and of the Council of 24 October 1995 on the protection of individuals with regard to the processing of personal data and on the free movement of such data.

Legislation guaranteeing equality in education exists in Bulgaria,[96] Hungary,[97] Latvia,[98] Lithuania,[99] Poland,[100] Spain[101] and Turkey.[102] Legislation on court procedure in Bulgaria,[103] the Czech Republic,[104] Estonia[105] and Latvia[106] guarantees that the courts shall implement the law equally with respect to all.

Legislation on radio and television broadcasting prohibits discriminatory messages in the media in Bulgaria,[107] the Czech Republic,[108] Hungary,[109] Poland,[110] Slovenia[111] and Turkey.[112] Regulation of advertising in Bulgaria (Rules of Commerce),[113] the Czech Republic[114] and Portugal[115] prohibits discriminatory advertising.

---

96 Article 4 in both the National Education Act (Promulgated 1991, last amended 1999, DV 86/18.10.1991, DV 68/30.07.1999) and the Higher Education Act (Promulgated 1995, last amended 2001, DV 112/27.12.1995, amended DV 22/9.03.2001).

97 Paragraph 7 of Article 4 of Act LXXIX of 1993 on Public Education.

98 Article 3 of the Education Law.

99 Law on Education, new version of 2 July 1998, Official Publication, 1998, No 67–1940.

100 Article 13, Act on the System of Education.

101 Articles 1.1 and 2.3, Law 1/1990 on the Education System.

102 The National Education Fundamental Act (No 1739).

103 Judiciary Act, Promulgated 1994, last amended 2001, DV 59/22.07.1994; amended DV 25/16.03.2001, entered into force 31.03.2001.

104 Law No 99/1963 of the Coll., the Civil Procedure Code, as Subsequently Amended.

105 Article 6 of the Code of Civil Procedure.

106 Article 4 (2) of the Judicial Powers law.

107 Articles 6, 10, 17 and 76 in the Radio and TV Act (Promulgated 1998, last amended 2000, DV 138/24.11.1998; amended DV 79/29.09.2000).

108 Law No 468/1991 of the Coll., the Law on Radio and Television Broadcasting, as subsequently amended; Article 5.

109 Paragraph (2) of Article 3 of Act 1 of 1996 on Radio and Television Broadcasting.

110 Article 21, Act on Radio and TV Broadcasting.

111 The Media Act Official Gazette RS No 35/2001.

112 Article 4 of the Act on the foundation and broadcasting of radios and televisions (No 3984).

113 Article 29 of the Consumer Protection and Rules of Commerce Act (Promulgated 1999, DV 30/2.04.1999, entered into force 3.07.1999).

114 Law No 40/1995 of the Coll., the Law on Regulation of Advertisement and on the Amendment to the Law on Radio and Television Broadcasting, as Subsequently Amended; Article 2.

115 Advertising Code (Legislative Decree 275/98, 9 September).

The Acts on the Protection of Children in Bulgaria[116] and Hungary[117] guarantee equality for children. The Health Care Acts in Bulgaria[118] and Hungary[119] guarantee equality in access to health care services.

The Laws on Elections in Bulgaria,[120] Lithuania[121] and Poland[122] guarantee equal treatment in presidential and parliamentary elections. The Laws on Religious Freedoms in Bulgaria,[123] Lithuania,[124] Portugal[125] and Spain[126] provide for equality among different religious groups. The Social Assistance Laws in Bulgaria[127] and Lithuania[128] guarantee equal access to social assistance for everyone.

In Bulgaria,[129] Denmark,[130] Greece,[131] Italy,[132] Lithuania[133] and Spain,[134] the laws on the legal status of aliens guarantee their equality with nationals. In Bul-

---

116 Article 10 of the Protection of the Child Act (Promulgated 2000, DV 48/ 13.06.2000).

117 Article 3 Par (2) of Act No XXXI of 1997 on the Protection of the Child.

118 Article 28 of the National Health Act (Promulgated 1973, last amended 2000, DV 88/6.11.1973, entered into force 1.01.1974, amended DV 10/4.02.2000, DV 36/ 2.05.2000).

119 Article 7 of Act CLIV of 1997 on Health Care.

120 Article 3 of the Electing a Great National Assembly Act, Promulgated 1990, last amended 2001. e, DV 28/6.04.1990, entered into force 6.04.1990, amended DV 24/ 13.03.2001.

121 Article 3 of the Law on Presidential Elections, Official Publication, 1993, No 2–29; Law on Elections to the Seimas, New version of 18 July 2000, Official Publication, 2000, No 59–1760, Law on Elections to the Municipal Councils, New version of 19 October 1999, Official Publication, 1999, No 93–2710.

122 Art. 134.1 Act on Elections.

123 Article 4 of the Denominations Act, Promulgated 1949, last amended 1998, DV 48/ 1.03.1949 ã., Decision 5/92 of the Constitutional Court of Republic of Bulgaria – DV 49/16.06.1992; amended DV 11/ 29.01.1998.

124 The law on Religious Communities and Associations.

125 Law 16/2001, 22 June.

126 Articles 1 and 2, Organic law 7/1980, 5 July, on religious freedom.

127 Article 3 of the Social Assistance Act, Promulgated 1998. DV 56/19.05.1998.

128 Law on the fundamentals of the State Social Care System.

129 The Foreigners in the Republic of Bulgaria Act, Promulgated 1998, last amended 2001, DV 153/23.12.1998, amended DV 42/27.04.2001, entered into force 27.04.2001.

130 Act on prohibition against different treatment on grounds of race etc.

131 Law 927/1979 on the prevention of activities related to racial or religious discrimination.

132 Act No 286 of 1998 regulating immigration and the legal condition of foreigners.

133 Law on the legal status of Aliens in the Republic of Lithuania.

134 Organic Law 8/2000, 22 December, on the rights and freedom of aliens in Spain and their social integration.

garia,[135] Denmark[136] and Lithuania[137] there are also laws regarding the status of refugees that guarantee the principle of anti-discrimination for refugees.

1.4 Administrative law provisions

Administrative law provisions guaranteeing the principle of equal treatment exist in Austria,[138] Belgium,[139] Bulgaria,[140] the Czech Republic,[141] Denmark (as an unwritten general principle), and Hungary.[142]

In Austria there are also penal sanctions for discriminating against persons requiring services intended for general public use.[143] In the Netherlands equal treatment constitutes a General Principle of Proper Administration.

1.5 International law

All European States have ratified the UN International Convention on the Elimination of All Forms of Racial Discrimination and all of the other major United Nations human rights treaties that guarantee equal treatment and prohibit discrimination.[144]

As members of the Council of Europe, all EU Member States and candidate countries have ratified the European Convention on Human Rights and Fundamental Freedoms. In 2000, the Council of Europe adopted Protocol No12 to the European Convention on Human Rights prohibiting all forms of discrimina-

---

135 Refugee Act, Promulgated 1999, last amended 1999, DV 53/11.06.1999, entered into force 1.08.1999, amended DV 97/9.11.1999.

136 Integration Act.

137 The law on Refugee Status in the Republic of Lithuania.

138 Article IX (1) EGVG, BGBL. Nr. 50/1991.

139 Article 16 of the royal decree of 2 October 1937 introducing the Public Servants Statute, amended by Article 5, A of the royal decree of 26 September 1994, entered into force on 1 October 1994.

140 The Civil Servant Act, Promulgated 1999, last amended 2000. DV 67/27.07.1999, entered into force 28.08.1999, amended DV 25/16.03.2001, entered into force 1.09.2000.

141 Law No 71/1967 of the Coll., the Code on the Administrative Procedure (Administrative Code), as Subsequently Amended; Article 4.

142 Article 3 of Act LXXV of 1996 on the Supervision of Labour Affairs.

143 Article IX (1) No 3 EGVG, BGBL. Nr. 50/1991.

144 The relevant UN Treaties: Convention on the Elimination of All Forms of Racial Discrimination (CERD of 21 December 1965), Covenant on Civil and Political Rights (CCPR of 16 December 1966), Covenant on Economic, Social and Cultural Rights (CESCR of 16 December 1966), and the Convention on the Elimination of All Forms of Discrimination against Women (CEDAW of 18 December 1979).

tion. The Convention's present provision on discrimination is limited in scope as it prohibits discrimination only where rights recognised by the Convention are affected. The new Protocol removes that restriction and provides that no one can be discriminated against by any public authority on any ground. Protocol No12 has been signed by 28 of the Council's 43 Member States and ratified by four (Croatia, Cyprus, Georgia and San Marino). It will come into force when ten States have ratified it. Ten EU Member States and most candidate countries have signed it, indicating the intention of these countries to ratify the Protocol. Bulgaria, Denmark, France, Lithuania, Poland, Spain, Sweden and the United Kingdom have not yet signed the Protocol.

The following States have recognised the competence to receive and process individual communications of the Committee on the Elimination of Racial Discrimination: Belgium, Bulgaria, the Czech Republic, Denmark, Finland, France, Germany, Ireland, Italy, Hungary, Luxembourg, the Netherlands, Poland, Portugal, Slovakia, Spain and Sweden.

However, the practical implications of adherence to international human rights standards for the national legal framework have thus far been somewhat limited. As the transposition of obligations under international law into national law depends on the model selected to this end under national constitutional law, the application of the guarantees on equal treatment and prohibition of discrimination in the UN treaties and the European Convention differs from one State to the next.

1.6 Summary

It can be concluded that in all European States at least the foundations of a legal framework that guarantees the principle of non-discrimination on the grounds of race, ethnic origin, religion and belief are in place. The nature of the framework differs widely among the European States. In some, the emphasis is on criminal law, in others there is a range of applicable civil and administrative provisions, and in a small number of countries specific equal treatment and non-discrimination legislation has been enacted. Clearly, the nature of the legislation has implications for the material scope of protection against discrimination as well as the legal remedies that are available to combat discrimination.

The inconsistent manner in which basic guarantees are provided across Europe makes it difficult to compare and contrast these. While there are numerous situations to which anti-discrimination provisions are applicable, their adequacy in combating racial and/or religious discrimination varies greatly from country to country and often they do not conform to the standards set by the EC Racial Equality Directive.

2. Implementation

Where anti-discrimination legislation is in place, what is the gap between the formal legislation and its actual implementation? Has research been done at national level that explains this gap?

It is a well-known fact that fundamental rights, although theoretically provided for in legislation, can be hard to obtain for the individual in practice, and indeed there appear to be shortcomings in the implementation of anti-discrimination law in all European States covered by this study. The following points can be made with regard to the implementation of anti-discrimination legislation in European States.

2.1 Austria

Austria's elaborate penal law system was the result of the country's Second World War legacy. It was designed in 1947 to eradicate national-socialist ideology, propaganda and other acts of hatred. When during the 1990s the relatively high minimum sentences that had been in place were considerably reduced, the efficacy of the system was raised.

The criminal law and penal administrative provisions that go beyond those providing protection against neo-national-socialist activities were enacted in order to implement the International Convention on the Elimination of all forms of Racial Discrimination. These, however, have suffered from what is assumed to be a lack of effective enforcement and/or a lack of sufficient knowledge about them on the part of victims and some members of the judiciary alike.

According to a report from 1996,[145] 'the legal restrictions governing immigrants in relation to...employment and works councils are so severe that it may be argued that legislation against "informal" discrimination would be of little value until the system of legal discrimination had been dismantled'. The situation has changed little since then. This assessment is also true with regard to other key areas of social integration, such as housing and social security.

2.2 Belgium

The wording of the Law of 30 July 1981 on the prevention of certain acts inspired by racism or xenophobia ensures that its scope is wide, and thus has the potential to enable a great number of concrete manifestations of racism and xenophobia to be combated. However, the implementation and effectiveness of

145 John Wrench, European Foundation of the improvement of Living and Working Conditions in 16 European Countries, p.72.

this legislation is in reality deficient in several respects. Evidence of this is to be found notably in the reports on Belgium by the European Commission Against Racism and Intolerance[146] and the International Committee on the Elimination of Racial Discrimination.[147]

In its analysis of the Law of 30 July 1981,[148] the Centre for Equal Opportunities and Opposition to Racism demonstrated three main problems with the application of the law: the initial filtering of complaints from victims by the police, the involvement of the public prosecutor's office and the large number of complaints that end in a withdrawal of proceedings, as well as the problem of the burden of proof.[149] While the first two problems require a change in mentality and a greater will on the part of the judiciary, the third could clearly form the subject of a legislative amendment.

It is hoped that protection against discrimination will improve considerably if the proposed general civil law Act to combat discrimination is adopted.

2.3 *Bulgaria*

The existing anti-discrimination legislation in Bulgaria is not effectively enforced. Rarely are civil actions brought alleging discrimination, and no cases are won on such allegations. Judges, as well as other authorities, are largely unaware of the principle of equal treatment and where allegations of discrimination are brought before them they tend to ignore these, thereby infringing the victim's right of access to court. Courts tend to fail to discuss allegations of discrimination, or simply to rule that there is no discrimination in the case, often in contradiction to adduced evidence, without giving reasons for such a finding. Moreover, the victims of racial discrimination do not have adequate access to the courts since, in the vast majority of cases, they do not have sufficient means to engage in proceedings.

Criminal remedies are also inadequately employed. Prosecutors and courts tend to refuse to take the racist nature of crimes into account, bringing charges under common crimes provisions instead, which contain no sentencing enhancements for racist motives, thus leaving criminal racial discrimination totally without remedy. The judiciary, as well as other authorities, are on record as having

146 ECRI, Second Report on Belgium, 18 June 1999, CRI (2000) 2.

147 CERD, Concluding Observations of the Committee on the Elimination of Racial Discrimination: Belgium. 23/04/97, CERD/C/304/Add.26.

148 See the Centre for Equal Opportunities and Opposition to Racism website: http://www.antiracisme.be.

149 For more on the problems of applying the Law of 30 July 1981, see O. De Schutter, 'Avis concernant certaines propositions visant à améliorer la loi du 30 juillet 1981 tendant à réprimer certains actes inspirés par le racisme ou la xénophobie', Rapport annuel 1997 C.E.C.L.R., Brussels, 1997, p.20.

claimed that crimes against Roma, for instance, are not racially motivated since Roma do not belong to a separate race. Indeed, domestic officials put forth the assertion that there are no separate races to be encountered in Bulgaria.[150] Administrative remedies are not effective in combating discrimination either. No administrative proceedings are instituted for violations of provisions prohibiting discrimination and no sanctions have ever been imposed for violations of the principle of equal treatment.

2.4 Czech Republic

While the Constitutional order and legal system of the Czech Republic do embody the principle of equal treatment between persons irrespective of racial or ethnic origin, comprehensive legislation ensuring equality does not yet exist. Similarly, general difficulties with legal aid and access to justice impede the protection of equal rights.

2.5 Denmark

In Denmark, specific legislative or administrative protection against racial, ethnic and religious discrimination is applicable in most circumstances. However, the existing mechanisms and procedures designed to deal with complaints of racial and religious discrimination are not working appropriately. The first problem is thought to be that Denmark has implemented the international human rights standards on non-discrimination almost exclusively by criminal law. This makes it crucial that the victim of discrimination has confidence in the police who receive the complaint. Psychological barriers may prevent migrants and ethnic or other minorities from approaching the police with complaints and the police and law enforcement agencies may be reluctant to investigate the complaints they receive. Civil court proceedings are expensive and the possibilities of free legal aid are limited, although recently it was decided to give legal aid to individuals who bring a complaint before international human rights committees.[151]

2.6 Estonia

Estonian courts have only rarely heard cases involving inter-ethnic offences regulated by the Criminal Code, and too often they, as well as the State prosecutors, deny that certain offences qualify as ethnically or racially motivated. Because Estonian legislation does provide detailed definitions of actions that

---

150 In a number of informal communications.

151 Act No 940 (1999).

could violate the rights and dignity of people on the basis of ethnic or racial origin, it is clear there is a lack of effective remedies in such cases. While Estonian law foresees the possibility of legal action for a victim using ordinary civil and criminal procedures, a high standard of proof must be overcome in both procedures. Furthermore, there is a lack of awareness among the public regarding their rights in this area. National and local authorities deny the existence of any problems in the field of discrimination in Estonia and pay no attention to any research in this regard.[152]

2.7 *Finland*

A central problem in Finland appears to be the widespread phenomenon of non-reporting of incidents of discrimination or harassment to the police. There is a clear gap in the number of crimes motivated by racism that are reported to the police and the occurrence of violence or harassment on racist grounds reported in studies of crime victims. Another major problem experienced by immigrants and members of ethnic minorities is a widespread sense that vocational training and competence acquired abroad is not accepted or valued in the Finnish labour market. It is a form of indirect discrimination, which is difficult to prove and remedy, but one that appears to be a major obstacle to entry into the labour market for immigrants.

2.8 *France*

The provisions of the French Penal Code which make discrimination illegal are relatively new. Moreover, they have formed the subject of numerous amendments in terms of legislation, a fact attributable to the nature of the subject being socially and politically highly sensitive.

In practice, it should be noted that the application of anti-discrimination legislation remains very modest. The difficulty of providing proof of discriminatory conduct is very often cited to explain the weakness of the legislation. However, it should also be pointed out that combating discrimination is not the prerogative of the criminal judge. In fact, many types of discriminatory conduct do not fall within the scope of any penal text and, in any case, the criminal sanction does not exclude the intervention of the civil or administrative judge who may, if need be, declare the discriminatory act null and void and award compensation to the victim (basing the decision, depending on the case, on the provisions of the Labour Code or the Administrative Code). Thus, while criminal judgements are

152 See e.g. information Estonian Foreign Minister on International Documents to Combat Racism and Intolerance at http://racoon.riga.lv/minelres/archive//05252001–09:09:48–18823.html (visited 31 July 2001).

rare, there is plenty of jurisprudence from the Social Chamber of the Court of Cassation in this area relating to discrimination in the field of employment.

2.9 Germany

The anti-discrimination clauses of the German Basic Law form the cornerstone of Germany's legal framework, most notably Articles 3.1 and 3.3 buttressed by the provisions of the criminal code which penalise *inter alia* the incitement to racial hatred and any kind of libel or slander. According to German Constitutional doctrine, Articles 3.1 and 3.3 have limited direct horizontal effect.

During recent years, with the increase in racist attacks on ethnic grounds, there have been many criminal cases reported in which racism played a decisive role in motivating the perpetrator of these crimes. Nevertheless, there is little case law in civil or administrative law concerning ethnic discrimination.

2.10 Greece

The application of Law 927/1979 (amended by Article 24 of Law 1419/1984) on the prevention of acts or activities related to racial or religious discrimination[153] has proven to be insufficient to ensure the prevention of acts and activities relating to racial or religious discrimination, because the prosecution of offences covered by this law can only take place if a complaint is lodged by the injured party. In view of the socio-economic vulnerability suffered by the majority of potential victims of racial discrimination and the absence of legal aid, their right of recourse to legal action is in fact no more than a virtual right. The prevention of all forms of racial discrimination is undermined by the fact that human rights organisations, immigrants' rights organisations and non-governmental organisations involved in combating racism and xenophobia cannot institute or support legal actions in this regard. Thus it is hardly surprising that, to date, very few complaints have been lodged based on this law.[154]

---

153 This refers to Law 927/1979 'On the prevention of acts or activities related to racial discrimination' (JO 139/A of 28 June 1979) and Law 1419/1984 'Amendments to the provisions of the Penal Code, the Code of Criminal Procedure and other provisions' (JO 28/A, 14 March 1984) of which Article 24 stipulates that the provisions of Law 927/1979 shall also be applicable in cases of religious discrimination and specifies that the concept of racial discrimination covers the race as well as the ethnic origin of the persons concerned. The fight against racial discrimination was recently reinforced by the ratification of the International Covenant on Civil and Political Rights on 16 December 1996 (ratified by Law 2462/1997).

154 In fact, two complaints were lodged in 1986 and 1993, by the Central Jewish Council against the journal Stochos.

2.11 Hungary

Hungary claims to possess one of the most elaborate legal and institutional frameworks the protection of minorities. However, in spite of the relatively comprehensive Hungarian framework for minority rights protection and the patchwork of anti-discrimination laws, the annual reports by the Minorities Ombudsman have repeatedly indicated that Roma experience widespread discrimination that cannot be addressed either by the minority self-government system or the existing legal and institutional framework. These findings are supported by the everyday experience of various NGOs engaged in human rights activities.[155]

2.12 Ireland

As much of the relevant legislation was adopted recently, it will be some time yet before there is firm evidence as to how the provisions will work out in practice and their judicial interpretation. Despite progress on the legislative front, there have been no developments to amend the Constitution of Ireland 1937 in order to update its equality and anti-discrimination provisions. The recent Report of the Constitution Review Group made a number of important recommendations for amendments to relevant Articles of the Irish Constitution. To date, however, no action has been taken to implement those recommendations.

2.13 Italy

As the principal legislation concerning discrimination based on racial or ethnic origin was introduced in 1998 in the context of a major statute regulating the whole of immigration law, the period in which the Act has been in force is too short to establish its actual impact. Empirical research to establish the diffusion of discriminatory practices has been done in relation to very narrow fields and not on the basis of the present legislation.

In many areas of Italy, there is a growth in xenophobic attitudes, partly with the encouragement of right-wing political groups. The press have reported discriminatory acts (in the form of local regulations) by public administrators linked to political parties. Current legislation has no significant deterrent effect against such acts, since they are mostly manifestations of the political climate.

155 Regular publications documenting rights abuses in Hungary include: the yearly White Booklet, published by the Legal Defence Bureau for National and Ethnic Minorities (NEKI); Chronicle of Everyday Events, published by the Roma Press Centre; Fundamentum, the monthly INDOK publication; the European Roma Rights Center's quarterly Roma Rights. Discrimination cases are also monitored by the Hungarian Helsinki Committee and the Roma Civil Rights Foundation (RPA).

Although the administrator tends to be aware of the illegality (the acts having been declared void by governmental supervising authorities), he is often interested in having his decision reported in the press to re-affirm his anti-immigration policy to the public and future voters.

2.14 Latvia

Despite the general equality clause in the Constitution and non-discrimination clauses in various other laws, surveys indicate the existence of a significant gap between the legislation and its implementation. There is a near total lack of any discrimination-related case law. While some research has been done analysing the Latvian legislation from the gender perspective[156] and also the factual situation in this field,[157] no research has been done analysing the situation in the sphere of discrimination based on racial and ethnic origin.

2.15 Lithuania

The actual implementation of the principle of equal treatment between persons irrespective of racial or ethnic origin in Lithuania is said to come close to existing legislative provisions, although there is room for improvement. Access to justice remains a problem, especially for vulnerable groups. Contributing factors are the low level of public trust in the law and legal institutions as effective tools in fighting discrimination, as well as an underdeveloped mechanism of providing legal aid and legal information to vulnerable groups. Improving the professional qualification of judges and other lawyers is also a continuous challenge.

2.16 Luxembourg

The Law of 9 August 1980, passed to enforce the New York Convention on the Elimination of all forms of Racial Discrimination of 1966 and amended by the Law of 27 July 1993 and by the Law of 19 July 1997, introduced Article 454 and subsequent articles into the Penal Code, creating as specific offences and applying penal sanctions to various acts of discrimination. To date, only one decision founding on Article 454 and subsequent articles of the Penal Code (specifically on the basis of Article 457-1) has been delivered.

Fear or lack of information on the part of the victims are possible reasons for this jurisprudential deficiency. Another reason lies in the wording of the articles themselves.

---

156 Dace Kavasa, Analysis of Latvian Legislation in Gender Perspective, unpublished.

157 Framework Document on the Implementation of Gender Equality, Ministry of Welfare of the Republic of Latvia, 2000, unpublished.

2.17 The Netherlands

In the Netherlands, general civil law has been proven to provide effective remedies against discrimination. Particular difficulties in implementing the legislation relate primarily to proving indirect discrimination. Other difficulties in using the legal system are the costs of litigation and the length of procedures. Although there is a system of legal aid, especially middle and lower income groups have difficulties in meeting the costs of litigation and paying a lawyer. Also, the length of procedures is such that victims of discrimination are compensated for damages only a considerable time after the discriminatory event (sometimes up to several years), which may discourage victims from taking legal action. Victims of racial discrimination and anti- discrimination bureaux still complain that the criminal law is insufficiently used to combat racial discrimination. At the same time anti-discrimination bureaux do admit that the performance has improved, and that criminal law is not necessarily the best remedy against discrimination.

2.18 Poland

Notwithstanding the absence of specific anti-discrimination legislation in Poland, the existing substantive law and its implementation can be assessed favourably. For example, the law provides preferential treatment for the minorities in some areas. The major exception is the socially disadvantageous situation of the Roma community.

There are few activities in the area of countering gender discrimination in Poland. The legislation is not satisfactory and in addition, the implementation of the legislation also requires improvement. The existing instances of such discrimination appear to be the most important barrier to the ratification of Protocol No12.

2.19 Portugal

There is no relevant jurisprudence on discrimination and a suggested reason for this is that discrimination arises mainly in the context of working and living conditions and not explicitly discriminatory activities. Where there are problems, attempts are being made to resolve them administratively or by imposing fines on the offenders. Criticism may also be levelled at the slow and bureaucratic operation of the alien reception services.

2.20 Romania

The Ordinance No 137 of 31 August 2000 on the prevention and punishment of all forms of discrimination provides for the possibility to seek remedies in cases of discrimination. As yet only two cases have been registered by the courts, both regarding discriminatory behaviour against Roma. They are still pending, therefore it is too soon to make a prediction regarding their evolution and solution. However, it is stressed that neither Romanian lawyers nor NGOs nor judges currently have the necessary expertise and experience in handling discrimination cases.

2.21 Slovakia

In Slovakia relevant anti-discrimination provisions are scattered across the whole legal domain. They provide general protection in very general and declaratory language against discriminatory practices at various levels. However, in many cases it is very hard to obtain an effective remedy, even where discrimination has been proven. The Slovak legal system relies mostly on the State authorities responsible for the implementation of laws to check legal and physical entities, rather then on the initiative of victims. Apart from reporting discriminatory practices to the authorities, the victims very often do not have appropriate access to the court, either due to the fact that there is no such access or, in searching for a remedy, the locus standi is complicated.

2.22 Slovenia

There is a notable gap between the declared anti-discrimination principles and the regulation of the status of minorities living in Slovenia in practice. This arises from the fact that the assured status of collective rights is granted only to certain minority groups. One of the reasons for such a small number of reported cases in the field of ethnic or racial discrimination is the fact that the racial element of some cases is ignored. According to the available data, there have not been any relevant court cases reported on the issue of the violation of gender equality as a criminal offence to date.

2.23 Spain

There is little jurisprudence in Spain pertaining to racial and religious discrimination. The reason behind this is partly the fact that certain offences, whilst committed for racist reasons, are dealt with judicially on the basis of the injury caused so that the racist motive is not recorded. There are concerns that preliminary investigations are not always rigorous enough, and that improvements could be made in researching evidence and dealing with witnesses.

There is a need for definite instructions and appropriate training to be given to the responsible authorities. The problem of lack of human and financial resources in the Spanish legal system also plays a role. More awareness of the existing legal tools and the potential for their application is required. Some interesting jurisprudence on equality between men and women has been developed by the Constitutional Court.

2.24 *Sweden*

The gap between the formal legislation and its implementation is substantial in Sweden. The two areas of law in which anti-discrimination legislation relating to ethnicity and religion is found are labour law and criminal law. The effectiveness of the laws in both of these fields can be questioned.

The law on measures against discrimination in the workplace on the grounds of, among others, race, ethnic origin and religious faith, came into effect in 1999. There is some indication that the new law is effective in that there is an increasing number of settlements in relation to complaints concerning workplace discrimination. Many victims of discrimination, while aware of the laws, are also aware that the laws have limits.

Thus far, the government, as well as the research community, has rejected the use of situation testing, which seems to be one of the few effective ways to expose the implementation gap. Similar gaps seem to exist in relation to the anti-discrimination laws counteracting discrimination in the workplace on the basis of gender, disability and sexual orientation.

2.25 *Turkey*

There are anti-discrimination provisions in the Constitution of Turkey and a number of codes prohibit discrimination on a number of grounds. The Constitutional provision is regarded by the courts as a general principle of law and is utilised in various contexts, ranging from labour law to administrative disputes. However, in neither civil law nor administrative law is there an independent prohibition of discrimination on the grounds of ethnic origin or race. The relevant article of the Criminal Code is unfortunately utilised only to penalise expressions criticising state policies in relation to ethnic and religious groups.

One of the basic problems in Turkey concerning discrimination on the grounds of ethnic origin or race is that, despite the guarantee of the principle of equality, the existing provisions are inadequate to ensure the application of the principle of anti-discrimination. In addition, sufficient awareness does not exist among those who are in the position to enforce the principle of anti-discrimination on the basis of ethnic origin and race, such as State officials, judges, and lawyers. This lack of awareness is mainly caused by the State policy of non-recognition of the presence of discrimination in practice and the denial of the inadequacy of current legislation.

2.26 United Kingdom

The main legislation in the United Kingdom relies on the civil law to provide protection against racial discrimination. The Race Relations Act 1976 has been reasonably effectively implemented, largely due to the fact that the Act established the Commission for Racial Equality (CRE), which is a non-departmental public body, whose powers and duties are prescribed in the 1976 Act and whose role is to ensure the correct implementation of the Act.

The main area in which the law has been used to challenge unlawful discrimination is employment. All employment and employment related discrimination cases are heard in an employment tribunal, and, over the years, as the number of discrimination cases has increased, some tribunal members in areas with large ethnic minority populations have developed wide knowledge and understanding of racial discrimination issues. In the employment tribunals, fewer than ten per cent of all racial discrimination cases are successful, although generally some 35–40 per cent are settled on terms that give the complainant a sum (often substantial) of money, but without a finding of discrimination.

The direct connection between discrimination on grounds of religion or belief and the long political conflict in Northern Ireland has yielded both stronger anti-discrimination legislation and a more active, positive, involvement by government.

3. Definition of 'Direct' and 'Indirect' Discrimination

Is there a definition of direct and indirect discrimination in your national legal system? Is there a need to introduce definitions of direct and indirect discrimination, as defined in Articles 2.2(a) and (b) of the Directive, into national legislation?

In answer to the question of whether the concepts of direct and indirect discrimination based on racial or ethnic origin and religion exist in the various national legal systems, several situations can be identified:

1. Direct discrimination is covered by a definition, but there is no distinction between direct and indirect discrimination, and no definition of indirect discrimination. This is the case in Luxembourg[158] (though in relation to gender, indirect discrimination is recognised within work relationships)[159] and Romania.[160]

---

158 Article 454 of the Penal Code.

159 In the Law on Equal Treatment between men and women as regards access to employment, vocational training and promotion and working conditions, as amended on 8 December 1981.

160 Article 1 of the Ordinance 137.

2. A distinction is made, but not defined. Indirect discrimination is not defined and it is not specified that there can be objective justification for indirect discrimination where there is a legitimate aim that is pursued with appropriate and necessary means. This is the case in Italy[161] and Portugal.[162] In the Austrian legal system the only reference to the concept of direct and indirect discrimination is in Article 6(2) of the Treaty of Vienna of 1955 (which has constitutional status) which prohibits direct and indirect discrimination of citizens in all areas of law based on their race, sex, language or religion. No definitions are given.
3. A distinction is made and both concepts are defined. This applies to Bulgaria (the ICERD definitions are incorporated into national law; indirect discrimination is defined in the Labour Code), Denmark (indirect discrimination is covered under some specific legislation,[163] the concept of discrimination should be interpreted in accordance with the legislation on gender equality, which defines both concepts), France (distinction is not made in the legislation, but in the case law, rendering an explicit definition under law desirable), Finland[164] (though indirect discrimination requires further specification), Germany (distinction is made in case law in relation to gender, but in principle could be applied in cases of racial and religious discrimination, distinction in terms of justification of direct or indirect discrimination not yet determined), Ireland[165] (though the justification test is not objective), the Netherlands[166] (under criminal law indirect discrimination cannot be objectively justified, but under civil law provisions there is an objective justification test in line with the Directive as outlined below), Spain[167] (definitions are given for what is to be seen as 'discrimination' as a whole and for indirect discrimination of workers), Sweden[168] (indirect discrimination is covered under employment legislation but not criminal law), and the United Kingdom[169] (though the definition of indirect discrimination is not as wide as that in the Directive). In

161 Article 43 of the Act no 286 of 1998 regulating immigration and the legal condition of foreigners.

162 Article 3 of Law 134/1999.

163 Section 1 (1) of the Act on Prohibition against Differential Treatment in the Labour Market.

164 Chapter II Section 6 of the Constitution combined with Government Bill (HE 1/1998) for the Constitution.

165 Sections 6 (1), 22 (1) and 31 (1 and 2) of the EEA 1998; section 3 (1 and 2) ESA 2000.

166 Article 90quater of the Criminal Code, Article 1 of the Equal Treatment Act.

167 Article 23.1 of the Organic Law on the rights and freedoms of aliens in Spain.

168 Article 8.1. of the Act on measures against ethnic discrimination in working life.

169 Section 1 (1)(a) and (b) read with Section 3(4) of the 1976 Act and Articles 3(1)(a) and (b) and Article 3(3) of the 1997 Order.

Belgium it is expected that both direct and indirect discrimination will soon be defined in legislation in accordance with the EC Directive.[170]
4. Indirect discrimination is covered by a definition, but no definition of direct discrimination or distinction between the two concepts exists. This is the case in Hungary.[171]
5. A notion of the concepts can be found in domestic law, but without any distinction between them and no definitions. This seems to be the situation in Estonian, Latvian, Lithuanian, Polish, Slovakian and Slovenian law.
6. No distinction is made and none of the concepts are defined. This applies to the Czech Republic, Greece, and Turkey.

A serious problem in several States, including Bulgaria, is that the courts and other authorities are not sufficiently familiar with international instruments and the case law of ECHR institutions, and are not accustomed to applying international law, including definitions. This must be addressed to ensure that international norms are applied at the domestic level.

A good example of the provision in law for the 'objective justification' of indirect discrimination, as is foreseen in Article 2b) of the Directive, is the Netherlands. Here, a distinction between criminal and civil law must be made. As under the Directive, under Dutch criminal law, indirect *discrimination* constitutes discrimination and is therefore forbidden altogether. When the effect of an apparently neutral provision, criterion or practice is discriminatory, the provision, criterion or practice cannot be objectively justified.

Under the Dutch Equal Treatment Act (civil law) indirect *distinction* can be objectively justified. According to Article 2.1 of the Equal Treatment Act, 'the prohibition of discrimination shall not apply to indirect distinction which is objectively justified'. If the conclusion under the Equal Treatment Act is 'there is indirect distinction', the objective justification test of Article 2.1 needs to be applied.

To this end, the Commission on Equal Treatment, established to implement the Act, uses the following criteria:

a. There should be no discrimination whatsoever related to the goal of the indirect distinction
b. The means which are chosen to reach the goal should respond to real needs of the organisation/person who uses the means
c. The means should be appropriate and necessary to reach the goal.[172]

170 On adoption of the proposed law on combating discrimination.

171 Act XXII, Article 5 (2) of 1992 on the Labour Code 1992.

172 These criteria stem from the history of the Parliamentary approval of the Equal Treatment Act, as well as jurisprudence of the European Court of Justice in Luxembourg (Case 170/84 *Bilka Kaufhaus* v *Weber von Hatrz*; Case 171/88 *Rinner-Kühn* v *FWW Spezial Gebäudereinigung GmbH & Co*).

Direct distinction cannot be objectively justified. In relation to direct distinction, law can only make exceptions (see for example the exception in Article 2 of the Act itself).[173]

It should be noted that in Hungary, Latvia and Lithuania there are draft laws incorporating definitions of direct and indirect discrimination and complying with the demands of the Racial Equality Directive that are pending entry into force.

Are there comparable definitions in national law in relation to gender discrimination?

Most Member States can point to definitions of direct and indirect discrimination in relation to gender discrimination, although in the countries cited in sections 1 and 2 above, the concept of indirect discrimination needs to be defined more clearly, as is the case with discrimination on the grounds of race and religion (Italy is satisfactory in this respect). The case law of the European Court of Justice has clearly been influencial in this respect. The candidate countries all lack definitions of the concepts in their gender laws. In Bulgaria there is a draft law pending in Parliament that defines both concepts and in Romania there is a draft law on equal opportunities between women and men that includes definitions that contradict those presently existing in Romanian law.

It can be concluded that the concepts of direct and indirect discrimination are familiar to the majority of Member States, but that most States need to take action to define these concepts more clearly in law. All of the candidate countries will, to a greater or lesser degree, need to take action to comply with the demands of the Directive.

4. Harassment

Is unlawful harassment an identifiable concept in national law? Is there a definition of harassment in the national law that corresponds to that in the Directive? Is it necessary to introduce such a definition into national legislation?

The concept of unlawful harassment, in the meaning of unwanted conduct related to racial or ethnic origin and religion, is employed by very few national legal systems in the EU. In Belgium harassment has been a criminal offence under the Penal Code since 1998. However, protection is weakened by the fact that charges must be brought by the victim, and the current draft law includes provisions to strengthen the definition of harassment in order to comply with

173 See for example Article 2.4 and the other exceptions allowed by Article 2 of the Equal Treatment Act in relation to sex (2.2), and nationality (2.5).

the Directive.[174] In Ireland[175] the legislative provisions on harassment focus on the effect on the individual and do not conform to the Directive in so far as it requires there to be the purpose or effect of creating an intimidation, hostile, degrading, humiliating or offensive environment.

In the Netherlands, the Equal Treatment Commission has twice ruled that harassment in the workplace falls under the scope of the definition of distinction under the Equal Treatment Act (on racial harassment and sexual harassment respectively), and has indicated that it will ensure that the definition covers not only employment but all other areas to which the Equal Treatment Act is applicable. In Portugal the concept of harassment stems from a rather theoretical interpretation of the wide definition of discrimination.[176] In Sweden there is a definition of harassment in employment law,[177] and there is a duty on employers to investigate and take measures against harassment.[178] In the United Kingdom harassment is prohibited in both civil and criminal law.[179]

The concept remains to be introduced in the other Member States' law relating to discrimination on the grounds of race and religion. In Austria the notion of harassment on racial grounds seems to be evolving with reference to employment situations. In many countries it is suggested that existing criminal law could cover the acts defined as harassment in the Directive. In Finland certain situations of harassment could be covered by criminal law that prohibits threats, slander or insult, and in Italy harassment could be established on the basis of the provisions of the Criminal Code concerning crimes against honour. The Slovak language does not possess a legal term corresponding to the concept of 'harassment' in English, but uses several different terms to express the meaning of this concept. Thus, depending on the circumstances, 'unwanted conduct', described in Article 2(3) of the Directive, could be considered to be a crime, a misdemeanour or a ground for bringing a civil defamation action (action on the protection of personhood).

---

174 M.B., 17 December 1998 inserted Article 442 bis into the Penal Code; Article 2, paragraph 4 in the Mahoux Bill on combating discrimination, Article 5 ter of the Draft Bill on strengthening anti-racism legislation.

175 Section 32 of the EEA 1998 and Section 11 of the ESA 2000.

176 Law 134/99, 28 August.

177 §4 of the 1999 Act on measures against ethnic discrimination in working life.

178 Article 13 of the 1999 Act on measures against ethnic discrimination in working life.

179 Cases Strathclyde Regional Council v Porcelli [1986] IRLR 134, Burton & Rhule v De Vere Hotels [1996] IRLR 596, Sidhu v Aerospace Composite Technology Ltd. [2000] IRLR 602, the protection from Harassment Act 1997 (www.hmso.gov.uk/acts/acts 1997/1997040.htm), the 1986 Public Order Act and the Crime and Disorder Act 1998 (www.hmso.gov.uk/acts/acts 1998/19980037.htm).

In the Slovenian legal system there are rules defining different levels of harassment in the Penal Code and the Executing Criminal Sanctions Act.[180] In Turkey too, it is claimed that there are criminal provisions that can be considered to contain the same elements as the Directive.

Although there is no direct definition of harassment in Lithuanian law, it can be derived from the relevant legal norms.[181] In Polish law there is no delineated concept of unlawful harassment, but the Penal Code does outlaw serious forms of harassment on the grounds of racial and ethnic origin and also those of political and religious affiliation, although it is narrower than the concept of harassment laid down in the Directive.[182]

In Bulgaria, Estonia,[183] Hungary, Latvia and Romania the legal systems do not contain any provisions defining or dealing with harassment.

Are there comparable definitions in national law in relation to gender discrimination?

The gender legislation in most of the EU Member States includes unlawful harassment (at least in employment situations), with the exception of the legislation in Finland, Greece and Italy. Gender legislation in France includes the concept of harassment, but is of a more restrictive nature than Article 2.3 of the Directive.

---

180 Unlawful harassment is defined as torture in Article 10(3) of the Executing Criminal Sanctions Act, and as 'cruel behaviour' under Article 146 of the Penal Code, and in specific cases of cruel behaviour against children as 'neglect of the youngsters and cruel behaviour' (Article 201/2). Further, the violation of human dignity by the abuse of official status and official rights is a criminal offence under Article 270 of the Penal Code.

181 The Law of the Republic of Lithuania of 31 August 2000 on the Amendment of Article 72 of the Criminal Code and the Supplementation of the Code by Article 72(1) (Official Publication, 2000, No 78–2363) provides a definition of unlawful conduct that is comparable to unlawful harassment. A comparable definition is contained in Article 169 of the new Criminal Code (Official Publication, 2000, No 89–2741). The Law of the Republic of Lithuania of 18 November 1997 on the Supplementation of the Code of Administrative Violations by Articles 214(12), 214(13), the Abolition of Article 214(1) and Amendment of Articles 224, 259(1), and 320 all provide definitions of unlawful conduct relevant to the concept of harassment.

182 Use or threat of use of force is covered by Chapter XVI, Art. 119 of the Penal Code concerning crimes against peace, humankind and war crimes and insult and infringement of personal integrity appear in the Chapter XXXII, Article 257 of the Penal Code on offences against public order.

183 However, certain cases of harassment may be caught by other provisions such as the Law on Cultural Autonomy of the National Minorities, Articles 113, 128, 129 and 130 of the Criminal Code, and Article 23 of the Law on General Principles of the Civil Code.

The situation in the candidate countries is contrary to that in the Member States. The gender legislation in only a few States includes unlawful harassment. Poland has existing provisions referring to sexual harassment, but as they are spread across various pieces of legislation, they do not provide a homogenous approach.

In the Czech Republic measures against sexual harassment were recently taken. It is proposed that these could provide a model for unlawful harassment on other grounds. Article 7(2) of the Labour Code prohibits the 'lowering of human dignity' in labour relations. Undesirable sexual behaviour in the workplace that is uninvited, inappropriate, or offensive or which could reasonably be perceived as a condition influencing the employment relationship is defined as such lowering of human dignity. The Lithuanian law on Equal Opportunities of Women and Men provides a definition of unlawful conduct in relation to gender discrimination, including sexual harassment.[184]

5. Instruction to Discriminate

Is it unlawful under national law to give instruction to discriminate on the grounds of racial or ethnic origin or religion and belief? Is it deemed to be discrimination? Is there a need to introduce a similar principle in national law?

Legislation in Austria,[185] Ireland,[186] Lithuania,[187] Romania,[188] Slovakia[189] and the United Kingdom[190] explicitly prohibits instruction to discriminate. In the UK, a relationship of authority must be established, or at least one person must be accustomed to acting in accordance with the wishes of the other person (to amount to 'instruction' or 'procuring'). Of particular interest is the fact that it is not possible for an individual to bring a legal challenge on the grounds of

184 Articles 2 and 3.

185 §§ 12 and 13 of the Criminal Code and § 7 of the Administrative Penal Code.

186 Sections 8(4) and 14 Employment Equality Act 1998, section 13 Equal Status Act 2000.

187 The Law of the Republic of Lithuania of 31 August 2000 on the Amendment of Article 72 of the Criminal Code and the Supplementation of the Code by Article 72(1) provides a definition of unlawful conduct comparable to 'giving instructions to discriminate'. A comparable definition is contained in the new Criminal Code. In addition, Article 18 of the Criminal Code expands the notion of criminal offenders from executors to organisers, instigators and assistants. A comparable provision is contained in Article 24 of the new Criminal Code.

188 Ordinance 137.

189 Article 198a of the Criminal Code.

190 Sections 30 and 31 of the 1976 Act, Articles 30 and 31 of the 1997 Order and Article 35 of the 1998 Order (Religion).

instruction to discriminate: the statutory specialised body, the Commission for Racial Equality, must instead initiate proceedings.

In Austria, Belgium and Lithuania, the provision is included in criminal law only and is therefore not applicable beyond the area of criminal law. In Slovakia, instructing to discriminate in cases governed by civil law is generally prohibited as well, although access to an effective remedy in such cases is, in some cases, questionable. Under Slovenian law, instruction to discriminate is unconstitutional and punishable under Article 141 of the Penal Code. Estonian law classes instruction to discriminate on the grounds of racial or ethnic origin or sex as unlawful according to the general provisions of the Constitution (Article 12).

None of the other States explicitly prohibit such instruction, although it may in some instances be considered to fall under the general definition of discrimination. This is the case in the Netherlands. Further, there may be situations of instruction that can be caught by other provisions such as provisions on 'incitement' or comparable provisions, which are found in most Member States. In Spain, 'provocation', 'promotion', and 'incitement' to discriminate are prohibited.[191] Whether or not incitement covers instruction to discriminate is a matter of interpretation. In Belgium, whereas there is a general prohibition of 'incitement' to discriminate under Article 1 of the Law of 30 July 1981, in relation to public office there is an explicit prohibition of the instruction to discriminate.[192]

In particular, criminal law principles can be applied to prosecute the person issuing instructions, either as the sole perpetrator or as co-perpetrator (this is the case in Austria,[193] Belgium,[194] France,[195] Finland, Greece and Luxembourg).

Further, in Germany for example, instruction could be regarded as instigation to commit libel or slander under criminal law.[196]

In Bulgaria there seems to be a need to introduce express statutory language prohibiting instruction to discriminate as a form of discrimination. In practice, there is a significant level of instruction to discriminate evident in Bulgaria, particularly with respect to access to services available to the public, such as access to restaurants and bars, where managers or owners instruct staff not to admit people on an ethnic or racial basis. At present there is no protection against this form of discrimination.

As a result, with the exception of Ireland, Romania and the UK, all States

191 Articles 510.1 and 515.5 of the Penal Code.

192 Article 4 of the law of 30 July 1981.

193 §§ 12 and 13 of the Criminal Code.

194 Article 66 of the Penal Code.

195 The standard law (droit commun) on complicity is applicable to the offence of discrimination as established and rendered illegal by Article 225–1 and subsequent articles of the Penal Code.

196 Sections 26 and 185 of the Penal Code.

need to take action to *explicitly* include the prohibition of instruction to discriminate in *all* areas of law. A particular point that must be clarified is that instruction per se is enough, that is to say there is no need to establish actual discrimination, as is the case in several countries at present. For example in Italy, whereas the general definition of discrimination can be interpreted to include a prohibition of instruction, a causal relationship must be proven between an order and an actual act of discrimination.

Are there comparable definitions in national law in relation to gender discrimination?

States that do not prohibit instruction to discriminate on the grounds of sex are Bulgaria, the Czech Republic, Estonia,[197] Greece, France, Hungary, Latvia and Poland.

6. Scope – Fields of Application

Does the definition of 'racial and ethnic discrimination' and 'discrimination on the grounds of religion and belief' apply to all the fields of application listed in Article 3, both in the private and the public sectors? To which other fields of application does the definition apply?[198]

There is room for improvement to the domestic law of most European States in order to comply with the wide scope of Article 3.1 of the Directive. There is a patchwork of compliance in the respective States that in many instances does not precisely adhere to the Directive's requirements. In most of the European States the picture of which law applies to which field of application is rather complex. In countries that have enacted special non-discrimination legislation the situation is clearer. It should be borne in mind that in most European States, anti-discrimination legislation is a combination of constitutional, criminal, civil and administrative law and that not every field of application is covered by the same type of legislation. For example there may be specific legislation for discrimination related to employment, whereas education may be covered

197 An exception is the Law on Wages.

198 Article 3.1 Racial Equality Directive lists as fields of application a) conditions for access to employment, self-employment and occupation, b) access to vocational guidance, c) employment conditions, d) membership of organisations of workers or employers, e) social protection, including social security and health care, f) social advantages, g) education, and h) access to goods and services which are available to the public, including housing. Note that the corresponding provision in the Employment Equality Directive, Article 3.1, does not include e), f), g) or h) so protection from religious discrimination does not extent to these fields.

by criminal law or by a general principle of law laid down in the Constitution. Furthermore, it should be considered that in most countries the legislation has not yet been fully (or at all) tested in court.

Some remarks that can be made with regard to specific countries are as follows:

- Austrian laws either apply to the public or private sectors, but not to both: the Constitutional provisions apply to the public sector, the criminal law provisions to the private sector.
- The scope of Belgian law is wider than Article 3.1, but it should be noted that as this is criminal law, its sphere of implementation is limited. If adopted, the new draft civil legislation should rectify this.
- Bulgarian law covers all fields of application as a result of the incorporated definitions of international agreements signed and ratified by the government. However, as yet there has been no case law implementing either a prohibition or a definition of discrimination in any of the fields stated under Article 3.1 of the Directive.
- In the Czech Republic discrimination in the area of labour relations is outlawed. In other relevant areas, Czech law does not comply with the Racial Equality Directive.
- Danish law meets the scope of Article 3.1, although compliance with Article 3.1(d) requires review. Different aspects are to be found in a variety of laws.
- In Estonia, the Constitution could in principle be applied in all the fields listed in Article 3.1, in the state, municipal and private sectors alike. Under employment law it is illegal to give preference and to restrict rights on the grounds of *inter alia* nationality, colour or race.
- Finnish law does not cover Article 3.1(h), supply and access to goods and services.
- In French law compliance with Article 3.1 is met through a combination of legislative and legal principles.
- German legislation does not cover Article 3.1(d), membership of an organisation of workers or employers. Furthermore, in order to conclude that German law otherwise fully covers Article 3.1, the interpretation of general principles of law is required, rather than the referral to specific provisions of law.
- As Greek law literally follows Article 5 ICERD, it does not cover all fields of application of Article 3.1. Considerable amendments to the law are required to ensure conformity with Article 3.1.
- In Hungary the constitutional anti-discrimination provision is amplified by a patchwork of provisions in legislation governing different fields of social life. However, there is little back-up through sanctions, and the prohibitions are mostly declaratory. Social security, membership in a professional organisation and self-employment are not covered at all by the prohibition of discrimination.

- Irish law covers all fields of application of Article 3.1.
- If the relevant provisions of the 1998 Act regulating immigration and the legal condition of foreigners are interpreted widely, Italian law can also be understood to cover all those fields of application listed in Article 3.1.
- The Latvian Constitution includes provisions that cover all the fields mentioned in Article 3.1. However, these provisions cannot be applied in relation to actions by private persons.
- Lithuanian legislation covers all fields mentioned in Article 3.1 except (b) and (c).
- Luxembourg law covers all the fields of application, but as the legislation is criminal law, its application is limited.
- Legislation in the Netherlands conforms to Article 3.1, with the exception of Article 3.1(d), membership of an organisation of workers or employers, in civil cases. However, previous case law indicates that the Equal Treatment Commission is likely in the future to rule that such organisations are also subject to equal treatment legislation.
- The Polish Constitution covers all the fields of application mentioned in Article 3.1. The Labour Code also specifically prohibits discrimination.
- Portuguese law covers all fields of application of Article 3.1.
- Romanian legislation covers all the fields of application mentioned in Article 3.1.
- In Slovakia, it is not possible to determine decisively whether the definition of racial and ethnic discrimination applies to all the fields of application listed in Article 3.1 of the Directive because Slovak law, except for the Labour Code, does not give any such definition.
- In Slovenia, the requirements of the Racial Equality Directive have been included in the draft Employment Act and programmes, which have been adopted as national strategies.
- Spanish law covers all fields of application.
- Swedish law explicitly covers Articles 3.1(a) and (h). The other fields of application are a matter of interpretation of the relevant provisions in the Constitution, Criminal Code and Act on Measures against Ethnic Discrimination in Working Life.
- In Turkish law, Article 11 of the Constitution, that gives the Constitution both horizontal and vertical effect, makes the application of the principle of equal treatment possible in all fields, although none of the Turkish Codes regulating the fields mentioned in Article 3.1 contain specific provisions explicitly stating the principle of equality or prohibiting discrimination.
- UK law seems to cover all fields of application. The development of case law will provide further interpretation of the legislation.

Is gender discrimination covered in the same fields?

In some European countries, there are specific labour law provisions for the equal treatment of men and women, for example in Austria, Belgium,[199] Denmark,[200] Italy,[201] Luxembourg,[202] Sweden[203] and Lithuania.[204] In France, discrimination on the basis of gender is covered by both the Labour Code and the Penal Code. In Greece, gender discrimination is restricted to those areas of application established by Article 3 of the Council Directive 97/80/EC on the burden of proof in cases of discrimination based on sex. In Bulgaria, Ireland and Slovakia gender discrimination is covered in the same areas as discrimination on the grounds of race or religion. In the UK, the Government has indicated that it intends to amend the sex discrimination legislation when parliamentary time permits, in order to bring all public functions within its scope. In Northern Ireland there is currently consultation on a proposed Equality Bill, which may make similar changes for race, sex and disability. In Poland, gender discrimination is covered by the general anti-discrimination clause in the Constitution. In Turkey, the Labour Code prohibits wage differentiation on the grounds of gender.[205] The National Education Fundamental Act also enshrines the principle of equality between men and women in the field of education.[206]

---

199 Law regarding employment conditions, access to employment and opportunities for promotion, access to self-employment and the complementary social security structures in pursuance of the Law of 7 May 1999. In this respect, the effect of the Mahoux Bill on combating discrimination would be to expressly extend the prohibition of sex discrimination to include new areas.

200 Section 1(1) of the Act on Equal Treatment of Men and Women.

201 Gender discrimination is now explicitly forbidden by a statutory rule only in the field of labour law. However, in most of the cases described in the list of Article 3.1, gender discrimination would be illegal also on other grounds (the Constitutional provisions of equal treatment), although significant case law exists only in the field of labour law, since gender discrimination outwith work and working conditions is not yet viewed as a legal problem of the same weight.

202 Law of 8 December 1981, which imposes the principle of equal treatment between men and women 'in access to employment, in promotion, vocational guidance, training, advanced training and retraining, in access to independent occupation and in working conditions'(Article 1).

203 Equal Opportunities Act, which prohibits gender discrimination in working life.

204 Law on Equal Opportunities for Women and Men.

205 Article 26/4 of the Labour Code.

206 Articles 4 and 8.

7. Discrimination on the Ground of Nationality

To what extent, if any, does national legislation go beyond the Directive in prohibiting discrimination on the ground of nationality?

With the exception of Austria and Luxembourg, it is a basic legal principle in EU Member States that discrimination on the ground of nationality is prohibited unless the law provides otherwise. Legislation in most Member States thus goes beyond Article 3.2 of the Directive, which provides that the Directive does not cover difference in treatment based on nationality and is without prejudice to provisions and conditions relating to the entry and residence of third country nationals and stateless persons and any treatment resulting from the legal status of these persons.

Discrimination on the grounds of nationality is not outlawed in Bulgaria: non-nationals are only protected against discrimination on the grounds of nationality in the exercise of basic rights under binding instruments. There are two exceptions to the principle that discrimination on the basis of nationality is permissible: discrimination on the grounds of nationality is prohibited in the provision of urgent medical aid and health care under the National Health Act[207] and National Framework Contract.[208]

In Estonia, for example, the Constitution permits differential treatment of non-citizens with regard to the enjoyment of certain rights[209] although Estonian legislation is rather liberal in relation to the social and economic rights of the Soviet-era settlers.

It is relevant here to note that most EU Member States' anti-discrimination laws do apply to non-nationals of the State. In the candidate countries, the situation is slightly different. In most of the countries, anti-discrimination law does not apply to non-nationals of the State. Poland and Romania,[210] however, constitute exceptions, as anti-discrimination law applies to non-citizens as well as citizens. This means that, for example in Poland, a foreigner has, in principle, the same rights and obligations as Polish citizens with some exceptions.[211]

In Turkey, although the Constitution grants fundamental freedoms to 'all individuals', without making a distinction between nationals and non-nationals,

207 Article 28; Promulgated 1973, last amended 2000. DV 88/6.11.1973, entered into force 1.01.1974, amended DV 10/4.02.2000, 36/2.05.2000.

208 Promulgated 2000. DV 42/23.05.2000, in force from 23.05.2000 until 31.12.2000, amended DV 55/7.07.2000.

209 Articles 28, 29 and 31 of the Constitution.

210 Article 1 (2) of the Ordinance 137; Article 18 (1) of the Constitution.

211 The exceptions are: no electoral rights, no obligation for military service, no access to public service, limitations on the purchase of land.

there are a few exceptions to this general rule including that the fundamental rights of aliens may be restricted by law in a manner consistent with international law.[212]

8. Genuine and Determining Occupational Requirements

Do exemptions relating to genuine and determining occupational requirements exist at national level? Is it necessary to restrict any exemptions to meet those defined in Article 4?

With regard to genuine and determining occupational requirements, the European States can be categorised into three models as follows:

1. There are no specific exceptions or exemptions relating to genuine and occupational requirements (Austria, Bulgaria, Czech Republic, Greece, Lithuania, Luxembourg, Poland, Portugal, Romania, Slovakia, Spain and Turkey).
2. There is a general principle of law that is comparable to Article 4 of the Directive (Belgium, whose draft law follows Article 4 almost literally; France, where a legitimate objective is required,[213] although the scope of the requirement may need widening to meet Directive standards; Germany, where the general principle of equal treatment of equal cases is applied in accordance with the criteria of there being a legitimate objective and proportionality, Hungary,[214] and Italy, where the same general principle of equal treatment of equal cases is upheld).[215]
3. National legislation provides specific exemptions. Such is the case in Denmark[216] where there are exemptions for employers promoting political or religious views, although these exemptions do not seem to fulfil the requirements of there being a legitimate objective and proportionality, Estonia,[217] where the exemptions relate to gender, religion and language skills, Finland,[218] where there are exemptions relating to religion, such as a minister of religion,

212 Article 16 of the Constitution.

213 French law recognises what it defines as 'objective discrimination', even if this is connected to ethnic or religious criteria, provided this was the deciding employment criterion.

214 However, there is a general principle in Hungarian law, which is limited to labour law.

215 Article 43(1) 1998 Immigration Act.

216 Section 6 of the Act on prohibition against differential treatment in the labour market 1996.

217 Section 2 of Article 10 of the Law of Republic of Estonia on Employment Contracts.

218 Chapter 11, section 125 and Chapter 47, section 3 of the Constitution.

Ireland, where various exemptions may need to be reviewed to fulfil the two criteria, and the Netherlands,[219] where there is an exhaustive list of exempt occupations (actors and other artists if the part played so requires, models, in cases where certain specific features and appearances may reasonably be required, and beauty contests, where appearance is relevant in relation to the aim of the contest, providing services that can only be rendered by persons with certain features and/or appearance), as well as exemptions for religious orders.[220] These exemptions may warrant review in the light of the legitimate objective and proportionality criteria. Similarly, in Sweden there are various exemptions that may warrant review in the light of the legitimate objective and proportionality criteria. In the United Kingdom the various exceptions and exemptions may also require modification.

In Latvia, there is a list of 'hard jobs' and 'jobs in a harmful environment' where it is forbidden to employ women[221] (and also a list of jobs where it is forbidden to employ persons under the age of 18), adopted in accordance with the requirements of the Labour Code.[222] This list certainly is putting women at a disadvantage in the labour market as there is a whole range of jobs they cannot take up. There is, however, no such list in relation to race or ethnic origin. Similar provisions exist in Turkey.[223]

9. Positive Action

Are there any specific measures that aim to ensure or promote full equality or to compensate for disadvantages linked with racial or ethnic origin or religion or belief? Is the government considering adopting such measures?

The situation with regard to measures to ensure full equality in practice to prevent or compensate for disadvantages linked to racial or ethnic origin or religion or belief can be categorised as follows:

1. Recognition in the form of a general rule that positive action is allowed to compensate for disadvantages, as well as specific (legal or policy) measures for certain groups and/or situations. This applies to Denmark (in the labour market, although the rule is more restrictive than the principle contained in

219 Article 2.4 of the Equal Treatment Act, Article 2 of the Equal Treatment Decree.

220 Articles 3 and 5 of the Equal Treatment Act.

221 Hard Jobs and Jobs in a Harmful Environment where it is Forbidden to Employ Women, adopted by the Decision of the Council of Ministers No 292, 24 July 1992, Zinotajs [Official Reporter] No 42, 1992.

222 Article 168 of the Labour Code.

223 Articles 68 and 69(1) of the Labour Code.

the Directive),[224] Ireland,[225] Luxembourg,[226] the Netherlands,[227] and Spain (where a general principle was established by a ruling of the Constitutional Court).[228] It will also apply to Belgium if the current draft law is adopted.[229]

2. Legislation/policies for specific situations, areas of application or ethnic groups. This applies to Austria (various specific ethnic groups),[230] Finland (policy measures to promote the recruitment of ethnic minorities in the public service),[231] France (specific measures in the field of education and housing),[232] Germany (legislation for specific ethnic groups),[233] Greece (specific legislation for the Muslim population in Thrace and measures aimed at the members of the Roma community),[234] Hungary (government programme with the objective of improving the situation for Roma), Lithuania (government programme seeking to improve the situation for Roma), Poland[235] (detailed below), Portugal (*inter alia* vocational and other training designed to increase job opportunities),[236] Romania (government programme aimed at improving the situation for Roma), Slovenia (where an article of the

---

224 Articles 6 and 9 of the Act on Prohibition against Differential Treatment in the Labour Market.

225 For the traveller community and disadvantaged groups of persons: section 33 of the EEA 1998, sections 9 and 14 of the ESA 2000, Housing (Travellers Accommodation) Act.

226 *Inter alia* Law of 29 April 1999 amending the Grand-Ducal Regulation of 12 May 1972 determining the regulations governing the employment of foreign workers on the territory of the Grand Duchy of Luxembourg.

227 Article 2.3 of the Equal Treatment Act.

228 Judgement 114/83 on positive action measures in favour of women.

229 There is no legal basis for current measures but Article 3 bis of the Mahoux Bill provides for this.

230 Croats, Slovenes, Hungarians, Czechs, Slovaks and Roma are recognised either directly by the Constitution or according to the Ethnic Group Act of 1976 (BGBl. 396/1976 as amended by BGBl. 314/1988).

231 Government Action Plan of 22 March 2001.

232 Education Priority Zones, educational success contracts (Minister of Education circular, 10 July 1998); Centres for Training and Information on the Schooling of Children of Migrants; Specific assistance policy for housing for migrants (circulars of 9 June 1988 and 15 February 1998 and the agreement of 14 May 1997 between the Minister for Housing and the Social Economy for Housing Union); Interministerial Committee for Housing Immigrant Populations (created by the decree of 9 June 1998); Social Action Fund for Immigrant Workers and their Families.

233 Under regional (Länder) legislation.

234 Law 2341/1995, JO 208/A, 6 October 1995.

235 Article 133.2 Act on Elections.

236 Law-making judgement 140/93, 6 July.

Constitution stipulates the essential characteristics of the implementation of special rights of national minorities[237] and there is a government programme aimed at improving the situation for Roma), Sweden (specific legislation in the field of employment)[238] and the United Kingdom (specific legislation in the field of education, training and welfare, encouragement of employer).[239]
3. No general rule or specific measures are in place. This applies to Bulgaria, the Czech Republic, Estonia, Italy, Latvia, Slovakia and Turkey.[240]

The Constitutions in Romania[241] and Slovakia[242] (if interpreted literally) prohibit the use of positive discrimination. Nevertheless, in Romania, as mentioned above, there is a government programme for the improvement of the situation for Roma. In Slovakia, the Constitution itself contains provisions, which derogate from the rule, permitting positive discrimination for women, juveniles and disabled persons. They enjoy more extensive health protection and special working conditions.[243]

In Poland, on the political level, preference is granted to national minorities, in that their electoral committees are exempt from the requirement to collect at least five per cent of votes cast in order to be taken into account for the distribution of seats in the lower chamber of Parliament. In the field of education and culture, in order to compensate for their higher operating costs, schools of national minorities receive an extra 20 per cent subsidy in comparison to other schools. The State budget also invests in schools, and subsidises the production and publishing of textbooks. Furthermore, the Ministry of Culture and National Heritage subsidises minority press and other publications and sponsors cultural events organised by national and ethnic minorities.[244] In 2001 the government agreed to launch a pilot programme for 2001-2003 to promote Roma in the fields of education, employment, healthcare, living conditions, security and culture.

---

237 Article 64 of the Constitution of the Republic of Slovenia.

238 Articles 4-7 of the Act on measures against the ethnic discrimination in working life.

239 Sections 35, 37 and 38 of the 1976 Act and Articles 35 and 37 of the 1997 Order.

240 Positive action is allowed only in relation to disabled people and formerly convicted people to promote equal opportunity in employment in Turkish law.

241 Article 6 (2).

242 Article 12 paragraph 2.

243 Section 38 of the Constitution reads '(i) Women, minors and disabled persons shall enjoy more extensive health protection and special working conditions. (ii) Minors and disabled persons shall enjoy special protection in employment relations and special assistance in vocational training'. Article 41 paragraph 2 reads 'Pregnant women shall be entitled to special treatment, terms of employment and working conditions'.

244 In 2000, 2,4 million PLZ were devoted to subsidising minorities press and publications and another 2,4 million PLZ to organising cultural events of minorities, altogether amounting to 4,8 million PLZ, that is, 1,2 million USD.

Are there are comparable measures in relation to gender discrimination?

Positive measures to ensure equal treatment between women and men are permitted and exist in almost all the EU Member States. Different kinds of positive action has been taken in the candidate countries, notably in the Czech Republic, Lithuania, Slovakia and Slovenia in to improve the situation of women.

It is clear that the level and willingness to adopt positive action within the scope of the Directive varies considerably between the States. Very generally, it can be said that the Member States are more willing to take positive action than the candidate countries where there seems to be widespread governmental resistance against taking positive measures, with the exception of Poland and Slovenia. Nevertheless, in some countries, the governmentally supported programmes for the improvement of the situation for Roma represent a positive step in the fight against discrimination of minorities.

10. Minimum Requirements

Are there any measures that protect the principle of equal treatment at national level that go beyond the minimum requirements of the Directive?

Legislation in most EU Member States does in certain respects go further than the Directive requires, most commonly in relation to the fields of application under Article 3.1 and in providing for positive action which is not mandatory under the Directive. In addition, often the legislation that guarantees non-discrimination on the grounds of race or ethnic origin also guarantees non-discrimination on other grounds including religion or belief, disability, age and sexual orientation.

In Belgium, the scope of the Law of 30 July 1981 is broader than that of the Directive in that it classifies as offences incitement or publicity given with the intention of resorting to racial discrimination, hatred or violence against a person, a group, a community or their members; and membership of a group or organisation which clearly and repeatedly practices discrimination or segregation or advocates this in the circumstances set out in Article 444 of the Penal Code, or supports such a group or organisation. Further, the Law of 10 April 1995[245] requires political parties to include a commitment to respect the rights and freedoms guaranteed by the Convention for the Protection of Human

245 Law of 10 April 1995 inserting an Article 15bis into the Law of 4 July 1989 on the limitation and control of electoral expenses for Federal Parliament elections as well as on financing and the transparency of accountability of political parties and amending the consolidated Laws of 12 January 1973 on the Council of State. For the opinion of the legislative section of the Council of State on the subject of this law, see: Doc. parl., Chambre, 1992–93, n° 1113/3.

Rights and Fundamental Freedoms. The proposed legislation foresees the extension of the scope of prohibited racial and ethnic discrimination yet further.

In Ireland, one important provision of the Equal Status Act 2000 goes beyond the Directive: under Section 3(1)(b), discrimination is held to have occurred when one person who is associated with another person is treated less favourably, by virtue of that association, than a person who is not thus associated is, has been or would be treated. It is also required that similar treatment of that other person on any of the discriminatory grounds listed in the legislation would constitute discrimination. This provision was applied by an Equality Officer in a recent decision where it was held that the complainant had been discriminated against through his association with a member of the Traveller Community.[246] The law in the UK is similar. It can be argued that in fact the Directive's description of discrimination covers such scenarios, since the definition merely requires that the discrimination occurs 'on grounds of race or ethnic origin', which does not require that the person discriminated against is themselves of a particular race or ethnic origin.

In the candidate countries, only with regard to Estonia, Poland and Slovenia can it be said that there is legislation that goes beyond the minimum requirements of the Directive. On the whole, the principle of equal treatment at national level falls short of the Directive.

In Poland, although generally the law does not go further than the Directive requires, there are areas that are not included in the Directive but that are provided for by law: electoral rights, protection of 'sensitive data' linked to national or ethnic origin, and the provision of an interpreter for a person taking part in court proceedings who does not have sufficient knowledge of the Polish language.

11. Legal Remedies

Are legal procedures available for the enforcement of the obligations under the Directive for those who consider themselves wronged?

The national legal systems in all the European States provide legal remedies for those who consider themselves wronged. However, the adequacy and effectiveness of these are often subject to criticism. With regard to the candidate countries, it can generally be said that while legal procedures exist in theory, in practice it is often hard for the persons concerned to access them.

In those countries where the material scope of the Directive (see Article 3.1) is not fully covered, there are gaps in the legal remedies provided for those who consider themselves wronged.

---

246 John Ward & Michael Ward v The Boathouse Pub: Equality Officer Decision DEC–S2001–001.

In those European States where the anti-discrimination law is mainly criminal law, victims are faced with the difficulty that criminal procedure laws must be followed which leave the victim little or no room for initiative and control over the proceedings after lodging the complaint. Any decision to investigate the complaint, to prosecute or continue with proceedings lies with the police and public prosecutor, which can prove very unsatisfactory for the victim. This applies for example to Luxembourg, where civil proceedings are only available in labour cases.[247] A problem in, for example, Bulgaria is furthermore that, although there are anti-discrimination provisions in the criminal code, the lack of implementation of these limits the law-enforcement authorities' understanding of the issues of discrimination and racially motivated crime, which in turn means that there is no case law on criminal provisions prohibiting racially motivated crime and criminal labour discrimination.

Regular civil law procedures can be cumbersome, time consuming and expensive, and are therefore deemed by some commentators to be inadequate and ineffective. Where it is necessary to instruct lawyers, these proceedings can furthermore be expensive and inaccessible for victims of discrimination.

Special procedures tailored to overcome such obstacles are considered to be more effective. This can be said for example of the procedure before the Netherlands Equal Treatment Commission.[248] One disadvantage of this procedure, however, is that the Commission cannot award damages, and therefore, following a decision of the ETC, normal civil court proceedings must be instigated for any damage claims. In Poland, a complaint to the Ombudsperson for Human Rights may prove to be an effective tool. Although the Ombudsperson cannot issue a legally binding decision, the office can investigate the case and exert pressure on the bodies responsible for inappropriate conduct or it can instigate legal measures.[249]

Overall, while there is recourse to legal procedures in cases of discrimination as required by the Directive in the EU Member States, their adequacy and effectiveness is sometimes questionable. Most of the candidate countries still fall short of the requirements set by the Directive when it comes to the access to legal remedies for discrimination.

247 Law of 6 December 1989 on labour jurisdiction.

248 See annex II in the Netherlands' country report for the brochure of the Equal Treatment Commission. The brochure, meant for potential victims and those who defend their interests, outlines the basic functions of the Commission and informs on what to do to file a complaint.

249 See Article 12–14 Act on Ombudsperson for Human Rights.

12. Engagement of Legal Entities in Legal Proceedings

Is it possible for national associations or other legal entities to engage in legal proceedings for the enforcement of rights under the Directive?

In the Czech Republic, Germany, Greece and Hungary, legal entities cannot engage in legal proceedings for the enforcement of rights under the Directive.

The law does, on the contrary, allow associations or other legal entities to engage in legal proceedings for the enforcement of rights under the Directive in Denmark (with the approval of the victim), France, the Netherlands (in civil law under certain conditions including that there is no objection from the person affected, and criminal law if the public prosecutor decides not to prosecute)[250] and Portugal (unless there is opposition from the wronged person).[251] In Ireland the Equality Authority may provide assistance and instigate proceedings, and the Human Rights Commission can institute and support proceedings in relation to human rights cases. In the United Kingdom statutory bodies (the Commission for Racial Equality and the Equality Commission for Northern Ireland), professional bodies and trade unions can all bring cases if they have the approval of the victim. Trade unions can also represent employees in labour disputes in Bulgaria, Italy, Latvia, Slovakia and Sweden.

Presumably in all countries individual lawyers working for associations of other legal entities have the capacity to engage in proceedings. This is certainly the case in Estonia, Finland and Latvia.

In Austria, legal entities can engage in legal proceedings in those cases for which no legal representation is required (*i.e.* before lower courts). In Belgium any registered charity and any non-profit-making association that has existed as a legal entity for at least five years at the time of the acts in question and which includes in its statutes the protection of human rights or combating discrimination, may take legal action in any dispute to which the anti-racism law might be applied, if their statutory objectives are compromised,[252] and any organisation representing workers and employers, professional organisations and organisations representing the self-employed may now also take legal action in any disputes to which Article 2bis of the law against racism may be applied where the victim has given his approval.

Romanian Law gives non-governmental organisations active standing in courts, as parties, in cases when the discrimination has taken place within their

250 Articles 305a and b, book 3 of the Civil Code, Article 12 Criminal Procedure Code. The National Ombudsman can also investigate an act of administrative authority under Article 12 National Ombudsman Act.

251 Law 20/96, 6 July.

252 Article 5, first paragraph, of the 1981 Act on the Punishment of Certain Acts Motivated by Racism or Xenophobia.

domain of activity and prejudices a community or a group of persons, and also where the discrimination prejudices one single person, if the person delegates the organisation to that effect.[253]

The Polish Code of civil procedure allows non-profit social organisations to bring a claim on behalf of individuals or join such proceedings.[254] If a social organisation does not participate in the proceedings, it can still act as *amicus curiae* and present its opinion on the case to the court.[255] Similarly, social organisations are allowed to start or to join administrative proceedings[256] and representatives of social organisations may also be admitted to criminal proceedings.[257]

In Lithuania, the possibility for associations, organisations or other legal entities to engage in any judicial and/or administrative procedure either on behalf or in support of the complainant is provided for in the laws regulating the civil,[258] the criminal[259] and the administrative procedures,[260] as well as the procedure of settling labour disputes.[261]

Thus there are European States in which the law clearly accords legal entities the power to defend the rights protected by the Racial Equality Directive. However, in others the restrictions to which entities are subject must be removed to secure compliance with Article 7.2.

13. Time Limits

What time limits apply to the bringing of an action?

There are few noteworthy features to be mentioned with regard to the period of time during which proceedings must be instigated. As regards proceedings within civil law or criminal law, generally the normal time limits apply. In specific anti-discrimination legislation there tend to be comparable time limits.

An unusual provision under the Netherlands Equal Treatment Act (ETA) is that the Equal Treatment Commission shall not conduct an investigation when '...the time, which has elapsed since the discrimination took place, is such that an investigation can no longer reasonably be conducted'.[262]

253 Article 22 of Ordinance 137/2000.

254 Article 8 Code of Civil Procedure.

255 Article 63 Code of Civil Procedure.

256 Article 31.1 Code of administrative procedure.

257 Articles 90 and 91 Code of Criminal Procedure.

258 Articles 55 and 56 Civil Procedure Code of the Republic of Lithuania.

259 Article 63 Criminal Procedure Code of the Republic of Lithuania.

260 Article 56 Law of the Republic of Lithuania on the Administrative Proceedings.

261 Article 3 Law on the Settling of Labour Disputes.

262 Article 14.

Under the UK anti-discrimination legislation,[263] a complaint of discrimination in employment must be submitted to the employment tribunal not later than three months less one day from the date of the alleged act of discrimination. For all non-employment case, that is cases concerning education, housing, goods, facilities or services and all other public functions, a complaint must be made not later than six months less one day from the act of discrimination. However, if the person seeking to bring a complaint applies to the Commission for Racial Equality/NI Equality Commission before the expiry of the six month time limit, the overall time limit is extended by two further months. The CRE/ECNI is able to extend that period to three months. Furthermore, the tribunal or the court may allow a case to be heard even if it had been submitted outside the statutory time limit where the tribunal or court is satisfied that in all the circumstances it is just and equitable to do so.[264]

In Latvia it is said that, when the new Labour Law enters into force, there will be time limits specific to equality of treatment claims, but only for a small category of cases.

14. The Burden of Proof

Does the principle of sharing the burden of proof in cases of racial and religious discrimination exist in national law?

The principle of the easing or sharing the burden of proof in cases of racial and religious discrimination exists in Denmark (where it is limited to wage differentiation),[265] Estonia (where it is limited to the Law of Wages),[266] Hungary (limited to Labour Law and the service relationship of the professional armed forces),[267] Ireland (in practice, although explicit provisions to this end are required), Italy (where it is limited to employment),[268] Latvia (where it is limited to Labour Law),[269] Lithuania[270] (where it is limited to non-judicial proceedings), the Neth-

263 Section 68(1) of 1976 Act and Article 65(1) of the 1997 Order.

264 Section 66(4), 68(2), (3) and (6) of the 1976 Act, Articles 64(4) and 65(2), (3) and (7), of the 1997 Order and Article 46(2) and (5) of the 1998 Order.

265 Section 2(4) of the Act on Prohibition against Differential Treatment in the Labour Market.

266 Article 51, Law of Wages.

267 Act LXXV of 1996 on Labour Supervision, Article 8, Par. (4) and Act LXIII of 1996 on the Service Relationship of Professional Members of Armed Organs.

268 Art. 44, comma 9 of the Act no 286 of 1998 regulating immigration and the legal condition of foreigners.

269 Article 29 of the Labour Law.

270 Article 15 of the Law on the Settling of Labour Disputes, Article 12 of the Law on Administrative Disputes Commission.

erlands (based on a Supreme Court ruling, not on legislation),[271] Spain (limited to social law),[272] Sweden (limited to employment)[273] and the United Kingdom.[274] In Belgium the draft law foresees the sharing of the burden of proof,[275] and in the Czech Republic there is a proposal for amendment to the Civil Procedure Code to this end. In Slovakia, where the Constitutional Court has ruled that the reversal or easing of the burden of proof itself would not be unconstitutional, such a provision is also contained in the new Labour Code.[276]

In Latvia, a new Administrative Procedure Law is currently being drafted. If adopted, this law would introduce the principle of 'objective examination' in the administrative procedure. According to this principle, the task of the court would be to exercise control over the lawfulness, and justification, of the administrative act or factual conduct of the administrative body. This means that the decision of the court would not be taken within the framework of the evidence produced by the parties, but on the objective evaluation of the circumstances of the case and on the evidence collected on its own initiative, if needed. The whole procedure before the court would put the burden of proof upon the administrative body. The administrative procedure would be applicable not only in relation to civil servants, who may challenge discriminatory decisions, but to any administrative decision that may have a direct or indirect discriminatory effect upon an individual within the framework of the Racial Equality Directive.

Are there comparable provisions in national law in relation to gender discrimination?

In terms of gender discrimination, all the EU Member States have introduced provisions on the shift of the burden of proof in cases involving gender discrimination in order to comply with the Council Directive on the burden of proof.[277]

---

271 Based on the ruling of the Supreme Court in the so-called *Binderen* case (HR 10.12.'82, NJ 1983, 687).

272 Article 55 of the law on the Workers' Statute and in the case of gender discrimination Article 96 of the Law of Social Procedure (R.D.L. 521/1990).

273 See preparatory works of the 1999 Act on measures against ethnic discrimination in working life.

274 The position under current UK law regarding the burden of proof in discrimination cases was set out by the Court of Appeal in the case of *King* v *Great Britain China Centre* [1991] IRLR 513, which was approved by the House of Lords in *Zafar* v *Glasgow City Council* [1998] IRLR 36.

275 Article 10 paragraph 3 of the Mahoux Bill.

276 Section 13 of the new Labour Code.

277 Council Directive 97/80/CE of 15 December 1997 on the burden of proof in cases of discrimination on the grounds of sex.

Among the candidate countries there is only an easing or reversal of the burden of proof in cases of gender discrimination in Latvia (in Labour Law),[278] and in draft form in Lithuania (in a draft for amendments to the Law of equal opportunities between Women and Men) and Slovenia (in the draft Employment Relations Act on burden of proof in cases of discrimination on the basis of gender).

Most EU Member States and candidate countries have to take action, either to introduce provisions or to adapt and improve existing provisions as far as the easing of the burden of proof in discrimination (on the basis of racial or ethnic origin) cases is concerned.

15. Victimisation

Is the Directive's definition of victimisation to be found in national law?

A definition of victimisation exists in Ireland,[279] the Netherlands (limited to employment),[280] Portugal (limited to employment),[281] Slovakia (general provision in the Constitution),[282] Sweden (limited to employment)[283] and the United Kingdom.[284] Such legislation is in the process of being drafted in Belgium,[285] and in Hungary in the Minorities Ombudsman's draft for an anti-discrimination law.[286] In Latvia provisions related to victimisation are found in the Labour Law[287] and case law implies that Latvian courts may rely on the general prohibition of discrimination under Article 1 of the Labour Code to extend protection to persons who have been subject to victimisation even in the absence of any specific legal provisions.

278 Article 29(3) of the Labour Law.

279 Section 74(2) of the EEA 1998 and Section 3(2)(j) of the ESA 2000.

280 In Article 8.1 of the Equal Treatment Act.

281 General labour law (Workers' Guarantees) and Article 4 of law 134/99, 28 August.

282 Article 12 paragraph 4 of the Constitution.

283 Article 12 of the Act on measures against ethnic discrimination in working life.

284 Section 2 of the 1976 Race Relations Act (GB) and Article 4 of the 1997 Race Relations Order (NI).

285 Art. 11 bis in the Mahoux Bill.

286 Article 11.

287 Articles 8.2 and 9 of the Labour Law.

Are there comparable definitions in national law in relation to gender discrimination?

Generally speaking, in the field of gender discrimination, it can be said that most Member States seem to include provisions concerning victimisation in their legislation on gender discrimination. Finland, Greece and Italy, however, have no provisions concerning victimisation in their legislation. In Austria, it is said that a notion of victimisation is part of the laws on sexual harassment.

A definition of victimisation can be found in the Lithuanian Law on equal opportunities for Women and Men.[288]

The standard of compliance with Article 9 seems to be low across Europe. Most Member States and candidate countries have to take action, either to introduce provisions or to adapt and raise the standard of existing provisions.

16. Ensuring Public Awaremes

Which steps are necessary to ensure sufficient public awareness of existing laws? What arrangements currently exist to ensure that anti-discrimination legislation has been or will be brought to the attention of the public? Does the government need to act to ensure that by means of information and training, and where necessary by effective sanctions, all officials and other representatives of the public authorities at every level abstain from any racially or religiously discriminatory speech or behaviour in the exercise of their functions?

Public awareness of existing laws is regarded as very low in most European countries. In some Member States, in particular those that adopted legislation in the last few years, even the legal profession is said not to be fully aware of the legislation.

Public awareness is also generally low in the candidate countries, although some communities – especially Roma – are exceptionally well informed.

That said, most Governments do undertake to promote the awareness of the principles of equal treatment and non-discrimination and of the relevant legal norms.

However:

- There seems to be no systematic assessment of effectiveness and impact.
- There is often no systematic and structural involvement of the civil society sector.
- There is little or no gathering of best practices in this area.
- Funding for awareness-building initiatives is often limited and *ad hoc*.

288 Articles 5 and 6.

To help solve such problems, various *modus operandi* are suggested in the different countries. Accessing the public via radio, newspapers and television is a good way to inform the public about existing laws, as well as producing information material and educating professionals. A substantial challenge is to educate young people and students and to shape their attitudes by showing them positive examples of non-discriminatory practices, positive discrimination and tolerance. Only laws implemented by people with a positive mindset can ensure that the desired level of tolerance is reached. The laws must not only be publicly known, but also voluntarily accepted.

Another important point that has been made is the importance of making laws and regulations more accessible to the minorities by translating them into minority languages. Illiteracy in some communities, however, can make the dissemination of information extremely difficult.

In Estonia, within the framework of the State Integration Programme (with the support of foreign donations) several advertising campaigns were organised, several television programmes produced, and printed information prepared to meet the goals of the sub-programme 'Social competence'. The campaigners sought to promote tolerance and to overcome psychological alienation of the Russian-speaking communities. The State budget also supported some media projects. At the same time, however, national authorities are not eager to discuss the problems of minority population in the field of discrimination.

In France trade unions are now undertaking several discrimination awareness-raising and training initiatives for employees.

In Latvia, the measures for informing the population on issues of non-discrimination in general or in specific areas such as labour relationships or pensions have so far included publishing a number of information brochures with the involvement of the Government as well as with extensive involvement of private donor organisations. No brochure, however, has been specifically devoted to the issue of the prohibition of discrimination on the grounds of race, ethnic origin or gender.

In Lithuania, the newly adopted legislation is being widely discussed in the mass media, including television, radio and the press, which is the most popular and trusted means of getting information. Legal education, in either general or specific fields, is given by a number of NGOs. The Lithuanian Lawyers' Society was granted money by the State Fund for Support of the Press, Radio and Television for a series of articles with commentaries on the latest legislation in 2001. The Open Society Fund of Lithuania has been supporting a programme on national television entitled 'The Lawyer's Advice' which explains various legal issues in a form accessible to the general public.

Independent specialised bodies, whose mandate includes the promotion of equality, and non-governmental organisations working in the field are instrumental in raising public awareness. For example, in the UK since legislation outlawing racial discrimination was first introduced in 1965 there has been one or two statutory bodies with mandates to enforce the legislation and/or to promote racial equality and good race relations. Since around 1968 there has existed a number of local voluntary organisations funded by the national statutory agency with a role to provide information at a local level about rights against discrimination as well as to foster good community relations.

In Hungary, the most well known public institution with capacity to address cases of discrimination is the Minorities Ombudsman. Through frequent media attention and well-established contacts with the non-governmental sector, the Minorities Ombudsman has become a respected and popular public institution during the past five years.

These factors contribute to the relatively high number of complaints about discrimination that the Ombudsman deals with. This could serve as a role model for other candidate countries.

With regard to informing and training officials, all EU Member States claim to implement some kind of training programmes for law enforcement personnel and sometimes for judiciary personnel.

In many candidate countries it is said that discriminatory behaviour among public officials is widespread and that there seems to be a significant insensitivity on the part of public authorities towards anti-discrimination issues.

In these countries the administration, law enforcement agencies and the judiciary must be taught about anti-discrimination issues. Some of the governments of the candidate countries do not appear to apply any measures to promote awareness of the principles of equal treatment and non-discrimination and of the relevant legal norms, whereas in other countries the governments seem to have woken up to the issues and at least some measures have been taken.

In the short term the importance of educating the administration, law enforcement agencies and the judiciary about anti-discrimination issues cannot be underestimated. It must be realised that discrimination is a breach of basic human rights that cannot be tolerated in a democratic society. In the long term it is of utmost importance to educate and change the attitudes of young people towards discrimination of minorities and to shape their attitudes by showing them positive examples of non-discriminatory practices, positive discrimination and tolerance.

17. Promotion of Social Dialogue

Are there any measures to promote the social dialogue on the issues of the Directive at national level?

In all the EU Member States there is a form of dialogue between the two sides of industry on equal treatment and anti-discrimination issues. Depending on the specific *modus operandi* in the Member State in the relationships between the partners in industry, equal treatment and non-discrimination can be part of a structured dialogue, or it may be discussed on an ad hoc or case-to-case basis. There are examples of the dialogue resulting in various types of concrete measures and/or instruments, such as the inclusion of measures in collective agreements, as in France, the joint production of information packs, as in Ireland, or the adoption of codes of conduct as is the case in the Netherlands. The active involvement of the government in stimulating concrete measures, especially including measures in collective agreements, depends on the traditional freedom of bargaining of the partners. Whereas the governments in France and Luxembourg can influence the dialogue rather strongly, this would be out of the question in Germany.

While in most candidate countries[289] there is some kind of tri-party system for discussions between representatives of the state, employers and employees, these systems are not geared towards combating discrimination and guaranteeing equal treatment. In Slovenia, there are specialised courts for labour and social affairs that, in addition to the judge, must comprise of representatives of workers and of employers. In Romania, there is a committee on equal opportunities, but it focuses mainly on gender issues. In Poland, the tri-party system is said not to be working satisfactory because of political tension among the parties involved.

It is not asserted with reference to the candidate countries that the State is taking any concrete measures to actively promote dialogue on the issues of the Directive, suggesting that there are, for the moment, other matters that are considered to be more important within the economic and social fields.

18. Promotion of Dialogue with Non-Governmental Organisations

Are there any measures to promote the dialogue with non-governmental organisations at national level?

There is considerable variation in the measures being taken to promote dialogue with non-governmental organisations in the EU Member States. The measures range from structuring a dialogue at national level as in Greece, structuring the dialogue at local (municipal level) as in Denmark or Finland, to ad hoc dialogue, and providing substantial financial support to NGOs as in the Netherlands.

There is some kind of dialogue between public authorities and NGOs in all of the candidate countries with the exception of Latvia, where no stable collaboration between NGOs, local governments and State institutions takes place. Most of the countries have formal dialogue between authorities (various levels) and the NGOs, but for example in Romania and Poland, the formalised struc-

289 There is no reference to such a system in the Czech republic, Estonia and Romania.

ture no longer seems to work in a satisfactory manner. The most common type of institution for dialogue is an inter-ministerial committee for the Roma communities in many of the candidate countries, accompanied by an Ombudsman for Human Rights. In Slovakia there is no guarantee of formal dialogue by the government. In the Czech Republic there is a system in which the government gives financial support to NGOs in the form of grants.

Where there is a lack of dialogue, sometimes, as in Romania, it is as much a case of non-existing structures on the part of the NGOs as on the governmental side.

19. Specialised Bodies

Is there a specialised body to promote equal treatment irrespective of race or ethnic origin at national level?[290] *If so, what are its powers and duties? Is such a body effective? If not, would the government need to act in order to give this body such specific powers? What would be the procedure?*

In Belgium,[291] Finland,[292] Ireland,[293] Netherlands,[294] Sweden[295] and the United Kingdom,[296] there are specialised bodies of the type required under Article 13 of the Directive. The respective mandates of these bodies are laid down in legislation.

In the nine remaining EU Member States bodies that perform some of the tasks of the specialised body referred to in Article 13 do exist, but their mandates do not fully meet the requirements of the Directive.[297] Providing indepen-

290 It is interesting to note that there is no article in the Employment Equality Directive that corresponds to Article 13 of the Racial Equality Directive requiring the designation of a specialised body.

291 The Centre for Equal Opportunities and Opposition to Racism.

292 The Chancellor of Justice of the Government and the Parliamentary Ombudsman; Act on a Minority Ombudsman (660/13.7.2001).

293 The Equality Authority.

294 The Equal Treatment Commission.

295 The Ombudsman against ethnic discrimination and the Board against discrimination.

296 The Commission for Racial Equality (GB); The Equality Commission for Northern Ireland (NI).

297 Austria: People's advocate, Denmark: Board for Ethnic Equality, France: High Council for Integration/National Consultative Commission on Human Rights, Greece: Ombudsman, Germany: Commissioner for foreigners' affairs, Italy: Commission for Integration policies, Luxembourg: National Council for Aliens /Special Permanent Commission against Racial Discrimination, Portugal: High Commissioner for Immigration and Minorities, Spain: Ombudsman.

dent assistance to victims of discrimination in pursuing their complaints, as well as conducting independent surveys on discrimination is not usually part of their tasks.

Of the candidate countries there is none that fully complies with Article 13. In Romania Ordinance 137/2000 provides for the establishment of a National Council for Fighting against Discrimination as an independent specialised body. However, at the time of writing this had not yet been realised. It is common that there is some kind of Ombudsman-type institution, to which the public can turn with their complaints.[298] The competences of the Ombudsmen differ from country to country.

In some of the candidate countries bodies that perform some of the tasks referred to in Article 13 exist, but as in most Member States, the mandates of these bodies do not fulfil the requirements of the Directive. It seems to be hard to evaluate the performance of these institutions, partly because they are (in many cases) quite new and the amount of cases concerning discrimination is so far very limited, and partly because they are not specialised bodies.

Non-compliance with the requirements of the Directive is particularly grave with regard to the (lack of) independence of the bodies and the fact that they are not in a position to represent victims of discrimination.

Nine Member States will therefore still have to act either to establish a specialised body or to designate the performance of the functions referred to in Article 13 to an existing body. The candidate countries will all have to take measures to transform or instate a body that meets the requirements set out in Article 13.

20. Priority of the Equal Treatment Provisions over Other Legislation

Is action needed to ensure that national law guaranteeing equal treatment between individuals, irrespective of racial or ethnic origin and religion or belief, takes priority over other laws, regulations or administrative provisions? Do national legislative or administrative procedures provide for declaring null and void those provisions in agreements, contracts or rules that relate to professional activity, workers and employers that are contrary to the principle of equal treatment?

---

298 In the Czech Republic: the Public Defender of Rights, Estonia: Legal Chancellor, Hungary: the Ombudsman for Civil Rights (General Ombudsman), the Deputy Ombudsman for Civil Rights and the Ombudsman for the Rights of National and Ethnic Minorities (Minorities Ombudsman) (at present the post of the Ombudsman for Data Protection is not filled), Latvia has no Ombudsman position, but the National Human Rights Office and State Labour Inspectorate, Poland: Ombudsperson for Human Rights, Romania: Ombudsman, Slovenia: the Human Rights Ombudsman.

In Finland and Sweden action needs to be taken to explicitly establish the principle that national law guaranteeing equal treatment irrespective of racial or ethnic origin and religion and belief takes priority over other laws.

Ireland, the Netherlands, and the United Kingdom are required to amend existing provisions in their equal treatment legislation that prevent the equal treatment provisions from taking priority over other legal provisions.

No further action is required of the other Member States.

There does not seem to be any need for any of the candidate countries to take action, as the principle of equal treatment enjoys Constitutional status in all of the countries. However in Romania, there are still a few laws that are discriminatory, for example the law on Financial Guard (gender discrimination). This law specifically mentions that only men may become financial guards.

With regard to the issue of declaring provisions in agreements etc. that are contrary to the principle of equal treatment null and void, action to anchor this principle firmly in the law only appears to be necessary in Finland.

In Slovakia neither the State, nor any other party, which is not directly affected by an individual act of discrimination can challenge for example a business contract which contains a discriminatory clause.

21. Effective, Proportionate and Dissuasive Sanctions

Is there a need for further effective, proportionate and dissuasive sanctions, penalties and remedies? Do equivalent provisions already exist at national level in other areas?

The legal systems of most European States provide for various types of sanctions, ranging from fines and imprisonment under criminal law, to payment of compensation for damages to the victim under civil law.

The following remarks can be made:

- In Austria and Luxembourg the law relating to racial and religious discrimination is mainly criminal law, and the sanctions are mainly criminal law sanctions. The introduction of civil law provisions that also provide for sanctions that are endemic to civil law proceedings may be needed to make sanctions effective and proportionate.
- In Estonia the courts are loath to find any basis for the payment of moral damages in civil cases.
- The legal systems of Germany and Greece do not provide for a comprehensive system of sanctions at all. Action is needed in this respect.
- In countries which have some degree of experience with the application of sanctions under the various areas of law, such as the Netherlands, Sweden and the United Kingdom, it is questioned whether sanctions under criminal law are the most effective.

- In countries where there is special legislation with regard to racial discrimination, such as Ireland, the Netherlands, Sweden and the United Kingdom, there is some debate as to whether the sanctions, penalties and remedies under the special legislation are effective, proportionate and dissuasive. Very little information seems to be available to make a proper assessment in this respect.
- Although basic sanctions are included in most of the candidate countries' legal systems, there seem to be problems with the practical application in many cases, such as in Bulgaria, the Czech Republic, Hungary, Lithuania, Latvia, Romania and Slovakia.
- In Estonia and Poland, the inclusion of sanctions, penalties and other remedies in the acts of domestic law that are to be drafted to implement the Directive is necessary.
- The principle of equal treatment irrespective of ethnic origin or race is not established in Turkish law as a separate concept with comprehensive legislation. Accordingly, effective and proportionate sanctions, penalties and remedies do not exist.

PART III

A COMPARATIVE PERSPECTIVE

Mark Bell

8. SETTING STANDARDS IN THE FIGHT AGAINST RACISM: A COMPARISON OF THE EUROPEAN UNION AND THE COUNCIL OF EUROPE

The 1990s witnessed a proliferation of legal responses to evidence of persistent racism and intolerance throughout Europe. The actions taken in the past decade have been distinguished by the new recognition that combating racism cannot be confined to purely national measures. Instead, both the European Union and the Council of Europe have firmly entered this arena. The two organisations pursue diverse strategies, naturally reflecting their different powers and responsibilities. Nonetheless, there are many areas where these activities overlap. This chapter examines the efforts by both entities to shape national legislation on racial discrimination. It begins with a brief summary of the principal aspects of each organisation's anti-racism policy, followed by an examination of their approaches to various aspects of law on discrimination. Specifically, it will consider the definition of discrimination; the scope of protection; mechanisms for enforcement of the law; and the provision for proactive measures. Throughout the analysis, there will be a critical focus on the consistency and coordination of the interventions of the EU and the Council of Europe.

1. Forging a Policy Framework against Racism

1.1 The European Union

Various commentators have documented the increasing prominence of combating racism within European Union law and policy.[1] A number of key stages in

1 T. Hervey, 'Putting Europe's house in order: racism, race discrimination and xenophobia after the Treaty of Amsterdam' in D. O'Keeffe and P. Twomey (eds), *Legal issues of the Amsterdam Treaty* (Hart Publishing, Oxford, 1999), p. 329; S. McInerney, 'Equal treatment between persons irrespective of racial or ethnic origin: a comment'

Jan Niessen, Isabelle Chopin (eds.), The Development of Legal Instruments..., *213-233*

the development of the Union's role occurred in the late 1990s. Most significantly, the EU Member States agreed in the 1999 Treaty of Amsterdam to confer a specific legal competence on the Union for combating racial discrimination within the framework of the EC Treaty,[2] as well as establishing separate powers for the Union in the EU Treaty to fight racism and xenophobia under the aegis of policies on 'police and judicial cooperation'.[3] The EC Treaty provision, Article 13, has hitherto received the greatest attention, in particular because it paved the way for the adoption in June 2000 of the Racial Equality Directive.[4] This now forms the cornerstone of the Union's policy against racism, requiring the prohibition by all Member States of direct and indirect discrimination based on racial or ethnic origin in a wide range of areas.[5] It was complemented in November 2000 by the Framework Directive, which forbids discrimination in employment and vocational training on grounds of religion or belief, age, disability or sexual orientation.[6]

In addition to the new legislation adopted in 2000, the Member States agreed the declaration of the EU Charter of Fundamental Rights.[7] The Charter is, as yet, only a political statement of the fundamental rights recognised by the Union. As such, the rights contained therein are not legally binding; individuals cannot directly enforce them. Nonetheless, the Charter rights already appear to enjoy a persuasive value before the EU courts.[8] Irrespective of the legal value of the Charter, it contains provisions that are clearly relevant to combating racial discrimination. Specifically, Article 21(1) states:

(2000) 25 *European Law Review* 317; S. McInerney, 'Bases for action against race discrimination in EU law' (2002) 27 *European Law Review* 72.

2 Article 13 EC.

3 Article 29 EU.

4 Directive 2000/43/EC of 29 June 2000 implementing the principle of equal treatment between persons irrespective of racial or ethnic origin, [2000] OJ L180/22.

5 See further, E. Guild, 'The EC Directive on race discrimination: surprises, possibilities and limitations' (2000) 29 *Industrial Law Journal* 416; A. Tyson, 'The negotiation of the European Community Directive on Racial Discrimination' (2001) 3 *European Journal of Migration and Law* 199.

6 Directive 2000/78/EC of 27 November 2000 establishing a general framework for equal treatment in employment and occupation, [2000] OJ L303/16. See further, D. Schiek, 'A New Framework on Equal Treatment of Persons in EC Law?' (2002) 8 *European Law Journal* 290.

7 [2000] OJ C364/1.

8 The Court of Justice has not yet based its own decisions on the Charter, however, it has been relied upon by the Court of First Instance: Case T-54/99 *max.mobil Telekommunikation Service GmbH v Commission* [2002] ECR II-313. Several Advocates-General have also referred to the Charter in their interpretations of Community law: for example, Case C-173/99 *BECTU* [2001] ECR I-4881.

> Any discrimination based on any ground such as sex, race, colour, ethnic or social origin, genetic features, language, religion or belief, political or any other opinion, membership of a national minority, property, birth, disability, age or sexual orientation shall be prohibited.

In addition to the high-profile adoption of the Article 13 Directives, the Union has gradually put in place other elements of an overall framework on racism. Since 1997, there has been an institutional commitment to promoting research and analysis of racial discrimination in the form of the EU Monitoring Centre on Racism and Xenophobia.[9] The Commission has simultaneously developed a range of specific actions on racism and discrimination,[10] as well as integrating race equality objectives into wider policies and programmes.[11] The EU institutions are now seeking to build upon the Racial Equality Directive with a new legislative intervention focusing on racism and the criminal law. In 2001, the Commission proposed the adoption of a 'Framework Decision' on racism and xenophobia.[12] Framework Decisions are instruments provided for under the EU Treaty. They bear certain similarities to Directives; in particular, a minimum level of harmonisation is established and this must be then transposed into national law during a specified time period. However, the enforcement mechanisms are quite different from those applicable to Community law instruments. In particular, the Commission cannot bring infringement proceedings to compel a Member State to implement correctly the Framework Decision, nor will there be the possibility for litigants to rely directly on its provisions in national legal proceedings.[13]

The proposed Framework Decision aims to establish minimum requirements with regard to the designation in national criminal law of racist and xenophobic offences. Amongst those under discussion are offences of incitement to discrimination, violence or hatred; dissemination of racist publications and material; and condoning or denying war crimes and genocide, including the Holocaust.

---

9 Regulation 1035/97/EC establishing a European Monitoring Centre for Racism and Xenophobia, [1997] OJ L151.

10 Decision 2000/750/EC of 27 November 2000 establishing a Community action programme to combat discrimination (2001 to 2006), [2000] OJ L303/23.

11 For example, integrating ethnic minorities into the labour market has been included as an objective in the EU annual employment guidelines: Council Recommendation of 18 February 2002 on the implementation of Member States' employment policies, [2002] OJ L60/70.

12 Commission, 'Proposal for a Council Framework Decision on combating racism and xenophobia' COM (2001) 664.

13 See further, J. Monar, 'Justice and Home Affairs in the Treaty of Amsterdam: reform at the price of fragmentation' (1998) 23 *European Law Review* 320.

At the time of writing, the Framework Decision is pending before the Council and negotiations on an agreed text are at an advanced stage.

1.2 The Council of Europe

Unlike the experience of the European Union, racial discrimination has been addressed in the work of the Council of Europe since its inception. Article 14 of the European Convention on Human Rights provides

> The enjoyment of the rights and freedoms set forth in this Convention shall be secured without discrimination on any ground such as sex, race, colour, language, religion, political or other opinion, national or social origin, association with a national minority, property, birth or other status.

Nonetheless, the potential of the Convention to be used in combating racism has not been fully explored. In part, this can be attributed to the ancillary character of Article 14, which prohibits discrimination in the provision of the other rights guaranteed by the Convention, whilst not actually providing an autonomous right to non-discrimination. It is not sufficient for a litigant to demonstrate that they have suffered differential treatment as a result of grounds listed in Article 14; instead, they must first establish that the activity to which the difference of treatment relates falls within the ambit of another Convention right.[14] Given that the Convention mainly focuses on the protection of civil and political rights, and not social rights – for example, access to healthcare – this places a significant limit on the scope of the non-discrimination guarantee. Moreover, the subsidiary nature of Article 14 has meant that in practice the Court of Human Rights often does not proceed to examine issues of discrimination if it has already found a violation of another part of the Convention.[15]

In 1993, the Member States of the Council of Europe recognised the limitations of the status quo and agreed a package of new measures on combating racism.[16] This included the establishment of an expert advisory committee – the European Commission on Racism and Intolerance (ECRI). ECRI's work has been characterised by the systematic review of the legal situation on racial discrimination in each of the Member States. This 'country-by-country' approach results in periodic reports on every state and the process is now in its second cycle.[17] The

14 *Gaygusuz v Austria* [1996] 23 European Human Rights Reports (EHRR) 364, 380.

15 For example, *Smith and Grady v UK* [1999] 29 EHRR 493.

16 Vienna Declaration reproduced at: (1993) 4 *Netherlands Quarterly of Human Rights* 513. See further, R. Cholewinski, *Migrant workers in international human rights law – their protection in countries of employment* (Clarendon Press, Oxford, 1997) 275.

17 Available at: <www.coe.int/T/E/human_rights/Ecri/1-ECRI/2-Country-by-country_approach/default.asp#TopOfPage>.

reports provide independent and critical analysis, which in turn supplies ECRI with a foundation for issuing a series of general policy recommendations.[18] These have culminated in a 2002 recommendation setting out a comprehensive scheme of model legislation on racism that all states should seek to enact.[19] Whilst not legally enforceable, the 'model legislation' recommendation provides a new benchmark against which national practice can be evaluated.

The recommendations operate as a vital complement to the agreement in 2000 of Protocol 12 to the Convention.[20] This Protocol aims to remedy the constraints imposed by existing Article 14, namely by providing a freestanding right to non-discrimination. Article 1(1) states 'the enjoyment of any right set forth by law shall be secured without discrimination on any ground such as sex, race, colour, language, religion, political or other opinion, national or social origin, association with a national minority, property, birth or other status.' Protocol 12 has been signed by 26 of the 44 Member States of the Council of Europe, but it has been ratified by just 2 states (Georgia and Cyprus).[21] It will only enter into force once ratified by 10 states.

2. Defining Racism and Discrimination

This section examines the concepts of racism and discrimination adopted by the EU and the Council of Europe. It concerns both the forms of difference of treatment that are regarded as 'racist' in nature, as well as the various facets of 'discrimination'.

2.1 Racism and Racial Discrimination

There is surprisingly little consensus on what the notions of racism or racial discrimination embrace. At the global level, the International Convention on the Elimination of All Forms of Racial Discrimination (ICERD) refers to differences in treatment linked to 'race, colour, descent or national or ethnic origins'.[22]

18 For example, ECRI general policy recommendation no. 6: combating the dissemination of racist, xenophobic and antisemitic material via the internet, CRI (2001) 1.

19 ECRI general policy recommendation no. 7 on national legislation to combat racism and racial discrimination, CRI (2002) 41, 13 December 2002.

20 See further, U. O'Hare, 'Enhancing European Equality Rights: a New Regional Framework' (2001) 8 *Maastricht Journal of European and Comparative Law* 133; M. Bell, 'Combating racism through European laws: a comparison of the Racial Equality Directive and Protocol 12' in I. Chopin and J. Niessen (eds), *Combating racial and ethnic discrimination: taking the European legislative agenda further* (Migration Policy Group and Commission for Racial Equality, London, 2002), p. 7.

21 Available at <http://conventions.coe.int/Treaty/EN/CadreListeTraites.htm>.

22 Article 1(1).

As already noted, Article 14 of the Convention (and Protocol 12) additionally refer to language, religion or association with a national minority. ECRI's model legislation chooses to provide a non-exhaustive list of characteristics linked to racism; it refers specifically to race, colour, language, religion, nationality or national or ethnic origins.[23]

In contrast to these fairly broad definitions, the Racial Equality Directive limits its protection to discrimination based on 'racial or ethnic origin'.[24] It expressly excludes difference of treatment linked to nationality[25] and discrimination based on 'religion or belief' is dealt with separately through the Framework Directive. Confusingly, the proposed EU Framework Decision interprets 'racism and xenophobia' in quite a different manner to the scheme established by the Article 13 Directives. The Commission seeks to define racism and xenophobia as 'the belief in race, colour, descent, *religion or belief*, national or ethnic origin as a factor determining aversion to individuals or groups'.[26]

The underlying importance of these linguistic semantics especially relates to two aspects of racism: nationality and religion. With regard to the former, the explanatory memorandum to the ECRI model legislation recognises that there will be a wider range of circumstances where differences of treatment based on nationality can be justified, as opposed to characteristics such as race or ethnicity.[27] For example, most states place limits on access to domestic labour markets by reference to nationality; third country nationals will normally first require a work permit. Whilst this practice is a common element of immigration policy and very likely to be regarded as justifiable, other differences of treatment within employment – for example, lower pay rates or less favourable working conditions for migrant labour – appear arbitrary forms of discrimination. Yet, the EU Racial Equality Directive does not aim to penalise such practices.[28] The treatment of third country nationals cannot be easily separated from issues relating to ethnic inequality.[29] There is a considerable overlap between minority ethnic communities in Europe and communities of third country nationals, although

23 Para. 1(a), ECRI general policy recommendation no. 7.

24 Article 1, Directive 2000/43/EC.

25 Article 3(2), *ibid.*

26 Author's emphasis. Article 3(a), COM (2001) 664.

27 Explanatory memorandum to ECRI general policy recommendation no. 7 on national legislation to combat racism and racial discrimination, CRI (2002) 41, p. 11.

28 The Commission has proposed a wide-ranging right to equal treatment for third country nationals who are long-term residents in the Union (i.e. five years legal and continuous residence): Article 12, COM (2001) 127.

29 Para. 16, 2001 World Conference against Racism, Racial Discrimination, Xenophobia and Related Intolerance, Declaration and Programme of Action. Available at: <http://www.un.org/WCAR/>.

the extent of this varies at the national level depending on issues such as patterns of migration and domestic law on access to nationality. The EU legislative instruments fail to engage with this reality, struggling instead to maintain paper walls between impermissible race and ethnic discrimination on the one hand, and legitimate nationality discrimination on the other. There is a wilful blindness to the problems this poses in practice. For example, if an Algerian woman is refused an apartment available to rent it is quite difficult to distinguish meaningfully between whether this is due to her north African ethnic origin or her nationality.

Similar issues of overlapping forms of discrimination arise in relation to religion. Again there is an attempt in the EU instruments to separate religious and racial discrimination. This is most manifest in the negotiations on the Framework Decision. Although it is currently proposed to maintain religion in the definition of 'offences concerning racism and xenophobia', this is subject to the option for individual Member States to exclude criminal liability for conduct related to 'religious conviction' where 'this is not a pretext for directing acts against a group of persons or a member of such group defined by reference to race, colour, descent, or national or ethnic origin'.[30] This complex exception indicates that Member States understand that the total omission of religion would make it easy for offenders to avoid the scope of the law by framing racist statements or publications by reference to religious communities. Paradoxically, at least some Member States nonetheless wish to be able to treat certain aspects of incitement to religious hatred as not racist in nature. For instance, incitement to hatred of Scientologists would probably fall outside the scope of the Framework Decision as it is currently formulated. However, many borderline areas will remain: for example, incitement to hatred of Islamic converts of European ethnic origin. It is particularly undesirable that criminal offences are defined in such an opaque manner, given that citizens need to understand their responsibilities under the law. More generally, it reveals ambivalence on the part of the Union with regard to the necessity to combat religious hatred and intolerance. Clarity in this area is especially important in the light of enhanced religious sensitivities since 11 September 2001. In contrast, already in April 2000, ECRI produced a general policy recommendation on combating intolerance and discrimination against Muslims,[31] firmly indicating that combating racism must include issues of religious discrimination.

---

30 Article 8(1)(a), Council, 'Note from Presidency to Coreper/Council' 14665/02 DROIPEN 86, 25 November 2002.

31 ECRI general policy recommendation no. 5: combating intolerance and discrimination against Muslims, CRI (2000) 21.

2.2 Defining Discrimination

Further divergence can be identified in respect of the definition of discrimination. In general, the Council of Europe has adopted a more flexible approach than the stance of the European Union, however, this tends to reflect the wider scope of its instruments.

2.2.1 Direct Discrimination

The definition of discrimination in the Council of Europe instruments has been largely shaped by the interpretation of Article 14 of the Convention by the Court of Human Rights

> A difference of treatment is discriminatory if it has no objective and reasonable justification, that is if it does not pursue a legitimate aim or if there is not a reasonable relationship of proportionality between the means employed and the aim sought to be realised.[32]

This interpretation is regarded as equally applicable to Protocol 12, which (like Article 14) does not provide any definition of discrimination. Moreover, ECRI have adopted a very similar formula in their recommendation as to how national legislation should define direct discrimination.[33] The explanatory memorandum to the model legislation suggests that justification of direct discrimination 'should be interpreted as restrictively as possible',[34] but this remains a matter left to national discretion. The Article 13 Directives take a different and more rigorous approach to direct discrimination. Direct discrimination is defined as where 'one person is treated less favourably than another is, has been or would be treated in a comparable situation on grounds of racial or ethnic origin'.[35] Although both Directives provide a number of express exceptions to the ban on direct discrimination,[36] it is otherwise presumed that direct discrimination is not open to justification.

2.2.2 Indirect discrimination

The case-law of the Court of Human Rights provides little guidance on its approach to indirect discrimination; in earlier decisions it failed to apply particular scrutiny to prima facie instances of indirect racial discrimination.[37] How-

32 Opinion of the European Court of Human Rights on draft Protocol 12 to the European Convention on Human Rights, Doc 8606, 5 January 2000, para 5.

33 Para. 1(b), recommendation no. 7.

34 Para. 8, explanatory memorandum.

35 Article 2(2)(a), Directive 2000/43/EC. See also Article 2(2)(a), Directive 2000/78/EC.

36 For example, difference of treatment based on nationality.

37 For example, *Abdulaziz, Cabales and Balkandali v UK* [1985] 7 EHRR 471, 504.

ever, ECRI's model legislation recommends that national laws define indirect discrimination as

> Cases where an apparently neutral factor such as a provision, criterion or practice cannot be as easily complied with by, or disadvantages, persons belonging to a group designated by a ground such as race, colour, language, religion, nationality or national or ethnic origin, unless this factor has an objective and reasonable justification. This latter would be the case if it pursues a legitimate aim and if there is a reasonable relationship of proportionality between the means employed and the aim sought to be realised.'[38]

This is quite similar to the definition provided in the Article 13 Directives. The Racial Equality Directive refers to practices that 'would put persons of a racial or ethnic origin at a particular disadvantage compared with other persons'.[39] The reference to *particular* disadvantage suggests a slightly higher threshold than ECRI proposes, as its definition covers anything that produces disadvantage. In contrast, the Directives are more demanding in terms of justification, requiring measures to be 'appropriate and necessary',[40] whereas ECRI's text simply demands a 'reasonable relationship of proportionality'. In the absence of judicial interpretation, though, it is difficult to determine how significant these textual differences will prove to be in practice.

2.2.3 Other aspects of discrimination

The Article 13 Directives identify two further forms of unlawful discrimination: harassment and instruction to discriminate. Although the Court of Human Rights has not yet dealt with these issues under Article 14 of the Convention, ECRI's model legislation endorses the view that it is not sufficient to rely purely on concepts of direct and indirect discrimination in national law. ECRI essentially recommend that states adopt the definition of harassment provided in the Article 13 Directives: conduct with 'the purpose or effect of violating the dignity of a person and of creating an intimidating, hostile, degrading, humiliating or offensive environment.'[41] It should be noted, however, that ECRI suggest to apply this to a variety of actors over which the employer exercises a certain degree of control – for example, clients and co-workers.[42] In contrast, the Article 13 Directives leave such details to national discretion.

38 Paragraph 1(c), recommendation no. 7.

39 Article 2(2)(b), Directive 2000/43/EC.

40 *Ibid.*

41 Art 2(3), *ibid.*

42 Para. 35, explanatory memorandum.

ECRI's model legislation also goes further in supporting a ban on 'segregation; discrimination by association; announced intention to discriminate; instructing another to discriminate; inciting another to discriminate; aiding another to discriminate'.[43] Some of these activities may fall within the scope of the Racial Equality Directive, depending on how broadly the Court of Justice interprets its provisions. Discrimination by association can occur, for example, where a person from a minority ethnic community is refused entry to a bar and other people who are not from minority communities are similarly refused access by reason of being in the company of someone from a minority community.[44] Considering the English version of the Racial Equality Directive, discrimination based on association would seem to be forbidden – it contains a wide reference to discrimination 'on grounds of racial or ethnic origin'.[45] However, the Italian version of the Directive is not amenable to such an interpretation because it speaks more narrowly of less favourable treatment 'because of *his* race or ethnic origin'.[46] It will ultimately fall to the Court of Justice to resolve this linguistic divergence.

Segregation is not explicitly addressed in the Racial Equality Directive. Nonetheless, evidence of involuntary segregation can still be found in Europe; for example, the treatment of many Roma children in the Hungarian education system.[47] The Directive has not been written with a view to tackling such practices. Instead, it is based on a comparative approach to discrimination, which focuses on the less favourable treatment of a particular individual or group. As a consequence, 'separate but equal' policies present a challenge to the identification of a comparator who is being treated more favourably. However, segregation often results in unequal treatment in practice: for example, a poorer standard of education for students from minority communities.[48] Where this can be established, there will be evidence of less favourable treatment contrary to the Directive.

In summary, the Council of Europe instruments present a broader approach to the concept of racism, readily accepting that characteristics such as language, religion and nationality can be the object of racial discrimination. Yet, the definition of discrimination remains more flexible, most notably as a result of

---

43 Para. 6, recommendation no. 7.

44 This has been held to be contrary to Irish anti-discrimination law in respect of persons associating with members of the Travelling community: *Ward and Ward v Quigley*, DEC-S2001-001, Equality Officer Decision of 16 March 2001, available at: <http://www.odei.ie>.

45 Art 2(2)(a), Directive 2000/43/EC.

46 Author's emphasis and translation: 'sussiste discriminazione diretta quando, a causa della sua razza od origine etnica, una persona è trattata meno favorevolmente'.

47 Para. 30, ECRI, 'Second report on Hungary', CRI (2000) 5.

48 *Ibid.*

the wider possibility for states to justify differences in treatment linked to these grounds. The Union has focused instead on establishing a strict level of protection in respect of a narrow range of grounds. This may be more effective for individuals who experience 'classical' forms of racism – for example, the exclusion of 'blacks' from a discotheque. It does not, though, engage with the evolving nature of racism and discrimination.

3. Building a Comprehensive Web of Protection

Having examined the definitions of discrimination, this part turns to the scope of legal protection. First, it considers the material scope of anti-discrimination legislation – the areas that should be covered. Second, it examines the nature of the legal instruments to be adopted, with special attention to the roles for civil and criminal law.

3.1 Material Scope

ECRI's model legislation is predicated upon an 'integrated approach' with legislative provisions 'in all the branches of the law, i.e. constitutional, civil, administrative and criminal law'.[49] This resounds well with the autonomous right to non-discrimination promised by Protocol 12. It prohibits discrimination in 'the enjoyment of any right set forth by law',[50] as well as providing that 'no one shall be discriminated against by any public authority'.[51] Taken together, there is a vision of Protocol 12 as an umbrella guarantee, overseeing the comprehensive legislation that states should adopt on the basis of the model provided by ECRI.

In contrast, EU action is inherently restrained by the limits of the legal competence conferred by the founding Treaties. Both the Racial Equality Directive and the Framework Employment Directive apply to a wide range of activities connected with employment and training.[52] In addition, the Racial Equality Directive applies to 'social protection, including social security and healthcare, social advantages, education, access to and supply of goods and services which are available to the public, including housing.'[53] This is a similar scope to that recommended by ECRI's model legislation, the main distinction being that ECRI additionally include 'public services'.[54] This extra element is intended to

49 Para. 3, explanatory memorandum.

50 Article 1(1).

51 Article 1(2).

52 Article 3(1): Directives 2000/43/EC and 2000/78/EC.

53 Article 3(1)(e)-(h), Directive 2000/43/EC.

54 Para. 7 recommendation no. 7.

cover activities such as law enforcement (including prisons) and immigration.[55] Whilst law enforcement activities largely fall outside the scope of the EC Treaty, the same cannot be said in respect of immigration and asylum. The absence of these areas from the material scope of the Racial Equality Directive is an undoubted weakness.

3.2 *The role for different branches of the law*

A new dimension emerging in European standard-setting on racism is the balance between different areas of law. National legal traditions vary greatly in this area, from states that focus on civil law remedies,[56] to those that have placed the accent on criminal law sanctions.[57] The Racial Equality Directive leaves this choice to the discretion of Member States, subject to the requirement that the sanctions selected must be 'effective, proportionate and dissuasive'.[58] Given the difficulties experienced by some states in using criminal sanctions to combat discrimination,[59] it is unlikely that a purely penal law framework would be the most effective response to the Directive.

If the Racial Equality Directive allows room for flexibility, the proposed Framework Decision will establish with more clarity the Union's view of the role criminal law should play in combating racism. The Council has focused its discussions on prohibiting three broad types of racist or xenophobic conduct:

1. Public incitement to discrimination, violence or hatred;
2. The commission of an act by public dissemination of tracts, pictures or other material;
3. Public condoning, denial or gross trivialisation of genocide, war crimes, crimes against humanity and the Holocaust.[60]

In addition, the Framework Decision contains provision for taking racist or xenophobic motivation into account as an aggravating factor in the commission of any other criminal offence.[61]

ECRI's model legislation recommends that states go significantly further in mobilising the criminal law to combat racism. Specifically, ECRI propose that

55 Para. 26, explanatory memorandum.

56 For example, UK and Ireland. See further, M. Bell, *Anti-discrimination law and the European Union* (OUP, Oxford, 2002).

57 For example, France and Spain, *ibid.*

58 Article 15, Directive 2000/43/EC.

59 Para. 4, ECRI, 'Second report on Belgium' CRI (2000) 2; para. 7, ECRI, 'Second report on France' CRI (2000) 31.

60 Article 1, Council, above n 30.

61 Article 4, *ibid.*

states forbid:

- Racist insults, defamation and threats;
- The public expression with a racist aim of racist ideologies;
- The creation of, support for or participation in groups that promote racism;
- Racial discrimination in the exercise of a public office.[62]

The requirement to penalise racist groups is a notable difference between ECRI's model legislation and the current draft of the EU Framework Decision. In this respect, ECRI are supported by ICERD, which includes a requirement to 'declare illegal and prohibit organisations ... which promote and incite racial discrimination'.[63] It is striking that although all EU Member States have ratified ICERD, they are not prepared to include this requirement in EU legislation.[64]

Taking an overview, both through Protocol 12 and the model legislation, the Council of Europe is taking a more comprehensive approach to legal protection against racial discrimination. Its standards are intended to apply throughout the law and all areas of public activity. In contrast, the Union has thoroughly addressed discrimination in the labour market, but is only moving hesitantly to tackle forms of discrimination in other areas. The Racial Equality Directive marked a major step forward in this respect and sets an important precedent for EU anti-discrimination law in general. However, highly sensitive areas, such as policing and immigration, remain untouched even though these are central to ensuring harmonious ethnic relations. The Framework Decision will represent another step in building a more holistic framework of EU protection, however, this not an instrument amenable to individual enforcement and it must be noted that the Member States are proceeding very cautiously in the negotiation of its contents.

4. Enforcement of Anti-Discrimination Law

A persistent problem with all areas of anti-discrimination law is securing effective means of putting the standards in the law into everyday practice. Earlier European legal interventions on gender equality suffered from a failure to pay sufficient attention to enforcement mechanisms, leaving these to the discretion of national authorities.[65] Similarly, although ICERD contributed to the prolif-

---

62 Para. 18, recommendation no. 7.

63 Article 4(b).

64 In fact, this offence was contained in the Commission proposal for the Framework Decision, but has since been deleted during the Council negotiations: Article 4(f), COM (2001) 664.

65 J. Blom, B. Fitzpatrick, J. Gregory, R. Knegt and U. O'Hare, *The Utilisation of Sex Equality Litigation in the Member States of the European Community* V/782/96-EN (Report to the Equal Opportunities Unit of DG V, 1995).

eration of national laws against racism during the 1970s, much of this legislation was rarely invoked.[66] As a consequence, the Racial Equality Directive has been praised for its attention to tools for practical implementation.[67]

The Directive requires states to take a number of measures that are aimed at facilitating successful individual litigation. In civil litigation, there is provision for a shift in the burden of proof from the complainant to the respondent, once the former has established 'facts from which it may be presumed that there has been direct or indirect discrimination'.[68] For example, where an individual from a minority ethnic community is refused entry to a bar on the grounds of not having sufficient identification to prove his age, but other persons of different ethnic origin are not being required to produce such identification, then a prima facie case of racial discrimination has been established and it will be for the bar to demonstrate that they have not committed unlawful discrimination.[69]

In addition, the Directive obliges states to ensure that complainants are protected against any victimisation as a consequence of making a complaint, and it specifies that the remedies for a finding of unlawful discrimination must be 'effective, proportionate and dissuasive'.[70] Although this provides a degree of discretion for national authorities, the Court of Justice has usefully deployed the 'effectiveness' standard in gender equality case-law in order to enhance sanctions in national law. For example, it has insisted that an individual who suffers discrimination in the recruitment process, but who would not have gained the position even in the absence of discrimination, is nonetheless entitled to a certain level of financial compensation.[71]

With regard to individual litigation, the ECRI model legislation endorses all the above aspects of the Directive. However, it recommends a number of additional steps that states should take to improve individual enforcement of anti-discrimination law. First, it proposes that 'fast-track' procedures be available in respect of discrimination cases, including the possibility of interim remedies to protect the individual's position – for example, an injunction against dismissal or termination of a rental contract.[72] In addition, ECRI suggest that free legal

66 Commission, 'Legal Instruments to Combat Racism and Xenophobia' (Office for the Official Publications of the European Communities, Luxembourg, 1992) p. 18.

67 C. Barnard, 'The changing scope of the fundamental principle of equality?' (2001) 46 *McGill Law Journal* 955, 973.

68 Article 8(1), Directive 2000/43/EC.

69 This was applied in an Irish case on refusal of access to a bar for an Azerbaijani national: *Sajjadi v The Turk's Head*, DEC-S2002-101, Equality Officer Decision of 31 July 2002. Available at: http://www.odei.ie

70 Article 15, Directive 2000/43/EC.

71 Case C-180/95 *Draehmpaehl v Urania Immobilienservice OHG* [1997] ECR I-2195.

72 Para. 10, recommendation no. 7.

aid be available to complainants, including court-appointed lawyers and interpretation facilities, as required.[73] The Starting Line Group[74] and the European Parliament[75] had both suggested provision of legal aid should be included in the Racial Equality Directive, but the Council of Ministers rejected this proposal.

Another novel feature of the Racial Equality Directive was the clear recognition that even with the measures listed above, enforcement would still prove difficult if it was purely dependent on individual litigation. Therefore, it presents two alternative strategies to supplement individual complaints. First, states must permit associations with a 'legitimate interest' in enforcing the Directive to 'engage, either on behalf or in support of the complainant, with his or her approval, in any judicial and/or administrative procedure'.[76] It seems reasonable to assume that such organisations would include trade unions and groups working against racism. Second, states are placed under a duty to create 'a body or bodies for the promotion of equal treatment'.[77] These agencies must have a broad remit to conduct research and make recommendations on combating racism, but a core responsibility is to provide 'independent assistance to victims of discrimination in pursuing their complaints'.[78]

As before, the ECRI model legislation includes the above elements from the Racial Equality Directive, but encourages states to do more. With regard to legal standing for associations, ECRI recommend that these should be able to bring cases 'even if a specific victim is not referred to'.[79] ECRI also foresee a broader mandate for the equal treatment body. It proposes that such bodies should be given 'investigation powers' as well as the right to 'initiate, and participate in court proceedings'.[80] In fact, ECRI already identified the important role to be played by such bodies in their 1997 recommendation on 'specialised bodies to combat racism'. This supports a role for such bodies in hearing and considering complaints, including the power to issue 'binding and enforceable decisions'.[81] However, the explanatory memorandum to the model legislation clarifies that if

73 Para. 26, recommendation no. 7.

74 I. Chopin and J. Niessen (eds), *Proposals for legislative measures to combat racism and to promote equal rights in the European Union* (Commission for Racial Equality, London, 1998) p. 29.

75 Amendment 41, [2001] OJ C59/271.

76 Article 7(2), Directive 2000/43/EC.

77 Article 13(1), *ibid.*

78 Article 13(2), *ibid.*

79 Para. 25, recommendation no. 7.

80 Para. 24, recommendation no. 7.

81 Principle 3(f), ECRI general policy recommendation no. 2: Specialised bodies to combat racism, xenophobia, antisemitism and intolerance at national level, CRI (97) 36.

adjudication functions are to be attributed to a specialised body, this must be separate from the agency responsible for the promotion of equal treatment and assistance of individuals.[82]

5. Developing a Proactive Agenda

In the previous sections, a reasonable degree of consensus has been observed between the Racial Equality Directive and Framework Decision on the one hand, and the ECRI model legislation on the other. In places, both EU law and the Council of Europe instruments alternatively impose higher standards, however, the general contours are similar. Where the instruments more clearly depart is in relation to what may be termed the 'proactive agenda'. This section is concerned with measures that move beyond negative prohibitions on discrimination, instead going towards obligations to take positive steps to realise equality. Three areas will be examined: positive action; contract compliance and positive duties.

5.1 Positive action

The taking of targeted actions to compensate for the effects of past disadvantage and to facilitate equal participation is by now a familiar element of the equality policy agenda. ICERD implies that positive action may be a duty of the state in some circumstances: Article 2(2) provides that 'State parties *shall*, when the circumstances so warrant, take, in the social, economic, cultural and other fields, special and concrete measures to ensure the adequate development and protection of certain racial groups and individuals belonging to them'.[83] This approach is followed in the ECRI model legislation, which demands that 'the law *should* provide that the prohibition of racial discrimination does not prevent the maintenance or adoption of temporary special measures'.[84] In other words, there must be legal space provided to permit positive action under appropriate circumstances. In contrast, the Racial Equality Directive simply states that 'the principle of equal treatment shall not prevent any Member State from maintaining or adopting specific measures'.[85] Thus, it remains at the discretion of each state to determine whether or not positive action will be permissible in the national legal system.

82 Para. 55, explanatory memorandum.

83 Author's emphasis.

84 Author's emphasis, para 5, recommendation no. 7.

85 Article 5, Directive 2000/43/EC.

5.2 Contract compliance

An even greater difference in approach can be found in relation to contract compliance schemes. This can be broadly understood to refer to programmes that seek to link respect for anti-discrimination law with participation in public contracts. Normally, this implies that the state uses its purchasing power to impose certain requirements and duties on firms in receipt of public contracts. This strategy is firmly embraced in the ECRI model legislation, which recommends that 'the law should place public authorities under a duty to ensure that those parties to whom they award contracts, loans, grants or other benefits respect and promote a policy of non-discrimination'.[86] Furthermore, failure to comply with these conditions should lead to termination of the contract.[87]

ECRI's strong endorsement of contract compliance contrasts with EU law, which does not promote the use of such policies and, in some circumstances, prevents public authorities adopting these programmes. The principal reference point here is the body of EU public procurement legislation. This was developed as part of the internal market programme, with a view to opening the market in public contracts to firms throughout the Union and displacing the traditional tendency of public bodies to give preference to local and national tenders. To this end, the award of contracts is predominantly based on criteria of economic efficiency and there is limited space for taking into account wider social policy priorities.[88] Although there has been considerable discussion and case-law concerning the precise requirements of the EU legislation,[89] the Commission's view is that social considerations generally cannot be taken into account in selecting a successful tender.[90] This restriction is balanced by two main possibilities for a degree of contract compliance. First, firms that have breached social legislation (including anti-discrimination law) may be excluded from entering the competition.[91] Second, the contract awarded may contain clauses requiring the pursuit

86 Para. 9, recommendation no. 7.

87 *Ibid.*

88 R. Fee, 'Contract compliance: subnational and European influences in Northern Ireland' (2002) 12 *Journal of European Social Policy* 107, 115.

89 J. Fernández Martín, *The EC public procurement rules: a critical analysis* (Clarendon Press, Oxford, 1996), chapter 2; J. Cormack and J. Niessen, 'Public procurement and anti-discrimination legislation' in I. Chopin and J. Niessen, *Combating racial and ethnic discrimination: taking the European legislative agenda further* (Commission for Racial Equality and Migration Policy Group, London, 2002), p. 35.

90 Interpretative Communication of the Commission on Community law applicable to public procurement and the possibilities for integrating social considerations into public procurement, [2001] OJ C333/27, para 1.3.

91 Para 1.3.1, *ibid.*

of social objectives in its completion – for example, the promotion of ethnic diversity.[92]

If a broad perspective is adopted, it is possible to identify opportunities for states to pursue the forms of contract compliance endorsed by ECRI without falling foul of EU public procurement law. Yet, the ambiguity surrounding the exact scope of EU law in this area certainly does not encourage states to adopt such policies. Indeed, at least one national authority has justified its failure to institute contract compliance schemes by citing EU law.[93]

5.3 *Positive duties*

Perhaps the most original component of the ECRI model legislation is the recommendation that 'the law should place public authorities under a duty to promote equality and to prevent discrimination in carrying out their functions'.[94] This is joined by an obligation to keep all forms of legislation under review for discriminatory effects.[95] The explanatory memorandum spells out the full implications of what ECRI envisions. Specifically, it suggests that all public authorities be placed under a duty to design legally binding equality programmes and that these should be regularly monitored and enforced by national equality bodies.[96] This is not an approach hitherto considered by the European Union, however, it bears marked similarities to recent legislative initiatives in the UK.

In Northern Ireland, in 1998, all public authorities were placed under a duty to promote equality of opportunity across a wide range of grounds, including 'racial group'.[97] This was initially implemented by each body publishing an 'equality scheme'.[98] These were subject to review by the Equality Commission for Northern Ireland and they set out how the authority intends to promote equality, including arrangements for monitoring outcomes and consulting with relevant communities.[99] Analogous arrangements were established in Great Britain as a result of the Race Relations (Amendment) Act 2000. This placed a wide range of public authorities under a general obligation 'to promote equality of opportunity and good relations between persons of different racial groups'.[100]

---

92 Para. 1.6, *ibid.*

93 Para. 5.25, Northern Ireland Office, 'Partnership for Equality – a White Paper' Cm 3890 (The Stationary Office, London, 1998).

94 Para. 8, recommendation no. 7.

95 Para. 13, *ibid.*

96 Para 27, explanatory memorandum.

97 Section 75(1), Northern Ireland Act 1998.

98 Schedule 9, Northern Ireland Act 1998.

99 *Ibid.*

100 Section 71(1)(b), Race Relations Act 1976 (as amended).

The general duty has been supplemented by specific duties issued by the government in respect of sectors such as education and healthcare.[101] These impose more detailed requirements in terms of what actions the relevant authorities must take to comply with the equality duty. Whilst it remains too early to assess the long-term effectiveness of these complex and innovative arrangements, they have at least generated considerable momentum in compelling public organisations to review their practices and to place greater priority on securing equality of opportunity throughout their service delivery.

The fact that similar, but quite different models have been adopted between Northern Ireland and Great Britain demonstrates the impossibility of mechanically reproducing these arrangements across Europe. Nevertheless, the positive duty approach provides a constructive response to the underlying weakness in relying on individual litigation as the predominant means of achieving equality. Even with the range of initiatives already taken to make anti-discrimination law more accessible and easy to enforce, it remains difficult to circumvent some basic financial and emotional costs for litigants. Therefore, it is sensible and forward-looking to devise complementary strategies. The positive duty proposed by ECRI is framed in wide and flexible terms that render it amenable to adaptation to the specific circumstances of the national environment. It contains significant potential and promises a different path from the litigation-oriented model found within EU legislation.

6. Between Convergence and Divergence: The EU and the Council of Europe

Taking an overview, it would be easy to criticise the EU instruments for generally adopting a more cautious approach in comparison to that recommended by ECRI. Admittedly, ECRI's model legislation goes significantly further than even the combined effects of the Article 13 Directives and the prospective Framework Decision. Yet, the fundamental differences in the nature of these instruments cannot be ignored. Crucially, the Union's legislation is binding, enforceable and the product of agreement between national governments. Unsurprisingly, Member States are typically reluctant to make sweeping new commitments that will impose major change on existing national practices. Whilst acknowledging its various omissions and weaknesses, the Racial Equality Directive in fact demands all EU states (present and future) alter their laws on racism. It is greatly strengthened by the efforts to improve individual enforcement within the national legal system and by its location within Community law, where a range of mechanisms exist through which states can be compelled to implement the Directive in full.[102]

101 Race Relations Act 1976 (Statutory Duties) Order 2001 (No. 3458).

102 See further, Bell, above n. 20, p. 30.

The Council of Europe also enjoys the power to adopt binding and enforceable legal instruments, of which the Human Rights Convention is the best example. Protocol 12 will significantly strengthen the capacity of the Convention to be utilised in combating racism, assuming it eventually enters into force. The comprehensive nature of its non-discrimination guarantee provides a striking contrast to the 'bits and pieces' approach found in EU legislation. Nonetheless, its wide, constitutional scope is balanced by the absence of detailed obligations. Protocol 12 is a flexible instrument, which will have to be melded over time by national courts and the Court of Human Rights.

By comparison, ECRI's recommendations inhabit territory much closer to the work of the Union. Overall, the model legislation recommendation seeks to promote higher standards than those found in the Racial Equality Directive and the Framework Decision. Again, this is understandable given the nature of the instruments. The EU legislation establishes strict minimum requirements, whereas ECRI seeks to identify best practice. Its tools for enforcement are not grounded in litigation, but rather the power of persuasion through peer review and regular monitoring. If the model legislation is deployed as a benchmark for ECRI's individual country reports, then states will feel political pressure to address its contents and to justify falling below its threshold. Moreover, ECRI's recommendations equip national non-governmental organisations with reference points that can legitimise their campaigns for law reform. ECRI's working methods are in fact increasingly found within EU regulatory practices. In various policy fields, the Union has shifted its emphasis away from the adoption of hard law instruments and towards more flexible mechanisms of policy coordination.[103] This technique, often referred to as the 'open method of coordination' (OMC), is characterised by EU level policy guidelines and periodic national reports on their implementation.[104] The cycle is completed by EU evaluation of the national reports and recommendations to individual states for further action. Issues connected with combating racism arise in a number of different OMCs – such as employment promotion[105] and social inclusion.[106] At present, there is not a specific OMC dedicated to anti-discrimination, although a European Parliament Committee has previously proposed this.[107] Therefore, ECRI's

103 E. Szyszczak, 'Social policy in the post-Nice era' in A. Arnull and D. Wincott (eds), *Accountability and Legitimacy in the EU* (OUP, Oxford, 2002) p. 330.

104 C. de la Porte, 'Is the open method of coordination appropriate for organising activities at European level in sensitive policy areas?' (2002) 8 *European Law Journal* 38.

105 Commission Staff Working Paper, 'Assessment of the implementation of the 2001 employment guidelines' SEC (2001) 1398, p. 64.

106 De la Porte, above n 104, p. 52.

107 Committee on Employment and Social Affairs, 'A framework for action on non-discrimination at EU level based on Article 13 of the Amsterdam Treaty' Working Document, PE 229.570, 25 March 1999, p. 6.

contribution provides a useful synergy with the legislative programme of the Union.

The omission in the current scheme is any external analysis and review of EU action on racism. Following the current enlargement, more than half of the states in the Council of Europe will be working within the legal framework provided by the Union. On the one hand, this will facilitate ECRI's work, because many of its recommendations will be simultaneously obligations under the Racial Equality Directive and the Framework Decision. On the other, there is the risk that states treat compliance with EU legislation as a sufficient response to racism; indeed, this may become a justification for failure to adopt higher standards. A more problematic situation is where EU law directly contradicts ECRI's standards. The overview provided in this chapter reveals that this is not yet a common problem, but there exist areas of considerable divergence. For example, the Union's outlook on public procurement remains entrenched in economic rationality, unlike the socially purposive view from ECRI. EU law reinforces legal inequality between EU citizens and third country nationals,[108] whereas ECRI start from the position that difference of treatment based on nationality is racial discrimination, unless objectively justified. In order to influence effectively practice in the EU Member States, the Council of Europe increasingly needs to be able to shape the legal and policy choices made at Union level. Specifically, it would be valuable if ECRI's periodic reports extended to a review of the Union's law and practice. Whilst this is not currently possible, given that the Union is neither a signatory of the Human Rights Convention, nor a member of the Council of Europe, it is important that accession by the EU to the Convention is once again under review.[109] This would provide a better guarantee of long-term coherence and cooperation in the fight against racism.

---

108 For example, the exclusion of third country nationals from the right to free movement.

109 European Convention, 'Final report of Working Group II' CONV 354/02, 22 October 2002.

Ann Dummett

9. IMPLEMENTING EUROPEAN ANTI-DISCRIMINATION LAW: A CRITICAL ANALYSIS

This chapter is an appraisal and critique of the legislative developments concerning racial and ethnic discrimination in 26 European states. It is based on reports comparing existing legislation in these countries with the requirements of the Council Directive implementing the principle of equal treatment between persons irrespective of racial and ethnic origin (Racial Equality Directive).[1]

This analysis, like the reports themselves, has to be treated with caution for several reasons. First, the reports deal with the situation up to September 2001; since then, there have been changes in some states' laws and systematic efforts in others to draft legislative changes in line with the Racial Equality Directive and the Employment Equality Directive.[2] In other states there has so far been no movement. Direct comparisons between countries may be misleading. At the same time there have been changes in the governments of several states, which can affect the prospects of legal change and perhaps affect even more the climate in which changes are implemented. Secondly, the reports vary in the

1 For the 15 EU Member States see, Isabelle Chopin and Jan Niessen (eds), Anti-discrimination legislation in EU Member States. A comparison of national anti-discrimination legislation on the grounds of racial or ethnic, religion or belief with the Council Directives. European Monitoring Centre on Racism and Xenophobia. The reports are available electronically (www. eumc.eu.int) in English and French and each individual report in the language of the respective Member State. The reports on the eleven candidate countries are available from the website of the Migration Policy Group (www.migpolgroup.com). These countries include: Bulgaria, Czech Republic, Estonia, Hungary, Latvia, Lithuania, Poland, Romania, Slovakia, Slovenia, and Turkey.

2 Council Directive establishing a general framework for equal treatment in employment and occupation (OJ L 303, 27/11/2000).

Jan Niessen, Isabelle Chopin (eds.), The Development of Legal Instruments..., *235-253*

kind of information they convey. Their purpose is to describe legal frameworks, and while some keep strictly to this purpose, saying little or nothing about the persons affected by discrimination, others provide some background information which helps the reader to interpret the impact of existing law and to assess how legal changes may affect vulnerable minorities. It is important here that the concept of minorities is not the same in all countries: in some, there are certain officially recognised minority groups with special rights, but persons who do not belong to one of these recognised groups yet who may suffer discrimination (e.g. Asian immigrants and asylum seekers) are left out of account. Therefore, my comments incorporate a few facts about the situations in some countries to place beside the legal material. None of these comments should be taken to provide a comprehensive account of the situation in any country: they merely indicate the kind of factors that need taking into account. Concepts of what constitutes discrimination also apparently vary between countries. More will be said below of this difficulty, which raises problems about whether compliance with the Directives is truly achieved once new laws are passed. I have not dealt with the material country-by-country but according to themes and questions which the reports suggest. As a result, the major achievements in anti-discrimination law, which some countries have made, are not given as much attention, perhaps, as they deserve. However, the reports themselves indicate very well such differences in achievement amongst states. The purpose of my account is to demonstrate the great variety that exists between the countries where the Directives are to be complied with, their differences of attitude and understanding of terms, and the policy problems that may arise from all these perceptions. At the same time, I must stress however that great efforts are being made in many places to overcome these problems.

While every country claims that it already outlaws racial discrimination, it is clear from the reports that in some of them implementation hardly exists. All the states concerned (except the UK), and both EU members and applicants for membership, have written constitutions stating that all citizens shall be equal and listing the types of discrimination between them that shall not be allowed: racial, religious and sex discrimination are included in the lists. But it is rare for constitutional provisions to be directly applicable to an individual case in any court. Similarly, states have adhered to international agreements on human rights and racial discrimination; but their provisions are in such general terms that they are of little practical help. International agreements and constitutions declare excellent principles but without specific legislation applying those principles, racial and ethnic discrimination cannot be effectively outlawed.

1. Historical Differences

A major difficulty in ensuring compliance with the Directives is that the concept of what discrimination is varies enormously between countries. These perceptions have been formed by differing histories. Over the last 15 years or so, perceptions in west European countries have come closer to each other than they used to be. But fundamental attitudes have been formed by earlier histories.

The overseas empires of the UK, the Netherlands and France left a legacy of imperial attitudes towards specific peoples in Africa, Asia and the Caribbean, countered by the views of movements for colonial freedom. Non-European origins and skin colour were important factors in British and Dutch history, whereas the French have always rejected accusations of racism by pointing out that the acceptance of French culture by colonial peoples made skin colour irrelevant to progress. All three powers took for granted the superiority of Europeanness, whether racial or cultural, and their imperial policies left a legacy of bitterness in many of the countries they had ruled. Their attitudes to religion were not all the same: French hostility to Islam, on the part of both Catholic Right and the secular Left, has deep roots and has complicated the racial situation.

In all three countries the history of empires has been crucial to the assumptions on all sides of the debate. But in the applicant countries of Eastern Europe, the history of empire turns such assumptions upside down. In the Baltic states of Estonia and Latvia, the vulnerable groups are mainly Russian or Ukrainian and are associated with old imperialisms rather than old victims. In eastern and southeastern states generally, ethnic discord is the result of centuries of rival, fierce nationalisms within the former Turkish, Russian and Austro-Hungarian empires.

These differences affect the terminology used in each country and can easily create misunderstanding. They could cause problems with popular and political interpretation of the directives. 'Nationality' is a particularly awkward term. For the EU, nationality means citizenship. But in Romania, for example, the Constitution refers several times to 'national minorities' but does not define these and makes no distinction between them and ethnic minorities. A glance at history will show why. For centuries within the Turkish Empire, Romania had consisted of Moldavia and Wallachia. In 1878 it was recognised as an independent state and gained some territory from part of the Dobrudja. After the First World War it gained several more territories, the most important being Transylvania which had a large Hungarian population: it had formerly been part of the Austrian empire. In 1940, Romania had to cede some lands to Soviet Russia and to Bulgaria. It now contains a considerable number of different ethnic groups, as people in the West would call them, but which are often referred to within the country as nationalities. Moreover, history has remained alive in the complicated relationships between these groups. Each national group is entitled to one representative in the Romanian Parliament.

The report on Romania in this study says that 'during the last ten years, when the issue of discrimination has been brought to the public attention, the Roma have been the only ones constantly claiming to be discriminated against'.

The Hungarian minority and its representatives, although at the very beginning considered as being discriminated against, afterwards preferred to consider the Hungarians as being 'under-represented in some sectors', such as the police and government agencies. Other minorities have stressed that they have not felt discriminated against and that their main concern is the preservation of their languages and cultural traditions. But superimposed on these historical minorities are 'new minorities' who have settled since 1990, including Arabs, Kurds and Chinese. These have the same legal rights as the historical minorities, provided that they hold Romanian citizenship, which many but not all have acquired through naturalisation. We are not told directly how they perceive discrimination, though it is said in the report that the Roma are the only group who have complained of it.

Evidently, the historical minorities do not have the same understanding of 'discrimination' as the framers of the EC Directive, to whom under-representation would be a discriminatory issue. The different perceptions of nationality could be important in negotiating legal changes. The report says that in Romania, as in other central and east European states, nationality denotes ethnic origin while citizenship means Romanian legal status independently of ethnic origin. The distinction is made not only legally but 'is employed in daily life by political parties, media and the public at large'. Passports issued a few years ago followed the western usage in having an item on 'nationality', which required a statement of citizenship. The Hungarian minority complained of 'forced assimilation'. The Romanians complained that they were being confused with the Roma minority, since the passports used the abbreviation 'Rom' for Romanian and 'Rom' is the word for Roma in the Romanian language. The passports had to be withdrawn.

Citizenship raises a different kind of problem in Estonia. Estonia was part of the old Russian Empire for centuries. It became an independent state in 1920 but was re-absorbed into Soviet Russia in 1940. It regained its independence in 1991. Naturally, after long periods as part of a much larger sovereign state, its population had become mixed with that of the dominant power, and non-Estonians make up one-third of the residents, most of this third being Russian. Resentment of former Soviet occupation goes along with strong Estonian nationalism. The report records that in 1992 'only citizens of pre-World War Two republic of Estonia, as of the moment it collapsed, and their successors, were declared citizens of the Republic of Estonia'. As a result about 22 per cent of the population are stateless. Non-Estonians have to apply for residence permits.

There is no systematic anti-discrimination law in the country, though there are a number of provisions to safeguard basic rights, such as the right for everyone to have access to the courts. However, it is clear that discrimination based on nationality (in the sense of citizenship as well as of national origin) is built into the system by law.

The situation in Latvia is similar. One-quarter of the population consists of 'non-citizens', a named category for former USSR citizens who were living in Latvia on 1 July 1991 and have not obtained citizenship of any other country. Non-citizens can be naturalised as Latvians if they pass examinations in Latvian language and history.

Interestingly, the impression conveyed by the other Baltic state, Lithuania, is very different. Lithuania was a major state in medieval Eastern Europe. Its relations with Poland over a long period have been more important than with Russia, and its independence was threatened by Poland after the First World War. In 1939, Lithuania concluded a separate pact with Germany, and in October that year regained her ancient capital of Vilna from Poland. Fifty years of Soviet occupation did not leave the same legacy as in Latvia and Estonia. The report lists its ethnic minorities as: Russians 6.9 per cent, Poles 1.5 per cent, and then other groups at one per cent each or less. The legal framework described in the report is markedly more liberal and sophisticated than those of many eastern and southern states, though the author admits that implementation is limited because of a 'low level of public trust in law and legal institutions as effective tools in fighting discrimination'.

2. Discrimination in Theory and Practice

Broadly speaking, the variations in perception of what constitutes unfair discrimination in applicant states are likely to cause problems in application of the Directive. Lawyers and NGOs may have a clearer understanding than others of the problem, but officials, the police and many institutions will still be heavily influenced by traditional attitudes. On the other hand, equality between men and women is usually (though not always, according to some of these reports) better understood and is already the subject of existing laws to counter discrimination. Also, in general, equality at work is recognised as an important issue everywhere, though its achievement is far from perfect.

Differences between Member States and applicant states should not obscure the fact that among Member States there are considerable differences in understanding what constitutes discrimination and of how to deal with it. France, for example, has for a long time emphasised the dangers of written and spoken expressions of racism rather than the dangers of discriminatory behaviour. Physical attacks on members of minorities have often not been considered racist unless the attackers specifically use racist language. The report on France comments that 'anti-discrimination legislation remains very modest. The difficulty of providing proof of discriminatory conduct is most often cited to explain the weakness of the legislation'. But this explanation cannot be convincing when the difficulties of proof are no different in countries which have well established systems of law against discriminatory conduct. We must look for other explanations to show why the French system is so different from, for instance, the

Dutch and British systems. The French dislike the idea that they could possibly be racist: racism is abhorrent to them. But, as mentioned already above, they perceive racism much more as a matter of the spoken and written word than as a form of behaviour. Moreover, individual complaints of unjust discrimination have usually to be made to state officials, in particular the police. Generally speaking, the most vulnerable minorities in France are exceedingly reluctant to approach the police, for fear of being removed from the country. When the report was written, there was no central body of the kind recommended in the Directive to deal with complaints, and so it is not surprising that the number of complaints made has been ridiculously small.

3. Immigration

It is not easy in any country to inspire confidence among the minorities in any government-funded or government-appointed institution dealing with racism. This is chiefly because governments themselves discriminate, or are perceived to discriminate, on racial grounds, mainly in the field of immigration and asylum law. The message conveyed in these laws goes out not only to the immigrant and immigrant-descended group in the population but to the citizen majority; both groups understand that certain types of people, defined by colour or descent, are officially considered undesirable. (The point was made very clearly in a meeting I attended in 1967, when the British government was considering an anti-discrimination law, which applied to employment. 'Why,' asked an employer, 'can't I say I don't want these people in my firm when the government says it doesn't want them in the country?')

An anti-discrimination law cannot work really effectively unless it has the confidence of the people it is intended to protect. It also needs the co-operation of all those who have the power to discriminate: employers, landlords, school authorities, providers of industrial training, trade unions, public officials and others. Confronting this latter group with accusations is not enough to stop discrimination: their active participation in promoting racial equality must be sought.

At present, immigration and asylum laws are a serious obstacle to confidence on one side and voluntary co-operation on the other, because of the hostile messages they send out about minorities — not just about those who are in fact immigrants or asylum-seekers but about anyone who holds citizenship but who is associated in the public's mind with those groups. Individuals who are merely thought to look or sound like immigrants or asylum-seekers suffer from these attitudes. But that is not all. The framework of immigration and asylum laws confers an inferior status on those who have not been granted permanent legal residence: limiting their right to work, their benefits and their access to family reunion. It also threatens their security of residence.

Thus what everyone can see is a two-tier system within each country, not openly defined as such but visible in practice: a system which proclaims belief in equal treatment but which effectively prefers those who belong to a majority.

The European Commission and Parliament have for some years been making commendable efforts to bring legally resident third-country nationals closer to equal status with EU nationals. One result of these efforts has been to make anomalies more obvious. EU nationals have the right to be joined in the state they belong to by close family members: spouse, children, parents and others under only very few conditions. However, under national laws an EU national married to a third-country national has no right to bring in a spouse, or any other relative who lacks an EU nationality, in many Member States. The only recourse is to move from one EU state to another, bring in a spouse under EU law to the new state, where national law must give way to EU law and allow the spouse in. In other words, EU law is much more liberal than many national laws on the right to family reunion. To force couples to live apart is a particularly distressing form of discrimination but state governments have not recognised this fact, since they keep migration law in a separate compartment, mentally and departmentally, from laws on equal treatment. But to the minorities themselves, the effects of discrimination are all one: inequality of treatment.

The policy implications here are that national governments need to look not only at the specific, technical requirements of the anti-discrimination Directives but at their policies and practices overall. Some have already been attempting to do this, but progress is very uneven.

4. Institutional Differences

Belgian law provides a strong example of systematic efforts over quite a long period to enact comprehensive laws against racial discrimination and to encourage positive efforts to promote equality. The Belgian background is unusual in that for decades before laws concerning those of non-European origin were considered the Belgian federal state had been struggling with measures to promote equality between its Flemish, Walloon (French-speaking) and German-speaking communities. There was therefore much experience of the difficulties raised by non-discrimination policies and public reactions to them. Then Belgium acted in 1981 to produce a specifically anti-racist law, and in 1993 created a national centre for Equal Opportunities and Opposition to Racism whose role has since been enlarged and strengthened. In most respects, Belgian law already conforms to the requirements of the Race Equality Directive and in some ways goes beyond it. There is a striking contrast here with many other European states, both EU members and applicants.

However, the author of the Belgian report comments that the implementation and effectiveness of the legislation has been deficient in several respects. Attempts to overcome these deficiencies are already being made, but some of the problems are said by the Belgian author to require 'a change in mentality and a greater political will' rather than legislative change.

This is an important point. The Belgian authorities have demonstrated their own political will and have accepted many of the suggestions and criticisms made by anti-racists, for example by making access to Belgian nationality, formerly closely restricted, much easier so as to allow the minorities to exercise political rights and have access to public employment. But implementation of the law depends not only on public authorities and their rules but also on the attitudes and activities of a host of individuals in both public and private sectors. The Belgian author mentions a case where police refused to report on the facts of a car accident involving a Belgian and an alien, and 'the alien was eventually involved in violence at the police station during which he was seriously injured'. This case came to court, which found in favour of the alien, who had been rendered unable to work as well as being deprived of the right to make a statement after the car accident. Behind this one brief example lies a huge problem, in Belgium and elsewhere: the attitudes and actions of many police officers all over Europe. Given that police in all countries have a large responsibility for dealing with aliens and ethnic minorities, this problem is going to be a serious obstacle to implementation of anti-discrimination laws even when these have everywhere been strengthened: a point to be discussed further below.

The Netherlands has a structure of anti-discrimination law fully as developed as Belgium's and in some ways adding to it. The Netherlands does not have Belgium's federal structure or linguistic history, but it has lively local government and an important historical tradition of tolerance, especially religious tolerance. There are active local anti-discrimination bureaux. Its central body for assisting victims of discrimination deals not only with race and religion but also with all kinds of unjust discrimination including discrimination between men and women. Discrimination is dealt with in both the Civil and Criminal Codes. A notable feature of the Dutch system is the large body of case law, unusual in Europe, which has been built up since the 1980s.

Structurally very different, again, is the United Kingdom, which has the longest-established laws on race in Europe. The first Race Relations Acts, of 1965 and 1968, did not go very far, but the 1976 Act (amended in 2000), produced a comprehensive structure including a central body to assist victims with their complaints, investigate public and private bodies suspected of discriminating, and promote harmonious relations between groups. However, the peculiar constitutional structure of the UK has produced anomalies. There is no written constitution to appeal to. Moreover, Northern Ireland is treated differently in many respects from Great Britain (i.e. England, Scotland and Wales). For some years, racial discrimination was not unlawful in Northern Ireland but religious discrimination was. Race has now been brought under the legislation for Northern Ireland, but so far religion has been left out of the British system.

Religious hostilities have not been as strong in Britain as in many parts of the continent, though in Northern Ireland they are paramount. There, the social and political divisions are between Catholic and Protestant Christians and over a long period have repeatedly erupted in violence. But Britain itself has become increasingly secularised over the last fifty years, with hostility or indifference towards all religions often manifest. Hostility to Islam is often a product of racial hostility as much as of religious prejudice. Since September 11 2001, people who look as though they might be Arabs have suffered verbal and sometimes physical abuse in the streets, while people with Muslim names have increasingly faced difficulty when applying for jobs. There is likely to be difficulty in many parts of Europe in distinguishing between racial and religious discrimination once new laws are applied.

These differences of background and structure between three countries with relatively advanced systems of anti-discrimination law illustrate some of the problems which face Europe in general in implementing the Directives. All three countries have to make adjustments in order to comply with the Directives. All three, despite their efforts, are able to deal with only a small proportion of the discrimination which exists. All three have faced problems in informing and convincing the public of the nature and value of their work.

The adjustments they have to make are, however, made easier by three factors: general acceptance of the need for anti-discrimination law; a history going back for a long period (up to 25 years) of making the law work and understanding its difficulties, and familiarity with the assumptions of the Directives. Other states, which have to comply with the Directive, face a host of problems. Not just their legal systems but also their legal habits of thought are challenged. Everyday attitudes to different groups are greatly varied: one person may be appalled by anti-Semitism but tell you all gypsies are thieves; another will be equally hostile to Catholics and Muslims as supposed enemies to enlightened thought and the secular state. The need to deal fairly with all, providing where necessary for compensatory or positive action, may often be difficult to appreciate.

Probably the establishment of a responsible, independent central body in each state will be one of the most useful measures to deal with these difficulties, and analogies with sex discrimination law one of the most powerful arguments in favour of the new measures generally.

5. What Will Compliance Mean?

Germany, largest of the EU states, has to make considerable changes to its legal system and also in many generally accepted assumptions. The concept of racism is particularly repellent to most Germans now because of the Nazi past, but racism is seen as starkly evil, a matter of false doctrines and physical violence, rather than as everyday distinction between, for example, German and foreign applicants for a home or a job. None the less, the courts have been dealing with some racial distinctions by stretching the application of the Basic Law Articles 3.1 and 3.3 on equality before the law. Most of the case law developed under these Articles has been on sex discrimination. Most importantly, the Basic Law deals with rights of citizens against public authorities and does not apply to relations between private citizens, where the predominant rule is freedom of contract between persons, e.g. in providing goods and services.

A major problem for the Germans is dealing with religious discrimination. Labour law requires that there be no discrimination between persons on the grounds of religion, but the Christian churches have a constitutional right to self-determination in their own affairs, which include the running of church institutions such as hospitals, schools and kindergartens: indeed the church plays such a large role in providing such institutions that it is a serious disadvantage to be excluded from access to or employment in any of them.

While various laws of limited application render discrimination on grounds of origin or religion unlawful, these do not appear to be frequently enforced. There is often no readily available recourse for the individual who feels discriminated against.

Germany has a federal structure within which each Land (region) has its own constitution and law-making power, and some of the Länder have been more active than others in working against discrimination. NGOs in Germany have also been active, sometimes with Federal or Land financial support. But overall Germany faces a huge task in complying with the Directives, not only in drafting the technical details but also in revising generally held assumptions about the citizen, the state, the churches and rival claims of fairness.

However, Germany is committed to complying with the Directives, and work has been proceeding on the means to do this. Elsewhere, there are fewer signs of readiness to comply. Spain, for example, at the time the above report was written had taken no steps. Spanish law has numerous anti-discrimination provisions, but these are scattered through many different laws, are unfamiliar to lawyers, and have produced very few complaints. The justice system as a whole is slow and in need of reform, and efforts are being made to tackle this. The letter of the law on the rights of aliens is quite impressive, and discrimination on grounds of nationality is explicitly banned, as is discrimination on grounds of ideology, religion or belief, race or ethnic origin. As in many other Member States, progress against sex discrimination has been much greater than in other fields. Labour law deals in addition with grounds of political opinion, trade union membership, national descent and social background. But the report makes only one brief reference to the Roma, an important element in the Spanish settled population, urging the need for more resources for their education. Overall, the impression is of a good basis for compliance with the Directives but at the same time the need for a great deal of work on implementation of existing law. The Spanish report does not mention any differences between various immigrant groups, such as Latin Americans, Moroccans and east Europeans, or Spanish attitudes to them.

The Portuguese report is more informative on the general situation, describing differences between immigrant groups (those from former colonies in Africa and from Macao, also Brazilians and east Europeans) and making the important point that the living and working conditions of immigrants are generally worse than those of the Portuguese, with the Africans in particular suffering from underemployment, accommodation in shanty-towns, low academic achievement among their children and social marginalisation. The east Europeans, it is said, are better received than the Africans but are usually employed well below the level of their skills. (The same things could be said of immigrants and their descendants in most European states, but the other reports do not state explicitly this background to anti-discrimination legislation.)

'There is no relevant jurisprudence', says the author, 'on discrimination because it arises mainly from working and living conditions and not from explicitly discriminatory procedures'. Discriminatory acts are punishable by summary fines. Thus, although the report describes legal structures in place for dealing with discrimination, the overall impression is that it is dealt with very little, and that the existence of structures is supposed to guarantee that action is being taken. There is an obvious danger (and this is true of many countries besides Portugal) that any legal changes made to comply formally with the Directives will be thought by the authorities to fulfil all responsibility for achieving equality between ethnic, racial and immigrant groups. What is necessary is for the information and motivation that lie behind the Directives to be appreciated by lawmakers.

6. Poverty and Powerlessness

Despite constitutional statements about equality for all, the fact is that all European societies are unequal, chiefly because of divisions between rich and poor. To be poor is not only to be lacking in money: it is to lack security, self-confidence, friends in high places, hopeful career prospects, good housing and advantages for one's children. A large proportion among the minorities consists of poor people, whose problems are compounded by racial or ethnic prejudice. The situation varies greatly between countries and localities, but it presents a problem, which anti-discrimination laws alone cannot solve. Something can be done by strong laws dealing with employment (in both recruitment and working conditions), with housing, and promoting positive action where necessary, but there are deeper difficulties, with large consequences for social policy, which have to be understood if governments are going to be serious about tackling inequality.

This needs to be said if anti-discrimination laws are to be administered sympathetically and if they are not to prove disappointing. Poverty goes along with powerlessness, which is shared by the poorest among host populations, among whom there are often recruits to extreme-Right, violent racist organisations.

7. Roma/Gypsies/Travellers

The misery and inequality suffered by Gypsies (Roma, Sinti and other groups) show in their most extreme form the problems created by a combination of poverty and discrimination. Gypsies in Europe have suffered persecution for many centuries, and even in countries where there is already an effort to deal fairly with immigrant groups who arrived in recent times they still get mistreated and are frequently ignored by campaigners for equality. They are probably the poorest and most powerless of all the groups who need the protection of the law.

Their problems are the most difficult to tackle because they have suffered persecution for so long. In Austria, for example, (not the country with the worst record) only ten per cent of gypsy children complete compulsory education. Obviously, even without open discrimination against them, their chances of employment will therefore be low. Situations vary in different countries due to enter the EU within a few years. In Hungary, for example, according to Anti-Semitism World Report[3] 'an estimated 80 per cent of Roma live below the poverty line … 50 to 80 per cent of Rom children do not complete elementary school … Due to unemployment, homelessness, extreme poverty and a large number of dependants, many Roma live in permanent fear of destitution and famine. Petty crime has markedly increased among them … Over 50 per cent of the prison population are Roma'. In the Czech Republic, many Roma lost their citizenship in June 1994 and thus lost their right to state benefits: some live by rummaging in dustbins for food and clothing. Those who fled from Slovakia have no permanent residence permit and no entitlement to medical care, social security, housing or education.

While some positive efforts are being made in both these countries and in other applicant nations, their impact is very small in comparison with the enormous disadvantages the Roma suffer. It is going to be very difficult to build confidence among them for any government measures. Similar problems, though less obviously harsh, exist in member states. Two important factors here are the bureaucratic powers of the local government institutions, often very hostile to Gypsies, and the impact of restrictive asylum policies on east European Gypsies seeking refuge in west European states.

In France, Ireland and the United Kingdom, people with a nomadic way of life are not designated an ethnic group but come under a general heading of travellers. Since the French government favours their settling rather than stay-

3 The report is no longer available in book form but can be found on www.axt.org.uk. Some of the information in it (on various forms of racism as well as anti-Semitism) has not been updated since 1996.

ing on the road, many measures effectively harass those who move about: sites where they can pause are in short supply, and activities that could earn them money are closely restricted. In the UK similarly, travellers cannot stay on unauthorised sites, and these sites are enough to meet only half the demand, are often in unhealthy locations and are over-regulated. As the police frequently move on groups of travellers, children lose the chance of attending school. The Roma and Irish among travellers *can* complain of discrimination as they are recognised as ethnic groups by UK law but they have not gained much from this since there is widespread hostility to them. In Ireland, most travellers are Irish, not Roma, and they are specially designated in the law as members of the 'travelling community', for example in the Unfair Dismissals Act. A traveller may not legally be refused service in a pub unless the publican has justifiable reason to believe the particular individual being refused would be a source of trouble. The above report also points to some positive efforts to provide Traveller accommodation.

For the future, there are now some encouraging efforts at international level to deal with the problems faced by Gypsies. But at the same time, enlargement of the EU will mean that Gypsies in applicant states, who have sometimes successfully sought asylum in existing member states, will no longer be able to do so.

8. Political Backgrounds

Not only the historical background but also the present-day political background in each country is of great importance to the prospect for anti-discrimination laws.

Ireland, with a series of liberal laws on equality and rights in recent years, is favourably placed for making the Directives work. By contrast, the political climate in Italy is highly unfavourable since l'Ulive was ousted and the Berlusconi-Fini-Lega-Nord government took over. Major legislation against racial or ethnic discrimination had been passed in 1998 but had not been in force long enough for results to be fairly assessed when the government changed in 2000. A further measure, extending protection to those discriminated against on grounds of religion, gender, sexual orientation, political opinion, age etc, had been planned by the former government. However the electoral success of Berlusconi and his allies has not only put a halt to progress here but has encouraged the racism and xenophobia expressed in some of their campaigning statements. No measures have been taken to comply with the Directives. Although there is a solid statutory base for work against discrimination, the slow and uncertain workings of the Italian legal system combined with the political climate make optimism difficult.

In many formerly Communist states (also in Greece) commentators have noticed an increase in recent years of powerful nationalism bordering on xenophobia. Anti-Semitism has resurfaced, often cutting across political party lines.

9. The Need for Precise Definitions

In some member states (e.g. Greece) and the applicant states (e.g. Slovakia, Poland, Slovenia and the Czech Republic) there is no definition in legislation of what constitutes either direct or indirect discrimination. So although discrimination is claimed outlawed in these countries under the provisions of international agreements and constitutional statements, there is no firm ground on which any complaint can stand.

It seems that the concept of racial discrimination is not widely understood; being interpreted sometimes as racial violence, sometimes as racist statements. In Slovakia, another substantive law besides the law against discrimination has to be violated at the same time before action can be taken, and then the action is by officialdom and not by the victim who, even in the unlikely event of a favourable decision, gets no compensation.

The Race Equality Directive begins, very properly, by defining what it means by racial or ethnic discrimination. Moreover, it refers to 'persons', that is individuals, and not to minorities or groups. In many European states (including those just mentioned) anti-discrimination measures are perceived and framed as rules concerning particular minorities. Anyone suffering discrimination who does not belong to a named group gets left outside whatever benefits the laws confer.

For example, in Slovenia (which has attempted several positive measures) there are special, legally defined rights for the Italian, Hungarian and Roma minorities, but not for the migrants and refugees who have moved there from other parts of Yugoslavia, nor for anyone else. A case is mentioned in the report of a violent attack on two black residents of the country, and this comes as a shock to the reader who would not otherwise know of any black residents there at all. In Greece, there are some legal guarantees for the Muslim population in Thrace (deriving from the Treaty of Lausanne in 1923) and some positive measures for Roma, but no special measures for Macedonians or Albanians, or for the numerous immigrants from Asia.

Compliance with the Directive should require clear definitions of discrimination, and relate it to 'persons' rather than minorities or groups. Indeed this may be the single most important point to be met by EU and applicant states.

10. Levels of Awareness

The Bulgarian report is unusually forthright in saying, 'There is no enforcement of existing anti-discrimination legislation in Bulgaria...Judges...are largely unaware of the principle of equal treatment... no individual victims bring cases, except for persons supported by human rights protecting NGOs and the latter are very few in number… The judiciary [have] claimed that crimes against Roma, for instance, are not racially motivated since Roma do not belong to a separate race' – and so on. Briefly, it appears that none of the legal machinery against discrimination really works.

The reports show that awareness of the problem of racial discrimination depends considerably on the judiciary. In countries where the courts have already for some years had to deal with discrimination cases, their rulings have necessarily affected the views of lawyers and politicians and even of journalists, seeping through to a wider public.

One of the arguments used most often in Britain when race relations' legislation was introduced was that, apart from its direct legal effect, it would have an educative effect on the public. There was some truth in this. Once racial discrimination had been officially made undesirable by parliament, not just in declarations but also in detailed law making, opinion began to shift in favour of racial equality. The reporting of particular cases required that personal stories should be told of how discrimination affected individuals and families. It also demonstrated how discrimination actually worked. Once the issue had been made personal in this way, public understanding could improve. No longer did 'discrimination' seem like an abstract issue. It portrayed human faces. Not that discrimination was abolished, but it became unrespectable. The legislation also made possible widespread collection of information on the incidents and character of discrimination.

All this was greatly helped by the parallel enforcement of laws against discrimination between men and women. There have been numerous court cases, often owing their success more to European case law than to the original British legislation, and the net effect has been to keep discrimination issues before the courts and the public. In countries where some anti-discrimination law exists but is not implemented this effect is obviously absent. Neither the public nor the judges themselves have the opportunity to learn about how discrimination works or how widespread it is.

Proving a case of indirect discrimination relies not only on reversal of the burden of proof but on the collection of information that goes outside an individual's particular experience: information on an institution's habitual practices, on the situation of minorities in a particular area or on the education, employment, housing or healthcare of whole communities.

NGOs can and do play an important part in collecting and distributing such information. Some lack the resources to do so, but they can lobby other organisations and institutions to provide facts and figures. Many NGOs have played a part in bringing cases to court, not only as officially recognised bodies in the legal process but as informal advisers giving help and encouragement to victims of discrimination. The importance of encouragement cannot be overestimated. It is exceedingly difficult for many victims to make complaints or bring cases even where the law allows them to do so: they need courage and perseverance and also informed advice. NGOs working at local level are especially useful here, as they are familiar with factors which more remote, national organisations do not know about but which may strongly affect a case. NGOs can also raise awareness locally through other activities. And at national level they can attempt to bring pressure on politicians and to publicise discrimination issues in the media. Such activities, which can also come from individual journalists, church representatives and so on, will be essential in making new laws work. In countries where national minorities have a special position, there is a danger that much of the energy which goes into NGOs elsewhere may be concentrated on specific minorities rather than on discrimination in general, particularly towards immigrants. There are however already signs in some places that their concerns are being broadened. This could be an important side effect of the Racial Equality Directive.

NGO effort at international level is increasingly important, particular concerning the Roma. The Helsinki Committee has been doing much to raise awareness and to promote practical measures.

11. Anti-Semitism and Xenophobia

Anti-Semitism is still alive throughout Europe, though with varying impact. Highly publicised incidents, such as desecration of Jewish cemeteries, may represent the work only of small, extreme-Right groups, but anti-Semitism also exists among sections of the public and even parliamentarians, usually on the Right but sometimes on the Left. Because state authorities since 1945 have done much to condemn anti-Semitism and outlaw certain expressions of it, its continuing importance is not always recognised.

Anti-Semitic statements can easily be transferred to hatred of foreigners. This happened in Austria where Jörg Haider's party successfully played on widespread anti-foreigner prejudice towards refugees to recruit sympathisers with old, anti-Semitic nationalism and pan-Germanism. France's Bruno Mégret congratulated Haider in 1999, with a commitment to bringing together 'Europe's nationalist Right-wing forces'. But while neo-Nazi activity is against the criminal law in Austria, neither civil nor criminal law has formally outlawed discrimination.

In Greece, 92 per cent of the country's Jews were deported to concentration camps in 1943 against the protests of intellectuals and church leaders. But anti-Semitism has nevertheless continued alongside growing xenophobia. The Orthodox Church officially condemns both, but individual churchmen have encouraged anti-Semitism, e.g. calling Jews Christ-killers and questioning their loyalty to the state. Ninety five per cent of Greeks are of Orthodox religion, and there is a strong tendency to identify the Church with the nation.

Similarly, in Poland many nationalists associate Polish-ness with the Catholic Church. Jews count as a national minority rather than a religious one, and there is still hostility to the few who are left in the country, e.g. over the Auschwitz site. But in many other countries, where anti-Semitism is officially condemned, it can still be used by propagandists for xenophobia and the justification of different forms of racism and xenophobia.

The Scandinavian countries have a much better record than most, though their strong traditions of equality and generous social legislation allow a degree of freedom of speech which has permitted neo-Nazi groups to use them as bases for anti-Semitic and other racist propaganda. The Swedish public, according to opinion polls, by a large majority rejects anti-Semitism and racism, and recognises the existence in the country of discrimination. Sweden has accepted many foreign immigrants and refugees and the tone of the Swedish report is optimistic. There is a strong anti-fascist movement, which has held successful demonstrations. In Finland, Jews have long been involved in public life, and in 1995 a law was passed against incitement to hatred against any national, racial, ethnic or religious group. Denmark too has strong liberal and anti-racist traditions, but in recent years support has grown for certain Right-wing parties and immigration law has expressed some growing hostility to foreigners.

The high level of toleration towards foreigners in Sweden is matched only, according to Eurobarometer in 1997, by Luxembourg. Luxembourg has the highest percentage of foreigners in its workforce (about 25 per cent) of any European state.

12. Turkish Accession

The report on Turkey was compiled before a change of government produced new hopes for human rights there. As Turkish accession has now been postponed, there is plenty of time for work to be done on compliance with the Directives, and much must be done both to alter the legal framework radically and to tackle old-established attitudes.

The Turkish situation has for a long time displayed the difference between theoretical and practical equality. The most delicate issues are religious toleration and the situation of the Kurds. The report describes how 312 Article 2 of the Criminal Code penalises incitement to hatred or hostility on the basis of a difference between social classes, races, religions, denominations or regions, but points out that in a number of cases concerning this article 'the judicial authorities used the provision to penalise expressions criticising State policies'. Turkish law also uses the principle of maintaining the integrity of the Turkish state to prevent assertions of Kurdish identity as a national group. No political party may assert that any national minorities exist in the country or propose the creation of minorities. There are limitations on religious freedom, including a denial of property rights to certain religious minorities. It is, then, not surprising that neither civil law nor administrative law contains an independent prohibition of discrimination on the grounds of ethnic origin or race, or that the Constitutional Court in 1998 closed down a group called the Welfare Party, saying it had become the centre of activities contrary to the principle of secularism.

Yet the Constitution lays down the principle of equality before the law. The uselessness of such a declaration of principle is particularly glaring in the Turkish case but other countries in Europe should take note that they will be judged for their compliance with the Directives on ordinary legislation and its application.

The prospect of Turkey's accession also requires adjustments of laws and attitudes in existing Member States: improved practices towards Muslims, recognition of Turkey's national role and Islam's religious role in European history and the realisation that Turks will be EU citizens and not third-country nationals or immigrants. These adjustments may be hard to make in many countries, including France and Germany, but they will be an important test of the significance and practicability of the Directives.

13. Effective Compliance

Member States and new states are not all showing equal concern for complying with the Directives, but the very existence of these European measures has given a strong push in the direction of overcoming racial and religious discrimination. The main points to watch will be:

- The appointment of truly independent central national bodies empowered to assist individuals and make surveys;
- Adequate protection and compensation for victims;
- Effective guidance for judges, public officials and police;
- Clear definitions of discrimination against persons rather than groups;
- Use, where appropriate, of existing laws on gender discrimination to provide examples and arguments;
- Readiness to co-operate with NGOs at international, national and local level;
- Willingness to examine existing laws and policies across the board for discriminatory effects, notably immigration and asylum laws.

If cases of discrimination are later perceived to increase, this may be a very good sign, showing that victims are taking courage to pursue their claims and the authorities are ready to hear them.

It is important that the public should see the new laws as establishing fairness for everyone rather than a privileged position for members of certain racial or religious groups, and so the new laws should be framed and understood to mean that members of established majorities can complain of discrimination if need arises. A comparison can be drawn here (as is in many other instances) with laws on sex equality: while most cases involve the rights of women, some deal with the rights of men to equal treatment,

Effective compliance will require much more than the framing of new national laws. No doubt it will take time in many countries for the message, as well as the substance, of the Directives to take effect, but this message is vital in a Europe, which is now irreversibly multiracial, multifaith, and, despite restrictive laws on entry, open to the world.

ANNEXES

COUNCIL DIRECTIVE 2000/43/EC

of 29 June 2000

implementing the principle of equal treatment between persons irrespective of racial or ethnic origin

THE COUNCIL OF THE EUROPEAN UNION,

Having regard to the Treaty establishing the European Community and in particular Article 13 thereof,

Having regard to the proposal from the Commission ([1]),

Having regard to the opinion of the European Parliament ([2]),

Having regard to the opinion of the Economic and Social Committee ([3]),

Having regard to the opinion of the Committee of the Regions ([4]),

Whereas:

(1) The Treaty on European Union marks a new stage in the process of creating an ever closer union among the peoples of Europe.

(2) In accordance with Article 6 of the Treaty on European Union, the European Union is founded on the principles of liberty, democracy, respect for human rights and fundamental freedoms, and the rule of law, principles which are common to the Member States, and should respect fundamental rights as guaranteed by the European Convention for the protection of Human Rights and Fundamental Freedoms and as they result from the constitutional traditions common to the Member States, as general principles of Community Law.

(3) The right to equality before the law and protection against discrimination for all persons constitutes a universal right recognised by the Universal Declaration of Human Rights, the United Nations Convention on the Elimination of all forms of Discrimination Against Women, the International Convention on the Elimination of all forms of Racial Discrimination and the United Nations Covenants on Civil and Political Rights and on Economic, Social and Cultural Rights and by the European Convention for the Protection of Human Rights and Fundamental Freedoms, to which all Member States are signatories.

(4) It is important to respect such fundamental rights and freedoms, including the right to freedom of association. It is also important, in the context of the access to and provision of goods and services, to respect the protection of private and family life and transactions carried out in this context.

(5) The European Parliament has adopted a number of Resolutions on the fight against racism in the European Union.

(6) The European Union rejects theories which attempt to determine the existence of separate human races. The use of the term 'racial origin' in this Directive does not imply an acceptance of such theories.

(7) The European Council in Tampere, on 15 and 16 October 1999, invited the Commission to come forward as soon as possible with proposals implementing Article 13 of the EC Treaty as regards the fight against racism and xenophobia.

(8) The Employment Guidelines 2000 agreed by the European Council in Helsinki, on 10 and 11 December 1999, stress the need to foster conditions for a socially inclusive labour market by formulating a coherent set of policies aimed at combating discrimination against groups such as ethnic minorities.

(9) Discrimination based on racial or ethnic origin may undermine the achievement of the objectives of the EC Treaty, in particular the attainment of a high level of employment and of social protection, the raising of the standard of living and quality of life, economic and social cohesion and solidarity. It may also undermine the objective of developing the European Union as an area of freedom, security and justice.

(10) The Commission presented a communication on racism, xenophobia and anti-Semitism in December 1995.

(11) The Council adopted on 15 July 1996 Joint Action (96/443/JHA) concerning action to combat racism and xenophobia ([5]) under which the Member States undertake to ensure effective judicial cooperation in respect of offences based on racist or xenophobic behaviour.

(12) To ensure the development of democratic and tolerant societies which allow the participation of all persons irrespective of racial or ethnic origin, specific action in the field of discrimination based on racial or ethnic origin should go beyond access to employed and self-employed activities and cover areas such as education, social protection including social security and healthcare, social advantages and access to and supply of goods and services.

([1]) Not yet published in the Official Journal.

([2]) Opinion delivered on 18.5.2000 (not yet published in the Official Journal).

([3]) Opinion delivered on 12.4.2000 (not yet published in the Official Journal).

([4]) Opinion delivered on 31.5.2000 (not yet published in the Official Journal).

([5]) OJ L 185, 24.7.1996, p. 5.

(13) To this end, any direct or indirect discrimination based on racial or ethnic origin as regards the areas covered by this Directive should be prohibited throughout the Community. This prohibition of discrimination should also apply to nationals of third countries, but does not cover differences of treatment based on nationality and is without prejudice to provisions governing the entry and residence of third-country nationals and their access to employment and to occupation.

(14) In implementing the principle of equal treatment irrespective of racial or ethnic origin, the Community should, in accordance with Article 3(2) of the EC Treaty, aim to eliminate inequalities, and to promote equality between men and women, especially since women are often the victims of multiple discrimination.

(15) The appreciation of the facts from which it may be inferred that there has been direct or indirect discrimination is a matter for national judicial or other competent bodies, in accordance with rules of national law or practice. Such rules may provide in particular for indirect discrimination to be established by any means including on the basis of statistical evidence.

(16) It is important to protect all natural persons against discrimination on grounds of racial or ethnic origin. Member States should also provide, where appropriate and in accordance with their national traditions and practice, protection for legal persons where they suffer discrimination on grounds of the racial or ethnic origin of their members.

(17) The prohibition of discrimination should be without prejudice to the maintenance or adoption of measures intended to prevent or compensate for disadvantages suffered by a group of persons of a particular racial or ethnic origin, and such measures may permit organisations of persons of a particular racial or ethnic origin where their main object is the promotion of the special needs of those persons.

(18) In very limited circumstances, a difference of treatment may be justified where a characteristic related to racial or ethnic origin constitutes a genuine and determining occupational requirement, when the objective is legitimate and the requirement is proportionate. Such circumstances should be included in the information provided by the Member States to the Commission.

(19) Persons who have been subject to discrimination based on racial and ethnic origin should have adequate means of legal protection. To provide a more effective level of protection, associations or legal entities should also be empowered to engage, as the Member States so determine, either on behalf or in support of any victim, in proceedings, without prejudice to national rules of procedure concerning representation and defence before the courts.

(20) The effective implementation of the principle of equality requires adequate judicial protection against victimisation.

(21) The rules on the burden of proof must be adapted when there is a prima facie case of discrimination and, for the principle of equal treatment to be applied effectively, the burden of proof must shift back to the respondent when evidence of such discrimination is brought.

(22) Member States need not apply the rules on the burden of proof to proceedings in which it is for the court or other competent body to investigate the facts of the case. The procedures thus referred to are those in which the plaintiff is not required to prove the facts, which it is for the court or competent body to investigate.

(23) Member States should promote dialogue between the social partners and with non-governmental organisations to address different forms of discrimination and to combat them.

(24) Protection against discrimination based on racial or ethnic origin would itself be strengthened by the existence of a body or bodies in each Member State, with competence to analyse the problems involved, to study possible solutions and to provide concrete assistance for the victims.

(25) This Directive lays down minimum requirements, thus giving the Member States the option of introducing or maintaining more favourable provisions. The implementation of this Directive should not serve to justify any regression in relation to the situation which already prevails in each Member State.

(26) Member States should provide for effective, proportionate and dissuasive sanctions in case of breaches of the obligations under this Directive.

(27) The Member States may entrust management and labour, at their joint request, with the implementation of this Directive as regards provisions falling within the scope of collective agreements, provided that the Member States take all the necessary steps to ensure that they can at all times guarantee the results imposed by this Directive.

(28) In accordance with the principles of subsidiarity and proportionality as set out in Article 5 of the EC Treaty, the objective of this Directive, namely ensuring a common high level of protection against discrimination in all the Member States, cannot be sufficiently achieved by the Member States and can therefore, by reason of the scale and impact of the proposed action, be better achieved by the Community. This Directive does not go beyond what is necessary in order to achieve those objectives,

HAS ADOPTED THIS DIRECTIVE:

CHAPTER I

GENERAL PROVISIONS

Article 1

Purpose

The purpose of this Directive is to lay down a framework for combating discrimination on the grounds of racial or ethnic origin, with a view to putting into effect in the Member States the principle of equal treatment.

Article 2

Concept of discrimination

1. For the purposes of this Directive, the principle of equal treatment shall mean that there shall be no direct or indirect discrimination based on racial or ethnic origin.

2. For the purposes of paragraph 1:

(a) direct discrimination shall be taken to occur where one person is treated less favourably than another is, has been or would be treated in a comparable situation on grounds of racial or ethnic origin;

(b) indirect discrimination shall be taken to occur where an apparently neutral provision, criterion or practice would put persons of a racial or ethnic origin at a particular disadvantage compared with other persons, unless that provision, criterion or practice is objectively justified by a legitimate aim and the means of achieving that aim are appropriate and necessary.

3. Harassment shall be deemed to be discrimination within the meaning of paragraph 1, when an unwanted conduct related to racial or ethnic origin takes place with the purpose or effect of violating the dignity of a person and of creating an intimidating, hostile, degrading, humiliating or offensive environment. In this context, the concept of harassment may be defined in accordance with the national laws and practice of the Member States.

4. An instruction to discriminate against persons on grounds of racial or ethnic origin shall be deemed to be discrimination within the meaning of paragraph 1.

Article 3

Scope

1. Within the limits of the powers conferred upon the Community, this Directive shall apply to all persons, as regards both the public and private sectors, including public bodies, in relation to:

(a) conditions for access to employment, to self-employment and to occupation, including selection criteria and recruitment conditions, whatever the branch of activity and at all levels of the professional hierarchy, including promotion;

(b) access to all types and to all levels of vocational guidance, vocational training, advanced vocational training and retraining, including practical work experience;

(c) employment and working conditions, including dismissals and pay;

(d) membership of and involvement in an organisation of workers or employers, or any organisation whose members carry on a particular profession, including the benefits provided for by such organisations;

(e) social protection, including social security and healthcare;

(f) social advantages;

(g) education;

(h) access to and supply of goods and services which are available to the public, including housing.

2. This Directive does not cover difference of treatment based on nationality and is without prejudice to provisions and conditions relating to the entry into and residence of third-country nationals and stateless persons on the territory of Member States, and to any treatment which arises from the legal status of the third-country nationals and stateless persons concerned.

Article 4

Genuine and determining occupational requirements

Notwithstanding Article 2(1) and (2), Member States may provide that a difference of treatment which is based on a characteristic related to racial or ethnic origin shall not constitute discrimination where, by reason of the nature of the particular occupational activities concerned or of the context in which they are carried out, such a characteristic constitutes a genuine and determining occupational requirement, provided that the objective is legitimate and the requirement is proportionate.

Article 5

Positive action

With a view to ensuring full equality in practice, the principle of equal treatment shall not prevent any Member State from maintaining or adopting specific measures to prevent or compensate for disadvantages linked to racial or ethnic origin.

Article 6

Minimum requirements

1. Member States may introduce or maintain provisions which are more favourable to the protection of the principle of equal treatment than those laid down in this Directive.

2. The implementation of this Directive shall under no circumstances constitute grounds for a reduction in the level of protection against discrimination already afforded by Member States in the fields covered by this Directive.

CHAPTER II

REMEDIES AND ENFORCEMENT

Article 7

Defence of rights

1. Member States shall ensure that judicial and/or administrative procedures, including where they deem it appropriate conciliation procedures, for the enforcement of obligations under this Directive are available to all persons who consider themselves wronged by failure to apply the principle of equal treatment to them, even after the relationship in which the discrimination is alleged to have occurred has ended.

2. Member States shall ensure that associations, organisations or other legal entities, which have, in accordance with the criteria laid down by their national law, a legitimate interest in ensuring that the provisions of this Directive are complied with, may engage, either on behalf or in support of the complainant, with his or her approval, in any judicial and/or administrative procedure provided for the enforcement of obligations under this Directive.

3. Paragraphs 1 and 2 are without prejudice to national rules relating to time limits for bringing actions as regards the principle of equality of treatment.

Article 8

Burden of proof

1. Member States shall take such measures as are necessary, in accordance with their national judicial systems, to ensure that, when persons who consider themselves wronged because the principle of equal treatment has not been applied to them establish, before a court or other competent authority, facts from which it may be presumed that there has been direct or indirect discrimination, it shall be for the respondent to prove that there has been no breach of the principle of equal treatment.

2. Paragraph 1 shall not prevent Member States from introducing rules of evidence which are more favourable to plaintiffs.

3. Paragraph 1 shall not apply to criminal procedures.

4. Paragraphs 1, 2 and 3 shall also apply to any proceedings brought in accordance with Article 7(2).

5. Member States need not apply paragraph 1 to proceedings in which it is for the court or competent body to investigate the facts of the case.

Article 9

Victimisation

Member States shall introduce into their national legal systems such measures as are necessary to protect individuals from any adverse treatment or adverse consequence as a reaction to a complaint or to proceedings aimed at enforcing compliance with the principle of equal treatment.

Article 10

Dissemination of information

Member States shall take care that the provisions adopted pursuant to this Directive, together with the relevant provisions already in force, are brought to the attention of the persons concerned by all appropriate means throughout their territory.

Article 11

Social dialogue

1. Member States shall, in accordance with national traditions and practice, take adequate measures to promote the social dialogue between the two sides of industry with a view to fostering equal treatment, including through the monitoring of workplace practices, collective agreements, codes of conduct, research or exchange of experiences and good practices.

2. Where consistent with national traditions and practice, Member States shall encourage the two sides of the industry without prejudice to their autonomy to conclude, at the appropriate level, agreements laying down anti-discrimination rules in the fields referred to in Article 3 which fall within the scope of collective bargaining. These agreements shall respect the minimum requirements laid down by this Directive and the relevant national implementing measures.

Article 12

Dialogue with non-governmental organisations

Member States shall encourage dialogue with appropriate non-governmental organisations which have, in accordance with their national law and practice, a legitimate interest in contributing to the fight against discrimination on grounds of racial and ethnic origin with a view to promoting the principle of equal treatment.

CHAPTER III

BODIES FOR THE PROMOTION OF EQUAL TREATMENT

Article 13

1. Member States shall designate a body or bodies for the promotion of equal treatment of all persons without discrimination on the grounds of racial or ethnic origin. These bodies may form part of agencies charged at national level with the defence of human rights or the safeguard of individuals' rights.

2. Member States shall ensure that the competences of these bodies include:

— without prejudice to the right of victims and of associations, organisations or other legal entities referred to in Article 7(2), providing independent assistance to victims of discrimination in pursuing their complaints about discrimination,

— conducting independent surveys concerning discrimination,

— publishing independent reports and making recommendations on any issue relating to such discrimination.

CHAPTER IV

FINAL PROVISIONS

Article 14

Compliance

Member States shall take the necessary measures to ensure that:

(a) any laws, regulations and administrative provisions contrary to the principle of equal treatment are abolished;

(b) any provisions contrary to the principle of equal treatment which are included in individual or collective contracts or agreements, internal rules of undertakings, rules governing profit-making or non-profit-making associations, and rules governing the independent professions and workers' and employers' organisations, are or may be declared, null and void or are amended.

Article 15

Sanctions

Member States shall lay down the rules on sanctions applicable to infringements of the national provisions adopted pursuant to this Directive and shall take all measures necessary to ensure that they are applied. The sanctions, which may comprise the payment of compensation to the victim, must be effective, proportionate and dissuasive. The Member States shall notify those provisions to the Commission by 19 July 2003 at the latest and shall notify it without delay of any subsequent amendment affecting them.

Article 16

Implementation

Member States shall adopt the laws, regulations and administrative provisions necessary to comply with this Directive by 19 July 2003 or may entrust management and labour, at their joint request, with the implementation of this Directive as regards provisions falling within the scope of collective agreements. In such cases, Member States shall ensure that by 19 July 2003, management and labour introduce the necessary measures by agreement, Member States being required to take any necessary measures to enable them at any time to be in a position to guarantee the results imposed by this Directive. They shall forthwith inform the Commission thereof.

When Member States adopt these measures, they shall contain a reference to this Directive or be accompanied by such a reference on the occasion of their official publication. The methods of making such a reference shall be laid down by the Member States.

Article 17

Report

1. Member States shall communicate to the Commission by 19 July 2005, and every five years thereafter, all the information necessary for the Commission to draw up a report to the European Parliament and the Council on the application of this Directive.

2. The Commission's report shall take into account, as appropriate, the views of the European Monitoring Centre on Racism and Xenophobia, as well as the viewpoints of the social partners and relevant non-governmental organisations. In accordance with the principle of gender mainstreaming, this report shall, *inter alia*, provide an assessment of the impact of the measures taken on women and men. In the light of the information received, this report shall include, if necessary, proposals to revise and update this Directive.

Article 18

Entry into force

This Directive shall enter into force on the day of its publication in the *Official Journal of the European Communities*.

Article 19

Addressees

This Directive is addressed to the Member States.

Done at Luxembourg, 29 June 2000.

For the Council

The President

M. ARCANJO

COUNCIL OF EUROPE CONSEIL DE L'EUROPE

PROTOCOL NO. 12 TO THE CONVENTION FOR THE PROTECTION OF HUMAN RIGHTS AND FUNDAMENTAL FREEDOMS AND EXPLANATORY REPORT

PROTOCOL NO. 12 TO THE CONVENTION FOR THE PROTECTION OF HUMAN RIGHTS AND FUNDAMENTAL FREEDOMS

The member states of the Council of Europe signatory hereto,

Having regard to the fundamental principle according to which all persons are equal before the law and are entitled to the equal protection of the law;

Being resolved to take further steps to promote the equality of all persons through the collective enforcement of a general prohibition of discrimination by means of the Convention for the Protection of Human Rights and Fundamental Freedoms signed at Rome on 4 November 1950 (hereinafter referred to as "the Convention");

Reaffirming that the principle of non-discrimination does not prevent States Parties from taking measures in order to promote full and effective equality, provided that there is an objective and reasonable justification for those measures,

Have agreed as follows:

ARTICLE 1 – GENERAL PROHIBITION OF DISCRIMINATION

1. The enjoyment of any right set forth by law shall be secured without discrimination on any ground such as sex, race, colour, language, religion, political or other opinion, national or social origin, association with a national minority, property, birth or other status.

2. No one shall be discriminated against by any public authority on any ground such as those mentioned in paragraph 1.

ARTICLE 2 – TERRITORIAL APPLICATION

1. Any state may, at the time of signature or when depositing its instrument of ratification, acceptance or approval, specify the territory or territories to which this Protocol shall apply.

2. Any state may at any later date, by a declaration addressed to the Secretary General of the Council of Europe, extend the application of this Protocol to any other territory specified in the declaration. In respect of such territory

the Protocol shall enter into force on the first day of the month following the expiration of a period of three months after the date of receipt by the Secretary General of such declaration.

3. Any declaration made under the two preceding paragraphs may, in respect of any territory specified in such declaration, be withdrawn or modified by a notification addressed to the Secretary General. The withdrawal or modification shall become effective on the first day of the month following the expiration of a period of three months after the date of receipt of such notification by the Secretary General.

4. A declaration made in accordance with this article shall be deemed to have been made in accordance with paragraph 1 of Article 56 of the Convention.

5 Any state which has made a declaration in accordance with paragraph 1 or 2 of this article may at any time thereafter declare on behalf of one or more of the territories to which the declaration relates that it accepts the competence of the Court to receive applications from individuals, non-governmental organisations or groups of individuals as provided by Article 34 of the Convention in respect of Article 1 of this Protocol.

ARTICLE 3 – RELATIONSHIP TO THE CONVENTION

As between the States Parties, the provisions of Articles 1 and 2 of this Protocol shall be regarded as additional articles to the Convention, and all the provisions of the Convention shall apply accordingly.

ARTICLE 4 – SIGNATURE AND RATIFICATION

This Protocol shall be open for signature by member states of the Council of Europe which have signed the Convention. It is subject to ratification, acceptance or approval. A member state of the Council of Europe may not ratify, accept or approve this Protocol without previously or simultaneously ratifying the Convention. Instruments of ratification, acceptance or approval shall be deposited with the Secretary General of the Council of Europe.

ARTICLE 5 – ENTRY INTO FORCE

1. This Protocol shall enter into force on the first day of the month following the expiration of a period of three months after the date on which ten member states of the Council of Europe have expressed their consent to be bound by the Protocol in accordance with the provisions of Article 4.

2. In respect of any member state which subsequently expresses its consent to be bound by it, the Protocol shall enter into force on the first day of the month following the expiration of a period of three months after the date of the deposit of the instrument of ratification, acceptance or approval.

ARTICLE 6 – DEPOSITARY FUNCTIONS

The Secretary General of the Council of Europe shall notify all the member states of the Council of Europe of:

a. any signature;
b. the deposit of any instrument of ratification, acceptance or approval;
c. any date of entry into force of this Protocol in accordance with Articles 2 and 5;
d. any other act, notification or communication relating to this Protocol.

In witness whereof the undersigned, being duly authorised thereto, have signed this Protocol.

Done at Rome, this 4th day of November 2000, in English and French, both texts being equally authentic, in a single copy which shall be deposited in the archives of the Council of Europe. The Secretary General of the Council of Europe shall transmit certified copies to each member state of the Council of Europe.

Annex

EXPLANATORY REPORT

TO PROTOCOL NO. 12 TO THE CONVENTION FOR THE PROTECTION OF HUMAN RIGHTS AND FUNDAMENTAL FREEDOMS

I. The Protocol No. 12 to the Convention for the Protection of Human Rights and Fundamental Freedoms was drawn up within the Council of Europe by the Steering Committee for Human Rights (CDDH). It was opened to signature by the member States of the Council of Europe on 4 November 2000.

II. The text of the explanatory report prepared by the CDDH and adopted by the Committee of Ministers of the Council of Europe on 26 June 2000 does not constitute an instrument providing an authoritative interpretation of the text of the Protocol although it may facilitate the understanding of the Protocol's provisions.

INTRODUCTION

1. Article 1 of the Universal Declaration of Human Rights proclaims: "All human beings are born free and equal in dignity and rights". The general principle of equality and non-discrimination is a fundamental element of international human rights law. It has been recognised as such in Article 7 of the Universal Declaration of Human Rights, Article 26 of the International Covenant on Civil and Political Rights and in similar provisions in other international human rights instruments. The relevant provision in the European Convention on Human Rights (ECHR) in this respect is Article 14. However, the protection provided by Article 14 of the Convention with regard to equality and non-discrimination is limited in comparison with those provisions of other international instruments. The principal reason for this is the fact that Article 14, unlike those provisions in other instruments, does not contain an independent prohibition of discrimination, that is, it prohibits discrimination only with regard to the "enjoyment of the rights and freedoms" set forth in the Convention. Since 1950, certain specific further guarantees concerning only equality between spouses have been laid down in Article 5 of Protocol No. 7 to the ECHR.

2. Various ways of providing further guarantees in the field of equality and non-discrimination through a protocol to the Convention have been proposed or studied from the 1960s onwards by both the Parliamentary Assembly and the competent intergovernmental committees of experts of the Council of

Europe. An important fresh impetus was given by work carried out in recent years in the field of equality between women and men and that of combating racism and intolerance. The European Commission against Racism and Intolerance (ECRI), the Steering Committee for Equality between Women and Men (CDEG) and the Steering Committee for Human Rights (CDDH), have actively considered a possible reinforcement of ECHR guarantees in these two areas.

3. Participants at the 7th International Colloquy on the European Convention on Human Rights (Copenhagen, Oslo and Lund, from 30 May to 2 June 1990) affirmed that the principles of equality and non-discrimination are fundamental elements of international human rights law. With regard to the possibility of broadening, through the development of the Strasbourg case-law, the protection offered by Article 14 of the Convention beyond the above-mentioned limit (see paragraph 1 above), participants recognised that there was little scope for further expansion of the case-law on this score since the prohibition in Article 14 is clearly accessory to the other, substantive guarantees in the Convention.

4. Since 1990, the examination of a possible strengthening of the Convention's guarantees with regard to equality and non-discrimination was initially pursued separately, and from specific standpoints, by the Steering Committee for Equality between Women and Men and the European Commission against Racism and Intolerance.

5. In the course of its work, the CDEG underlined the fact that there is no legal protection for equality between women and men as an independent fundamental right in the context of the binding instruments of the Council of Europe. Considering that a legal norm to that effect is one of the prerequisites for achieving de jure and de facto equality, the CDEG focused the major part of its activities on the inclusion in the European Convention on Human Rights of a fundamental right of women and men to equality. The work of the CDEG resulted in a reasoned proposal to include such a right in a protocol to the ECHR. In 1994, the Committee of Ministers instructed the Steering Committee for Human Rights to consider the necessity for and the feasibility of such a measure, taking into consideration, inter alia, the report submitted by the CDEG. On the basis of the work of its Committee of Experts for the Development of Human Rights (DH-DEV), the CDDH agreed in October 1996 that there was a need for standard-setting work by the Council of Europe in the field of equality between women and men but expressed reservations, from the point of view of the principle of universality of human rights, about a draft protocol based on a sectoral approach. Further to a request made by the CDDH, the Committee of Ministers sub-

sequently (in December 1996) instructed the CDDH to examine, and submit proposals for, standard-setting solutions regarding equality between women and men other than a specific draft protocol to the ECHR.

6. In the meantime, work in the Council of Europe on the problem of racism and intolerance had intensified as a direct result of the 1st Summit of Heads of State and Government of its member States, held in Vienna on 8 and 9 October 1993. The Declaration and Plan of Action on combating racism, xenophobia, anti-Semitism and intolerance adopted at this meeting expressed alarm over the resurgence of these phenomena as well as the development of a climate of intolerance. As part of a global approach for tackling these problems set out in the Plan of Action, the heads of state and government agreed to establish the European Commission against Racism and Intolerance and gave it, among other things, the task of working on the strengthening of the guarantees against all forms of discrimination and, in that context, studying the applicable international legal instruments with a view to their reinforcement where appropriate.

7. Having studied all existing international human rights instruments which deal with discrimination issues, ECRI submitted its findings to the Committee of Ministers. ECRI considered that the protection offered by the ECHR from racial discrimination should be strengthened by means of an additional protocol containing a general clause against discrimination on the grounds of race, colour, language, religion or national or ethnic origin. In proposing a new protocol, ECRI recognised that the law alone cannot eliminate racism in its many forms vis-à-vis various groups, but it stressed also that efforts to promote racial justice cannot succeed without the law. ECRI was convinced that the establishment of a right to protection from racial discrimination as a fundamental human right would be a significant step towards combating the manifest violations of human rights which result from racism and xenophobia. It emphasised that discriminatory attitudes and racist violence are currently spreading in many European countries and observed that the resurgence of racist ideologies and religious intolerance is adding to daily tension in our societies an attempt to legitimise discrimination.

8. In the light of ECRI's proposal, the Committee of Ministers decided in April 1996 to instruct the Steering Committee for Human Rights to examine the advisability and feasibility of a legal instrument against racism and intolerance taking account of ECRI's reasoned report on the reinforcement of the non-discrimination clause of the ECHR.

9. On the basis of preparatory work done by the DH-DEV, which included the identification of arguments for and against possible standard-setting

solutions (namely, an additional protocol based on ECRI's proposal; an additional protocol broadening, in a general fashion, the field of application of Article 14; a framework convention or other convention; or a recommendation of the Committee of Ministers), the CDDH adopted, in October 1997, a report for the attention of the Committee of Ministers concerning both the question of equality between women and men and that of racism and intolerance. The CDDH was of the opinion that an additional protocol to the ECHR was advisable and feasible, both as a standard-setting solution regarding equality between women and men and as a legal instrument against racism and intolerance.

10. It was on the basis of this report that, at the 622nd meeting of the Ministers' Deputies (10-11 March 1998), the Committee of Ministers gave the CDDH terms of reference to draft an additional protocol to the European Convention on Human Rights broadening in a general fashion the field of application of Article 14, and containing a non-exhaustive list of discrimination grounds.

11. The CDDH and its committee of experts, the DH-DEV, elaborated the draft protocol and an explanatory report in 1998 and 1999. As had been the case during previous stages of this activity, the CDEG and ECRI were associated with this work through their representatives. During this period, further support for the rapid conclusion of the elaboration of the draft protocol was expressed by the participants at the European regional colloquy "In Our Hands – The Effectiveness of Human Rights Protection 50 Years after the Universal Declaration" (Strasbourg, 2-4 September 1998), organised by the Council of Europe as a contribution to the commemoration of the 50th anniversary of the Universal Declaration of Human Rights, and in the political declaration adopted by the Committee of Ministers on 10 December 1998 on the occasion of the same anniversary.

12. The CDDH, after having consulted the European Court of Human Rights and the Parliamentary Assembly, finalised the text of the draft protocol at an extraordinary meeting held on 9 and 10 March 2000 and decided to transmit it, together with the draft explanatory report, to the Committee of Ministers.

13. The Committee of Ministers adopted the text of the Protocol on 26 June 2000 at the 715th meeting of the Ministers' Deputies and opened it for signature by member states of the Council of Europe on 4 November 2000.

* * *

COMMENTARY ON THE PROVISIONS OF THE PROTOCOL

PREAMBLE

14. The brief Preamble refers, in the first recital, to the principle of equality before the law and equal protection of the law. This is a fundamental and well-established general principle, and an essential element of the protection of human rights, which has been recognised in constitutions of member states and in international human rights law (see also paragraph 1 above).

15. While the equality principle does not appear explicitly in the text of either Article 14 of the Convention or Article 1 of this Protocol, it should be noted that the non-discrimination and equality principles are closely intertwined. For example, the principle of equality requires that equal situations are treated equally and unequal situations differently. Failure to do so will amount to discrimination unless an objective and reasonable justification exists (see paragraph 18 below). The Court, in its case-law under Article 14, has already made reference to the "principle of equality of treatment" (see, for example, the Court's judgment of 23 July 1968 in the "Belgian Linguistic" case, Series A, No. 6, paragraph 10) or to "equality of the sexes" (see, for example, the judgment of 28 May 1985 in the case of Abdulaziz, Cabales and Balkandali v. the United Kingdom, Series A, No. 94, paragraph 78).

16. The third recital of the preamble refers to measures taken in order to promote full and effective equality and reaffirms that such measures shall not be prohibited by the principle of non-discrimination, provided that there is an objective and reasonable justification for them (this principle already appears in certain existing international provisions: see, for example, Article 1, paragraph 4, of the International Convention on the Elimination of All Forms of Racial Discrimination, Article 4, paragraph 1, of the Convention on the Elimination of All Forms of Discrimination against Women and, at the regional level, Article 4, paragraph 3, of the Framework Convention for the Protection of National Minorities). The fact that there are certain groups or categories of persons who are disadvantaged, or the existence of de facto inequalities, may constitute justifications for adopting measures providing for specific advantages in order to promote equality, provided that the proportionality principle is respected. Indeed, there are several international instruments obliging or encouraging states to adopt positive measures

(see, for example, Article 2, paragraph 2, of the International Convention on the Elimination of All Forms of Racial Discrimination, Article 4, paragraph 2, of the Framework Convention for the Protection of National Minorities and Recommendation No. R (85) 2 of the Committee of Ministers to member states on legal protection against sex discrimination). However, the present Protocol does not impose any obligation to adopt such measures. Such a programmatic obligation would sit ill with the whole nature of the Convention and its control system which are based on the collective guarantee of individual rights which are formulated in terms sufficiently specific to be justiciable.

ARTICLE 1 – GENERAL PROHIBITION OF DISCRIMINATION

17. This article contains the main substantive provisions of the Protocol. Its wording is based on the following general considerations.

18. The notion of discrimination has been interpreted consistently by the European Court of Human Rights in its case-law concerning Article 14 of the Convention. In particular, this case-law has made clear that not every distinction or difference of treatment amounts to discrimination. As the Court has stated, for example, in the judgment in the case of Abdulaziz, Cabales and Balkandali v. the United Kingdom: "a difference of treatment is discriminatory if it 'has no objective and reasonable justification', that is, if it does not pursue a 'legitimate aim' or if there is not a 'reasonable relationship of proportionality between the means employed and the aim sought to be realised'" (judgment of 28 May 1985, Series A, No. 94, paragraph 72). The meaning of the term "discrimination" in Article 1 is intended to be identical to that in Article 14 of the Convention. The wording of the French text of Article 1 ("sans discrimination aucune") differs slightly from that of Article 14 ("sans distinction aucune"). No difference of meaning is intended; on the contrary, this is a terminological adaptation intended to reflect better the concept of discrimination within the meaning of Article 14 by bringing the French text into line with the English (see, on this precise point, the Court's judgment of 23 July 1968 in the "Belgian Linguistic" case, Series A, No. 6, paragraph 10).

19. Since not every distinction or difference of treatment amounts to discrimination, and because of the general character of the principle of non-discrimination, it was not considered necessary or appropriate to include a restriction clause in the present Protocol. For example, the law of most if not all member states of the Council of Europe provides for certain distinctions based on nationality concerning certain rights or entitlements to benefits. The situations where such distinctions are acceptable are sufficiently safe-

guarded by the very meaning of the notion "discrimination" as described in paragraph 18 above, since distinctions for which an objective and reasonable justification exists do not constitute discrimination. In addition, it should be recalled that under the case-law of the European Court of Human Rights a certain margin of appreciation is allowed to national authorities in assessing whether and to what extent differences in otherwise similar situations justify a different treatment in law. The scope of the margin of appreciation will vary according to the circumstances, the subject-matter and its background (see, for example, the judgment of 28 November 1984 in the case of Rasmussen v. Denmark, Series A, No. 87, paragraph 40). For example, the Court has allowed a wide margin of appreciation as regards the framing and implementation of policies in the area of taxation (see, for example, the judgment of 3 October 1997 in the case of National and Provincial Building Society and Others v. the United Kingdom, Reports of Judgments and Decisions 1997-VII, paragraph 80).

20. The list of non-discrimination grounds in Article 1 is identical to that in Article 14 of the Convention. This solution was considered preferable over others, such as expressly including certain additional non-discrimination grounds (for example, physical or mental disability, sexual orientation or age), not because of a lack of awareness that such grounds have become particularly important in today's societies as compared with the time of drafting of Article 14 of the Convention, but because such an inclusion was considered unnecessary from a legal point of view since the list of non-discrimination grounds is not exhaustive, and because inclusion of any particular additional ground might give rise to unwarranted a contrario interpretations as regards discrimination based on grounds not so included. It is recalled that the European Court of Human Rights has already applied Article 14 in relation to discrimination grounds not explicitly mentioned in that provision (see, for example, as concerns the ground of sexual orientation, the judgment of 21 December 1999 in the case of Salgueiro da Silva Mouta v. Portugal).

21. Article 1 provides a general non-discrimination clause and thereby affords a scope of protection which extends beyond the "enjoyment of the rights and freedoms set forth in [the] Convention".

22. In particular, the additional scope of protection under Article 1 concerns cases where a person is discriminated against:

i. in the enjoyment of any right specifically granted to an individual under national law;
ii. in the enjoyment of a right which may be inferred from a clear obligation of a public authority under national law, that is, where a public author-

ity is under an obligation under national law to behave in a particular manner;

iii. by a public authority in the exercise of discretionary power (for example, granting certain subsidies);

iv. by any other act or omission by a public authority (for example, the behaviour of law enforcement officers when controlling a riot).

23. In this respect, it was considered unnecessary to specify which of these four elements are covered by the first paragraph of Article 1 and which by the second. The two paragraphs are complementary and their combined effect is that all four elements are covered by Article 1. It should also be borne in mind that the distinctions between the respective categories i-iv are not clear-cut and that domestic legal systems may have different approaches as to which case comes under which category.

24. The wording of Article 1 reflects a balanced approach to possible positive obligations of the Parties under this provision. This concerns the question to what extent Article 1 obliges the Parties to take measures to prevent discrimination, even where discrimination occurs in relations between private persons (so-called "indirect horizontal effects"). The same question arises as regards measures to remedy instances of discrimination. While such positive obligations cannot be excluded altogether, the prime objective of Article 1 is to embody a negative obligation for the Parties: the obligation not to discriminate against individuals.

25. On the one hand, Article 1 protects against discrimination by public authorities. The Article is not intended to impose a general positive obligation on the Parties to take measures to prevent or remedy all instances of discrimination in relations between private persons. An additional protocol to the Convention, which typically contains justiciable individual rights formulated in concise provisions, would not be a suitable instrument for defining the various elements of such a wide-ranging obligation of a programmatic character. Detailed and tailor-made rules have already been laid down in separate conventions exclusively devoted to the elimination of discrimination on the specific grounds covered by them (see, for example, the Convention on Elimination of All Forms of Racial Discrimination and the Convention on the Elimination of All Forms of Discrimination against Women, which were both elaborated within the United Nations). It is clear that the present Protocol may not be construed as limiting or derogating from domestic or treaty provisions which provide further protection from discrimination (see the comment on Article 3 in paragraph 32 below).

26. On the other hand, it cannot be totally excluded that the duty to "secure" under the first paragraph of Article 1 might entail positive obligations. For example, this question could arise if there is a clear lacuna in domestic law protection from discrimination. Regarding more specifically relations between private persons, a failure to provide protection from discrimination in such relations might be so clear-cut and grave that it might engage clearly the responsibility of the State and then Article 1 of the Protocol could come into play (see, mutatis mutandis, the judgment of the Court of 26 March 1985 in the case of X and Y v. the Netherlands, Series A, No 91, paragraphs 23-24, 27 and 30).

27. Nonetheless, the extent of any positive obligations flowing from Article 1 is likely to be limited. It should be borne in mind that the first paragraph is circumscribed by the reference to the "enjoyment of any right set forth by law" and that the second paragraph prohibits discrimination "by any public authority". It should be noted that, in addition, Article 1 of the Convention sets a general limit on state responsibility which is particularly relevant in cases of discrimination between private persons.

28. These considerations indicate that any positive obligation in the area of relations between private persons would concern, at the most, relations in the public sphere normally regulated by law, for which the state has a certain responsibility (for example, arbitrary denial of access to work, access to restaurants, or to services which private persons may make available to the public such as medical care or utilities such as water and electricity, etc). The precise form of the response which the state should take will vary according to the circumstances. It is understood that purely private matters would not be affected. Regulation of such matters would also be likely to interfere with the individual's right to respect for his private and family life, his home and his correspondence, as guaranteed by Article 8 of the Convention.

29. The first paragraph of Article 1 refers to "any right set forth by law". This expression seeks to define the scope of the guarantee provided for in this paragraph and to limit its possible indirect horizontal effects (see paragraph 27 above). Since there may be some doubt as to whether this sentence on its own covers all four elements which constitute the basic additional scope of the Protocol (the question could arise in particular with respect to elements iii and iv – see paragraph 22 above), it should be recalled that the first and second paragraphs of Article 1 are complementary. The result is that those four elements are at all events covered by Article 1 as a whole (see paragraph 23 above). The word "law" may also cover international law, but this does not mean that this provision entails jurisdiction for the European Court of

Human Rights to examine compliance with rules of law in other international instruments.

30. The term "public authority" in paragraph 2 has been borrowed from Article 8, paragraph 2, and Article 10, paragraph 1, of the Convention and is intended to have the same meaning as in those provisions. It covers not only administrative authorities but also the courts and legislative bodies (see paragraph 23 above).

ARTICLE 2 – TERRITORIAL APPLICATION

31. This is the territorial application clause contained in the Model Final Clauses adopted by the Committee of Ministers in February 1980. Paragraph 5 follows closely Article 56, paragraph 4 of the Convention.

ARTICLE 3 – RELATIONSHIP TO THE CONVENTION

32. The purpose of this article is to clarify the relationship of this Protocol to the Convention by indicating that all the provisions of the latter shall apply in respect of Articles 1 and 2 of the Protocol. Among those provisions, attention is drawn in particular to Article 53, under the terms of which "Nothing in this Convention shall be construed as limiting or derogating from any of the human rights and fundamental freedoms which may be ensured under the laws of any High Contracting Party or under any other agreement to which it is a Party". It is clear that this article will apply in the relations between the present Protocol and the Convention itself. It was decided not to include a reference to Article 16 of the Convention in this Protocol.

33. As has already been mentioned in paragraph 21 above, Article 1 of the Protocol encompasses, but is wider in scope than the protection offered by Article 14 of the Convention. As an additional Protocol, it does not amend or abrogate Article 14 of the Convention, which will therefore continue to apply, also in respect of States Parties to the Protocol. There is thus an overlap between the two provisions. In accordance with Article 32 of the Convention, any further questions of interpretation concerning the precise relationship between these provisions fall within the jurisdiction of the Court.

ARTICLE 4 – SIGNATURE AND RATIFICATION

ARTICLE 5 – ENTRY INTO FORCE

ARTICLE 6 – DEPOSITARY FUNCTIONS

34. The provisions of Articles 4 to 6 correspond to the wording of the Model Final Clauses adopted by the Committee of Ministers of the Council of Europe.

ECRI

European Commission against Racism and Intolerance
Commission européenne contre le racisme et l'intolérance

CRI (2003) 8

European Commission against Racism and Intolerance

ECRI GENERAL POLICY RECOMMENDATION N°7 ON NATIONAL LEGISLATION TO COMBAT RACISM AND RACIAL DISCRIMINATION

Adopted on 13 December 2002

Strasbourg, 17 February 2003

COUNCIL OF EUROPE CONSEIL DE L'EUROPE

Secretariat of ECRI
Directorate General of Human Rights – DG II
Council of Europe
F - 67075 STRASBOURG Cedex
Tel.: +33 (0) 3 88 41 29 64
Fax: +33 (0) 3 88 41 39 87
E-mail: combat.racism@coe.int

Visit our web site : www.coe.int/ecri

The European Commission against Racism and Intolerance (ECRI):

Recalling the Declaration adopted by the Heads of State and Government of the member States of the Council of Europe at their first Summit held in Vienna on 8-9 October 1993;

Recalling that the Plan of Action on combating racism, xenophobia, antisemitism and intolerance set out as part of this Declaration invited the Committee of Ministers to establish the European Commission against Racism and Intolerance with a mandate, inter alia, to formulate general policy recommendations to member States;

Recalling also the Final Declaration and Action Plan adopted by the Heads of State and Government of the member States of the Council of Europe at their second Summit held in Strasbourg on 10-11 October 1997;

Recalling that Article 1 of the Universal Declaration of Human Rights proclaims that all human beings are born free and equal in dignity and rights;

Having regard to the International Convention on the Elimination of All Forms of Racial Discrimination;

Having regard to Convention No 111 of the International Labour Organisation concerning Discrimination (Employment and Occupation);

Having regard to Article 14 of the European Convention on Human Rights;

Having regard to Protocol No 12 to the European Convention on Human Rights which contains a general clause prohibiting discrimination;

Having regard to the case-law of the European Court of Human Rights;

Taking into account the Charter of Fundamental Rights of the European Union;

Taking into account Directive 2000/43/EC of the Council of the European Union implementing the principle of equal treatment between persons irrespective of racial or ethnic origin, and Directive 2000/78/EC of the Council of the European Union establishing a general framework for equal treatment in employment and occupation;

Having regard to the Convention on the Prevention and Punishment of the Crime of Genocide;

Recalling ECRI's general policy recommendation No 1 on combating racism, xenophobia, antisemitism and intolerance and ECRI's general policy recommendation No 2 on specialised bodies to combat racism, xenophobia, antisemitism and intolerance at national level;

Stressing that, in its country-by-country reports, ECRI regularly recommends to member States the adoption of effective legal measures aimed at combating racism and racial discrimination;

Recalling that, in the Political Declaration adopted on 13 October 2000 at the concluding session of the European Conference against racism, the governments of member States of the Council of Europe committed themselves to adopting and implementing, wherever necessary, national legislation and administrative measures that expressly and specifically counter racism and prohibit racial discrimination in all spheres of public life;

Recalling also the Declaration and the Programme of Action adopted by the World Conference against Racism, Racial Discrimination, Xenophobia and Related Intolerance held in Durban, South Africa, from 31 August to 8 September 2001;

Aware that laws alone are not sufficient to eradicate racism and racial discrimination, but convinced that laws are essential in combating racism and racial discrimination;

Stressing the vital importance of appropriate legal measures in combating racism and racial discrimination effectively and in a way which both acts as a deterrent and, as far as possible, is perceived by the victim as satisfactory;

Convinced that the action of the State legislator against racism and racial discrimination also plays an educative function within society, transmitting the powerful message that no attempts to legitimise racism and racial discrimination will be tolerated in a society ruled by law;

Seeking, alongside the other efforts underway at international and European level, to assist member States in their fight against racism and racial discrimination, by setting out in a succinct and precise manner the key elements to be included in appropriate national legislation;

Recommends to the governments of member States:

a. to enact legislation against racism and racial discrimination, if such legislation does not already exist or is incomplete ;

b. to ensure that the key components set out below are provided in such legislation.

Key elements of national legislation against racism and racial discrimination

I. Definitions

1. For the purposes of this Recommendation, the following definitions shall apply :

   a) "racism" shall mean the belief that a ground such as race[1], colour, language, religion, nationality or national or ethnic origin justifies contempt for a person or a group of persons, or the notion of superiority of a person or a group of persons.

   b) "direct racial discrimination" shall mean any differential treatment based on a ground such as race, colour, language, religion, nationality or national or ethnic origin, which has no objective and reasonable justification. Differential treatment has no objective and reasonable justification if it does not pursue a legitimate aim or if there is not a reasonable relationship of proportionality between the means employed and the aim sought to be realised.

   c) "indirect racial discrimination" shall mean cases where an apparently neutral factor such as a provision, criterion or practice cannot be as easily complied with by, or disadvantages, persons belonging to a group designated by a ground such as race, colour, language, religion, nationality or national or ethnic origin, unless this factor has an objective and reasonable justification. This latter would be the case if it pursues a legitimate aim and if there is a reasonable relationship of proportionality between the means employed and the aim sought to be realised.

II. Constitutional law

2. The constitution should enshrine the principle of equal treatment, the commitment of the State to promote equality as well as the right of individuals to be free from discrimination on grounds such as race, colour, language, religion, nationality or national or ethnic origin. The constitution may provide that exceptions to the principle of equal treatment may be established by law, provided that they do not constitute discrimination.

[1] *Since all human beings belong to the same species, ECRI rejects theories based on the existence of different "races". However, in this Recommendation ECRI uses this term in order to ensure that those persons who are generally and erroneously perceived as belonging to "another race" are not excluded from the protection provided for by the legislation.*

3. The constitution should provide that the exercise of freedom of expression, assembly and association may be restricted with a view to combating racism. Any such restrictions should be in conformity with the European Convention on Human Rights.

III. Civil and administrative law

4. The law should clearly define and prohibit direct and indirect racial discrimination.

5. The law should provide that the prohibition of racial discrimination does not prevent the maintenance or adoption of temporary special measures designed either to prevent or compensate for disadvantages suffered by persons designated by the grounds enumerated in paragraph 1 b) (henceforth: enumerated grounds), or to facilitate their full participation in all fields of life. These measures should not be continued once the intended objectives have been achieved.

6. The law should provide that the following acts, *inter alia*, are considered as forms of discrimination: segregation; discrimination by association; announced intention to discriminate; instructing another to discriminate; inciting another to discriminate; aiding another to discriminate.

7. The law should provide that the prohibition of discrimination applies to all public authorities as well as to all natural or legal persons, both in the public and in the private sectors, in all areas, notably: employment; membership of professional organisations; education; training; housing; health; social protection; goods and services intended for the public and public places; exercise of economic activity; public services.

8. The law should place public authorities under a duty to promote equality and to prevent discrimination in carrying out their functions.

9. The law should place public authorities under a duty to ensure that those parties to whom they award contracts, loans, grants or other benefits respect and promote a policy of non-discrimination. In particular, the law should provide that public authorities should subject the awarding of contracts, loans, grants or other benefits to the condition that a policy of non-discrimination be respected and promoted by the other party. The law should provide that the violation of such condition may result in the termination of the contract, grant or other benefits.

10. The law should ensure that easily accessible judicial and/or administrative proceedings, including conciliation procedures, are available to all victims of discrimination. In urgent cases, fast-track procedures, leading to interim decisions, should be available to victims of discrimination.

11. The law should provide that, if persons who consider themselves wronged because of a discriminatory act establish before a court or any other competent authority facts from which it may be presumed that there has been direct or indirect discrimination, it shall be for the respondent to prove that there has been no discrimination.

12. The law should provide for effective, proportionate and dissuasive sanctions for discrimination cases. Such sanctions should include the payment of compensation for both material and moral damages to the victims.

13. The law should provide the necessary legal tools to review, on an ongoing basis, the conformity with the prohibition of discrimination of all laws, regulations and administrative provisions at the national and local levels. Laws, regulations and administrative provisions found not to be in conformity with the prohibition of discrimination should be amended or abrogated.

14. The law should provide that discriminatory provisions which are included in individual or collective contracts or agreements, internal regulations of enterprises, rules governing profit-making or non-profit-making associations, and rules governing the independent professions and workers' and employers' organisations should be amended or declared null and void.

15. The law should provide that harassment related to one of the enumerated grounds is prohibited.

16. The law should provide for an obligation to suppress public financing of organisations which promote racism. Where a system of public financing of political parties is in place, such an obligation should include the suppression of public financing of political parties which promote racism.

17. The law should provide for the possibility of dissolution of organisations which promote racism.

IV. Criminal law

18. The law should penalise the following acts when committed intentionally:

a) public incitement to violence, hatred or discrimination,
b) public insults and defamation or
c) threats

against a person or a grouping of persons on the grounds of their race, colour, language, religion, nationality, or national or ethnic origin;

d) the public expression, with a racist aim, of an ideology which claims the superiority of, or which depreciates or denigrates, a grouping of persons on the grounds of their race, colour, language, religion, nationality, or national or ethnic origin;

e) the public denial, trivialisation, justification or condoning, with a racist aim, of crimes of genocide, crimes against humanity or war crimes;

f) the public dissemination or public distribution, or the production or storage aimed at public dissemination or public distribution, with a racist aim, of written, pictorial or other material containing manifestations covered by paragraphs 18 a), b), c), d) and e);

g) the creation or the leadership of a group which promotes racism ; support for such a group ; and participation in its activities with the intention of contributing to the offences covered by paragraph 18 a), b), c), d), e) and f);

h) racial discrimination in the exercise of one's public office or occupation.

19. The law should penalise genocide.

20. The law should provide that intentionally instigating, aiding, abetting or attempting to commit any of the criminal offences covered by paragraphs 18 and 19 is punishable.

21. The law should provide that, for all criminal offences not specified in paragraphs 18 and 19, racist motivation constitutes an aggravating circumstance.

22. The law should provide that legal persons are held responsible under criminal law for the offences set out in paragraphs 18, 19, 20 and 21.

23. The law should provide for effective, proportionate and dissuasive sanctions for the offences set out in paragraphs 18, 19, 20 and 21. The law should also provide for ancillary or alternative sanctions.

V. Common provisions

24. The law should provide for the establishment of an independent specialised body to combat racism and racial discrimination at national level (henceforth: national specialised body). The law should include within the competence of such a body: assistance to victims; investigation powers; the right to initiate, and participate in, court proceedings; monitoring legislation and advice to legislative and executive authorities; awareness-raising of issues of racism and racial discrimination among society and promotion of policies and practices to ensure equal treatment.

25. The law should provide that organisations such as associations, trade unions and other legal entities which have, according to the criteria laid down by the national law, a legitimate interest in combating racism and racial discrimination, are entitled to bring civil cases, intervene in administrative cases or make criminal complaints, even if a specific victim is not referred to. If a specific victim is referred to, it should be necessary for that victim's consent to be obtained.

26. The law should guarantee free legal aid and, where necessary, a court-appointed lawyer, for victims who wish to go before the courts as applicants or plaintiffs and who do not have the necessary means to do so. If necessary, an interpreter should be provided free of charge.

27. The law should provide protection against any retaliatory measures for persons claiming to be victims of racial offences or racial discrimination, persons reporting such acts or persons providing evidence.

28. The law should provide for one or more independent bodies entrusted with the investigation of alleged acts of discrimination committed by members of the police, border control officials, members of the army and prison personnel.

Explanatory Memorandum to ECRI general policy recommendation N°7 on national legislation to combat racism and racial discrimination

Introduction

1. This general policy recommendation (hereafter: the Recommendation) focuses on the key elements of national legislation to combat racism and racial discrimination. Although ECRI is aware that legal means alone are not sufficient to this end, it believes that national legislation against racism and racial discrimination is necessary to combat these phenomena effectively.

2. In the framework of its country-by-country approach, ECRI regularly recommends to member States of the Council of Europe the adoption of effective legal measures aimed at combating racism and racial discrimination. The Recommendation aims to provide an overview of these measures and to clarify and complement the recommendations formulated in this respect in ECRI's country-by-country reports. The Recommendation also aims to reflect the general principles contained in the international instruments mentioned in the Preamble.

3. ECRI believes that appropriate legislation to combat racism and racial discrimination should include provisions in all branches of the law, i.e. constitutional, civil, administrative and criminal law. Only such an integrated approach will enable member States to address these problems in a manner which is as exhaustive, effective and satisfactory from the point of view of the victim as possible. In the field of combating racism and racial discrimination, civil and administrative law often provides for flexible legal means, which may facilitate the victims' recourse to legal action. Criminal law has a symbolic effect which raises the awareness of society of the seriousness of racism and racial discrimination and has a strong dissuasive effect, provided it is implemented effectively. ECRI has taken into account the fact that the possibilities offered by the different branches of the law are complementary. As regards in particular the fight against racial discrimination, ECRI recommends that the member States of the Council of Europe adopt constitutional, civil and administrative law provisions, and that, in certain cases, they additionally adopt criminal law provisions.

4. The legal measures necessary to combat racism and racial discrimination at national level are presented in the form of key components which should be contained in the national legislation of member States. ECRI stresses that the measures it recommends are compatible with different legal systems, be they common law or civil law or mixed. Furthermore, those components that ECRI considers to be key

to an effective legal framework against racism and racial discrimination may be adapted to the specific conditions of each country. They could thus be set out in a single special act or laid out in the different areas of national legislation (civil law, administrative law and penal law). These key components might also be included in broader legislation encompassing the fight against racism and racial discrimination. For example, when adopting legal measures against discrimination, member States might prohibit, alongside racial discrimination, other forms of discrimination such as those based on gender, sexual orientation, disability, political or other opinion, social origin, property, birth or other status. Finally, in a number of fields, member States might simply apply general rules, which it is therefore not necessary to set out in this Recommendation. This is the position, for example, in civil law, for multiple liability, vicarious liability, and for the establishment of levels of damages; in criminal law, for the conditions of liability, and the sentencing structure; and in procedural matters, for the organisation and jurisdiction of the courts.

5. In any event, these key components represent only a minimum standard; this means that they are compatible with legal provisions offering a greater level of protection adopted or to be adopted by a member State and that under no circumstances should they constitute grounds for a reduction in the level of protection against racism and racial discrimination already afforded by a member State.

I. Definitions

Paragraph 1 of the Recommendation

6. In the Recommendation, the term "racism" should be understood in a broad sense, including phenomena such as xenophobia, antisemitism and intolerance. As regards the grounds set out in the definitions of racism and direct and indirect racial discrimination (paragraph 1 of the Recommendation), in addition to those grounds generally covered by the relevant legal instruments in the field of combating racism and racial discrimination, such as race, colour and national or ethnic origin, the Recommendation covers language, religion and nationality[2]. The inclusion of these grounds in the definitions of racism and racial discrimination is based on ECRI's mandate, which is to combat racism, antisemitism, xenophobia and intolerance. ECRI considers that these concepts, which vary over time, nowadays cover manifestations targeting persons or groups of persons, on grounds such as race, colour, religion, language, nationality and national and ethnic origin. As a result, the expressions "racism" and "racial discrimination" used in the Recommendation encompass all the phenomena covered by ECRI's mandate. National origin is sometimes interpreted as including the concept of nationality. However, in order to ensure that this concept is indeed covered, it is expressly included in the list of grounds, in addition to national origin. The use of the expression "grounds such as" in the

---

[2] *ECRI understands the term "nationality" as defined in Article 2 a). of the European Convention on Nationality: " 'nationality' means the legal bond between a person and a State and does not indicate the person's ethnic origin".*

definitions of racism and direct and indirect racial discrimination aims at establishing an open-ended list of grounds, thereby allowing it to evolve with society. However, in criminal law, an exhaustive list of grounds could be established in order to respect the principle of forseeability which governs this branch of the law.

7. Unlike the definition of racial discrimination (paragraphs 1 b) and c) of the Recommendation), which should be included in the law, the definition of racism is provided for the purposes of the Recommendation, and member States may or may not decide to define racism within the law. If they decide to do so, they may, as regards criminal law, adopt a more precise definition than that set out in paragraph 1 a), in order to respect the fundamental principles of this branch of the law. For racism to have taken place, it is not necessary that one or more of the grounds listed should constitute the only factor or the determining factor leading to contempt or the notion of superiority; it suffices that these grounds are among the factors leading to contempt or the notion of superiority.

8. The definitions of direct and indirect racial discrimination contained in paragraph 1 b) and c) of the Recommendation draw inspiration from those contained in the Directive 2000/43/CE of the Council of the European Union implementing the principle of equal treatment between persons irrespective of racial or ethnic origin and in the Directive 2000/78/CE of the Council of the European Union establishing a general framework for equal treatment in employment and occupation as well as on the case-law of the European Court of Human Rights. In accordance with this case-law, differential treatment constitutes discrimination if it has no objective and reasonable justification. This principle applies to differential treatment based on any of the grounds enumerated in the definition of racial discrimination. However, differential treatment based on race, colour and ethnic origin may have an objective and reasonable justification only in an extremely limited number of cases. For instance, in employment, where colour constitutes a genuine and determining occupational requirement by reason of the nature of the particular occupational activities concerned or of the context in which they are carried out, differential treatment based on this ground may have an objective and reasonable justification. More generally, the notion of objective and reasonable justification should be interpreted as restrictively as possible with respect to differential treatment based on any of the enumerated grounds.

II. Constitutional law

9. In the Recommendation, the term "constitution" should be understood in a broad sense, including basic laws and written and unwritten basic rules. In paragraphs 2 and 3, the Recommendation provides for certain principles that should be contained in the constitution; such principles are to be implemented by statutory and regulatory provisions.

Paragraph 2 of the Recommendation

10. In paragraph 2, the Recommendation allows for the possibility of providing in the law for exceptions to the principle of equal treatment, provided that they do not constitute discrimination. For this condition to be met, in accordance with the definitions of discrimination proposed in paragraph 1 b) and c) of the Recommendation, the exceptions must have an objective and reasonable justification. This principle applies to all exceptions, including those establishing differential treatment on the basis of nationality.

Paragraph 3 of the Recommendation

11. According to paragraph 3 of the Recommendation, the constitution should provide that the exercise of freedom of expression, assembly and association may be restricted with a view to combating racism. In articles 10 (2) and 11 (2), the European Convention on Human Rights enumerates the aims which may justify restrictions to these freedoms. Although the fight against racism is not mentioned as one of these aims, in its case-law the European Court of Human Rights has considered that it is included. In accordance with the articles of the Convention mentioned above, these restrictions should be prescribed by law and necessary in a democratic society.

III. Civil and administrative law

Paragraph 4 of the Recommendation

12. The Recommendation provides in paragraph 4 that the law should clearly define and prohibit direct and indirect racial discrimination. It offers a definition of direct and indirect racial discrimination in paragraph 1 b) and c). The meaning of the expression "differential treatment" is wide and includes any distinction, exclusion, restriction, preference or omission, be it past, present or potential. The term "ground" must include grounds which are actual or presumed. For instance, if a person experiences adverse treatment due to the presumption that he or she is a Muslim, when in reality this is not the case, this treatment would still constitute discrimination on the basis of religion.

13. Discriminatory actions are rarely based solely on one or more of the enumerated grounds, but are rather based on a combination of these grounds with other factors. For discrimination to occur, it is therefore sufficient that one of the enumerated grounds constitutes one of the factors leading to the differential treatment. The use of restrictive expressions such as "difference of treatment *solely* or *exclusively* based on grounds such as ..." should therefore be avoided.

Paragraph 5 of the Recommendation

14. In its paragraph 5, the Recommendation provides for the possibility of temporary special measures designed either to prevent or compensate for disadvantages suffered by persons designated by the enumerated grounds, or to facilitate their full participation in all fields of life. An example of temporary special measures designed to prevent or compensate for disadvantages linked to the enumerated grounds: a factory owner who has no black employees among his managerial staff but many black employees on the assembly line might organise a training course for black workers seeking promotion. An example of temporary special measures designed to facilitate the full participation, in all fields of life, of persons designated by the enumerated grounds: the police could organise a recruitment campaign designed so as to encourage applications particularly from members of certain ethnic groups who are under-represented within the police.

Paragraph 6 of the Recommendation

15. The Recommendation specifically mentions in paragraph 6 certain acts which should be considered by law as forms of discrimination. In theory, the application of the general legal principles and the definition of discrimination should enable these acts to be covered. However, practice demonstrates that these acts often tend to be overlooked or excluded from the scope of application of the legislation. For reasons of effectiveness, it may therefore be useful for the law to provide expressly that these acts are considered as forms of discrimination.

16. Among the acts which the Recommendation mentions specifically as forms of discrimination, the following warrant a brief explanation:

- Segregation is the act by which a (natural or legal) person separates other persons on the basis of one of the enumerated grounds without an objective and reasonable justification, in conformity with the proposed definition of discrimination. As a result, the voluntary act of separating oneself from other persons on the basis of one of the enumerated grounds does not constitute segregation.

- Discrimination by association occurs when a person is discriminated against on the basis of his or her association or contacts with one or more persons designated by one of the enumerated grounds. This would be the case, for example, of the refusal to employ a person because s/he is married to a person belonging to a certain ethnic group.

- The announced intention to discriminate should be considered as discrimination, even in the absence of a specific victim. For instance, an employment advertisement indicating that Roma/Gypsies need not apply should fall within the scope of the legislation, even if no Roma/Gypsy has actually applied.

Paragraph 7 of the Recommendation

17. According to paragraph 7 of the Recommendation, the prohibition of discrimination should apply in all areas. Concerning employment, the prohibition of discrimination should cover access to employment, occupation and self-employment as well as work conditions, remunerations, promotions and dismissals.

18. As concerns membership of professional organisations, the prohibition of discrimination should cover: membership of an organisation of workers or employers, or any organisation whose members carry on a particular profession ; involvement in such organisations ; and the benefits provided for by such organisations.

19. Concerning education, the prohibition of discrimination should cover pre-school, primary, secondary and higher education, both public and private. Furthermore, access to education should not depend on the immigration status of the children or their parents.

20. As concerns training, the prohibition of discrimination should cover initial and on-going vocational training, all types and all levels of vocational guidance, advanced vocational training and retraining, including the acquisition of practical work experience.

21. As concerns housing, discrimination should be prohibited in particular in access to housing, in housing conditions and in the termination of rental contracts.

22. As concerns health, discrimination should be prohibited in particular in access to care and treatment, and in the way in which care is dispensed and patients are treated.

23. Concerning social protection, the prohibition of discrimination should cover social security, social benefits, social aid (housing benefits, youth benefits, etc.) and the way in which the beneficiaries of social protection are treated.

24. As concerns goods and services intended for the public and public places, discrimination should be prohibited, for instance, when buying goods in a shop, when applying for a loan from a bank and in access to discotheques, cafés or restaurants. The prohibition of discrimination should not only target those who make goods and services available to others, but also those who receive goods and services from others, as would be the case of a company which selects the providers of a given good or service on the basis of one of the enumerated grounds.

25. Concerning the exercise of economic activity, this field covers competition law, relations between enterprises and relations between enterprises and the State.

26. The field of public services includes the activities of the police and other law enforcement officials, border control officials, the army and prison personnel.

Paragraph 8 of the Recommendation

27. According to paragraph 8 of the Recommendation, the law should place public authorities under a duty to promote equality and to prevent discrimination in carrying out their functions. The obligations incumbent on such authorities should be spelled out as clearly as possible in the law. To this end, public authorities could be placed under the obligation to create and implement "equality programmes" drawn up with the assistance of the national specialised body referred to in paragraph 24 of the Recommendation. The law should provide for the regular assessment of the equality programmes, the monitoring of their effects, as well as for effective implementation mechanisms and the possibility for legal enforcement of these programmes, notably through the national specialised body. An equality programme could, for example, include the nomination of a contact person for dealing with issues of racial discrimination and harassment or the organisation of staff training courses on discrimination. As regards the obligation to promote equality and prevent discrimination, the Recommendation covers only public authorities; however, it would be desirable were the private sector also placed under a similar obligation.

Paragraph 10 of the Recommendation

28. According to paragraph 10 of the Recommendation, in urgent cases, fast-track procedures, leading to interim decisions, should be available to victims of discrimination. These procedures are important in those situations where the immediate consequences of the alleged discriminatory act are particularly serious or even irreparable. Thus, for example, the victims of a discriminatory eviction from a flat should be able to suspend this measure through an interim judicial decision, pending the final judgement of the case.

Paragraph 11 of the Recommendation

29. Given the difficulties complainants face in collecting the necessary evidence in discrimination cases, the law should facilitate proof of discrimination. For this reason, according to paragraph 11 of the Recommendation, the law should provide for a shared burden of proof in such cases. A shared burden of proof means that the complainant should establish facts allowing for the presumption of discrimination, whereupon the onus shifts to the respondent to prove that discrimination did not take place. Thus, in case of alleged direct racial discrimination, the respondent must prove that the differential treatment has an objective and reasonable justification. For example, if access to a swimming pool is denied to Roma/Gypsy children, it would be sufficient for the complainant to prove that access was denied to these children and granted to non-Roma/Gypsy children. It should then be for the respondent to prove that this denial to grant access was based on an objective and reasonable justification, such as the fact that the children in question did not have bathing hats, as required to access the swimming pool. The same principle should apply to alleged cases of indirect racial discrimination.

30. As concerns the power to obtain the necessary evidence and information, courts should enjoy all adequate powers in this respect. Such powers should be also given to any specialised body competent to adjudicate on an individual complaint of discrimination (see paragraph 55 of the present Explanatory Memorandum).

Paragraph 12 of the Recommendation

31. Paragraph 12 of the Recommendation states that the law should provide for effective, proportionate and dissuasive sanctions for discrimination cases. Apart from the payment of compensation for material and moral damages, sanctions should include measures such as the restitution of rights which have been lost. For instance, the law should enable the court to order re-admittance into a firm or flat, provided that the rights of third parties are respected. In the case of discriminatory refusal to recruit a person, the law should provide that, according to the circumstances, the court could order the employer to offer employment to the discriminated person.

32. In the case of discrimination by a private school, the law should provide for the possibility of withdrawing the accreditation awarded to the school or the non-recognition of the diplomas issued. In the case of discrimination by an establishment open to the public, the law should provide for the possibility of withdrawing a licence and of closing the establishment. For example, in the case of discrimination by a discotheque, it should be possible to withdraw the licence to sell alcohol.

33. Non-monetary forms of reparation, such as the publication of all or part of a court decision, may be important in rendering justice in cases of discrimination.

34. The law should provide for the possibility of imposing a programme of positive measures on the discriminator. This is an important type of remedy in promoting long-term change in an organisation. For instance, the discriminator could be obliged to organise for its staff specific training programmes aimed at countering racism and racial discrimination. The national specialised body should participate in the development and supervision of such programmes.

Paragraph 15 of the Recommendation

35. According to paragraph 15 of the Recommendation the law should provide that harassment related to one of the enumerated grounds is prohibited. Harassment consists in conduct related to one of the enumerated grounds which has the purpose or the effect of violating the dignity of a person and of creating an intimidating, hostile, degrading, humiliating or offensive environment. As far as possible, protection against harassment related to one of the enumerated grounds should not only target the conduct of the author of the harassment but also that of other persons. For instance, it should be possible for the employer to be held responsible, where applicable, for harassment by colleagues, other employees or third parties (such as clients and suppliers).

Paragraph 16 of the Recommendation

36. Paragraph 16 of the Recommendation states that the law should provide for the obligation to suppress public financing of political parties which promote racism. For example, public financing for electoral campaigns should be refused to such political parties.

Paragraph 17 of the Recommendation

37. Paragraph 17 of the Recommendation states that the law should provide for the possibility of the dissolution of organisations which promote racism. In all cases, the dissolution of such organisations may result only from a Court decision. The issue of the dissolution of these organisations is also dealt with under Section IV - Criminal law (see paragraphs 43 and 49 of the present Explanatory Memorandum).

IV. Criminal law

Paragraph 18 of the Recommendation

38. The Recommendation limits the scope of certain criminal offences set out in paragraph 18 to the condition that they are committed in "public". Current practice shows that, in certain cases, racist conduct escapes prosecution because it is not considered as being of a public nature. Consequently, member States should ensure that it should not be too difficult to meet the condition of being committed in "public". Thus, for instance, this condition should be met in cases of words pronounced during meetings of neo-Nazi organisations or words exchanged in a discussion forum on the Internet.

39. Some of the offences set out in paragraph 18 of the Recommendation concern conduct aimed at a "grouping of persons". Current practice shows that legal provisions aimed at sanctioning racist conduct frequently do not cover such conduct unless it is directed against a specific person or group of persons. As a result, expressions aimed at larger groupings of persons, as in the case of references to asylum seekers or foreigners in general, are often not covered by these provisions. For this reason, paragraph 18 a), b), c), and d) of the Recommendation does not speak of "group" but of "grouping" of persons.

40. The term "defamation" contained in paragraph 18 b) should be understood in a broad sense, notably including slander and libel.

41. Paragraph 18 e) of the Recommendation refers to the crimes of genocide, crimes against humanity and war crimes. The crime of genocide should be understood as defined in Article II of the Convention for the Prevention and Punishment of the Crime of Genocide and Article 6 of the Statute of the International Criminal Court (see paragraph 45 of the present Explanatory Memorandum). Crimes against humanity and war crimes should be understood as defined in Articles 7 and 8 of the Statute of the International Criminal Court.

42. Paragraph 18 f) of the Recommendation refers to the dissemination, distribution, production or storage of written, pictorial or other material containing racist manifestations. These notions include the dissemination of this material through the Internet. Such material includes musical supports such as records, tapes and compact discs, computer accessories (e.g. floppy discs, software), video tapes, DVDs and games.

43. Paragraph 18 g) of the Recommendation provides for the criminalisation of certain acts related to groups which promote racism. The concept of group includes in particular *de facto* groups, organisations, associations and political parties. The Recommendation provides that the creation of a group which promotes racism should be prohibited. This prohibition also includes maintaining or reconstituting a group which has been prohibited. The issue of the dissolution of a group which promotes racism is also dealt with under Section III - Civil and administrative law (see paragraph 37 of the present Explanatory Memorandum) and below (see paragraph 49 of the present Explanatory Memorandum). Moreover, the notion of "support" includes acts such as providing financing to the group, providing for other material needs, producing or obtaining documents.

44. In its paragraph 18 h) the Recommendation states that the law should penalise racial discrimination in the exercise of one's public office or occupation. On this point, the definitions contained in paragraphs 1 b) and c) and 5 of the Recommendation apply *mutatis mutandis*. Racial discrimination in the exercise of one's public office or occupation includes notably the discriminatory refusal of a service intended for the public, such as discriminatory refusal by a hospital to care for a person and the discriminatory refusal to sell a product, to grant a bank loan or to allow access to a discotheque, café or restaurant.

Paragraph 19 of the Recommendation

45. Paragraph 19 of the Recommendation provides that the law should penalise genocide. To this end, the crime of genocide should be understood as defined in Article II of Convention on the Prevention and Punishment of the Crime of Genocide and Article 6 of the Statute of the International Criminal Court, i.e. as "any of the following acts committed with intent to destroy, in whole or in part, a national, ethnical, racial or religious group, as such: killing members of the group; causing serious bodily or mental harm to members of the group; deliberately inflicting on the group conditions of life calculated to bring about its physical destruction in whole or in part; imposing measures intended to prevent births within the group; forcibly transferring children of the group to another group". The Recommendation refers only to penalisation of genocide and not of war crimes and crimes against humanity since these are not necessarily of a racist nature. However, if they do present such a nature, the aggravating circumstance provided for in paragraph 21 of the Recommendation should apply.

Paragraph 20 of the Recommendation

46. Paragraph 20 of the Recommendation provides that instigating, aiding, abetting or attempting to commit any of the criminal offences covered by paragraphs 18 and 19 should be punishable. This recommendation applies only to those offences for which instigating, aiding, abetting or attempting are possible.

Paragraph 21 of the Recommendation

47. According to paragraph 21 of the Recommendation, the racist motivation of the perpetrator of an offence other than those covered by paragraphs 18 and 19 should constitute an aggravating circumstance. Furthermore, the law may penalise common offences but with a racist motivation as specific offences.

Paragraph 22 of the Recommendation

48. According to paragraph 22 of the Recommendation, the law should provide for the criminal liability of legal persons. This liability should come into play when the offence has been committed on behalf of the legal person by any persons, particularly acting as the organ of the legal person (for example, President or Director) or as its representative. Criminal liability of a legal person does not exclude the criminal liability of natural persons. Public authorities may be excluded from criminal liability as legal persons.

Paragraph 23 of the Recommendation

49. According to paragraph 23 of the Recommendation, the law should provide for ancillary or alternative sanctions. Examples of these could include community work, participation in training courses, deprivation of certain civil or political rights (e.g. the right to exercise certain occupations or functions; voting or eligibility rights) or publication of all or part of a sentence. As regards legal persons, the list of possible sanctions could include, besides fines: refusal or cessation of public benefit or aid, disqualification from the practice of commercial activities, placing under judicial supervision, closure of the establishment used for committing the offence, seizure of the material used for committing the offence and the dissolution of the legal person (see on this last point paragraphs 37 and 43 of the present Explanatory Memorandum).

V. Common provisions

Paragraph 24 of the Recommendation

50. According to paragraph 24 of the Recommendation, the law should provide for the establishment of an independent specialised body to combat racism and racial discrimination at national level. The basic principles concerning the statute of such a body, the forms it might take, its functions, responsibilities, administration, functioning and style of operation are set out in ECRI's general policy recommendation no 2 on specialised bodies to combat racism, xenophobia, antisemitism and intolerance at national level.

51. The functions attributed to this body should be provided by law. The Recommendation enumerates a certain number of such functions. Assistance to victims covers provision of general advice to victims and legal assistance, including representation in proceedings before the courts. It also covers assistance in seeking friendly settlement of complaints.

52. As concerns investigation powers, in order that a national specialised body may conduct these effectively, it is essential that the law provides the latter with the requisite powers, subject to the rules of procedure of the national legal order. This includes powers granted in the framework of an investigation, such as requesting the production for inspection and examination of documents and other elements; seizure of documents and other elements for the purpose of making copies or extracts; and questioning persons. The national specialised body should also be entitled to bring cases before the courts and to intervene in legal proceedings as an expert.

53. The functions of the national specialised body should also include monitoring legislation against racism and racial discrimination and control of the conformity of legislation with equality principles. In this respect, the national specialised body should be entitled to formulate recommendations to the executive and legislative authorities on the way in which relevant legislation, regulations or practice may be improved.

54. As concerns awareness-raising of issues of racism and racial discrimination among society and promotion of policies and practices to ensure equal treatment, the national specialised body could run campaigns in collaboration with civil society; train key groups; issue codes of practice; and support and encourage organisations working in the field of combating racism and racial discrimination.

55. In addition to these functions, the national specialised body may be attributed other responsibilities. Moreover, another body could be entrusted with the adjudication of complaints through legally-binding decisions, within the limits prescribed by the law.

Paragraph 25 of the Recommendation

56. The Recommendation provides in its paragraph 25 that organisations such as associations, trade unions and other legal entities with a legitimate interest should be entitled to bring complaints. Such a provision is important, for instance, in cases where a victim is afraid of retaliation. Furthermore, the possibility for such organisations to bring a case of racial discrimination without reference to a specific victim is essential for addressing those cases of discrimination where it is difficult to identify such a victim or cases which affect an indeterminate number of victims.

Paragraph 27 of the Recommendation

57. According to paragraph 27 of the Recommendation, the law should provide protection against retaliation. Such protection should not only be afforded to the person who initiates proceedings or brings the complaint, but should also be extended to those who provide evidence, information or other assistance in connection with the court proceedings or the complaint. Such protection is vital to encourage the victims of racist offences and discrimination to put forward their complaints to the authorities and to encourage witnesses to give evidence. In order to be effective, the legal provisions protecting against retaliation should provide for an appropriate and clear sanction. This might include the possibility of an injunction order to stop the retaliatory acts and/or to compensate victims of such acts.

Proposal for a Council Framework Decision on combating racism and xenophobia

(2002/C 75 E/17)

COM(2001) 664 final — 2001/0270(CNS)

(Submitted by the Commission on 29 November 2001)

THE COUNCIL OF THE EUROPEAN UNION,

Having regard to the Treaty on European Union, and in particular Articles 29, 31 and 34(2)(b) thereof,

Having regard to the proposal from the Commission,

Having regard to the opinion of the European Parliament,

Whereas:

(1) Racism and xenophobia are direct violations of the principles of liberty, democracy, respect for human rights and fundamental freedoms and the rule of law, principles upon which the European Union is founded and which are common to the Member States.

(2) The Action Plan of the Council and the Commission on how to best implement the provisions of the Treaty of Amsterdam on an area of freedom, security and justice ([1]), the Conclusions of the Tampere European Council of 15 and 16 October 1999 ([2]), the European Parliament in its resolution of 20 September 2000 ([3]) and the Commission's Communication to the Council and the European Parliament on the biannual update of the Scoreboard ([4]) to review progress on the creation of an area of 'freedom, security and justice' in the European Union (second half of 2000) call for action in this field.

(3) Joint Action 96/443/JHA of 15 July 1996 adopted by the Council on the basis of Article K.3 of the Treaty on European Union, concerning action to combat racism and xenophobia ([5]) needs to be followed by further legislative action addressing the need for further approximation of law and regulations of Member States and for overcoming obstacles for efficient judicial cooperation which are mainly based on the divergence of legal approaches in the Member States.

(4) According to the evaluation of the 1996 Joint Action and work carried out in other international fora, such as the Council of Europe, some difficulties have still been experienced regarding judicial cooperation and therefore there is a need for further improvement of Member States' criminal laws in order to ensure the implementation of a comprehensive and clear legislation to combat racism and xenophobia effectively.

(5) It is necessary to define a common criminal law approach in the European Union to this phenomenon of racism and xenophobia in order to ensure that the same behaviour constitutes an offence in all Member States and that effective, proportionate and dissuasive penalties and sanctions are provided for natural and legal persons having committed or being liable for such offences.

(6) Racist or xenophobic motivation should be taken into account as an aggravating factor when imposing penalties for ordinary offences. This would constitute a direct response to perpetrators of such offences and have a deterrent effect.

(7) An offence concerning racism and xenophobia committed in the exercise of a professional activity, should be considered as an aggravating circumstance since it entails an abuse and is particularly reprehensible.

(8) It should be ensured that investigations and prosecutions of offences involving racism and xenophobia are not dependent on reports or accusation made by victims, who are often particularly vulnerable and reluctant to initiate legal proceedings.

(9) Judicial cooperation in criminal matters should be promoted to combat more effectively racist and xenophobic offences by establishing clear rules on jurisdiction and extradition.

(10) Operational contact points should be established for the exchange of information or adequate use should be made of existing cooperation mechanism.

(11) All Member States have ratified the Council of Europe Convention of 28 January 1981 for the protection of individuals with regards to automatic processing of personal data. The personal data processed in the context of the implementation of this Framework Decision will be protected in accordance with the principles of the said Convention.

([1]) OJ C 19, 23.1.1999, p. 1.

([2]) http://ue.eu.int/en/Info/eurocouncil/index.htm

([3]) OJ C 146, 17.5.2001, p. 110.

([4]) COM(2000) 782 final.

([5]) OJ L 185, 24.7.1996, p. 5.

(12) Since the objectives of ensuring that racism and xenophobia be sanctioned in all Member States by effective, proportionate and dissuasive criminal penalties and improving and encouraging judicial cooperation by removing potential obstacles, cannot be sufficiently achieved by the Member States individually, as rules have to be common and compatible, and can therefore better achieved at the level of the Union, the Union may adopt measures, in accordance with the principle of subsidiarity as referred to in Article 2 of the EU Treaty and as set out in Article 5 of the EC Treaty. In accordance with the principle of proportionality, as set out in the latter Article, this Framework Decision does not go beyond what is necessary in order to achieve those objectives.

(13) This Framework Decision is without prejudice to the powers of the European Community.

(14) Joint Action 96/443/JHA should be repealed since with the adoption of the Treaty of Amsterdam, of Council Directive 2000/43/EC of 29 June 2000 implementing the principle of equal treatment between persons irrespective of racial or ethnic origin [1] and of this Framework Decision, it has become obsolete.

(15) This Framework Decision respects the fundamental rights and observes the principles recognised in particular by the European Convention on Human Rights, in particular Articles 10 and 11 thereof, and by the Charter of Fundamental Rights of the European Union, and notably Chapters II and VI thereof,

HAS DECIDED AS FOLLOWS:

Article 1

Subject matter

This Framework Decision lays down provisions for approximation of laws and regulations of the Member States and for closer co-operation between judicial and other authorities of the Member States regarding offences involving racism and xenophobia.

Article 2

Scope

This Framework Decision applies to offences involving racism and xenophobia committed:

(a) within the territory of the Member States, or

(b) by nationals of a Member State where the act affects individuals or groups of that State, or

(c) for the benefit of a legal person established in a Member State.

Article 3

Definitions

For the purposes of this Framework Decision, the following definitions shall apply:

(a) 'racism and xenophobia' shall mean the belief in race, colour, descent, religion or belief, national or ethnic origin as a factor determining aversion to individuals or groups;

(b) 'racist or xenophobic group' shall mean as a structured organisation established over a period of time, of more than two persons, acting in concert to commit offences referred to in Article 4, paragraphs (a) to (e).

(c) 'legal person' shall mean any entity having such status under the applicable law, except for States or other public bodies in the exercise of State authority and for public international organisations.

Article 4

Offences concerning racism and xenophobia

Member States shall ensure that the following intentional conduct committed by any means is punishable as criminal offence:

(a) public incitement to violence or hatred for a racist or xenophobic purpose or to any other racist or xenophobic behaviour which may cause substantial damage to individuals or groups concerned;

(b) public insults or threats towards individuals or groups for a racist or xenophobic purpose;

(c) public condoning for a racist or xenophobic purpose of crimes of genocide, crimes against humanity and war crimes as defined in Articles 6, 7 and 8 of the Statute of the International Criminal Court;

(d) public denial or trivialisation of the crimes defined in Article 6 of the Charter of the International Military Tribunal appended to the London Agreement of 8 April 1945 in a manner liable to disturb the public peace;

(e) public dissemination or distribution of tracts, pictures or other material containing expressions of racism and xenophobia;

(1) OJ L 180, 19.7.2000, p. 22.

(f) directing, supporting of or participating in the activities of a racist or xenophobic group, with the intention of contributing to the organisation's criminal activities.

Article 5

Instigation, aiding, abetting and attempt

Member States shall ensure that instigating, aiding, abetting or attempting to commit an offence referred to in Article 4 is punishable.

Article 6

Penalties and sanctions

1. Member State shall ensure that the offences referred to in Articles 4 and 5 are punishable by effective, proportionate and dissuasive penalties.

2. Each Member State shall take the necessary measures to ensure that the offences referred to in Article 4(b) to (e) are punishable at least in serious cases, by custodial sentences which can give rise to extradition or surrender.

3. Each Member State shall take the necessary measures to ensure that the offences referred to in Article 4(a) and (f) are punishable by terms of deprivation of liberty with a maximum penalty that is not less than 2 years.

4. Member States shall ensure that ancillary or alternative sanctions such as community service or participation in training courses, deprivation of certain civil or political rights or publication of all or part of a sentence may be imposed or foreseen for the offences referred to in Articles 4 and 5.

5. Member States shall ensure that fines can be imposed or payment for charitable purposes accepted in respect of the offences referred to in Articles 4 and 5.

6. Member States shall ensure seizure and confiscation of any material or instruments to commit and proceeds obtained from offences referred to in Articles 4 and 5.

Article 7

Aggravating circumstance for racist offences

Member States shall ensure that in cases where the perpetrator of the offences referred to in Articles 4 and 5 is acting in the exercise of a professional activity and the victim is depending on this activity, the sentence can be aggravated.

Article 8

Racist and xenophobic motivation

Member States shall ensure that racist and xenophobic motivation may be regarded as aggravating circumstances in the determination of the penalty for offences other than those referred to in Articles 4 and 5.

Article 9

Liability of legal persons

1. Member States shall ensure that legal persons can be held liable for the forms of conduct referred to in Articles 4 and 5, committed for their benefit by any person, acting either individually or as part of an organ of the legal person, who has a leading position within the legal person, based on:

(a) a power of representation of the legal person, or

(b) an authority to take decisions on behalf of the legal person, or

(c) an authority to exercise control within the legal person.

2. Apart from the cases provided for in paragraph 1, Member States shall ensure that a legal person can be held liable where the lack of supervision or control by a person referred to in paragraph 1 has made possible the commission of the offences referred to in Articles 4 and 5 for the benefit of that legal person by a person under its authority.

3. Liability of a legal person under paragraphs 1 and 2 shall not exclude criminal proceedings against natural persons who commit offences or engage in the conduct referred to in Articles 4 and 5.

Article 10

Sanctions for legal persons

1. Member States shall ensure that a legal person held liable pursuant to Article 9(1) is punishable by effective, proportionate and dissuasive sanctions, which shall include criminal or non-criminal fines and may include other sanctions, such as:

(a) exclusion from entitlement to public benefits or aid;

(b) temporary or permanent disqualification from the practice of commercial activities;

(c) placing under judicial supervision;

(d) a judicial winding-up order;

(e) temporary or permanent closure of establishments which have been used for committing the offence.

2. Member States shall ensure that a legal person held liable pursuant to Article 9(2) is punishable by effective, proportionate and dissuasive sanctions or measures.

Article 11

Initiation of prosecutions

Each Member State shall ensure that investigations into or prosecution of offences referred to in Articles 4 and 5 shall not be dependent on the report or accusation made by a victim of the offence, at least in cases where offences referred to in Article 4, paragraphs (a), (e) and (f) have been committed in its territory.

Article 12

Jurisdiction

1. Each Member State shall establish its jurisdiction with regard to the offences referred to in Articles 4 and 5 where the offence has been committed:

(a) in whole or in part within its territory; or

(b) by one of its nationals and the act affects individuals or groups of that State; or

(c) for the benefit of a legal person that has its head office in the territory of that Member State.

2. When establishing jurisdiction in accordance with paragraph 1(a), each Member State shall ensure that its jurisdiction extends to cases where the offence is committed through an information system and:

(a) the offender commits the offence when physically present in its territory, whether or not the offence involves racist material hosted on an information system in its territory;

(b) the offence involves racist material hosted on an information system in its territory, whether or not the offender commits the offence when physically present in its territory.

3. A Member State may decide not to apply, or to apply only in specific cases or circumstances, the jurisdiction rule set out in paragraphs 1(b) and (c).

4. Member States shall inform the General Secretariat of the Council and the Commission accordingly where they decide to apply paragraph 3, where appropriate with an indication of the specific cases or circumstances in which the decision applies.

Article 13

Extradition and prosecution

1. A Member State which, under its law, does not extradi its own nationals shall establish its jurisdiction over th offences referred to in Articles 4 and 5 when committed b its own nationals on the territory of another Member Stat

2. Each Member State shall, when one of its nationals alleged to have committed, in another Member State, a offence referred to in Articles 4 and 5, and it does n extradite that person to that other Member State solely o the ground of his nationality, submit the case to i competent authorities for the purpose of prosecution if appr priate.

In order to enable prosecution to take place, the Member Sta in which the offence was committed shall forward to th competent authorities of the other State all the relevant th files, information and exhibits relating to the offence i accordance with the procedures laid down in Article 6(2) the European Convention on Extradition of 13 December 195 The requesting Member State shall be informed of the initiatio and outcome of any prosecution.

3. For the purpose of this Article, a 'national' of a Membe State shall be constructed in accordance with any declaratio made by that State under Article 6(1)(b) and (c) of th European Convention on Extradition.

Article 14

Political offences

Member States shall ensure that the offences referred to i Articles 4 and 5 are not regarded as political offences justifyin refusal to comply with requests for mutual legal assistance o extradition.

Article 15

Exchange of information

1. Member States shall designate operational contact point or may use existing operational structures for the exchange o information and for other contacts between Member States fo the purposes of applying this Framework Decision.

2. Each Member State shall inform the General Secretariat o the Council and the Commission of its operational contac points or operational structure for the purposes of paragrap 1. The General Secretariat shall notify that information to th other Member States.

3. Where a Member State has information relating to the storage in its territory of material containing expressions of racism and xenophobia for the purposes of distribution or dissemination in another Member State it shall provide that information to the other Member State to enable the latter to initiate, in accordance with its law, legal proceedings or proceedings for confiscation. For that purpose, the operational contact points referred to in paragraph 1 may be used.

Article 16

Implementation

1. Member States shall take the necessary measures to comply with this Framework Decision by 30 June 2004.

2. They shall communicate to the General Secretariat of the Council and to the Commission the text of any provisions they adopt and information on any other measures they take to comply with this Framework Decision.

3. On that basis, the Commission shall, by 30 June 2005, submit a report to the European Parliament and to the Council on the operation of this Framework Decision, accompanied where necessary by legislative proposals.

4. The Council shall assess the extent to which Member States have complied with this Framework Decision.

Article 17

Repeal of Joint Action 96/443/JHA

The Joint Action 96/443/JHA is hereby repealed.

Article 18

Entry into force

This Framework Decision shall enter into force on the third day following that of its publication in the *Official Journal of the European Communities*.

LIST OF CONTRIBUTORS

Mark Bell is a lecturer in law at the University of Leicester. In 2000, he was awarded a doctorate from the European University Institute, Florence in the area of European Union anti-discrimination law. In autumn 1997, he worked for five months in the European Parliament's research directorate. Within the field of EU law, his principal research interests include issues relating to equality and discrimination, and immigration and asylum. He is the author of "Anti-discrimination law and the European Union", Oxford University Press, 2002.

Giancarlo Cardinale studied law at the State University of Milan and specialised in Human Rights at the Universidad Pontificia of Salamanca. After working in the field of refugees and asylum for the British section of Amnesty International, he is currently legal and policy researcher at the Secretariat of the European Commission against Racism and Intolerance (ECRI) of the Council of Europe. In this capacity, his activities include the preparation of the necessary legal and policy background for ECRI's country-specific monitoring exercise and work on general policy recommendations.

Isabelle Chopin studied Law at the Université Paris V. She completed her studies in Brussels at the VUB in Legal European and International studies (PILC) Currently she is deputy director of the Brussels based Migration Policy Group. She acted as the Director of the Starting Line Group coalition and contributed to the adopted text of the Directive 2000/43/EC. She conducted research on the 15 EU Member States anti-discrimination legislation and is also working on the candidate countries through diverse projects looking at anti-discrimination legislation. She also co-ordinates the group of independent experts on race and ethnicity and religion and belief created by the European Commission looking at the transposition and implementation of the Racial Equality Directive and the Framework Directive.

Ann Dummett worked as Community Relations Officer for Oxford City from 1966 to 1969. After a period teaching in further education, she worked for the Institute of Race Relations and then the Joint Council for the Welfare of Immigrants in London, becoming Director of the Runnymede Commission on anti-racist measures in member states of the EC. From 1990 to 1998 she was consultant to the Commission for Racial Equality on its European policies. She was a founder member of the Starting Line Group. Besides numerous pamphlets and articles, her books include *A Portrait of English Racism* (Penguin 1973) and, with Andrew Nicol, *Subjects, Citizens, Aliens and Others* (Law in Context, Weidenfeld and Nicolsonn, 1990).

Janneke Gerards studied law at Maastricht University, The Netherlands, with a specialization in (comparative) constitutional law and civil rights. She started working as a Ph.D. candidate at the department of Public Law of Maastricht University after her graduation in 1998. In her thesis, she analysed the application of the equality principle in the case law of the US Supreme Court, the ECJ, the ECHR and the Dutch Courts, with the aim of developing a decision model for judges to apply in equality cases. In November 2002, she obtained her doctorate *cum laude* at Maastricht University. She is presently working as an associate professor in constitutional law at the department of Public Law of Leiden University, with a special interest in civil rights and equal treatment.

Per Johansson studied Swedish law at the University of Gothenburg and specialised in European Law at the University of Saarland. After working as a trainee judge at Varberg District Court, he is now working for the public affairs consultancy BKSH in Brussels. He has also worked for the European Commission, as a trainee in DG Employment and Social affairs and as an Editor for the Eurobarometer opinion poll for DG Press.

Jan Niessen studied sociology at the Free University of Amsterdam and received a Ph.D. on a study on Moroccan migration to Europe. Currently he is director of the Brussels based Migration Policy Group, an independent policy institute on migration and diversity. His activities include the organisation of experts meeting involving European and North American governmental and non-governmental organisations and the private sector, as well as the establishment of international expertise networks on migration, anti-racism, and diversity issues. For many years he chaired the Starting Line campaign. He is a member of the Editorial Board of the *European Journal of Migration and Law* and of the Board of Directors of *the Journal of International Migration and Integration.* He is also co-editor of this book series on migration and law. For the Council of Europe he wrote the report *Diversity and Cohesion new challenges for the integration of immigrants and minorities.* He advises public and private sector organisations on matters related to the inclusion of immigrants and minorities.

Sejal Parmar is an Emile Noël Fellow and European Union Fulbright Scholar at New York University School of Law for the 2003-2004 academic year. She holds law degrees from the European University Institute, Florence (Ph.D. in Laws, 2003) and the London School of Economics and Political Science (LL.B. with honours, 1998). During her doctoral studies, she was also a Marie Curie Fellow at the Amsterdam Centre for International Law and a Visiting Scholar at the University of Wisconsin-Madison Law School. Sejal has published on a range of human rights-related topics, including the relationship between international human rights law and the EU Charter of Fundamental Rights, EU anti-discrimination law and transnational dialogues in the human rights field. She is currently working on a postdoctoral research project on the EU's evolving role in international cooperation in the field of sustainable development.

Born in Groningen (The Netherlands) in 1960, **Jeroen Schokkenbroek** studied law at the University of Leiden (The Netherlands). From 1984 to 1993, he was lecturer in Constitutional and Administrative Law at the University of Leiden. Since 1993, he has occupied various functions in the Directorate (General) of Human Rights of the Council of Europe, including as co-Secretary of the drafting Committee of the Framework Convention for the Protection of National Minorities, as Secretary of the Steering Committee for Human Rights and as Head of the Minorities Section. He is currently Head of the Human Rights Law and Policy Division. A former President of the Dutch Section of the International Commission of Jurists, representative of the ICJ with the Council of Europe and editor-in-chief of the Netherlands Human Rights Law Journal (NJCM-Bulletin), Mr Schokkenbroek has published various books and articles in the field of human rights and constitutional law, including *Judicial Control of Restrictions on the Fundamental Freedoms of the European Convention on Human Rights, A Study of Strasbourg and Netherlands Case-Law* (doctoral thesis, in Dutch, Zwolle 1996) and contributed to P. Van Dijk and G.J.H. van Hoof, *Theory and Practice of the European Convention on Human Rights* (3rd ed.), Kluwer 1998.

Adam Tyson is responsible within the European Commission for developing and implementing Community policy under the non-discrimination provisions of the EC Treaty ("Article 13"), having drafted and negotiated with the Council of Ministers the Commission's proposals for the Directive on Racial Discrimination and the Community Action Programme to combat discrimination, devoted to research and policy exchange. Following the adoption of the anti-discrimination measures in 2000, his current responsibilities involve monitoring the transposition by the Member States of the two Directives prohibiting discrimination, developing European policy responses to equality issues and managing the Action Programme. He represents the European Commission on the Board of the Vienna-based European Monitoring Centre on Racism and Xenophobia. Adam previously worked at the UK Permanent Representation to the EU as the Counsellor for Employment and Social Affairs (1993-1999) and at the British Embassy in Brussels responsible for relations on employment and social affairs in the Benelux countries (1990-1993). From 1985 to 1990 he worked for the UK Department of Employment in a range of posts.

Additional Editors: **Alison Bird** and **Janet Cormack**, Migration Policy Group.

SELECTED BIBLIOGRAPHY

Alkema, E.A., 'Rechterlijk toezicht en de Europese vrijheidsrechten', in *Vrijheid en Recht ('s Jacobbundel)*, Zwolle 1975, 8.

Barnard, C., 'The changing scope of the fundamental principle of equality?' 46 *McGill Law Journal (2001)* 955, 973.

Barnard, C., 'The Economic Objectives of Article 119' in D. O'Keeffe and T. Hervey (eds.), *Sex Equality Law in the European Union*, Wiley 1996.

Barnard, C., and B. Hepple, 'Substantive Equality', (2000) 59 *Cambridge Law Journal* 562, 568.

Bell, M., *Anti-discrimination law and the European Union*, OUP, Oxford 2002.

Bell, M., 'Combating racism through European laws: a comparison of the Racial Equality Directive and Protocol 12' in I. Chopin and J. Niessen (eds.), *Combating racial and ethnic discrimination: taking the European legislative agenda further,* Migration Policy Group and Commission for Racial Equality, London 2002.

Berchtold, K., 'Council of Europe activities in the field of economic, social and cultural rights', in F. Matscher (ed.), *The Implementation of Economic and Social Rights*, Engel Verlag 1991, 355-370.

Blom, J., B. Fitzpatrick, J. Gregory, R. Knegt and U. O'Hare, *The Utilisation of Sex Equality Litigation in the Member States of the European Community* V/782/96-EN, Brussels: European Commission, 1996.

Bossuyt, M., *L'Interdiction de la discrimination dans le droit international des droits del'homme*, Brussels 1976.

Brems, E., 'The Margin of Appreciation Doctrine under the European Convention on Human Rights: Its Legitimacy in Theory and Application in Practice', *Zeitschrift für Ausländisches Recht und Völkerrecht*, 1996, 304.

Burkens, M.C., *Algemene leerstukken van grondrechten naar Nederlands constitutioneel recht*, Zwolle 1989.

Chalmers, D., 'The Mistakes of the Good European?' in S. Fredman (ed.), *Discrimination and Human Rights: The Case of Racism*, Oxford: Oxford 2001, 193.

Cholewinski, R., *Migrant workers in international human rights law – their protection in countries of employment*, Clarendon Press, Oxford 1997.

Chopin, I., and J. Niessen (eds.), *Proposals for legislative measures to combat racism and to promote equal rights in the European Union*, Commission for Racial Equality, London 1998.

Connolly, M., 'Discrimination Law: Victimisation', (2002) *Industrial Law Journal* 161.

Cormack, J., and J. Niessen, 'Public procurement and anti-discrimination legislation' in I. Chopin and J. Niessen, *Combating racial and ethnic discrimination: taking the European legislative agenda further*, Commission for Racial Equality and Migration Policy Group, London 2002.

Edel, F., 'Le protocole no. 12 à la Convention européenne des droits de l'homme', in: *Europe des libertés*, 2001, 11-16.

Ellis, E., *EC Sex Equality Law*, Oxford: Clarendon 1998.

Fee, R., 'Contract compliance: subnational and European influences in Northern Ireland' (2002) 12 *Journal of European Social Policy* 107.

Flynn, L., 'The Implications of Article 13 EC – After Amsterdam, will some forms of discrimination be more equal than others?', (1999) 36 *Common Market Law Review* 1127.

Frangakis, N., 'The prohibition of discrimination in the case-law of the European Court of Human Rights, and Protocol No 12 to the European Convention on Human Rights', in M. Gavouneli and V. Kyriakopoulos (eds.), *Olympia II: Human Rights in the 21st Century*, Athens/Komotini 2002, 153-177.

Fredman, S., 'Equality: A New Generation', (2001) 30 *Industrial Law Journal* 145.

Fredman, S., 'Reverse Discrimination in EU Law: A Critical Analysis' in J. Shaw (ed.), *Social Law and Policy in an Evolving European Union,* Hart: Oxford 2000, 171.

Fredman, S., *Women and the Law*, Clarendon: Oxford 1997.

Gomien, Harris and Zwaak, *Law and practice of the European Convention on Human Rights and the European Social Charter*, Strasbourg 1996.

Guild, E., 'Article 13: The European Commission's Anti-Discrimination Proposals', (2000) 29 *Industrial Law Journal* 79.

Guild, E., 'The EC Directive on race discrimination: surprises, possibilities and limitations', (2000) 29 *Industrial Law Journal* 416.

Harris, O'Boyle and Warbrick, *Law of the European Convention on Human Rights*, London 1995.

Helfer, L., 'Consensus, Coherence and the European Convention on Human Rights', (1993) *Cornell International Law Journal* 140.

Helfer, L., 'Note: Finding a consensus on equality: the homosexual age of consent and the European Convention on Human Rights', (1990) *New York University Law Review* 1044.

Heringa, A.W., 'Artikel 14 EVRM: een achtergestelde waarborg?', in Heringa and Myer (eds.), *45 Jaar Europees Verdrag voor de Rechten van de Mens*, Leiden 1996, 108.

Heringa, A.W., J. Schokkenbroek and J. van der Velde, *EVRM Rechtspraak & Commentaar*, Den Haag 1998.

McKea, W., *Equality and discrimination under international law*, 1995.

Heringa, A.W., and A. Woltjer, 'Gelijke behandeling in het sociale zekerheidsrecht: 'Straatsburg' scherpt de eisen aan', *Nederlands Juristenblad*, 1997, 1713.

Hervey, T., 'Putting Europe's house in order: racism, race discrimination and xenophobia after the Treaty of Amsterdam' in D. O'Keeffe and P. Twomey (eds.), *Legal issues of the Amsterdam Treaty*, Hart Publishing: Oxford 1999, 329.

Hervey, T.,'Small Business Exclusion in German Dismissal Law' (1994) *Industrial Law Journal* 267.

Kerdel, K., 'Meer gelijkheid in de bescherming tegen discriminatie? Protocol 12 bij het EVRM', *Nemesis* 2001 43.

Kewenig, W., *Der Grundsatz der Nichtdiskriminierung im Völkerrecht der internationalen Handelsbeziehungen*, 1972.

Loucaides, *Essays on the Developing Law of Human Rights*, London 1995.

Macdonald, 'The Margin of Appreciation', in Macdonald, Matscher and Petzold (eds.), *The European System for the Protection of Human Rights*, Dordrecht 1993.

Mancini, G., and S. O'Leary, 'The new frontiers of sex equality law in the European Union', 24 (1999) *European Law Review* 331.

Matscher, F., 'Betrachtungen über das Diskriminierungsverbot (Art. 14 EMRK) nach der neueren Praxis der Strassburger Instanzen', in Adamovich and Pernthaler (eds.), *Auf dem Weg zur Menschenwürde und Gerechtigkeit*, Vienna 1980, 637.

Mazey, S., *Gender Mainstreaming in the EU: Principles and Practice*, Kogan Page 2001.

McInerney, S., 'Bases for action against race discrimination in EU law' (2002) 27 *European Law Review* 72.

McInerney, S., 'Equal treatment between persons irrespective of racial or ethnic origin: a comment' (2000) 25 *European Law Review* 317.

Merrills, J.G., *The Development of International Law by the European Court of Human Rights*, Manchester 1993.

Monar, J., 'Justice and Home Affairs in the Treaty of Amsterdam: reform at the price of fragmentation' (1998) 23 *European Law Review* 320.

Moon, G., The Draft Discrimination Protocol to the European Convention on Human Rights: A Progress Report, *European Human Rights Law Review* (2000) 49-53.

O'Donnell, T.A., 'The Margin of Appreciation Doctrine: Standards in the Jurisprudence of the European Court of Human Rights', *Human Rights Quarterly* 1982, 477.

O'Hare, U., 'Enhancing European Equality Rights: a New Regional Framework' (2001) 8 *Maastricht Journal of European and Comparative Law* 133.

Partsch, K.J., 'Discrimination', in: Macdonald, Matscher and Petzold (eds.), *The European System for the Protection of Human Rights*, London 1993.

Pollack, M. and E. Hafnor-Burton, 'Mainstreaming Gender in the EU' (2000) 7 *Journal of European Public Policy* 432.

De la Porte, C., 'Is the open method of coordination appropriate for organising activities at European level in sensitive policy areas?' (2002) 8 *European Law Journal* 38.

Schiek, D., 'A New Framework on Equal Treatment of Persons in EC Law?' (2002) 8 *European Law Journal* 290.

Schokkenbroek, J., *Toetsing aan de vrijheidsrechten van het Europees Verdrag tot Beschermingvan de Rechten van de Mens*, Diss. Leiden 1996.

Schokkenbroek, J., 'Towards a Stronger European Protection against Discrimination: The Preparation of a new Additional Protocol to the European Convention on Human Rights', in G. Moon (ed.), *Race Discrimination: Developing and Using a New European Legal Framework*, Oxford 2000.

De Schutter, O., 'Avis concernant certaines propositions visant à améliorer la loi du 30 juillet 1981 tendant à réprimer certains actes inspirés par le racisme ou la xénophobie', Rapport annuel 1997 C.E.C.L.R., Brussels 1997.

Strasser, 'Remedies against racial discrimination and other forms of racism, xenophobia or intolerance under the ECHR', in Woltjer and De Beert (eds.), *Juridische middelen ter bestrijding van rassendiscriminatie en racial gemotiveerde geweldpleging*, Leiden 1996, 41.

Szyszczak, E., 'Social policy in the post-Nice era' in A. Arnull and D. Wincott (eds.), *Accountability and Legitimacy in the EU*, OUP: Oxford 2002.

Tomuschat, C., 'Europe – A common constitutional space', in De Witte and Forder (eds.), *The Common Law of Europe and the future of legal education*, Deventer 1992, 136.

Tyson, A., 'The negotiation of the European Community Directive on Racial Discrimination' (2001) 3 *European Journal of Migration and Law* 199.

Van Dijk, P., and G.J.H. van Hoof, *Theory and Practice of the European Convention on Human Rights*, Deventer 1997.

Velaers, J., *De beperkingen van de vrijheid van meningsuiting*, Antwerp 1991.

Waddington, L., and M. Bell, 'More Equal than Others: Distinguishing European Union Equality Directives' (2001) 38 *Common Market Law Review* 587.

INDEX

Immigration and Asylum Law and Policy in Europe

1. E. Guild and P. Minderhoud (eds.): *Security of Residence and Expulsion*. 2000

ISBN 90-411-1458-0

2. E. Guild: *Immigration Law in the European Community*. 2001

ISBN 90-411-1593-5

3. B. Melis: *Negotiating Europe's Immigration Frontiers*. 2001

ISBN 90-411-1614-1

4. R. Byrne, G. Noll and J. Vedsted-Hansen (eds.): *New Asylum Countries?* Migration Control and Refugee Protection in an Enlarged European Union. 2002

ISBN 90-411-1753-9

5. K. Groenendijk, E. Guild and P. Minderhoud (eds.): *In Search of Europe's Borders*. 2003

ISBN 90-411-1977-9

6. J. Niessen and I. Chopin (eds.): *The Development of Legal Instruments to Combat Racism in a Diverse Europe*. 2004

ISBN 90-041-3686-X

Martinus Nijhoff Publishers – LEIDEN/BOSTON

www.ingramcontent.com/pod-product-compliance
Lightning Source LLC
LaVergne TN
LVHW010624300926
849162LV00001B/59